The Remarkable Rise of Transgender Rights

Although medical identification and treatment of gender dysphoria has existed for decades, the development of transgender as a "collective political identity" is a far more recent construct. Over the past two and a half decades, the transgender movement has gained statutory nondiscrimination protections at the state and local levels, hate crimes protections in a number of states, inclusion in a federal law against hate crimes, legal victories in the courts, and increasingly favorable policies in bureaucracies at all levels. It has achieved these victories and other policy advances despite the difficulties in identifying the relatively small number of trans people and despite the widespread discrimination, poverty, and violence experienced by a large portion of the transgender community. This is a remarkable achievement in a majoritarian political system where public policy often favors those with important political resources that the transgender community lacks: access, money, and voters. *The Remarkable Rise of Transgender Rights* explains the rise of the transgender rights movement and explores how it operates despite its marginalized status within the current political opportunity structure.

Jami K. Taylor is Professor of Political Science and Public Administration at the University of Toledo.

Daniel C. Lewis is Associate Professor and Chair of the Department of Political Science and Faculty Fellow for the Community Policy Institute at Siena College.

Donald P. Haider-Markel is Professor and Chair of the Political Science Department at the University of Kansas.

The Remarkable Rise of Transgender Rights

Jami K. Taylor, Daniel C. Lewis, and
Donald P. Haider-Markel

University of Michigan Press
Ann Arbor

Copyright © 2018 by Jami K. Taylor, Daniel C. Lewis,
and Donald P. Haider-Markel

Published in the United States of America by the
University of Michigan Press
Manufactured in the United States of America
Printed on acid-free paper

A CIP catalog record for this book is available from the British Library.

Library of Congress Cataloging-in-Publication Data

Names: Taylor, Jami K., author. | Lewis, Daniel C., author. | Haider-Markel,
    Donald P., author.
Title: The remarkable rise of transgender rights / Jami K. Taylor, Daniel C.
    Lewis, and Donald P. Haider-Markel.
Description: Ann Arbor : University of Michigan Press, [2018] | Includes
    bibliographical references and index. | Identifiers: LCCN 2018023916 (print)
    | LCCN 2018036434 (ebook) | ISBN 9780472124275 (E-book) | ISBN
    9780472074013 (hardcover : acid-free paper) | ISBN 9780472054015 (pbk. :
    acid-free paper) | ISBN 9780472124275 (ebook)
Subjects: LCSH: Transgender people—Civil rights. | Transgender people—
    Legal status, laws, etc. | Sex and law. Classification: LCC HQ77.9 (ebook) |
    LCC HQ77.9 .T39 2018 (print) | DDC 306.76/8—dc23
LC record available at https://lccn.loc.gov/2018023916

*We dedicate this book to the many individuals who
have done the difficult and often thankless work of
making the world a better place for transgender people,
and to our families. Thank you.*

Contents

Transgender Identity and LGBT Rights

Introduction

When one of our coauthors, Jami Taylor, enrolled at North Carolina State University in 2001, she transitioned from male to female. This created an uproar in her department and at the university. Back then, there were few transgender people on campus. NC State did not even have a campus LGBT center. Even the state's gay rights group, Equality North Carolina, could not be described as transgender inclusive. Indeed, most folks had never met a trans person.[1] While there were some individuals who were openly hostile to her, most people honestly did not know what to make of the situation. Bathroom and locker room access was a major problem. To their great credit, the university and the department worked with her and tried to make accommodations where possible. However, the university's administration informed Jami that she could not enter the women's locker room until after she had completed sex reassignment surgery. It was the same for restrooms. She needed to use one of the few single person restrooms on campus.[2] At the time, she was thrilled that the university was this supportive, because many places were decidedly not. We share this story because it occurred in North Carolina, which in 2016 passed the nation's most egregious law targeting transgender people (HB2). This policy's most publicized effect denied most transgender people access to multiuser public restrooms that corresponded to their gender identity. This highly salient, politically inspired crackdown on transgender people effectively codified the bathroom accommodation that Jami begged and pleaded to get in 2001. Moreover, it created a national backlash. Businesses inside and outside the state were telling transgender people, regardless of their surgical status, that they could use whichever restroom they wanted. Both the president and the attorney general weighed in against the law, while Equality North Carolina was leading the charge against HB2. The state was the subject of boycotts and Governor Pat Mc-

Crory lost his reelection bid in large part because of his support for the law. With perspective, that is amazing progress. It is what winning looks like.

Indeed, the progress of transgender rights has been stunning. Most Americans today have at least heard the term transgender and they are increasingly knowledgeable about what it means (Public Religion Research Institute 2011b). However, a few decades ago, the term transgender had not yet been coined (Stryker 2008); there was no such thing as transgender rights.[3] Viewed from 2018, the change seems rapid and dramatic.

Beginning in the 1980s and 1990s, a new social movement developed around the concept of transgender (Stryker 2008). It was an informal umbrella term and a "collective political identity" (Currah, Juang, and Minter 2006b, xv) that brought together different groups who experience gender dysphoria. Those involved in this social movement share an interest in a fight for "a right to gender self-determination" (Currah, Juang, and Minter 2006b, xvi). It is a movement that is both distinct from the gay rights movement and increasingly intertwined with it due to mutual policy interests, common opponents, and gender stereotype-based discrimination that affects gay, bisexual, and trans people (e.g., Minter 2006; Taylor and Lewis 2014; Nownes 2014). The advances of the transgender movement and its allies in the combined lesbian, gay, bisexual, and transgender (LGBT) movement have been significant.

One important change has been the increasing visibility of transgender people and trans themes in our media and culture. For instance, *Time* magazine's June 9, 2014 issue gave transgender rights center billing for its cover story "Transgender Tipping Point." In that issue, Steinmetz (2014) chronicled the growing awareness of transgender rights and the plight of transgender people. Laverne Cox, a transgender actress starring in the hit television show *Orange Is the New Black*, was featured on the cover. For her role, Cox also became the first transgender person nominated for a Primetime Emmy Award (Gjorgievska 2014). The national media also fixated on the transition of Caitlyn Jenner (formerly Bruce Jenner), leading to a reality television show, *I Am Cait*. Major films in recent years, like *TransAmerica*, *The Adventures of Priscilla, Queen of the Desert*, and *Boys Don't Cry*, have focused on transgender themes. *Transparent*, a television show that explores the story of a family coming to terms with a transgender parent, won a Golden Globe Award in 2015 (Riley 2015). Transgender model Andreja Pejić prominently appeared in the fashion magazine *Vogue* (Gregory 2015). Transgender celebrities like Chaz Bono, Lana Wachowski, Janet Mock, and Jennifer Finney Boylan appear regularly in the media.

The social gains made by the transgender movement have mirrored changes in its access to the policy agenda and to related changes in public policy. Previously, the policy concerns of this group received little attention by policymakers. Transgender rights was a marginalized topic and on the fringes. Yet over the past two and a half decades the transgender movement has gained increasing access to policymakers. The movement has also achieved statutory nondiscrimination protections in several states and in many localities, often through the addition of the term "gender identity" to existing laws. The national government and several states have adopted hate/bias crimes protections with transgender-inclusive language. There have been legal victories in the courts and many favorable federal rules and policies. For instance, courts have increasingly supported transgender plaintiffs in Title VII discrimination cases (e.g., *Smith v. City of Salem* 2004) and under Title IX (e.g., *Whitaker v. Kenosha Unified School District* 2017). At the national level, Barack Obama's administration took many executive actions that improved the policy landscape for transgender people. For instance, the Social Security Administration (2016) made it easier for transgender people to amend their records and the Department of Housing and Urban Development (2012) developed a gay and transgender-inclusive equal access rule for all of its programs.

Although there have clearly been political and policy setbacks to the transgender movement, such as the 2016 passage of HB2 in North Carolina, these episodes have sometimes led to important political gains for the movement. For instance, after the passage of HB2 some Democrats in the North Carolina House of Representatives recanted their previous vote in support of the measure (e.g., Richardson 2016). Other Democrats in the state senate, who walked out rather than cast a controversial vote (B. Smith 2016), grew in their resolve to protect the LGBT community by later working to successfully repeal the measure in 2017 (Doran 2017). Interestingly, many Democrats who voted against the repeal of HB2 did so because it effectively returned policy to where it existed prior to 2015 and *did not go far enough* in protecting transgender and gay people from discrimination (Jarvis, Campbell, and Bonner 2017).

Even some Republican moderates now openly support transgender rights or at least attempt to block legislative harm to transgender people. For example, during Texas's special legislative session in the summer of 2017, a copycat version of HB2 was introduced and championed by social conservatives and the lieutenant governor. Yet the bill was ultimately scuttled by the Republican Speaker of the House, a relative moderate by Texas standards (Montgomery and Fernandez 2017). We saw a similar backlash by Republican elected officials when President Donald Trump "tweeted" that he was going to ban transgender troops in the military (May 2017). Many Republican members of Congress, a group not normally known for its warm embrace of transgender rights, balked at this abrupt policy change and the manner in which it was announced. Included in this group, surprisingly, were conservatives like Senator Orrin Hatch (R-Utah) and Senator Richard Shelby (R-Alabama). In the background of much of this strengthening resolve by Democrats and some Republicans is the increasing support for transgender and broader LGBT rights in the business community. Certainly, in the case of HB2 in North Carolina and the blockage of similar legislation in Texas, this was decisive (Montgomery and Fernandez 2017; Katz 2016). This support is a sign of important political progress for transgender rights given the position of privilege, access, and power that business enjoys in American politics (Lindblom 1977).

The movement achieved these cultural advances and policy changes despite the difficulties in identifying the relatively small number of trans people (Meier and Labuski 2013; Combs 2014) and despite widespread discrimination, poverty, and violence experienced by a large portion of the transgender community (Grant, Mottet, and Tanis 2011). This is a remarkable achievement in a majoritarian political system where public policy often favors those with important political resources that the transgender community lacks: access, money, and voters (Olson 1965; Schlozman 1984; Gilens 2012).

In this book, we explore the rise of the transgender rights movement and examine how it is operating so successfully despite its marginalized status within the current political opportunity structure. This book's central question can be described succinctly as "how are they doing that?" To begin to answer this question, we first review foundational concepts of social movements and discuss the concept of transgender in order to better understand the nature and origin of the transgender rights movement.

Introduction to Social Movements

Social movements are "collective attempts to promote or resist change in a society or a group" (Benford 1992, 1880). Movements can be regional, national, or global in scope and they might focus on political, religious, or social lifestyle issues. They can call for large or small changes in society. Some movements might focus on change in individuals rather than change in social or political structures. Movements can focus on broad agendas (e.g., the civil rights movement) or single issues (e.g., drunk driving reform). Social movements are commonly classified as revolutionary (e.g., Islamist movements) if they seek fundamental structural changes or reform oriented (e.g., the environmental movement or the gay rights movement) if they seek to modify existing social structures. Reform movements do not existentially threaten existing social institutions. Both revolutionary and reform movements may spawn countermovements (e.g., the Christian Right) that seek to preserve existing social practices and institutions (Benford 1992). Social movements are composed of individuals that sympathize with the movement, those that directly participate in movement activities, and social movement organizations that coordinate and structure activities, strategies, and tactics. In social science, we commonly call social movement organizations interest groups or pressure groups. These organizations are linkage groups that translate the interests of citizens to policymakers.

Research on movement formation finds that social movements form from a complex set of historical, cultural, and structural conditions. Macrostructural factors include the political opportunity structure, degree of political repression, existing indigenous organization, and state intervention into private spheres of life (Benford 1992). Political opportunity structure is broadly defined as "the institutional features or informal political alignments of a given political system" (McAdam 1995, 224). It can include factors such as the structure of government, the rules for decision-making, the strength of institutions, and the rules for political participation. Aspects of the political opportunity structure might be static, such as the institutional structure of government. It can also feature dynamic aspects, such as the way that political elites are divided or the presence of crises or focusing events (e.g., Smith and Fetner 2010). The opportunity structure describes how receptive and vulnerable the political system is to social movement protest (McAdam, McCarthy, and Zald 1988). A receptive or vulnerable political system encourages the development and survival of social movements and their social movement organizations (Meyer and Imig 1993).

Successful social movements provide a "proof of concept" effect in protest cycles that encourage other movements by signaling responsiveness in the system (e.g., Tarrow 1989). For example, the advances of the civil rights movement clearly encouraged mobilization of the feminist movement in the 1960s and 1970s (Minkoff 1997). Conversely, when political opportunities decline, fewer groups form. Existing groups and movements can waste away. In this regard, the external environment constrains the number of organizations that are active in the political system (Gray and Lowery 1996). Related to opportunity is threat. Perceived threats can contribute to social movement formation and activity. Groups often mobilize in response to new threats or disturbances to the status quo (Truman 1951). Smith and

Fetner (2010) note that political opportunity as an analytical tool has been criticized as being too vague and too broad because the varied contributory factors comprise most things external to the organization and they are often identified after the fact. However, Meyer and Minkoff (2004) note that structural factors clearly affect policy related outcomes. Within the public policy literature, the importance of political opportunity structures and the factors that affect them are commonly given significant attention (Button, Rienzo, and Wald 1997; Kingdon 1984). For instance, Benford (1992) notes a bell-shaped relationship between regime repression and collective action. Up to a point, repression can spur movement participation. However, as repression tactics become increasingly severe, the cost of participation can become too high. The scale of repression might also vary by the power of the group (Tilly 1978). Relatively weaker groups are more likely to be strongly repressed while collective action by stronger groups is facilitated. For example, Fording (1997) demonstrated that urban unrest in the United States during the 1960s only benefited African Americans in cities where they also had access to the ballot box. Powerless groups tend to be ignored if they have low levels of collective action.

Beyond the political opportunity structure, another important factor in developing social movements is the spread of information. Preexisting organizations can provide communications networks and provide an avenue for issue framing. They also can mobilize resources necessary to sustain a movement. For example, churches in the African American community filled these important roles during the civil rights movement (Morris 1984). Similarly, evangelical churches and conservative pastors played a role in the countermobilization of the Christian Right (Wald and Calhoun-Brown 2010). Globalization also aids in the spread of information and values, resulting in increased economic, cultural, and political interconnectedness across nations. Movements can learn from collective action in other nations and in other regions. This is furthered by the communications revolution and technologies like the Internet (Benford, Gongaware, and Valadez 2000).

Another factor that has promoted the rise of social movements is the increased role of the state. In industrialized societies, states have intervened into private domains of life to address perceived public problems, including aspects of sexuality and gender roles, which previously had been considered private matters. The socialization of conflict in previously private realms was both inspired by the development of social movements like the feminist, environmental, and gay rights movements and was motivational to these movements (Tarrow 1994). These so-called new social movement (NSM) oriented forms of collective action are often organized around the expressive goal of identity and on autonomy (Johnston, Larana, and Gusfield 1994). This perspective arose because of the inability of Marxist analysis to explain social protest that was not related to capitalist exploitation (Buechler 1995; Tarrow 1994).

Additionally, a common culture can be an important factor in social movement formation. It consists of the "shared mental worlds and their perceived embodiments" (Jasper 2010, 60). Among other things, it is found in the jokes, speeches, clothing, lifestyle choices, performing arts, rituals, events, visual symbols, texts, buildings, and memorials in a society that convey meaning (Jasper 2010). Culture provides a sense of commonality and promotes shared worldviews (Benford 1992). It shapes how we understand the world and interpret events (Faderman 1991). Culture affects our cognitive processes. Our emotions, which are "stances and reactions to the world that express how it matters for us" (Jasper 2010, 80), are in part grounded in cultural understandings as well. Shared economic activity, cultural expectations, legal status, and political status are not sufficient to create a shared collective identity. It requires shared experiences and emotions from those positions (Jasper 2010). Further, morality is in part grounded in culture. Moral shock can occur when events or actions fail to meet culturally informed expectations. This can facilitate social movement formation. Violations of values are one of the ways that conditions are transformed into problems that force themselves onto the policy agenda (Kingdon 1984). A sense of common culture can also spur social movement participation when there are minority cultural grievances against a dominant culture. At the microlevel, individuals can use relevant group frames or narratives to interpret events (Conover 1988).

Indeed, social movement organizations are actively involved in the process of framing through the use of rhetorical tools such as narrative, symbolism, and metaphor (Chong 1991). They tell stories of cause and effect, and identify villains, victims, and heroes (Stone 2012). The goal is to bring movement and individual interpretations into congruence via frame alignment (Chong 1991; Snow et al. 1986; Stryker 2000). The nature of these alignment strategies can affect tactics, the ability to form alliances, and access to the policymaking processes (Polletta and Jasper 2001). Further, framing helps to solve the recruitment and sustainment dilemmas that are required for social movements and their organizations to flourish (Chong 1991). By using various strategies and tactics, social movement organizations find a way to differentiate themselves from similar organizations (Gray and Lowery 1996). As Haider-Markel (1997) notes in his study of gay and lesbian rights groups, organizations might avoid direct competition with allied organizations through the development of issue niches (areas of specialization) while still pursuing some shared goals.

Effects of Social Movements

Social movements can lead to varying degrees of social and political change. Depending on the particular movement and its effectiveness, these changes might be seen at the individual, institutional, cultural, or political level. Yet, identifying these outcomes is difficult because some changes might not occur until well after the period of strong social movement activity (Benford 1992). For instance, the American feminist movement failed to ratify the Equal Rights Amendment, but its activity altered the social and legal status of women in ways that are still changing today—in 2015, for example, women became eligible for all combat positions in the U.S. armed forces (Tobia 2015). Such gender equality was not present and rarely demanded during the height of feminist activity in the 1970s. Additional challenges to assessing the impact of social movements include causal attribution, affect stability, goal adaptation by movements, interrelation of effects, and unintended effects (Giugni 1998). Benford, Gongaware, and Valadez (2000, 2724) contend that assessment of movement impact includes examining "explicit and implicit goals, the direction of those goals, and the intended and unintended outcomes of attempting to reach those goals." However, movement participants may have different goals and priorities (Giugni 1998, 383). Further, notions of success in goal achievement are relative. Different movement participants can interpret success or failure in different ways.

Several authors have examined ways to assess movement outcomes. Gamson (1990) noted that challenging groups might gain acceptance along two dimensions, as legitimate representatives of interests and through the introduction of new advantages. Together, these two dimensions yield four potential outcomes: (1) full response (complete success); (2) preemption (advantages without acceptance); (3) co-optation (acceptance without advantages); or (4) collapse (complete failure). Alternatively, Amenta, Carruthers, and Zylan (1992) identify three types of success: membership in the polity, co-option or recognition from opponents or the state, and concessions for the movement. In their study of the nuclear freeze movement, Rochon and Mazmanian (1993) looked at success in terms of policy change, changes in the policy process, and changes in social values. Changes in social values contribute to how political problems are defined, prioritized, and how the political agenda is set. Social values affect what is possible. In addition to having an indirect effect on policy change, changing social values is sometimes "a goal in its own right" (1993, 77). Nonetheless, political or policy outcomes are often used as measures of success (McCammon et al. 2001) even though social movements may be more effective in producing cultural change rather than structural change (Benford 1992). Indeed, changes in public opinion can serve as a movement goal (Giugni 1998). However, as noted by Rochon and Mazmanian (1993), changes in the policy process are also valuable to social movements. For example, increased requirements for public consultation can affect policy decision-making.

Social movement success may be related to the movement's resources (e.g., time, organization skills, and money) and its ability to mobilize those resources (e.g., McCarthy and Zald 1973). Gamson (1990) argued that single-issue groups are more successful than those who seek to address multiple concerns. Additionally, bureaucratized groups lacking factions are more successful. Further, movements that can deploy selective incentives are more likely to succeed. Controversially, movements that employ disruptive tactics might be more successful (Gamson 1990). Finally, one cannot understate the impact of the political context that a movement faces (e.g., Kitschelt 1986), including mass public opinion (Giugni 1998). It mediates the impact that a movement can have, and the political context has a large determinant on the possible outcomes (Amenta, Carruthers, and Zylan 1992).

In this book, we focus primarily on public policy as a measure of success for the transgender movement because of the pervasive influence of public policy on the lives of transgender people (e.g., Spade 2015). In particular, we concentrate on policies where the intended outcomes directly target or directly affect the transgender community, or both. Prior to 1990, there were few transgender-positive policies. As such, we document most policy change in this realm as a measure of success for this social movement. Of course, we also acknowledge that changing public opinion or the broader culture, or both, are goals of some social movements and explore these factors in chapters 2 and 3. Indeed, changing the public's views about gender and its relevance are goals of the transgender movement (e.g., Currah 2006). However, as policy scholars, we view public opinion and culture as inputs in the broader public policy process (Kingdon 1984). Indeed, public policy is affected by the social, political, economic, cultural, and governmental contexts in which it is made (Kraft and Furlong 2015). From this perspective, we regard the transgender social movement, and the individuals and the organizations (interest groups) that comprise it, as informal actors in the policy process. Like other organized interests, they are pursuing policy goals.

In its pursuit of policy goals, as we will discuss in the following chapter, the transgender movement became increasingly intertwined with the far larger gay and lesbian movement. Therefore, we are interested in how the transgender movement and the gay and lesbian movement became allies. This advocacy coalition (Sabatier and Weible 2007) pressed for policy changes in a host of domains and across many jurisdictions. Often, they battled an opposing coalition, the Christian Right (e.g., Wald and Calhoun-Brown 2010). Like many policy scholars (e.g., Mooney and Lee 1995), we believe that policymaking in this area is informed by morality politics. However, it is also possible that when the scope of conflict over transgender rights policies is contained, the contours of policymaking can and will be altered (Haider-Markel and Meier 1996). Thus, we are interested in how the transgender movement makes demands on the political system and which venues and which political actors are targeted. We explore the opportunities and hurdles that transgender advocates face across each of the branches of government and at different levels of government in the federal system. In short, this book seeks to explain how the transgender rights movement, despite its small size and political marginalization, has been able to secure a remarkable amount of transgender-inclusive policy in just a few decades.

Conceptualizing Transgender

Yet, before turning to those subjects, it is important to first review the concept of transgender and the origins of the transgender movement. Sex and gender are complex topics that are interrelated and central to the concept of transgender. Sex and gender are also confused with each other. Indeed, it is common in public and legal discourse to use the words interchangeably (Currah and Minter 2000). Historically and in the standard North American cultural view (Dettwyler 2011), sex has referred to the binary categorization of individuals based on biological factors such as chromosomes. However, not all individuals fit a binary definition of biological sex because chromosomes, hormone production, or hormone receptors may be atypical (Dettwyler 2011). Yet, despite prominent criticism from the intersex movement, most individuals are forced into the categories of male and female (Fausto-Sterling 1993). In the early 1900s, the word "sex" referred to male and female and the traits associated with men or women. It also encompassed their sexual behavior, with the understanding that "[t]he desires and practices known as masculine and feminine seemed to spring from the same processes that divided male and female" (Meyerowitz 2002, 3). However, this understanding of sex evolved over time. Research, such as Alfred Kinsey's work on sexual practices and Margaret Mead's examination of sex roles, helps to distinguish between biological sex, sexual behavior, and gender.

Broadly speaking, gender describes the social and cultural differences ascribed to one's sex. Gender is something that is developed via interactions with others across situations and over time (West and Zimmerman 1987). Butler (1990) notes that gender is performative. Gender shapes expectations of clothing, behavior, societal roles, and even sexual relationships. These rules for gender can change over time and across societies. For instance, as of 2015, women could serve as combat infantry in the U.S. Army (Tobia 2015), but were not allowed to drive a car in Saudi Arabia.

Most individuals adhere, to varying degrees, to the societal rules and expectations of gender. If they are born male or female bodied, they largely adhere to society's expectations for men or women. Their *gender expression*, the outward manifestation of masculinity or femininity, or both, is in conformance with societal expectations based on their assigned sex. Of course, sex is assigned when babies are classified as male or female according to external genitalia (Bishop and Myricks 2004). Additional clues about an individual's sex can be found in the secondary sex characteristics (e.g., breasts or facial hair), hormone levels, reproductive organs, and genetic makeup (Greenberg 1999). However, some people are *gender variant* because they break the cultural rules that are associated with gender. Others have a gender identification that does not align with the other markers of sex. These individuals may or may not express their gender in a societally conforming manner.

Gender identity is the internal sense of being male or female (Bullough 2000). It is a continuum rather than a dichotomy (e.g., Eyler and Wright 1997), and is another marker of one's sex. While a person's gender identification is influenced by how society constructs gender, it is likely "hardwired into the brain at birth" (Rudacille 2005, 292). When a person's gender identity is not congruent with the other markers of one's sex, that person might be described as *transgender*. Transgender refers "to individuals whose gender identity or expression does not conform to the social expectations for their assigned birth" sex (Currah, Juang, and Minter 2006b, xiv). However, it is an informal term without a precise conceptual definition (Combs 2014). Understandings vary by time and place, and by different academic disciplines. In the United States and in many other Western nations, transgender is thought of as a "collective political identity" (Currah, Juang, and Minter 2006b, xv). It is an umbrella term that encompasses many different identities, including gender queer, those who cross-dress, and transsexual individuals. The gender queer reject the binary gender system and offer "a third gender or non-gendered identity and presentation" (Combs 2014, 233). Individuals who cross-dress on a temporary basis are sometimes known by the synonym "transvestites." These individuals may occasionally adopt the dress of the opposite birth sex and might have a dual male and female identity (Combs 2014). According to the American Psychiatric Association's *Diagnostic and Statistical of Mental Disorders* (DSM-5), people with "a marked incongruence between one's experienced/expressed gender and assigned gender, of at least 6 months' duration" are said to have *gender dysphoria* (Kraus 2015).[4] People with gender dysphoria may seek varying degrees of medical treatment to bring relief from this condition. Those individuals are sometimes called transsexuals, but this term is increasingly viewed as archaic.

The origins of gender dysphoria are unclear. Studies have investigated biological and psychosocial causes (Zucker, Lawrence, and Kreukels 2016). Among the posited biological causes are prenatal exposure to abnormal levels of sex hormones that affect the development of certain brain structures relating to gender identity (Zhou et al. 1995; Kruijver et al. 2000). There are also hypothesized genetic causes (Green 2000; Henningsson et al. 2005; Bentz et al. 2008). Yet to date, Zucker, Lawrence, and Kreukels (2016) note that no gene has been found that explains gender dysphoria. They further state that for psychosocial factors to merit causal status, these factors would need to explain cross-gender identities in very young children. Otherwise, psychosocial processes might perpetuate the condition. Additionally, research into psychosocial causes in adults faces challenges posed by retrospective methodologies.

The prevalence of gender dysphoria is also uncertain. To date, no rigorous epidemiological studies have been conducted (Zucker and Lawrence 2009). Extant studies only focus on those who have either received medical treatment (e.g., Olsson and Möller 2003) or applied for a legal gender change (Dhejne et al. 2014), and they commonly only address samples within a single country (e.g., van Kesteren, Gooren, and Megens 1996). Further, methodological differences, social stigma, and differences in treatment access make meta-analyses of these studies difficult (Cohen-Kettenis and Gooren 1999). As such, estimates of prevalence vary considerably, from 1:2,900 to 1:100,000 for adults born male and 1:8,300 to 1:400,000 for adults born female (De Cuypere et al. 2007). In the United States, most studies rely on limited service provider data and self-reporting because there is little government-collected data (Zucker and Lawrence 2009). The most recent estimates, derived from the Centers for Disease Control and Prevention's Behavioral Risk Factor Surveillance System, find that 0.6 percent of the United States' population is transgender (Flores et al. 2016). This is nearly double the size of the previous estimates, highlighting the challenges of self-reported gender identity due to social stigma, changes in societal attitudes in recent years, and the diverse identities included under the informal term "transgender."

Regardless of origin or prevalence, a number of treatments are available to address severe impairment associated with gender dysphoria. However, treatment should be highly individualized due to varying personal circumstances and degrees of discomfort with one's gender dysphoria (World Professional Association for Transgender Health 2012). Despite the need for medical treatment and counseling by some portions of the transgender community, the medicalization and treatment of gender identity related conditions is contentious (Combs 2014). Medical treatments and transgender health care issues are explored further in chapter 10.

Transgender History and the Transgender Social Movement

A collective transgender *political* identity developed in the late 1980s and early 1990s (Stryker 2008), but gender variant people have existed throughout time and across cultures. Historically, examples include some ancient Egyptian, Assyrian, and Roman leaders, the twentieth-century jazz musician Billy Tipton, and many Civil War soldiers who were born female but served as men. Examples across cultures include the hijras in India and two-spirit individuals in Native American tribes (Feinberg 1996; Green 1998b). To varying degrees, these people have faced constraints imposed by gender expectations that have caused isolating personal struggles. This is complicated by the fact that societies, such as localities in the United States, also regulated what people could wear by passing laws that forbade crossdressing (Stryker 2008).

The process of translating these individual struggles with gender into "socialized conflict" (Schattschneider 1960) has been a long process involving multiple social movements. These social movements (women, gay and lesbian, and transgender) sometimes overlap, are sometimes allies, and are sometimes hostile to each other (Minter 2006; Wilchins 1997, 2004). Of course, the gay and lesbian movement is often linked with the transgender movement as the LGBT movement, but this is a relatively recent phenomenon—the incorporation just beginning in the 1990s. Moreover, the modern gay movement has its roots in the 1969 riots at the Stonewall Inn (New York City), which by many accounts were inspired by the violent reactions of transvestite patrons of the bar during an aggressive police raid (Feinberg 1992; Vaid 1995). In this book, we focus on the transgender movement, but also incorporate discussion of the movement's overlap with the women's movement and the gay and lesbian movement in later chapters.

Important in socializing conflict over gender identity was the scientific study of sex from the late 19th to the middle of the twentieth century that led to separation of sex into three separate, but interrelated concepts: biological sex, gender, and sexuality (Meyerowitz 2002). This medicalized the study of gender variance and trans identities (e.g., Bolin 1998). Researchers like Richard von Krafft-Ebing (*Psychopathia Sexualis*, 1886) and Karl Heinrich Ulrichs (*Researches on the Riddle of Man-Manly Love*, a series of tracts published between 1864 and 1880) were influential in the study of homosexuality and gender variance. This line of work helped the medical establishment become arbiters of what is sick or healthy in relation to human sexuality (Stryker 2008). Due to its social authority, the medical profession created "unjust and oppressive social hierarchies" (Stryker 2008, 36). Treatment providers' biases and sexism reflected the dominant culture from the 1960s through the 1980s (Denny 2006). This affected how treatment providers interpreted the actions of transsexual clients and, in turn, helped to shape the behavior of their patients. It further "sustained the Western paradigm that the sexes are oppositional and differences in behavior, temperament, character, emotions, and sexual orientation are constituted in biological polarity" (Bolin 1998, 68).

An important pioneer in trans related research was the German researcher Magnus Hirschfeld. As part of his research on individuals who cross-dress, Hirschfeld coined the word "transvestite" in 1910 (Stryker 2008, 38) and developed the idea that each person has a "unique combination of sex characteristics, secondary sex-linked traits, erotic preferences, psychological inclinations and culturally acquired habits and practices" (Stryker 2008, 39). His work would influence colleagues, and his Institute for Sexual Science served as a hub for research on sexual diversity prior to World War II. Notably, one person that was shaped by this work was Dr. Harry Benjamin. By the 1950s, Benjamin became the foremost expert on transsexuality and worked extensively with individuals wanting to undergo sex reassignment. He played an important role in developing diagnostic criteria and treatment protocols for trans patients.

Additionally, the treatment of transsexualism was enabled by the work of researchers who developed the understanding of endocrinology and the effects of estrogen and testosterone (Bolin 1998). Further, advances in anesthesia and surgical techniques to alter the genitalia of the intersexed and to help soldiers injured in both World Wars contributed to the development of sex reassignment surgeries (Bullough and Bullough 1998). However, while transsexualism resulted from the surgical and hormonal treatment of gender dysphoria, it was not conceptually developed (Bullough and Bullough 1998, 17). Rather, transsexualism was a creation of medical science, with treatment driving the diagnosis. This concern was reflected in withering criticism of transsexualism from feminists such as Janice Raymond (1979).

The number of individuals undergoing sex reassignment grew over time, with the overwhelming majority being male to female transgender persons (Bullough and Bullough 1998). This growth occurred despite regulatory concerns about doctors being criminally liable for creating mayhem if they performed genital modification on patients (e.g., Stryker 2008). Indeed, due to the regulatory climate in the United States, many of the medical procedures in the early years of treatment for transsexualism occurred in Europe. The most famous such case was Christine Jorgensen, a patient treated by Dr. Christian Hamburger in Denmark during the early 1950s (Docter 2008). Unlike in the United States, the Danish Sterilization and Castration Act of 1935 allowed for removal of genitals to reduce criminality or to provide relief from psychological disturbances (Bullough and Bullough 1998). The international intrigue that Christine Jorgensen spawned increased interest in transsexualism. New patients, particularly males desiring to be women, came forward. Books were written on the topic, notably *The Transsexual Phenomenon* by Harry Benjamin (1966). He also popularized the term transsexualism through his lectures on the topic (Bullough and Bullough 1998).

By the mid-1960s, large university medical centers in the United States began to open gender identity clinics with a significant focus on research (Denny 1992). The first center, at Johns Hopkins University, was funded in part by the Erickson Educational Foundation, an organization started by Reed Erickson, a wealthy female-to-male trans person (Bullough and Bullough 1998). The gender identity clinics normally contained interdisciplinary teams of doctors, therapists, and psychologists who worked with trans patients, but few had specialized training in transsexualism because the field was new. Access to their experimental care was also tightly regulated (Denny 1992).

The clinics maintained strict protocols that funneled certain types of people on the path to sex reassignment, but surgical treatment was denied to most. As noted by Denny (2006, 176–77), you had to be a "good" transsexual who manifested gender dysphoria at a young age, played with gender inappropriate toys, failed as a member of your birth sex, and had to pass as a member of the desired sex. The sexual orientation of patients was also sometimes a determinative factor in treatment decisions. This attitude contributed to recognized transsexual paths with rigid expectations and rites of passage (Bolin 1988). Because of the rigid expectations, some transsexual individuals used deception to gain access to care. Transsexuals accepted for treatment were also expected to not socialize with other transsexuals, creating a barrier to movement formation (Denny 2006). Bornstein (1994) describes how treatment protocols encouraged transsexual patients to create false histories and lie about their pasts in order to disappear into society after treatment. Individuals not accepted into the university-based gender identity programs were often left with illicit treatment options. They formed small communities of transsexuals who shared knowledge about treatment (Denny 2006).

Meanwhile, groups of crossdressers started to form in the 1950s and '60s (Stryker 2008). There was a movement to "redefine transvestism as a synonym for heterosexual male cross-dressing" (Stryker 2008, 49). As such, many of these groups explicitly barred gay or transsexual individuals, or both (Stryker 2008). A key pioneer in this culture was Virginia Prince, a trans person who transitioned to a female social role, but eschewed sex reassignment (Meyerowitz 2002). Prince started a long-running crossdresser-focused magazine called *Tranvestia* and the Foundation for Personality Expression, which would later be named Tri-Ess. With this platform, Prince openly campaigned *against* sex reassignment surgeries and tried to convince trans individuals to avoid that path (Meyerowitz 2002).

Prior to the 1990s, the terms "transgender" and "transgenderist" were used by individuals like Virginia Prince and Ari Kane to describe those who permanently changed their social genders (unlike crossdressing), but who did not envision medical sex reassignment (transsexuals) (Stryker 2008, 123). However, the current meaning of transgender grew out of separate communities of transsexuals and crossdressers in the mid-1980s and early '90s. In 1984, the first large organization for crossdressers and transsexuals was formed, the International Foundation for Gender Education (Denny 2006). It published the journal *Tapestry* (later, *Transgender Tapestry Journal*). Other combined transsexual and crossdresser groups formed with their own small newsletters. These groups and their publications provided a forum to discuss problems with treatment options, models of gender variance, and intercommunity differences (Denny 2006). Among the important differences that needed to be bridged were those between the homosexual and heterosexual trans communities (Frye 2000).

In a seminal article published in *Tapestry* and *Chrysalis Quarterly*, Holly Boswell (1991, 30) put forth transgenderism as a "bridge of consciousness between crossdressers and transsexual people who feel unnecessarily estranged within our own subcultures." Boswell's conception of transgenderism emphasized androgyny and defiance of binary cultural norms of gender. Her article put forth models of transgender identity, including the advanced crossdresser, the androgyne, and the pretranssexual person. Leslie Feinberg's 1992 publication *Transgender Liberation: A Movement Whose Time Has Come* brought this new conceptualization of transgender into the political sphere (Stryker 2008). Feinberg's Marxist interpretation discussed oppression and how trans people were subjected to cruelty. It also called for unity among trans people and harkened back to earlier uprisings, such as Stonewall. Led by activists such as the late Lou Sullivan and FTM International successor Jamison Green, a small but growing female-to-male transgender community was also becoming more prominent (Green 1998; Cameron 1996).

In addition, several scholars, such as Judith Butler (1990) with her conceptualization of gender as performance, created space for transgender within academic circles and contributed to how transgender people understood themselves (Stryker 2008). Queer theory was one such field (Wilchins 2004). Additionally, Sandy Stone (1991) produced a touchstone book chapter for transgender studies with *The Empire Strikes Back: A Posttranssexual Manifesto*. This work was an important rebuttal to feminist scholar Janice Raymond's attacks on transsexualism. It noted that transsexual invisibility and passing led to inauthentic relationships and lives. Stone called for transsexuals to be open about their lives.

Bolin (1998) described the revolutionary changes that this concept of transgender had on trans communities since her earlier work (1988). There now were more than two possibilities, and people were found all along the gender spectrum. Kate Bornstein (1994, 8) highlights this sentiment:

> I know I'm not a man—about that much I'm very clear, and I've come to the conclusion that I'm probably not a woman either, at least not according to a lot of people's rules on this sort of thing. The trouble is that we we're living in a world that insists we be one or the other—a world that doesn't bother to tell us exactly what the other is.

Activists like Riki Wilchins (1997) were exploring ways to undermine the gender binary. While the transgender movement contains many identities with different experiences, its participants share an interest in the fight for "a right to gender self-determination" (Currah, Juang, and Minter 2006b, xvi).

In addition to the undermining of binary gender concepts, Bolin (1998) argues that changes in the societal role of women were a significant factor in the development of the transgender concept. These changes have occurred in both the economic and social spheres. Changing standards of beauty have allowed more androgynous or muscular female body shapes to be viewed as attractive and acceptable. This has opened more space for male-to-female trans people to "pass" as the other sex.

Another factor that led to the rise of the transgender movement was the closure of most university-affiliated gender treatment centers during the 1980s. This, combined with the already strict requirements for acceptance, left many transsexual individuals without options for treatment (Bolin 1998; Denny 2006). However, non-university-affiliated treatment centers soon filled the void. These centers placed greater emphasis on their transsexual patients (Denny 1992) and had more flexible gender expression and identity requirements (Bolin 1998). As businesses, they were incentivized to provide care to cash paying customers. Many transsexuals also realized that disappearing into the woodwork was unacceptable and difficult, if not impossible. For instance, Lynn Conway, a computer scientist at the University of Michigan, found that she could not escape her earlier career as an engineer at IBM, even after decades of living quietly in stealth (Hiltzik 2000). This also happened to the model and actress Caroline Cossey (Nichols 2016). While Cossey's outing occurred before the rise of the World Wide Web, the Internet has made it easy to do background checks on individuals. Attempting to live in stealth leaves one in constant fear of the devastating financial, social, and emotional effects of being outed.

Another important factor in the development of the transgender movement was the creation of transgender conferences such as Southern Comfort, Be All You Can Be, Texas T-party, and California Dreaming (Frye 2000; Wilchins 2016). One might also include the numerous support groups that met in many locations around the nation. Preeminent transgender activist Riki Wilchins (2016) notes that while conferences, like Southern Comfort, are not political by design, they are political in nature because they bring marginalized people together. Jamison Green (2016) touched upon this theme as well when he discussed the importance of the first conference for transgender men in 1995 on subsequent organizing in the female-to-male community. Wilchins (2016) said, "It is hard to see that trans is just a personal issue when there were so many other transgender people there." Jamison Green (2016) added that the female-to-male transgender community learned a lot from the male-to-female support groups that often gathered. Of course, some transgender conferences were political by design. It was at the International Conference on Transgender Law and Employment Policy that the International Bill of Gender Rights was adopted in 1993 (Frye 2000).

Finally, movement development was aided by the communications revolution between the late 1980s and the 2000s (Frye 2000). From the old computer bulletin board systems where transgender people could trade information, to closed systems like Compuserve and America Online, to the later open Internet and its many webpages, improved communications made the diffusion of information easier and cheaper. It allowed individuals to search for information despite the social stigma attached to transsexualism or transgender identities. It gave scared and isolated individuals a feeling of anonymity to do research, to try out identities in online spaces, and to learn about treatment options. It let them know that they were not alone (Frye 2000). These services also allowed transgender individuals, such as Andrea James, to share information without the filters of doctors, therapists, and other gatekeepers.[5] Chat rooms like The Gazebo, started by Gwendolyn Ann Smith, or Donna's Den, put isolated transgender individuals in contact with one another (New York Times 2015). As a result, more transgender people began to come out (Frye 2000). The Internet would also be an important factor in transgender organizing (Shapiro 2004). Wilchins (2016) called the Internet "a facilitator" that helped to rapidly advance the organizing that had already started.

Discussion and Outline of the Book

The prior review provides a foundation for understanding the recognition and growth of transgender people and the transgender movement in the United States. In the chapters that follow, we more closely explore the rise of the transgender movement. We examine how a relatively small collection of individuals and groups came to have considerable political and policy success at such a rapid pace.

In chapter 1, we examine the rise of transgender as a political identity (Bornstein 1994; Feinberg 1998; Wilchins 1997; Murib 2015), social movement (Currah, Juang, and Minter 2006a; Stryker and Whittle 2006), and interest group system (Nownes 2010). We highlight the importance of transforming trans identities from a psychiatric/medical condition to a political movement (Minter 2006). Additionally, we address the history of organized transgender activism (Stryker 2008), the initial exclusion of transgender people from the gay and lesbian rights movement (Minter 2006), and the long road to inclusion under the umbrella of the LGBT rights movement (Taylor and Lewis 2014). Drawing from interviews with leading LGBT activists and some current and former elected officials, our argument posits that the alliance with the gay rights movement occurred for several reasons, such as the HIV/AIDS crisis, and this has significantly boosted transgender rights.

In section II, we turn to the role of public attitudes in transgender rights and politics. We provide insights about public attitudes on transgender rights by incorporating findings from three national public opinion polls administered in June 2015, October 2015, and June 2016. These surveys were authored by a team of researchers from across the country and funded by the University of Toledo, the University of Kansas, UCLA's Williams Institute, and Ohio University. The scholars joining us on these chapters are Barry Tadlock, Andrew Flores, and Patrick Miller. These public opinion scholars were important collaborators in our previously published polling research. In addition, Tadlock was a major contributor to our edited volume, *Transgender Rights and Politics: Groups, Issue Framing, and Policy Adoption* (University of Michigan Press, 2014). The chapters in this section shed new light on public attitudes toward the transgender community and transgender rights policies.

Chapter 2 provides a comprehensive descriptive exploration of public opinion toward transgender people and related policies, filling an important void in the literature. The survey data used in this chapter covers general feelings toward transgender people and transgender concepts. It also assesses public support for a wide range of relevant policies, such as gender-identity-inclusive protections against discrimination in employment and public accommodations, allowing military service by transgender individuals, and policies about public restroom usage by transgender people. Where appropriate, we also compare this to acceptance levels for gay and lesbian individuals. Further, we explore attitudes about preventing bullying of transgender students in public schools and public funding of sex reassignment surgeries via social programs, among other issues. Finally, we examine public support for policies that enable transgender people to change their sex on government documents and public support for transgender political candidates.

Chapter 3 explores the underlying factors that shape public attitudes on transgender issues. Research on attitudes toward gay rights generally finds that views are shaped by individual characteristics, values, psychological traits, and experiences such as contact with gay people (Brewer 2003, 2008; Olson, Cage, and Harrison 2006; Haider-Markel and Joslyn 2008; Lewis and Gossett 2008; Herek 2002; Lewis 2003). However, very few studies have examined whether, and how, these factors affect attitudes toward transgender rights. Based on existing theoretical frameworks, we explore the characteristics, experiences, and values that underlie these attitudes with data from our three surveys on transgender rights. In particular, our analyses focus on contact theory, political knowledge, political identity, religion, psychological traits (e.g., authoritarianism), and individual demographic characteristics.

In section III, we build on earlier research to examine transgender politics within different institutions to understand the growth of transgender rights based on political opportunity structures. This includes addressing transgender rights in direct democracy contests, in legal and judicial processes, and within legislative and executive branches of government. In the American context, federalism is also at play given that the fifty states, each with their own tripartite structure of government and diverse publics, have great latitude to create laws or policies that can hinder or advance transgender rights. States can also empower their localities to pass transgender-inclusive policies or prohibit them from doing so. Conversely, state officials might seek to thwart the actions of the national government.

Chapter 4 focuses on transgender politics within American legislative contexts. We employ and examine systematic data on when and how transgender issues have reached the political agenda of state and national legislatures. We also address the fate of these proposals over time. In addition, we dive deeper into the legislative process by providing a case study of a transgender-inclusive law that was passed by Congress.

Chapter 5 examines policymaking in the courts and the litigation-based strategies used by the LGBT movement. Joining us in writing this chapter is Jason Pierceson, a noted expert on LGBT issues in the judiciary. Here we connect transgender rights litigation to the larger LGBT movement and demonstrate that the typical critique of litigation-based movements is exaggerated. Indeed, given higher levels of challenge to binary conceptualizations of gender and the social ostracism experienced by transgender people, litigation may be essential for the creation of transgender policy. Based on interviews with activist lawyers, documents from litigation organizations, and an examination of legal documents, this chapter examines the reasons for this use of and recent turn to litigation.

Chapter 6 examines the role of the executive branch in the advancement of transgender rights. Joining us in writing this chapter is Mitchell Sellers, an important contributor to our previous edited volume and an expert on executive power in the states. We analyze bureaucratic rulemaking on transgender rights issues as well as presidential and gubernatorial use of unilateral powers to understand the current framework of transgender protections that arose within the executive branches of the nation and the states. In doing so, we advance work by Sellers (2014b) on the strategic use of transgender-inclusive executive orders by governors. The analysis includes interviews with leaders in national and state LGBT rights organizations, agency officials, and former Delaware governor Jack Markell (2009–17). Further, this chapter chronicles the myriad regulatory advances made on the federal and state levels, with particular emphasis on changes made during the Obama administration.

Chapter 7 explores the role of direct democracy institutions, such as ballot initiatives and referendums, in the fight for transgender-inclusive policy. These institutions provide another venue for policy advocates to pursue their goals. However, the literature on direct democracy highlights the potentially negative impact that these institutions may have on minority rights (Haider-Markel et al. 2007; Lewis 2013). When public opinion aligns against a particular minority group, governmental systems with direct democracy institutions may increase the probability of passing antiminority legislation compared to purely representative systems. This chapter assesses the effects of direct democracy on transgender rights policy by examining local ballot measures. We explore how LGBT groups and their political opponents have used these institutions and examine how policy development in this venue compares to policy outputs from representative governments.

In section IV, the final section of the book, we more closely examine specific policy areas relevant to transgender people, looking at both victories and the challenges for the future. We discuss the current state of transgender public policy (as of February 2018) and examine its controversies. In these short chapters, we highlight key issues in several policy domains.

Chapter 8 leads the discussion by examining the importance of legal forms of identification in American society. For instance, verification of one's identity might be required to gain access to public education, to vote, to obtain a marriage license, or to travel on airlines. While these everyday interactions are of little interest to most people, they are highly significant for many transgender individuals (e.g., Davis 2014). This chapter addresses trends in administrative regulations for securing driver's licenses, birth certificates, passports, and other critical governmental documents.

Chapter 9 provides an account of several major nondiscrimination policy areas: employment, public accommodations, housing, and credit. We examine the executive actions by the Obama and Trump administrations, the Civil Rights Act of 1964, and related court decisions. Of particular importance is the Supreme Court's ruling in *Price Waterhouse v. Hopkins* (1989) that made gender stereotyping a prohibited form of sex discrimination under Title VII. We also detail the dramatic 2016 repeal of the ban on transgender service members and its potential future. Beyond federal policy, we review current state laws in each policy area. This section also includes state court decisions and executive orders that cover gender identity in public employment. In addition, we address local transgender-inclusive laws and their implementation under home rule regimes.

Chapter 10 examines the evolution of gender-identity-related medical issues and addresses associated health care policies. Joining us on this chapter is Ryan Combs, another contributor from our previous volume and an expert on health policy. It begins with the exclusion of transgender related medical or psychological treatment under most private insurance policies in the United States. As a result, many transgender individuals are often unable to obtain treatment given the costs associated with various therapies (Currah and Minter 2000; Dasti 2002). We explore trends in this area along with changes that facilitated greater transgender access to health care under the Affordable Care Act. The chapter also addresses public programs such as Medicare and Medicaid (e.g., Dasti 2002; Minter 2003).

Recent attention to the recurring legal fights over accommodations and transgender K-12 students provides the introduction to chapter 11. We then turn to federal law, particularly Title IX and related case law (e.g., *Miles v. New York University* 1997). The chapter also examines state laws prohibiting discrimination in education as well as state and local antibullying policies. Beyond K-12 education, we address transgender identities in college and university settings. We discuss related trends, such as installing unisex bathrooms and gender-neutral housing, and we examine student records and privacy concerns. Finally, we address the increasingly common, yet highly controversial, issue of transgender people in athletics.

Chapter 12 examines transgender identities in the context of criminal justice policies and practices. We begin with discussion of the victimization of trans people in bias-motivated crimes and examine related transgender-inclusive hate crime laws at the national and state level. We then turn to the interactions of transgender people with the criminal justice system, beginning with police-transgender relations. Subsequently, we address transgender issues in federal and state prisons and cover relevant case law (e.g., *Fields v. Smith* 2011; *De'lonta v. Angelone* 2003; *De'lonta v. Johnson* 2013). The discussion includes incarceration policies, such as confinement with prisoners of the opposite gender or the placement of transgender inmates in administrative segregation. The chapter highlights policies and court decisions regarding treatment for a transgender prisoner's gender-identity-related medical issues.

Our concluding remarks in chapter 13 draw out the themes and lessons from the previous chapters. Our focus is on reinforcing the notion that there is great difficulty in creating a coherent policy framework for transgender identities in America's federal system. However, this fragmented policymaking system has also allowed transgender individuals to register surprising gains despite their limited resources, which is partly the result of the framers' intentions in dispersing power within the federal system.

CHAPTER 1

Rise of the Transgender Rights Movement and LGBT Rights

As David Meyer (2004) notes, the potential influence of a social movement and its outcomes are determined by interactions between the movement and the world around it. Indeed, one cannot explain the rise of the transgender movement without examining the context from which it arose. This requires exploring the factors affecting the development of the gay and lesbian rights movement, including the early exclusion and the subsequent incorporation of transgender rights into a broader LGBT rights movement. To answer the question of how transgender rights became intertwined with gay rights, we interviewed several activists and reviewed the literature in the field. These elite interviews were conducted with a mix of longtime transgender rights activists, LGBT rights professionals, policymakers, and academics. Appendix B discusses these interviews and our methodology. Throughout the chapter, we highlight the importance of the development of the transgender rights movement as part of a LGBT advocacy coalition. We examine the role of the academy, the HIV/AIDS crisis, movement professionalization, commonalities between gay and trans people, and the media in the development of transgender rights and LGBT rights.

LGBT Rights and Collective Identities

A critical foundation to all social movements is a collective identity. Snow (2001, 2) notes that its "essence resides in a shared sense of one-ness or we-ness anchored in real or imagined shared attributes and experiences among those who comprise the collectivity and in relation or contrast to one or more actual or imagined sets of 'others.'" These collective identities are often assumed to occur naturally among societal groups, but the new social movement tradition argues that collective identities are constructed and maintained by social movements themselves (e.g., Melucci 1995). Indeed, movements engage in boundary work that defines who they are and who they are not (Fominaya 2010). Gamson (1995, 393) notes that battles over group membership are part of determining "whose rights and freedoms are at stake in the movements." Further, social movements strategically deploy these collective identities in order to make public claims (Campbell 2003; Rupp and Taylor 1999). Collective identities with clear borders are sometimes required for political gains (Gamson 1995). Conversely, Snow et al. (1986) note that extension of a social movement's collective identity can alienate existing adherents and conscience constituents, dampening their participation and support. Thus, it is very important to examine how the LGBT movement emerged from the gay rights movement.

The 1969 Stonewall Rebellion is generally thought of as the birth of the modern gay rights movement, even though groups such as the Mattachine Society and the Daughters of Bilitis were already active well beforehand (Rimmerman 2015). This event took place during an era when the large "baby boom" generation was coming of age and revolutionary cultural changes were under way. Sexual mores were changing with the advent of the birth control pill. Gender norms were changing as well. Men were growing their hair longer and women were cutting their hair. Both men and women were donning more unisex clothing (Hillman 2011). Hair, clothing, appearance, and self-presentation were increasingly contested political battlegrounds where those who deviated from established norms were sometimes labeled as queers (Hillman 2015).

In addition, the gay rights movement of the late 1960s developed in the wake of the battles over civil rights, which sparked a cycle of protest where many contender groups (African Americans, Chicanos, Native Americans, women, gay men) were pressing for political and social change. As McAdam (1994) notes, the civil rights movement for African Americans shaped the gay rights movement and other leftist social movements that arose at the time. Importantly, all of these groups adopted a "civil rights master frame" (McAdam 1994, 42) that created a collective identity as victims of discrimination deserving of equal rights.

Yet, despite the emerging collective identity as a countercultural civil rights movement, the gay rights movement had many rifts. Like other social movements that emerged during this era, it has long been divided between assimilationists, who emphasized sameness with the dominant societal group (straight people), and liberationists, who emphasized differences (e.g., Gamson 1995; Rimmerman 2015). During the 1970s, there were also deep divisions between gay men and lesbian women because of misogyny in the gay rights movement (Rimmerman 2015). Due to the underlying sexism that lesbians felt, gay men and lesbian women tended to organize separately (Hillman 2011). However, gays and lesbians in the late 1970s sometimes worked together to battle political backlash. One such instance occurred in 1977 during Anita Bryant's Save Our Children campaign to repeal a gay rights ordinance in Dade County, Florida. Another important instance of coordination happened during the campaign to defeat the 1978 Briggs Initiative in California that would have banned gays and lesbians from working in public schools. Despite these limited efforts, the gay and lesbian communities often remained divided.

Gender division also extended to the trans community during this era (Valentine 2007). Both gay men and lesbians sometimes marginalized gender variant people, such as butch lesbians or effeminate gay men and transsexual individuals, due to assimilationist pressures. Sinfield (2004, 269) describes the sentiment as "people whose primary sense of themselves was firmly grounded in gender dissidence . . . were incidental, unintelligible, out-of-date, embarrassing." This marginalization occurred despite the contributions that trans individuals, such as Reed Erickson, had long provided to gay and lesbian rights advocacy and organizations (Devor and Matte 2004). In the 1970s, lesbian separatists also rebuked trans women, who felt that such individuals threatened women's spaces (Valentine 2007). Examples of this type of exclusion include the Michigan Womyn's Music Festival (1976–2015) and their womyn born womyn policy (Califia 1997) as well as protests over a trans woman's employment at the all-female company Olivia Records (Raymond 1979).[1] The gender bending practice of drag, which had long held a place in gay communities, was also controversial and often deemed not respectable (Hillman 2011). It invited police attention at a time when sodomy laws still existed in most states and some activists were conscious of how it was used to stereotype gay men as effeminate. Additionally, many lesbian feminists felt that drag mocked women because it trafficked in female sex stereotypes (Raymond 1996). Doctors who performed sex reassignment surgeries were also criticized by both gay liberationists and feminists because they were not sufficiently radical on matters of sex, gender, and sexuality (Meyerowitz 2002, 262).

With the demise of liberationist groups like the Gay Liberation Front in the early 1970s, gender transgression was outside the purview of "homosexual issues" (Hillman 2011, 178) for gay rights organizations. Devor and Matte

(2004) state that "[h]omosexual collective identity, especially in the days before queer politics, was largely framed as inborn, like an ethnicity, and based primarily on sexual desires for persons of the same sex and gender." As late as the 1990s, gay rights activists debated whether to make arguments about immutability, an essentialist argument, part of legal strategies (Halley 1994). Thus, transsexual people during this period were viewed as separate from gay rights activism (Valentine 2007). Additionally, the medical community generally told them to be secret (to not be public) about their transitions—they were told to lie about their past lives (Bornstein 1994), which contrasted sharply with the "being out" message of gay rights activists.

In the 1980s, the HIV/AIDS epidemic, with its highly disproportionate impact on gay men in the United States and the strengthening backlash to gay rights, created an existential threat to sexual minorities. Klarman (2013, 39) referred to AIDS as a "call to action." Infected individuals were dying in ever-larger numbers and there was no response by the government. As powerfully shown in the documentary film *How to Survive a Plague* and in numerous other works (e.g., Kramer 1985), people were scared, and they became angry at government indifference to their plight. Gays and lesbians put aside many of their differences in response to what pluralist group scholars, like Truman (1951), might refer to as a societal "disturbance." With little governmental response to the crisis, gay men and lesbians formed groups to take care of their own, creating a generation of lesbian and gay activists politicized by the HIV/AIDS crisis (Rimmerman 2015). More gay people (and transgender people) came out of the closet. Lesbian and gay activists also interacted with transgender people who were also affected by the disease. In addition to incentivizing the movement to expand and heal divisions, the epidemic also attracted the attention of economic elites and donors. As a result, the capacity of gay rights organizations significantly increased during this time (D'Emilio 2002).

Indeed, new advocacy groups mobilized in cities across the nation and a new wave of outsider politics was born. Some of these groups, notably ACT-UP, Queer Nation, and Lesbian Avengers, eschewed the assimilationist approaches of 1970s gay rights activism and engaged in more direct action tactics (Rimmerman 2015). Overall, gay rights organizations made important progress by the late 1980s and early 1990s. They found increasing access to political elites and were able to build political alliances. For example, the 1988 Democratic Party Platform included an AIDS plank and a pro–gay rights plank was added to the 1992 Democratic Party Platform (Democratic Party 1988, 1992). This access to party elites showed that there was openness in the political opportunity structure (Tarrow 1994).

As Califia (1997, 225) notes, the shifts in gay rights identities and advocacy tactics also played a role in the development of transgender rights organizations. Groups such as Transgender Nation and Transexual Menace successfully mobilized despite the diverse set of identities that would be encompassed by the label of transgender (Nataf 1996; Currah 2006). Different identities, from gay or straight identified transgender people, to postoperative male-to-female transsexuals, female-to-male transsexuals, nonoperative trans people, and the gender fluid were each fighting for self-expression and a "right to gender self-determination" (Currah, Juang, and Minter 2006b, xvi) and against social, political, and economic marginalization, stigmatization, and discrimination. They were able to project a unity that is necessary in political advocacy (Murib 2015), while at the same time sometimes criticizing the very identity politics models that other movements used (Wilchins 2004). Like activists from other movements who had challenged the socially constructed hierarchies of race, class, and gender, transgender activists were questioning the category of sex (Meyerowitz 2002, 285).

Transgender activists would challenge not only the injustices in governmental policies, inadequacies of doctors and medical treatment of transsexuals, harassment and violence, but they also challenged the gay and lesbian rights social movement. They confronted exclusion by prominent gay rights groups, such as Lambda Legal and the Human Rights Campaign (HRC), in their legal and legislative advocacy. They rebuked organizations like the Service Members Legal Defense Network, who appropriated transgender people or ignored their existence, such as what occurred to Calpernia Addams during the media and advocacy frenzy over the 1999 murder of her boyfriend, Pvt. Barry Winchell (France 2000). They also criticized the media for failing to report on the truths of transgender lives, for painting trans people as gay, or otherwise erasing them, in cases like the murder of Brandon Teena in 1993 (Minkowitz 1994). Protests about violence against transgender individuals, mistreatment by those with authority (such as the 1995 death of car accident victim Tyra Hunter at the hands of unsympathetic paramedics), or exclusion in legislation (such as the federal Employment Nondiscrimination Act and similar state-level bills) often proved to be rallying cries for the transgender community. Particularly for the latter, gay and lesbian rights groups were often the target of these protests (e.g., Johnson 2017).

According to Diego Sanchez (2016), the director of policy for PFLAG (originally Parents and Friends of Lesbians and Gays), a critical turning point in the battle with gay rights groups was the trans community's fight for inclusion in the 1993 March on Washington for Lesbian, Gay and Bi Rights. Frye (2000, 460) describes this as the "first national act of defiance" by transgender people. While they were excluded in name and some transgender activists had talked of lying down in front of the march in protest, they did get mention in the event's purpose and goals (Frye 2000). For this event, and in many organizations, transgender people, as former National Gay and Lesbian Task Force director Matt Foreman (2016) described, "demanded a seat at the table." Some gay rights organizations, such as the National Gay and Lesbian Task Force, responded relatively quickly to these advocacy efforts (Nownes 2014). Others did not. As noted by Taylor and Lewis (2014), this process of full incorporation into the policy core of the LGBT advocacy coalition would develop slowly during the 1990s and 2000s.

This gradual incorporation is evident in the evolution of state-level laws to protect gay and transgender people from discrimination in employment, hate crimes, and in relationship recognition (marriage, civil union, or domestic partnership). As seen in table 1.1, of the states that adopted laws prior to 1995 protecting gay people from discrimination, only one state, Minnesota, elected to also protect transgender people at the same time. This reflects both the lack of organized transgender advocacy and the lack of attentiveness to transgender rights within the gay rights coalition. However, between 1996 and 2005, as transgender people were increasingly pressuring gay rights organizations for inclusion in an LGBT advocacy coalition, three of the eight states passing gay inclusive nondiscrimination laws concurrently included transgender protections. Transgender rights were secondary concerns within the burgeoning coalition and, as such, would not be prioritized in the face of legislative opposition. Transgender people were thus excluded from protections in states like New York and Maryland. As transgender inclusion moved toward the policy core in the LGBT advocacy coalition between 2006 and 2015, four of the five states that passed comprehensive sexual-orientation-inclusive nondiscrimination protections were also concurrently inclusive of gender identity.[2] The only laggard in the latter period was Delaware, a state where there was significant legislative discomfort with transgender inclusion and where there was little trans involvement in the state's gay rights advocacy coalition (Peterson 2016; Taylor and Lewis 2014).[3]

Further evidence of this slow incorporation of transgender rights into the LGBT coalition can be seen in the timing of policy adoptions. States that adopted sexual orientation protections earlier tended to prioritize relationship recognition (domestic partnerships, civil unions, and same-sex marriage) ahead of gender-identity-inclusive protections. We see this pattern in places like Massachusetts, New York, Maryland, and Vermont. Also demonstrating the slow incorporation of transgender rights into the policy core of the advocacy coalition is the long delay in "coming back" to transgender nondiscrimination in most of the early states that adopted sexual-orientation-inclusive policies against discrimination. For the ten states that passed a sexual-orientation-only nondiscrimination measure prior to 2005 and subsequently added gender identity protections, the average delay was greater than fifteen years. Eventually, most early adopters passed transgender protections, but it was not until the LGBT coali-

TABLE 1.1. Nondiscrimination Policy Data

State	Sexual Orientation ND Law	Broad Relationship Recognition	Hate Crime Law (Gay/Trans)	Gender Identity ND Law	Years btw. Gay and Trans Laws	Relationship Recognition before Trans ND Law?
WI	1982	*2014*	2002	——	——	Yes
MA	1989	*2004*	2002/2011	2011	22	Yes
CT	1991	2005*	2004/2004	2011	20	Yes
HI	1991	2011*	2003/2003	2011	20	Same Session
CA	1992	1999*	1999/1999	2003	11	Yes
NJ	1992	2006*	2002/2008	2006	14	Same Session
VT	1992	2000*	2001/2001	2007	15	Yes
MN	1993	2013	1993/1993	1993	0	No
RI	1995	2011*	2001/2012	2001	6	No
NH	1997	2007*	2002	2018	21	Yes
NV	1999	2009*	2001/2013	2011	12	Yes
MD	2001	2012	2005/2005	2014	13	Yes
NY	2002	2011	2002	——	——	Yes
NM	2003	*2013*	2003/2003	2003	0	No
IL	2005	2011*	2001/2016	2005	0	No
ME	2005	2012	2001	2005	0	No
WA	2006	2009*	1993/2009	2006	0	No
CO	2007	2013*	2005/2005	2007	0	No
IA	2007	*2009*	2002	2007	0	No
OR	2007	2008*	2001/2008	2007	0	No
DE	2009	2011*	2001/2013	2013	4	Yes
UT	2015	*2014*	——	2015	0	Yes

Sources: Badgett and Herman (2011), National Gay and Lesbian Task Force (2014), National Council of State Legislatures (2014) and Taylor and Lewis (2014)

Notes: This table is updated from Taylor and Lewis (2014). States not listed here do not have a nondiscrimination law that covers sexual orientation or gender identity. MO (2001) has a fully inclusive hate crimes statute. AZ (2003), FL (2001), KS (2002), KY (2001), LA (2002), NE (2002), TN (2001), and TX (2002) offer hate crimes protections for sexual orientation. MI (2002) requires the collection of data for crimes committed on the basis of sexual orientation. The relationship recognition column refers to civil unions, broadly constructed domestic partnerships, and marriage. Dates in italics under relationship recognition refer to a court imposed relationship recognition rather than a statute or ballot initiative. We acknowledge that the state court system forced Vermont's legislature to at minimum grant civil unions. Asterisks denote civil unions or domestic partnerships. Same-sex marriage laws that were blocked by voters (e.g., California 2008 and Maine 2009) are not included. Utah's nondiscrimination laws do not include public accommodations.

tion fully incorporated trans identities that transgender rights became a core priority.

The ability of transgender activists to secure "a seat at the table," both directly and indirectly through influential voices within gay rights organizations, can be attributed to a process known as *co-optation* (Selznick 1948). This process is undertaken when organizations face threats to stability or existential threats, and in reaction absorb new elements into the policymaking team. This occurs when the legitimacy of the organization is called into question or when power centers exist outside the command of the leadership team. Both factors affected the inclusion of transgender rights into the gay rights movement. As noted earlier, transgender rights advocates sharply criticized many gay rights organizations during the 1990s and 2000s for their exclusionary practices in decision-making and on proposed legislation. As noted by former Equality North Carolina board member Addison Ore (2016), "There was a great deal of pressure for trans inclusion. At a community meeting . . . they let us have it. We felt under siege." These criticisms often surfaced in policy debates, such as during the proposed federal Employment Nondiscrimination Act (ENDA) in 1995 that would have banned sexual orientation employment discrimination (Frye 2000). HRC explicitly opposed gender identity or transgender inclusion in the 1995 bill (Frye 2000, 465), which led many gender-variant gay, lesbian, or bisexual people to voice displeasure with their exclusion from ENDA. They also voiced opposition at the exclusion of transgender people from ENDA. Further, this lack of inclusive advocacy exacerbated long-running race and class divisions in the gay rights movement that go back to its white middle class origins (Minter 2006; Vaid 2012).

These critiques continued, culminating in the 2007 fight over ENDA in which HRC faced severe criticism from a coalition of more than 400 LGBT rights organizations, United ENDA, about its opposition to transgender inclusion (Johnson 2017). Temple University professor and expert in transgender advocacy, Heath Fogg Davis (2016), described the battle "as a debacle" that deeply divided the LGBT social movement. Its largest advocacy organization, HRC, was at cross-purposes with a large coalition of other LGBT rights organizations on the issue of transgender inclusion. Although they all wanted transgender protections, they were sharply divided on tactics (inclusion in a single bill versus separate bills and almost certainly "coming back" for transgender people). Former Equality Ohio executive director Lynne Bowman (2016) stated that this episode forced "us to say that we are us." Longtime transgender activist Jamison Green (2016) referred to the episode as "a big wakeup call" for HRC. As noted by Mara Keisling (Johnson 2017), "HRC had totally lost touch with what the community was." The

2007 ENDA fight forced them to grapple with divisions in the LGBT rights movement and engage more meaningfully with transgender rights and with varieties of gender expression within gay and lesbian communities.

The fight over ENDA in 2007 also highlights the second factor associated with co-optation: the existence of power centers outside the control of national LGBT group leadership. Reflecting the division among gay and lesbian activists on transgender exclusion, United ENDA, a coalition of just about every other large national LGBT rights organization and the majority of statewide groups, assembled to challenge HRC and the views of some members of Congress (e.g., Representative Barney Frank) in the 2007 ENDA fight. This wide-ranging coalition took on the largest gay rights organization and had the credibility to point out the hypocrisy in HRC's ubiquitous use of equality symbols (including bumper stickers) even though the organization was demonstrably not applying that principle to trans and gender variant people. HRC's only transgender board member, Donna Rose, resigned in protest over the organization's decision to not oppose putting sexual orientation and gender identity in separate bills (Eleveld 2007a).

Donors and grantors form another type of power center commonly outside of leadership control. Speaking to the ability of United ENDA to disrupt fundraising efforts by HRC and Representative Frank, transgender activist Rebecca Juro stated (Johnson 2017):

> The reason why Barney Frank was able to introduce and get the kind of support he did in Congress was because there was a feeling [of] who cares, nobody knows about these people. . . . What that did was it said, "No, no, no, you're wrong." and people are going to call you out and it's going to cost you politically and people are going to show up at the Human Rights Campaign galas and make it difficult for you to solicit money for your campaign.

The impact of funders extends beyond the 2007 ENDA fight. From the 1980s through the early 2000s, LGBT major donors and funders might have been "ambivalent about transgender rights" (Taylor and Lewis 2014, 120), but, increasingly, institutional LGBT rights funders now require some level of accountability on transgender issues as part of the grant-making process (Anonymous 2016). Grantors might review the number of transgender people on the board, on the staff, and check with the local transgender community to get their perspective on organizational inclusion (Anonymous 2016; Suffredini 2016). This conditional funding pushes transgender inclusion within LGBT rights organizations and within the LGBT coalition.

The Importance of LGBT Advocacy to Transgender Rights

The trajectory of the transgender rights movement would be remarkably different if it had not successfully joined itself to the gay rights cause, creating a broader LGBT collective identity. However, we do not discount the impressive organizing that transgender groups have done on their own, such as assembling groups of transgender people to lobby members of Congress in the mid-1990s through today (e.g., Frye 2000). Groups like the American Educational Gender Information Service and Transexual Menace in the 1990s, the National Transgender Advocacy Coalition in the 2000s, or the Massachusetts Transgender Political Coalition and the National Center for Transgender Equality today, have done or continue to do important advocacy work. Indeed, Transgender Day of Remembrance, started by trans activist Gwendolyn Ann Smith, is solemnly commemorated in events nationwide.

Nonetheless, the transgender community is numerically very small. Recent scholarship by Flores et al. (2016) estimates that just 0.6 percent of Americans identify as transgender. That is approximately 1.4 million people. By comparison, the gay, lesbian, and bisexual communities are more than six times larger, comprising about 3.5 percent of the population (Gates 2011; 2017). Simply put, the LGB communities are much larger and have far more voters, financial resources, and activists than the transgender community has. Voters, particularly groups of organized voters, are critical to the fortunes of the elected officials that set policy (Mayhew 1974). As shown by Taylor et al. (2014), organized groups of LGBT voters have been able to wield important influence on local-level policy, particularly when faced with responsive strong mayor systems of government (see also Bailey 1999; Hertzog 1996).

The differences between the two communities' resources are also very stark. In part, this might be due to the poverty in the transgender community (James et al. 2016). The impact of this is immediately apparent in examining the financial data of LGBT nonprofit organizations, as derived from the National Center for Charitable Statistics' collection of IRS Business Master Files (BMF) 1995–2015 (see appendix A). Table 1.2 shows the sum of all income and assets for all transgender-only groups in our dataset, such as TransOhio or the Sylvia Rivera Law Project, and compares it to the resources of the single largest LGBT rights organization, the Human Rights Campaign.[4] Comparison with the Human Rights Campaign is apt because of their past exclusionary stances on transgender rights in public policy, such as the previously discussed ENDA proposal (e.g., Califia 1997; Taylor and Lewis 2014). Additionally, HRC lagged behind many other national gay rights organizations in adding transgender to its mission statement (Nownes 2014). This comparison clearly demonstrates that the financial resources of the transgender community are small. At the beginning of this period, HRC's income was typically well over 100 times that of all transgender rights groups combined. This ratio has declined in recent years to a 9:1 advantage, but it is still quite large. If we were to compare transgender resources to that of all gay rights groups in our dataset, the relative resources of the transgender community would be even smaller, at approximately 116:1 in 2015. Adding in the far more substantial resources of HIV/AIDS groups dwarfs the relatively meager resources of the transgender community.

This is important because these financial resources are the lifeblood of political advocacy: paying for staff, research, lobbying, organizing, media outreach, and fundraising. All of these activities are costly and each must be sustained to engage in successful advocacy for public policies. Without the financial resources of the gay and lesbian communities, transgender activists would lack the political resources necessary to perform the work of the

TABLE 1.2. Transgender Group Income and Asset Data versus Human Rights Campaign

Year	HRC Income	Trans Groups Income	Income Ratio	HRC Assets	Trans Groups Assets	Asset Ratio
1995	6,097,957	37,646	161.982	930,114	28,153	33.038
1996	6,551,025	37,646	174.016	712,931	28,153	25.323
1997	9,385,526	140,880	66.621	2,235,283	77,902	28.694
1998	13,009,580	157,463	82.620	2,509,446	82,137	30.552
1999	15,779,379	147,471	107.000	6,191,628	78,527	78.847
2000	16,523,757	109,825	150.455	8,030,535	50,374	159.418
2001	20,901,513	128,348	162.850	13,475,169	60,925	221.176
2002	24,623,438	381,463	64.550	16,646,898	77,522	214.738
2003	27,022,007	402,668	67.107	21,458,859	79,804	268.895
2004	29,438,187	604,060	48.734	46,547,909	166,809	279.049
2005	33,190,224	719,653	46.120	55,859,523	234,445	238.263
2006	33,113,856	1,581,906	20.933	47,654,369	614,313	77.573
2007	38,321,451	2,004,938	19.114	43,871,650	747,389	58.700
2008	43,318,146	3,769,488	11.492	40,855,061	2,062,934	19.804
2009	44,136,538	2,257,350	19.552	39,315,706	1,611,573	24.396
2010	36,800,109	3,723,435	9.883	42,129,604	2,372,596	17.757
2011	42,583,107	3,981,030	10.697	45,559,143	2,809,344	16.217
2012	45,346,279	4,892,180	9.269	42,994,076	3,334,946	12.892
2013	52,541,745	4,825,517	10.888	42,397,311	3,682,126	11.514
2014	56,439,923	5,959,453	9.471	48,908,648	5,030,428	9.723
2015	56,439,923	5,981,700	9.435	48,908,648	4,903,508	9.974

Source: Compiled by the authors from National Center for Charitable Statistics, IRS Business Master Files.
Notes: Income and asset amounts are in nominal form; HRC data includes 501(c)3 and 501(c)4 entities.

three-legged stool of advocacy campaigns—direct lobbying, advertising, and grassroots mobilization (Wright 2003). As stated by former Massachusetts Transgender Political Coalition leader Gunner Scott in 2005, "I think we're going to rely a lot on our allies. Our biggest obstacle is going to be financial resources" (Kiritsy 2005).

The costs of legislative advocacy are mirrored in judicial advocacy. Legal cases must be filed, briefs must be written, and cases settled or argued, and this all requires the work of lawyers. Several of the key lawyers advocating on behalf of transgender rights are currently employed or were employed by leading LGBT rights organizations. Among these lawyers are some of the architects of the transgender movement: Jennifer Levi, who directs GLAD's Transgender Rights Project; Shannon Minter, legal director of the National Center for Lesbian Rights; and Lisa Mottet, formerly of the National Gay and Lesbian Task Force and "the first attorney working full-time on transgender rights at the national level" (National Center for Transgender Equality 2017).

By joining with gay rights groups, transgender rights advocates have benefitted through incorporation into an existing social movement and into its social movement organizations. This has provided access to critical resources and professional networks. Sometimes, gay rights groups have even given money or other resources to support independent transgender advocacy organizations. For example, the Massachusetts Transgender Political Coalition, in a controversial decision, accepted a $25,000 grant in 2008 from the Human Rights Campaign (Jacobs 2008). The National Gay and Lesbian Task Force donated office space to help the National Center for Transgender Equality (Keisling 2017). As Kasey Suffredini (2016 interview) of Freedom for All Americans told us, "There just is not a big bucket of money for just trans issues." Joining with gay advocacy enabled more stability in transgender rights advocacy because of the tendency of established organizations to remain viable, compared to new organizations, during periods of social movement growth and decline (McCarthy and Zald 1977). They are able to do this because of greater legitimacy, more accomplishments, higher levels of professionalism, links to constituents, and fundraising prowess.

The financial resources of the gay rights movement, via campaign donations, also provide access to policymakers (e.g., Wright 2003). This is done through both direct and indirect campaign contributions and via a range of electioneering programs conducted by various nonprofit organizations and committees. Campaign contributions are distributed via political action committees. Issue advocacy campaigns are run by 501(c)(4) organizations. Voter education efforts are conducted by 501(c)(3) organizations. Additionally, direct financial contributions can be secured from group members or conscience constituents who are willing to speak on behalf of the cause. According to one report (Green 2016):

> Among the approximately 140 biggest donors who gave almost exclusively to Democrats in 2014, about 7 percent, or $13 million, came from 10 openly gay donors. More recent data isn't available. At least six more LGBT donors rank among the so-called bundlers who raised $50,000 or more for Hillary Clinton in her current run.

When compared to transgender group revenue information in table 1.2, the $13 million contributed to Democratic candidates by ten openly gay donors in 2014 is more than double the income of the entire transgender social movement in 2014. Gay and lesbian donors strongly helped President Obama during his 2012 campaign as well (Smith and Haberman 2011). This brought more access to policymakers than transgender people could have done alone. As we discuss in chapter 6, this access to the White House would play an important role in the advancement of transgender rights during President Obama's administration. Similarly, chapter 4, on legislative politics, explores how combined LGBT advocacy has helped to advance transgender rights during legislative efforts in Congress.

Yet joining the LGBT coalition was not without problems for transgender rights advocates. The small size and resource base of the transgender community made it difficult for transgender people to contribute vital political resources (financial support, voters, volunteers, board members) to LGBT rights organizations (Taylor and Lewis 2014). LGBT advocacy groups also had limited organizational, financial, and political resources, forcing them to prioritize some policy issues over others. Most notably, this included the publicly prominent issue of same-sex marriage, which "sucked all the air out the room" for LGBT advocacy (Palmquist 2016). This type of agenda prioritization occurred in Massachusetts, Maryland, Delaware, and nationally (Taylor and Lewis 2014). In discussing the battle for transgender rights in Massachusetts, Diego Sanchez (2016) said "transgender people had to stand down" until marriage equality was achieved. They had to "trust" gay rights advocates that they would not forget them after marriage. When faced with greater support from the larger gay and lesbian communities, the distribution of benefits in LGBT advocacy had to reflect the desires of their largest supporters. Otherwise, the frame extension to new issues, those of the transgender community, would alienate existing group members (Snow et al. 1986). Prior to *Obergefell v. Hodges*, this meant that same-sex marriage was prioritized over the passage of laws combating discrimination in employment or public accommodations, a set of policies rated more important by transgender people (Grant, Mottet, and Tanis 2011, 178). Since the achievement of marriage equality in 2015, LGBT rights advocacy groups have given far more attention to transgender rights (Haider-Markel and Taylor 2016).

Although the financial benefits of joining gay rights advocacy are clear and the lack of priority attached to transgender advocacy was sometimes concerning, the transgender community also benefited from association with the gay and lesbian community because gay people and identities tend to be more visible and more familiar to the public. As we will see in the following public opinion chapters, most people know a gay person, but they often do not know a transgender person. Further, as measured by feeling thermometers, gay people are also consistently better liked than are transgender individuals. Even today, much of the public has only a vague understanding of transgender identity (Public Religion Research Institute 2011b; Fausto-Sterling 2012). According to a 2011 Public Religion Research Institute poll, slightly more than two-thirds of Americans could identify the term transgender without assistance. Historically, understanding of transgender identity was even lower. In a 2002 poll conducted for HRC by Lake, Snell, Perry and Associates, 70 percent of respondents stated that they had heard the word "transgender." However, when asked to explain what it meant, 32 percent of those respondents failed to identify concepts associated with transgender identity. Thus, just 48 percent of the public could accurately identify the term in 2002. Indeed, the lack of understanding was so great that one of our coauthors, while attempting to learn about views on transgender rights, spent an afternoon in 2006 educating an opposition group, the North Carolina Family Policy Council, about transgender identity instead of learning anything about their position on the issue.[5] Organization personnel and their policy director were not very familiar with the term at the time.

Due to their greater numbers and public familiarity, gay people have been able to help transgender rights by providing a secondary contact effect on attitudes about transgender people and transgender rights (Flores 2015a; Tadlock et al. 2017). This might be achieved by the shared in-group identities that gay people have with others that makes those individuals more receptive to messaging about transgender rights (Harrison and Michelson 2017). In short, gay advocates have been ambassadors for transgender rights when transgender advocates could not speak for themselves or when they would have been less well received.

Indeed, as a former director of Equality Ohio described to us in 2012, Republican legislators were fine with talking about sexual orientation and gay people, but were personally uncomfortable with transgender people. Gay men and lesbian women have helped transgender people educate lawmakers and the public who, as one Delaware legislator told us in 2012, were "not up to speed on transgender issues." In addition, by having gay activists discuss transgender issues while they are also advocating for gay rights, it has been easier to spend less time on transgender issues. They might only use the terms "gender identity or gender expression", stating that those terms are "intertwined" and are needed to protect the full LGBT community, as one Equality Michigan staffer told us in 2012. Our Equality Ohio contact noted that sometimes with the focus on gender identity, there was tactical avoidance of the word transgender in lobbying efforts. When transgender is discussed by LGBT activists in conjunction with gay and lesbian rights, they can also more easily avoid a political vulnerability of the transgender community, its diversity (Sanchez 2016). Given the multitude of identities under this umbrella term, it is easier for the movement when gay activists talk about the need for LGBT protections and subsequently spend less time discussing particular transgender identities. They can highlight a transgender person who conforms to the binary gender system, like Chaz Bono or Janet Mock, and move on.

In general, it becomes problematic in lobbying when more time is spent on other identities under the transgender umbrella. As one Gender Rights Maryland board member told us in 2012, "people who want to smash the gender binary are doing us no favor [politically]." One of the key sponsors of North Carolina's HB2, Rep. Paul Stam (2016), noted these distinctions under the transgender umbrella. He said that his bill did not target those who had "undergone a full change of sex" with the controversial bathroom restrictions. He was much more concerned about those who wanted access to public accommodations based on internal gender identification and those who were in the process of transitioning but still had anatomical parts of their birth sex.

Further, the public, at least historically, has often conflated gay and transgender identities. This has sometimes helped transgender advocacy. Palm Center director Aaron Belkin (2016) described how this assisted with his organization's fight to end the ban on transgender soldiers. He said that after the end of the Don't Ask Don't Tell policy, many soldiers felt that "we had already had this conversation" concerning transgender troops who remained barred from service. Several of our contacts from the 2012 set of interviews noted that state legislators were often unaware of the distinctions between gay and transgender people. As we show in subsequent chapters, sometimes gender identity protections would also be defined under sexual orientation. Transgender advocacy, particularly when there was less awareness of transgender identity, benefitted from the strategic deployment of ambiguity by gay rights advocates (e.g., Stone 2012). Gay rights advocates could sometimes slip gender identity into bills without much fanfare. As one Equality Georgia staff member confided to us in 2012, "Our allies are all over the board. There is ignorance about trans. They are just doing this [supporting gender identity inclusion] because Equality Georgia says it is right." Indeed, many states that passed gender-identity-inclusive protections in the 2000s would package sexual orientation and gender identity together in their legislation (Taylor and Lewis 2014). These early city and state advances provided examples for policy learning and emulation for other jurisdictions. A Delaware state legislator in 2012 found this approach advantageous given that legislators often "look for cover" when taking positions. Of course, standalone legislation protecting transgender rights has been more difficult to pass. Even the first state to pass gay rights legislation, Wisconsin, has not "come back" to pass transgender nondiscrimination protections.

Public unfamiliarity with transgender issues may have been beneficial in some instances, but it likely also slowed the incorporation of transgender rights into the LGBT coalition and into public policy via policy elites. Delaware state senator Karen Peterson (2016), a longtime champion of LGBT rights, found that legislator knowledge about transgender issues has lagged behind that of gay rights issues. This sentiment was echoed by North Carolina House majority leader Paul Stam (2016), a conservative Republican, when he referred to gender identity based advocacy as "new." Although this lack of knowledge might have been beneficial at times, it could also block transgender inclusion as elites became just aware enough of transgender identities to recognize a difference with gays and lesbians. Both Senator Peterson (2016) and Governor Jack Markell (2016) described to us how this was the case with respect to the lack of transgender inclusion in Delaware's sexual-orientation-inclusive nondiscrimination law in 2009.

Adding the "T"

The incorporation of transgender rights in the LGBT rights advocacy coalition was not just a political strategy born of necessity, but rather resulted from the gradual intertwining of gay and transgender rights over time that has been driven by a variety of factors. A prominent argument explaining this phenomenon and offered by our interview subjects is that discrimination against both gay and transgender people stems from transgressing gender norms. Indeed, Matt Foreman (2016) said that when he was with the NYC Gay and Lesbian Anti-Violence Project, 100 percent of the victims of violent crime that he dealt with were gender nonconforming (whether gay, lesbian, bisexual, or trans). These victims shared a common source of oppression. They were beat up because they were perceived to be queer. From the gay man who sleeps with other men to the transgender woman dressed in stereotypically female attire, each transgressed what was viewed as appropriate behavior for a person of their birth sex.

However, recognition of this common source of bigotry did not immediately merge gay and transgender advocacy into a single movement. Instead, transgender advocacy was slowly incorporated with gay rights advocacy. Transgender rights advocates had to overcome what Foreman (2016) described as a bright line between sexual orientation and gender identity based discrimination. At first, "adding the T" to LGBT was often symbolic and this was much to the annoyance of many transgender activists and their allies. Yet, in recent years, transgender rights have moved to the policy core of many organizations.

So what was behind the shift? In our interviews and in the literature, several important factors emerged to help transgender activism gain inclusion in the LGBT advocacy coalition. These factors include the HIV/AIDS crisis, commonalities between the gay and transgender communities, academia and queer theory, media exposure, and increasing professionalization in transgender advocacy.

HIV/AIDS Crisis

Due to nonresponse by government and society's indifference to the HIV/AIDS crisis, gays and lesbians had to "do for themselves what mainstream society wouldn't" (Plumb 2000, 361). Stryker (2008) notes that the existential threat of HIV/AIDS pushed gays and lesbians to revamp the politics of homosexuality. They were forced to create alliances that moved beyond the narrow identity politics of race, gender, class, nationality, and sexual orientation. Longtime LGBT activist Liz Seaton (2016) stated that in reference to HIV/AIDS "everyone was being affected at the same time." To incorporate everyone in the fight against HIV/AIDS, they needed to move beyond assimilationist politics. Gay rights activists created advocacy organizations to protect and to care for those afflicted by the HIV/AIDS crisis. This new direction in the movement, along with the mobilization of new organizations such as ACT-UP and Queer Nation, "shifted internal gay, lesbian, and bisexual community politics in ways that allowed transgender issues to come back into the communities' dialogue" (Stryker 2008, 134). This insight was echoed by PFLAG's Diego Sanchez (2016), who viewed the HIV/AIDS crisis as a critical factor in joining transgender rights to gay rights. Addison Ore (2016), a former executive director for an HIV/AIDS service organization, Triad Health Project, and former board member for Equality North Carolina, adds that "Queer Nation and ACT-UP cracked the door open and others [trans people] came through too."

Service-oriented groups, like New York City's Lesbian and Gay Community Service Center, took notice that HIV/AIDS was ravaging transgender communities. In particular, male-to-female sex workers and those who shared needles for hormone injections were at heightened risk (Wilkinson 2006). These victims sought out help and advocated for inclusion in gay service organizations because "it was a place in which they thought they might be safe" (Blumenstein, Warren, and Walker 1998, 427). Addison Ore (2016) notes that service organizations, such as Triad Health Project, cared for an increasing number of transgender clients over the years and they have become more familiar with the needs of transgender patients. In addition, Ore stated that personal contact with transgender people, through her professional duties, made her a stronger advocate for transgender rights and inclusion. Her professional contact was important because social circles for segments of the LGBT community sometimes do not significantly overlap. Rather, she met nearly all of her transgender friends through her work with Equality North Carolina and the Triad Health Project.

AIDS service providers beyond the LGBT community were also incentivized to care for transgender populations. The Centers for Disease Control and Prevention (CDC) provided funding for HIV/AIDS services to transgender victims (Sanchez 2016). The CDC also set regulations in 1993 forcing states receiving federal HIV prevention resources to develop prevention plans in conjunction with the communities affected, and with experts (CDC 2012). As part of the prevention strategy, high-risk groups, including transgender people, were targeted for interventions (Stryker 2008). Further, AIDS funding entities directed money to "culturally competent" prevention and harm-reduction strategies aimed at transgender people (Stryker 2008, 132). Indeed, where there is funding, there is also an incentive for academic research. A voluminous academic literature addressing HIV/AIDS and transgender identities has thus been developed (e.g., Clements-Nolle et al. 2001). In studying that intersection, researchers also took notice of other problems facing the community, such as substance abuse and mental health concerns (e.g., Nemoto et al. 2005). Some of the data generated in health research, such as the CDC's Behavioral Risk Factor Surveillance System, have been used to generate estimates of the number of transgender people in the United States (Flores et al. 2016). Thus, AIDS funding became an important mechanism for bringing needed social and financial resources to transgender communities. In addition, Stryker (2008) notes that for communities of color, AIDS service centers became important venues for transgender advocacy.

Professionalization of Transgender Advocacy

Jamison Green (2016) discussed how early transgender advocacy was the work of volunteers who were "simply fed up." There was a "rising consciousness and there was no reason that we should be treated as we were." Informal groups like Transexual Menace and Transgender Nation engaged in direct action. However, these pioneers were faced with a monumental task of creating and sustaining a nascent movement to help a small number of geographically and socially isolated individuals where a collective identity did not fully exist. As we noted earlier, the transgender community was also resource-poor and organizations were always at high risk for organizational demise. Factionalization, particularly from transsexual separatists (Denny 2016), was also a risk given the heterogeneity under the transgender umbrella. Moreover, their overarching goal of a right to gender self-determination was a long-term vision. It was a project that might take decades given the size of the task and fluctuating social and political conditions. As such, sustaining a movement based on volunteers and informal organizations was difficult.

Professionalization can help to sustain movements facing difficult environmental conditions (Staggenborg 1988). As Taylor and Crossley (2013) note, it is during these abeyance periods that collective identity can be nurtured. Further, Staggenborg (1988) finds that professionalization of social movements facilitates coalition work and formalized organizations. Aspects of these insights are apparent in the history of the transgender rights movement, and professionalization contributed to its incorporation with LGBT advocacy.

An early attempt to increase professionalization was the founding of GenderPAC. In e-mail correspondence, Riki Wilchins (2016), the leading founder of GenderPAC, noted that the 1996 formalization of this organization marked the first time that the transgender community had consolidated its resources. They subsequently invited representatives from the National

Center for Lesbian Rights, BiNet USA, and the National Gay and Lesbian Task Force to join the GenderPAC board of directors. In coalition with those organizations, GenderPAC activists were later invited to speak at a 1997 conference of the National Organization for Women (NOW) and helped them pass a transgender-inclusive resolution. However, GenderPAC's relationship with the transgender community soured. GenderPAC and Wilchins (2004) eschewed identity politics and pursued gender rights more broadly. This led to a rebuke in 2001 from many transgender activists who felt that their community was being ignored by the organization (Koyama 2006). GenderPAC later shut its doors in 2009.

Because of the lack of a professionalized, transgender-focused presence in Washington, the National Center for Transgender Equality (NCTE) was formed in 2003 with the leadership and financial backing of Mara Keisling (Keisling 2017). In an interview about the founding of NCTE, Keisling noted that gay rights organizations and, in particular, the National Gay and Lesbian Task Force provided resources and mentorship to help the organization (Bugg 2004). Keisling also discussed how NCTE has been able to facilitate collaboration with gay rights groups and other progressive organizations. Keisling (2017) noted that "being the executive director of an organization gets you into meetings." Indeed, Keisling and NCTE have been a voice at the LGBT movement table and in progressive politics. They have focused on advancing transgender rights in concert with gay and lesbian rights. They have built relationships with other organizations. Its relative organizational stability and leadership allows NCTE to "play a long game" (Keisling 2017). Since they are professionalized, they do not suffer the problem of volunteer burnout when wins do not immediately materialize (Keisling 2017). Further, and unlike GenderPAC, they do not eschew identity politics and do not ignore the important role that identity formation can have in social movement participation (Polletta and Jaspar 2001). NCTE, like state-focused groups such as the Massachusetts Transgender Political Coalition, are unabashedly transgender-focused organizations, and they engage in identity work that helps to build and sustain transgender activism. These identity-based organizations are important because political actors generally respond to organized interests in society (e.g., Olson 1965).

NCTE's established presence in Washington can also provide education for lawmakers and staffers when called upon informally or in hearings. Many of the activists that we interviewed found that NCTE did not independently have a lot of influence on Capitol Hill or within the Obama administration. Instead, the primary LGBT rights players were larger groups like the Human Rights Campaign. However, it was commonly thought that

NCTE plays an important role in the LGBT coalition. It is an "agitator" that serves as a "watchdog in the advocacy community" (Rupert 2016) and in progressive politics. Because of its stable and professionalized leadership, the organization can coherently and consistently channel transgender concerns to the larger LGBT movement. They are also a readily accessible and quotable source for the news media.

Of course, the professionalization of other social movements has helped to advance transgender integration within the LGBT movement. There are careers within the social movement industry. McCarthy and Zald (1973, 15) referred to this as the "institutionalization of dissent." People can work in this field within a variety of organizations. Indeed, many of our interview respondents have held positions in multiple organizations at different points in their social movement careers. Transgender allies, such as these, are able to move between organizations with knowledge about transgender rights. They can, and have, positively shaped relations with the transgender community within multiple LGBT organizations. These LGBT organizations subsequently engage in increasingly transgender-inclusive advocacy through actions like framing, agenda setting, and lobbying.

Commonalities between Communities

Several of our interview respondents noted that gay and transgender people had much in common. Indeed, Matt Foreman (2016) noted that the old "distinctions between them do not make sense on the ground." More gay people, like himself, started to understand this and "evolved" over time due to the frame extension (Snow et al. 1986) by transgender rights advocates that compellingly discussed gay or lesbian identities as gender nonconformance (Minter 2006). Speaking to this point, longtime transgender rights activist Kylar Broadus (2016) stated that "not every gender transgressor is a transsexual . . . [but] gender ambiguity is there." Former Equality Maryland director Dan Furmansky (2016) talked about the "increasing fluidity on sexuality and gender." In addition, many transgender people are also gay, lesbian, or bisexual (Currah and Minter 2000), and fights over demarcating clearly between these identities were difficult and fraught (Halberstam 1998). Mara Keisling (2017) stated that many transgender people, particularly trans men, have come out as gay or lesbian prior to their transitions. Jamison Green (2016) also noted that transgender people had long been part of the queer community. All of these personal connections to the gay and lesbian communities are important in prejudice reduction between these communities (Allport 1954).

During our interview with a preeminent scholar on transgender rights, Paisley Currah (2016), he asked why the transgender movement joined gay and lesbian advocacy rather than the feminist movement.[6] Perhaps the answer to that question, in part, lies in the greater commonality in the agendas of gay and transgender people. When transgender rights advocacy became organized in the 1980s and 1990s, women's rights organizations had already achieved statutory inclusion in most nondiscrimination laws. So this was not an organizing issue for feminist organizations. In most places, gay people were fighting for many of the same policy issues that transgender people desired. From antidiscrimination laws, to hate crimes laws, to laws combating bullying in schools, to relationship recognition, to HIV/AIDS funding, there was great intersection between the policy needs of the gay and transgender communities. In short, it is probably easier to catch a ride in a car going to where you want to go than ask someone who is already there to come back and get you.

Kylar Broadus (2016) also notes that the gay and transgender communities were "bonded by hate." The Christian Right and its views on matters of sex, sexuality, and gender provided a unifying common opponent for gay and transgender people. As Lynne Bowman (2016) said, "We realized that we were hated by the same people." Until recently, the Christian Right rarely distinguished between what they considered various forms of sexual immorality. Dan Furmansky (2016) stated that the broader public has not distinguished between members of the LGBT community nor did they pay much attention to the internecine identity debates that have roiled LGBT activism: "They were all outcasts at the school lunch table." For those opposed to LGBT rights, or much of the public, they were all just faggots and queers.

Academia and Transgender Advocacy

Beyond the advocacy and service organizations active in the development of the LGBT rights movement, David Valentine (2007) argues that academia also played a role through its scholarship and in imposing the term "transgender" onto populations that did not embrace the term. They did this in service of a view that gender and sexuality are different areas of inquiry into the human condition. Despite that criticism, the role of academia in the advancement of transgender rights is often understated. From the beginning of the transgender rights movement, colleges and universities have facilitated many aspects of transgender rights. Our introduction discussed how colleges and universities legitimized transsexualism through the opening of treatment clinics. Additionally, the academy has provided a relatively safe platform for transgender academics to share information about transgender identity and to theorize about transgender rights. As transgender rights scholar and activist Dean Spade (2016) told us, "This is my paid gig that allows me to do the work."

One scholar that has had a large impact in bringing transgender to the masses is Jennifer Finney Boylan. A respected writer and tenured professor of English, she transitioned in the early 2000s and wrote the *New York Times* best-selling book *She's Not There: A Life in Two Genders,* a memoir about her life and transition (Boylan 2003). In writing about the commonality between transgender experiences and those of cisgender people, one of her goals is to humanize transgender people and their experiences for her audience (Boylan 2016). Boylan parlayed the success of this book into multiple appearances on the *Oprah Winfrey Show, Live with Larry King,* and the *Today Show,* and she writes for the *New York Times.* Boylan has also been featured in multiple documentaries and as a cast member in the reality TV series *I Am Cait.* In many ways, she has become one of the prominent faces of the transgender rights movement.

In addition to sharing their personal stories about transgender identity, academics have used their positions to advance transgender rights through more critical work that examines transgender issues in public policy, in society, and in LGBT rights. These scholars have focused on framing arguments that can be used to advance transgender rights and in discussing the nature of gender and gender transition (Currah 2016). This advocacy oriented approach has differed in some respects from gay and lesbian intersections with academia, where there has been comparatively more interest in social science research to buttress advocacy (Currah 2016). In short, many of the academics who have taken this approach, such as Dean Spade, Susan Stryker, Paisley Currah, and Heath Fogg Davis, are scholars and transgender advocates (Currah 2006, 6). They have played a vital role in creating academic space for transgender rights and transgender studies but also for engaging in praxis by applying their insights to advocacy and policymaking.

Transgender and transgender-affirming students have also been an important resource for the movement. As long ago noted by McCarthy and Zald (1973), students provide a useful source of activists for social movements because of their flexible schedules. In addition, because of the increasingly common student-as-consumer model in higher education, colleges and universities have progressively been more responsive to the needs and wants of students, including those who are transgender identified. Even prior to pressure from the Obama administration via a controversial Title IX interpretation, many colleges and universities had studied ways to make their campuses more welcoming to transgender students. Transgender students have also worked independently and in organized advocacy for campus policy changes. As such, there has been a rise in transgender-inclusive policies on campuses, such as gender-neutral dorms, nondiscrimination policies, guidance on preferred names, and the identification of single stall restrooms. Trainings about transgender identity for students, community, faculty, and staff have become ubiquitous. Additionally, academia has worked to make a future generation of gay rights activists more receptive to transgender rights through propagation of queer theory and the rise of campus centers for sexual minorities.

In the 1990s, gay and lesbian studies, which was premised on firm sex/gender and sexuality based categories, was transformed by the rise of queer theory in academia (Pierceson 2016). This area of study "focuses on mismatches between sex, gender and desire" (Jagose 1996, 3). It eschews the stability of sex, gender, and sexuality as categories and denies that they are essentialist in nature, but rather are performative (Butler 1990). Queer theory is arcane, often unintelligible to the average person, and not widely distributed (Spade 2016; Beemyn 2016; Wilchins 2016). Indeed, prominent transgender activist Riki Wilchins even felt compelled to write a book, *Queer Theory Gender Theory*, to explain it to a broader audience. However, it has been influential within academia and it is important to transgender rights. As Roen (2002, 502) pointed out, "Contemporary transgender politics are informed by postmodern conceptions of subjectivity, queer understandings of sexuality and gender." Further, Paisley Currah (2016) elaborates that queer theory was useful in attaching transgender to gay and lesbian politics, rather than a more assimilationist feminist politics. Queer understandings destabilized the fixed identities underpinning early 1990s gay advocacy when confronted by transgender and bisexual identities (Gamson 1995). The queer movement of the 1990s "worked to break down old divisions between sexual identity communities" (Stryker 2008, 26).

As queer theory developed in the "ivory tower," it has been passed on to younger activists through college and university curricula. Beemyn (2016) notes how queer studies has been institutionalized within the academy through LGBT centers, increasingly receptive women's and gender centers, and in the curriculum. In classrooms and coursework, faculty members expose their students to the ideas of queer theory in a variety of disciplines, such as gender studies, political science, and sociology. Beemyn (2016) notes that queer politics, if not necessarily queer theory, might even be discussed among students outside of their formal study. In particular, "Feinberg's *Stone Butch Blues* and Bornstein's *Gender Outlaw* had a big impact and these were required reading in queer circles in the 1990s" (Beemyn 2016). The young gay activists who were exposed to these ideas were sometimes affected by them. Renn (2007) describes the "queer activist" transformation of one of her research subjects:

> When Kevin came out as gay in college, he got involved in LGBT campus activism and in community activism. He came to understand that his gay identity was part of a larger picture of socially constructed gender and sexual identities and no longer felt comfortable only "working to get gays and lesbians accepted by society." (325)

As shown in that quote, the destabilization of sex, gender, and sexuality categories helped to encourage students to expand their advocacy beyond the narrow identity labels of gay or lesbian. The new ways to examine sex, gender, and sexuality also helped to make these individuals more receptive to transgender people and transgender rights (and to intersectional concerns). They worked with transgender individuals in student organizations that were increasingly LGBT focused (Beemyn 2016). Young gay people who join and lead campus LGBT organizations often find that the experience influences career goals and political aspirations, and that it connects them to other social justice movements (Renn 2007, 319). While engaged in college advocacy, they might work on transgender-inclusive policies such as gender-neutral restrooms or gender-neutral housing. They might fight to improve the hostile campus climate for trans individuals (Beemyn 2003; McKinney 2005). As Dan Furmansky noted (2016), college is where many people "get [a] fire in the belly" for LGBT advocacy work.

Those that would later go into social movement organizations were more likely to accept transgender claims than a generation of activists who were rooted in more traditional identity politics views of gay rights. Heath Fogg Davis (2016) identified this "generational replacement" in the movement. A longtime veteran of the LGBT rights movement observed that the gender nonconforming and queer language, as well as the expansion of gender identity in her organization's policies, "is often driven by college interns and young staff" (Bowman 2016). Replacement in organizations tends to be with younger individuals and career staff tend to be college graduates with "a greater openness to consideration of ideas" (Bowman 2016). Liz Seaton (2016), who was at the Human Rights Campaign in the early 2000s, found that "younger people were not stuck back" in older views about distinct advocacy for gay and transgender rights. There was more receptiveness to their interconnections. Another longtime LGBT rights activist, Ian Palmquist (2016), agreed that this exposure to queer theory in college left him and other gay rights activists more open to and knowledgeable about transgender identities. When they moved into social movement organizations as careers, they replaced a generation of activists who were somewhat less familiar with transgender identities. Of course, as noted by Shannon Minter (2016), many social movement leaders in the 1990s and early 2000s were not opposed to transgender rights. In addition, many, such as former Empire State Pride Agenda executive director Matt Foreman (2016), would later evolve on the inclusion of transgender rights.

As exposure to queer and trans understandings increased and as campus gay rights organizations and centers became transgender inclusive (Renn 2007; Beemyn 2016), a generation of gay rights activists became more familiar with, more comfortable with, and more receptive to the argument that discrimination against gay and transgender people occurs because they violate gender norms. The receptiveness to transgender inclusion became a norm for advocates. This facilitated transgender inclusion over time as more of these individuals assumed greater decision-making authority within advocacy organizations. This explanation for the slow but increasing acceptance of transgender rights within the LGBT advocacy community is one that resonated with several of our interview respondents who ran statewide LGBT rights organizations in the mid to late 2000s, including Dan Furmansky, Ian Palmquist, and Lynne Bowman. Independently of our research, Rebecca Juro echoed similar insights in an interview with *Washington Blade* reporter Chris Johnson (2017):

> Juro said college-aged LGBT activists just beginning to come into the movement have a much different view of trans inclusion than their LGBT elders. "They're all like, no, you cannot separate, we're all in this together and trying to say we'll get rights for gay people without trans people is unacceptable."

Transgender inclusion became a norm for many activists who have come of age since the 1990s. This affected their advocacy and their organizations. These individuals were able to provide leadership on transgender rights within their organizations and with their constituents. This has been important because not everyone in the gay and lesbian communities has always viewed transgender rights as connected to gay rights (Palmquist 2016; Foreman 2016). Furmansky (2016) noted that it would be the activist elite that helped tip the scales toward future transgender inclusion during the 2007 ENDA debate.

Media

A few of our interview respondents noted that the media was also an important factor in the increasing awareness of transgender issues in the general public as well as within gay and lesbian circles. Importantly, there are LGBT organizations that explicitly work to shape coverage of transgender issues, such as GLAAD (originally the Gay and Lesbian Alliance Against Defamation) (2016).[7] This has made it easier for LGBT advocates to engage in transgender advocacy. Indeed, King (1996, 150) states that

> [i]ndividual transvestites and transsexuals maybe be damaged by the [media] exposure they receive; but other transvestite and transsexual viewers or readers may be inspired or educated or entertained by it. The general public may be misled or misinformed but it may also be educated and enlightened.

Stryker (2008, 24–25) says that the media has paid attention to transgender issues since the 1950s, but that recent years have witnessed increasing attention and "increasingly positive representation." Regardless of whether they are misinforming or not, both print and broadcast media have increasingly covered transgender topics. To empirically confirm this trend, we performed a keyword search of the print edition of the *New York Times* and several leading broadcast media outlets using LexisNexis on terms related to transgender issues.[8] Figure 1.1 shows the results for the *New York Times* search between 1970 and 2015. Prior to the early 1990s, transgender issues received relatively sparse media coverage, with fewer than 100 mentions annually. However, after this early period, the coverage increased modestly until 2010. Since then, there has been a dramatic spike in coverage of these issues. Figure 1.2 reveals similar trends in broadcast media, particularly for CNN and NPR, though the data are somewhat limited in time and coverage.[9]

Tadlock (2014) analyzed the content of media stories on transsexual and transgender between 1992 and 2011, and found that the framing of transsexual and transgender rights differs from that of gay rights. Many research-

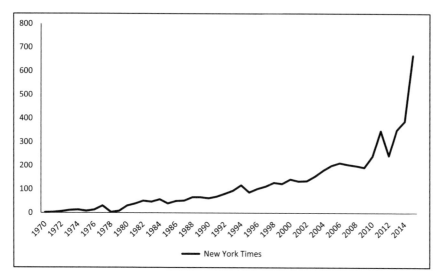

Figure 1.1 New York Times Coverage of Transgender. (Compiled by the authors from LexisNexis.)

Note: Print edition only. Vertical axis is the number of stories.

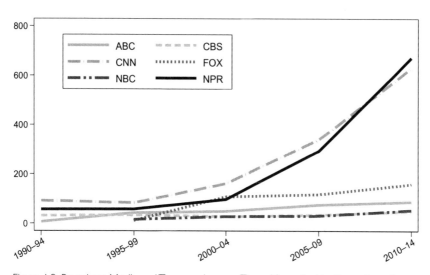

Figure 1.2. Broadcast Media and Transgender over Time. (Compiled by the authors from LexisNexis.)

Notes: CNN contains hits for news transcripts only. Online is not included. LexisNexis transcript holdings vary by outlet in terms of breadth and date of coverage. Vertical axis is the number of stories.

ers have found that equality and morality frames are the most common frames in media coverage about gay and lesbian issues (Brewer 2008; Pan et al. 2010; Tadlock, Gordon, and Popp 2007). However, Tadlock (2014) found that education and safety/security frames are also very prominent in stories about transsexual rights. Education frames were also featured in stories about transgender rights, but equality frames were commonly used as well. The prominence of education frames has been due to public's relative unfamiliarity with transgender people and their rights.

Liz Seaton (2016) noted that early talk shows, such as the *Phil Donahue Show* (1967–96) and the *Oprah Winfrey Show* (1986–2011), had an impact on getting transgender into the public conversation. As previously mentioned, noted transgender author Jennifer Finney Boylan was a guest on the latter show on multiple occasions. Kate Bornstein's *Gender Outlaw* (1994, 141) highlights her appearance on the *Geraldo* talk show as well. This insight about the impact of talk shows is consistent with Gamson's (1998) study of sexual nonconformists on talk shows, where he argues that these shows increased visibility for marginalized LGBT groups. Gamson's (1998, 234) content analysis of these shows, which were predominantly drawn from the 1990s, found that a variety of frames were used in the stories. These frames include boundaries distinguishing between transgender and natal men or women, the morality of sex reassignment, the etiology of transsexualism, therapeutic approaches to self-acceptance, gender displays highlighting pre- and post-transition, honesty, and tolerance. However, MacKenzie (1994) argued that talk shows are exploitative, often airing transgender stories for shock value and featuring negative and demeaning stereotypes of transgender individuals. In particular, MacKenzie (1994) discussed Phil Donahue's treatment of transgender actress and model Tula, where he focused on whether or not audience members would buy copies of *Playboy* that featured nude photos of the actress and how men would feel if they were intimate with her without being aware of her transgender status.

Media attention to transgender issues also extends beyond news outlets and talk shows. Transgender themes and characters have featured in a number of films and TV shows. The use of cisgender crossdressing has long been a staple in movies and TV. Examples of this include the classic films *Some Like it Hot* (1959), *Tootsie* (1982), *Mrs. Doubtfire* (1993), *Victor/Victoria* (1982), and even in numerous Bugs Bunny cartoons (e.g., *What's Opera, Doc?* 1957; *Mississippi Hare* 1949). However, this presentation of crossdressing in film and television was often done temporarily, for comedic value, and to reinforce gender norms in society (MacKenzie 1994). The use of drag has also featured in movies, albeit less frequently, in films like *La Cage aux Folles* (1978), *To Wong Foo, Thanks for Everything! Julie Newmar* (1995), *Torch Song Trilogy* (1988), or *The Birdcage* (1996). Many films of this genre are also comedies. Drag stage personas, such as television star RuPaul, have also been criticized for the way that their acts parody women and reinforce gender norms and male power (e.g., Raymond 1996). A few films have presented more serious examinations of transsexual characters, including *Transamerica* (2005) and the award-winning film *Boys Don't Cry* (1999). More recently, an AIDS stricken pre-op trans woman was a major character in the *Dallas Buyers Club* (2013).

Often, portrayals of transgender people in the media are used to arouse feelings of shock, outrage, betrayal, titillation, and confusion (Mackenzie 1994). Perhaps one of the best examples of this is seen with Jaye Davidson's character, Dil, in *The Crying Game* (1992) and "The Secret" that was used to hype the film (Welkos 1993). Almost by definition, reality television shows such as Caitlyn Jenner's *I Am Cait* (2015–16) are based on titillation. Additionally, films like *Silence of the Lambs* (1991), *Psycho* (1960), and *The Crying Game* portray trans people as dangerous, weird, disgusting, and sick (MacKenzie 1994, 137). Similarly, in her analysis of the films *Adventures of Priscilla, Queen of the Desert* (1994) and *Le Sexe des etoiles* (1993), Namaste (2000, 131) finds that they deploy negative stereotypes of transgender people. In particular, these films associate transgender characters with illusion, deception, and tragedy.

However, some more recent portrayals of transgender people have been more positive or, at worst, more realistic (Stryker 2008). Examples of this include Felicity Huffman's leading character in *Transamerica*, Laverne Cox's portrayal of Sophia Burset in the cable television show *Orange Is the New Black* (2013–), and Jeffrey Tambor's character Maura Pfefferman in the online show *Transparent* (2014–). Even when portraying tragedy, such as in *Soldier's Girl* (2003), which addresses the case of a murdered soldier involved with a transgender woman, films increasingly let transgender characters be relatable and sympathetic. They are less frequently a caricature. Transgender people increasingly consult on such projects. In the case of *Transparent*, transgender people are associate producers of the show (Bobrow 2016). In the genre of reality television, *I Am Cait* also explored aspects of transgender identity in more depth and with more honesty than some earlier examinations. It also incorporated the views of several trans women from different perspectives. However, it is important to note that most roles portraying transgender people are offered to cisgender actors.

To assess whether the public is receiving the framing messages sent by the media, we included an item in our June 2015 national survey asking the following question:

We are interested in how people get information about issues related to gender identity and transgender people. What are your top three sources of information (please rank 1, 2, and 3)?

Table 1.3 shows the response categories for information sources along with the percentage of respondents who rated it a most important source for information about transgender identities and the percentage of respondents who rated a particular category first, second, or third choice for learning about transgender identities. Various media sources comprise many of the most important sources of information for people about transgender identity and rights. Media coverage, and likely the increase in media coverage, has helped to increase awareness of transgender identity in the public. This type of parasocial contact, through the media, has been shown to have increased positive attitudes toward gay people and gay civil rights (Garretson

TABLE 1.3. Top Information Sources to Learn about Transgender

Information Source	1st choice	1st, 2nd, or 3rd choice
Online news sources	24.0	51.6
Social media like Facebook or Twitter	14.6	30.2
Entertainment TV shows, radio, or movies	12.8	34.4
Other news media	9.4	36.2
None of the above	8.2	10.3
Books and other printed material	5.0	17.8
Family	4.5	18.3
Friends or acquaintances who are gay	3.9	13.7
School or college	3.5	9.9
LGBT advocacy groups	2.6	10.5
Transgender people that I know	2.5	6.1
Religious texts	2.4	6.5
Religious organizations and leaders	1.8	8.9
Transgender celebrities	1.8	9.5
Friends or acquaintances who are not gay or transgender	1.4	9.4
Other advocacy groups	0.8	4.2
Government leaders	0.7	4.5

Source: CVR Survey, June 12–25, 2015.
Note: n = 2,067

2015; Schiappa, Gregg, and Hewes 2006). As positive depictions of transgender characters in the media increase, knowledge about and positive attitudes toward transgender people should increase.

Media coverage of transgender issues may also influence government action and policies. Liz Seaton (2016) noted that transgender inclusion in the 2009 Matthew Shepard Hate Crimes Act was not a foregone conclusion. Rather, coverage of the Angie Zapata murder case "sealed the deal" on transgender inclusion (Seaton 2016). Further, Jeff Graham (2016), the executive director for Georgia Equality, said that the print and broadcast media played an important role in convincing Georgia governor Nathan Deal to veto an anti-LGBT "religious liberty" bill in 2016. During the fight over whether to repeal HB2 in North Carolina, Republicans such as Governor Pat Mc-Crory were concerned about the onslaught of negative media coverage of the law (Rothacker 2017). This undoubtedly played an important part in the Republican-led General Assembly's decision to repeal the law.

Conclusion

In this chapter, we discussed the importance of LGBT advocacy to the transgender movement and addressed several factors that promoted a combined advocacy coalition under that acronym. Queer politics provided an opening for transgender rights to join with gay and lesbian advocacy. Transgender rights advocates argued that the root of gay and transgender oppression was found in the violation of gender norms. This argument was persuasive, but the process of transgender inclusion within LGBT advocacy still took time. It was facilitated by the HIV/AIDS epidemic, academia and the role of queer theory/politics, the professionalization of transgender and LGBT rights advocacy, commonalities between gay and transgender people, and increased media coverage of transgender identities and issues. Transgender advocacy has benefitted tremendously from this arrangement; it gained access to far greater resources than it would have on its own. Additionally, the transgender movement's linkage with existing LGB organizations allowed the movement to leverage the expertise and elite access of the LGB community, and it turned out that gay people were good ambassadors for transgender rights with the public and with legislators. In the following chapters, we address public opinion on transgender rights and how the combined LGBT movement made so many advances for the transgender community.

Public Attitudes on Transgender Rights

CHAPTER 2

Public Opinion about Transgender People and Policies

with Andrew Flores, Patrick Miller, and Barry Tadlock

As a relatively small minority group in a majoritarian democratic system, the success of the transgender rights movement is, in many ways, dependent on public attitudes toward the group and public preferences on relevant policies. Indeed, many of the transgender and broader LGBT rights movement's advocacy tactics target the public directly in order to sway public opinion in their favor. Evident in the rapid changes in same-sex marriage policies in the United States, public support or opposition to minority rights, in particular, can be a crucial linchpin in shaping public policies (D. Lewis 2011b). With transgender rights emerging as a more salient issue in recent years, public opinion is similarly likely to shape public policies regarding transgender rights (Flores, Herman, and Mallory 2015).

Yet, to date, public attitudes toward transgender people and rights have received scant attention from pollsters, policy advocates, and scholars (Flores 2015a). As such, we know very little about the content of public attitudes toward transgender people and their rights in the United States. The term "transgender" only appears in nationally representative surveys beginning in 2002 and the first publicly available survey dedicated to these issues was not fielded until 2005 (Norton and Herek 2013).[1] Several earlier surveys included questions related to transgender rights, but they are most often lumped in with broader LGBT rights investigations (e.g., asking about LGBT people as a group). Only a handful of survey items fielded before 2015 addressed transgender issues separately from issues related to sexual orientation.

A more extensive set of literature has explored attitudes toward gay rights. It examines a host of issues including group affect, nondiscrimination policy, hate crimes, and same-sex marriage (e.g., Brewer 2008). Further, the literature has addressed a myriad of factors shaping these attitudes, including race (Lewis 2003), gender (Herek 2002), partisanship (Brewer 2003; Garretson 2014), religion (Olson, Cadge, and Harrrison 2006), attributions for homosexuality (Haider-Markel and Joslyn 2005, 2008, 2013; Lewis 2009), and interpersonal contact (Bramlett 2012; Flores 2015a; Garner 2013; Herek and Capitanio 1996; Herek and Glunt 1993; G. Lewis 2011; Skipworth, Garner, and Dettrey 2010). Although attitudes toward the gay and lesbian community are correlated with attitudes toward transgender people, the few existing studies of public opinion toward the latter group suggest that there are important differences (Norton and Herek 2013; Lewis et al. 2017).

Thus, in this chapter, we provide a more comprehensive and systematic examination of the nature of public opinion toward transgender people and attitudes toward transgender rights policies. This will be followed in chapter 3 by an examination of why people differ in their views on these issues. Joining us in these analyses are Barry Tadlock, Andrew Flores, and Patrick Miller. Together, this team of researchers fielded a series of nationally representative opinion polls,[2] generously funded by the University of Kansas, the University of Toledo, UCLA's Williams Institute, and Ohio University. The first survey (n=1,940) was conducted online by Clear Voice Research (CVR) from June 12 to June 25, 2015.[3] The second survey, which employs a random probability sample and is nationally representative, was conducted via GfK's KnowledgePanel (n=1,020) from October 9 to October 11, 2015.[4] The third survey (n=1,291) was conducted online by CVR from June 18 to June 28, 2016.[5] In each survey, we asked participants to respond to a wide range of items relating to transgender people and policies affecting transgender rights, accounting for perhaps the most comprehensive national surveys of these topics to date. The surveys included items on group affect, personal comfort, nondiscrimination policies, transgender candidates, health policies, gender marker identification changes, bullying, societal roles, and public restroom access. Appendices E and F provide more information about our instruments. In addition to these three comprehensive surveys, we also supplement the analyses, where possible, with items from other national surveys.

In this chapter, we provide a descriptive analysis of American public opinion on transgender people and their rights, and start to explore the individual characteristics that are associated with attitudes about transgender people and related issues. Our examination begins with general attitudes and feelings toward transgender people and concepts, including questions of morality and acceptance. We then turn our attention to public policies, covering broad nondiscrimination laws as well as more specific policies, such as public restrooms, gender marker changes, health care, and school policies. In chapter 3, we more fully examine the factors that shape and underlie these attitudes.

Attitudes and Feelings toward Transgender People

We begin our exploration of public opinion on transgender rights by assessing general attitudes and feelings toward the concept of transgender and toward transgender people themselves. These general attitudes often inform and constrain more specific issue attitudes relevant to public policy and politics (Herek 2002; Peffley and Hurwitz 1985). One way to broadly assess general attitudes is by measuring group affect, or feelings toward various groups in society, with a feeling thermometer rating. Each of the surveys had questions asking respondents to rate a set of organizations and groups that are in the news on a 0 to 100 scale, with higher scores indicating warmer, more favorable feelings and lower scores indicating colder, more negative feelings. Respondents were instructed that a rating of 50 indicate feelings that are not particularly warm or cold (i.e., neutral feelings).

Figure 2.1 shows the average thermometer ratings of fifteen groups evaluated in the June 2016 survey. Compared to other groups, Americans tend to have relatively negative feelings toward transgender people, with an average rating of 46.3. This rating is on par with several politically polarizing groups, like Christian fundamentalists, the National Rifle Association, and the Democratic Party. In this survey, the average rating of transgender people is higher than both Muslims and atheists ($p < 0.001$)—two groups that Americans tend to view the most negatively (Edgell et al. 2016)—but surveys in prior years revealed ratings of transgender people on similar levels to these groups, in the mid-to-low forties. The average rating of transgender people is well below the most warmly evaluated groups, such as veterans, scientists, and the police. It is lower than interracial couples, a group that has faced significant societal discrimination in the past. The relatively negative feelings toward transgender people revealed in these surveys is consistent with earlier ratings from 2002 and 2011 (Human Rights Campaign 2002; 2011), which averaged 47.7 and 45, respectively. It is also consistent with our October 2015 survey conducted by GfK, in which Americans rated transgender people with an average thermometer rating of just 43. Thus, despite an increase in

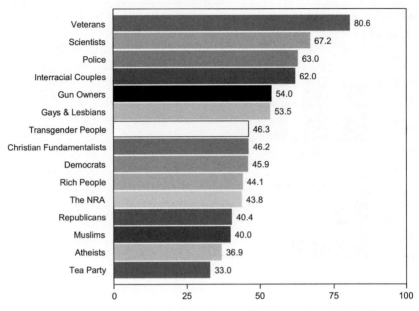

Figure 2.1. Thermometer Ratings of Various Groups. (CVR Survey, June 29, 2016.)

attention to and awareness of transgender people and issues in recent years, feelings toward this group have remained fairly low and stable over time.

Interestingly, the thermometer ratings also show that Americans tend to view transgender people more negatively than gay men and lesbians ($p < 0.001$). Despite their common association in the LGBT rights movement, many Americans make clear distinctions between the two groups (Lewis et al. 2017). Indeed, not only are the average ratings of gay men and lesbians significantly higher than the ratings of transgender people, but the average ratings of gays and lesbians are above 50—indicating somewhat warm feelings. This discrepancy in feeling thermometer scores between transgender people and gay men and lesbian women is consistent across our other 2015 survey as well, with the average rating of transgender people in that survey being about eight points lower than the average rating of gay men and lesbians.

While on average Americans tend to have relatively negative feelings toward transgender people, these feelings do vary across some demographic segments of society. For example, even though higher levels of education are correlated with greater support for gay and lesbian rights (Brewer 2008), we find little variation across different levels of educational attainment on feelings toward transgender people in our 2016 survey, as seen in figure 2.2.

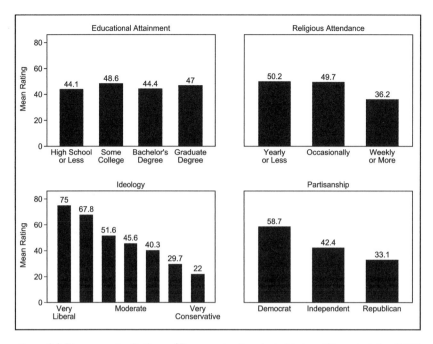

Figure 2.2. Thermometer Ratings of Transgender People, by Various Characteristics. (CVR Survey, June 29, 2016.)

However, the 2015 GfK survey does reveal some differences across educational attainment, with average ratings increasing from 37.2 for those with up to a high school diploma to 57 for those with graduate degrees. Religiosity, ideology, and partisanship are all associated with different levels of affect toward transgender people, patterns that were also evident in our earlier surveys. Respondents who attend religious services weekly or more frequently have colder feelings toward transgender people compared with those who attend less frequently. Ideological self-placement, measured on a seven-point scale ranging from very liberal to very conservative, shows a striking and consistent pattern. The most liberal respondents rate transgender people as a group at 75 while the most conservative respondents rate them at 22. A similar pattern is evident for partisanship. Republicans (including independents who lean toward the Republican Party) have much lower ratings for transgender people than nonleaning independents and Democrats (including independents who lean toward the Democratic Party). In addition to these factors, we also looked for differences by gender, age, and race. Women tend to report higher ratings than men, 49 to 43 ($p < 0.001$). The average rat-

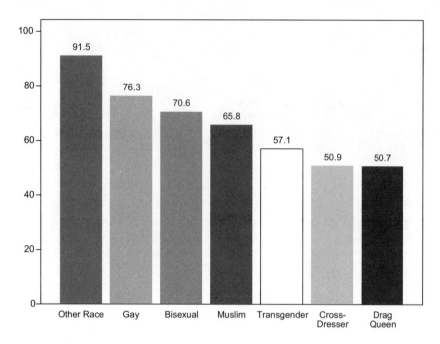

Figure 2.3. Personal Comfort around Various People. (GfK Survey, October 9–11, 2015.)
Note: Results from a survey item asking "Are you, personally, comfortable or uncomfortable when you are around someone who is . . . (select only response for each)?" Response categories include "comfortable," "somewhat comfortable," "somewhat uncomfortable," and "uncomfortable."

ings by older Americans (over forty-five) are slightly lower than those from younger respondents, but the pattern is not consistent across different age groups. There were no statistically significant differences across racial groups.

The relatively negative feelings of Americans toward transgender people *as a group* is also reflected in their attitudes toward interactions with transgender people *as individuals*. In the first two surveys from 2015, we investigated the personal comfort level of respondents around different types of people, asking whether they were "personally comfortable around someone who is [transgender]." Figure 2.3 shows the percentage of respondents that answered "comfortable" or "somewhat comfortable" in the October 2015 survey. Just 57.1 percent of respondents reported some degree of comfort around transgender people. This level of personal comfort is well below the percentages of Americans that are comfortable around people who are gay or bisexual. It is even below Muslims, who, as a group, were evaluated more negatively than transgender people on the thermometer rating scale. This suggests a level of personal discomfort with transgender people that is not

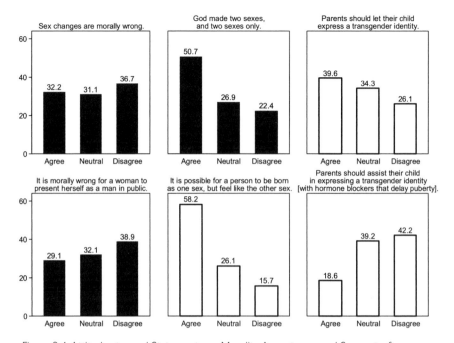

Figure 2.4. Attitudes toward Statements on Morality, Acceptance, and Support of Transgender People. (GfK Survey, October 9–11, 2015.)

Notes: Bars for negatively framed statements in black; bars for positively framed statements in white. "Agree" category includes respondents that "strongly agree," "agree," and "somewhat agree." "Disagree category includes respondents that "strongly disagree," "disagree," and "somewhat disagree." Neutral responses are "neither agree nor disagree."

evident for other groups that are evaluated negatively. The figure also reveals that the language used to refer to transgender people can generate different levels of personal comfort. Significantly, fewer respondents were comfortable around "crossdressers" and "drag queens." These terms have been commonly used to refer to transgender people, but may also be derogatory and invoke negative stereotypes. However, levels of comfort with someone who is "transsexual" (not shown), a somewhat dated term that is less often used in a derogatory manner, are almost the same as for transgender people.

To examine these general attitudes and feelings, we asked respondents about their level of agreement or disagreement with a set of statements addressing the perceived morality and acceptance of transgender as a concept.[6] A selection of these survey items from the 2015 GfK study, presented in figure 2.4, reveals a public that is not merely highly divided but also shows that many people do not hold clear opinions on these issues. For each of the statements, 26 to 39 percent of respondents chose the neutral option of "neither agree nor disagree." In terms of morality, the public is nearly evenly divided across the three response categories. The bar graphs on left show that 37 to 39 percent of respondents do not believe that transgender expression or sex changes are morally wrong, but 29 to 32 percent agree with these statements. The two middle graphs address the concept of nonbinary gender and produce contradictory responses. On one hand, 51 percent of respondents agree that "God only made two sexes, and two sexes only." On the other hand, a substantial majority (58 percent) also agree that "it is possible for a person to be born one sex but feel like the other sex."

The graphs on the right plot responses to statements regarding parental decisions related to raising a transgender child. As in the other graphs in figure 2.4, the responses reflect a divided public with fairly fluid opinions. The upper right graph shows a clear plurality of the sample agrees that parents should allow their child to express their transgender identity, though about a third remains neutral. However, when the statement includes the use of hormone blockers to delay puberty, the plurality shifts to those that disagree and the "neither agree nor disagree" option grows to nearly 40 percent. The public seems to be more willing to tolerate transgender expression, but is hesitant to embrace transgender medical treatments, at least for youth.[7] In the June 2016 survey, we repeated these questions, but did not allow for a neutral response. The pattern of supporting transgender expression, but opposing transgender medical treatment, holds. Two-thirds of the respondents agreed with allowing transgender expression, but 60 percent disagreed with using hormone blockers to delay puberty.

As with the thermometer ratings, variation in the attitudes about morality and support for transgender people is associated with individual characteristics. Table 2.1 shows how the responses to these statements vary across educational attainment, religious service attendance, and partisanship in our 2015 GfK data. Respondents with greater education tend to be more likely to view transgender people as moral and are more accepting of nonbinary gender identity. Educational attainment is also associated with increased willingness to allow children to express a transgender identity and to use hormone treatments, but the pattern is not nearly as consistent or stark as with the other statements in the table. Unsurprisingly, religious attendance is strongly associated with statements on the morality of transgender people, but it also seems related to acceptance of transgender concepts and the statements on parenting decisions. Similarly, partisanship also shows a strong association with responses to this set of statements. Again, the associations are somewhat weaker for the statements regarding parenting decisions, with

TABLE 2.1. Attitudes toward Statements on Morality and Acceptance of Transgender People, by Various Characteristics

	Education				Religious Attendance			Partisanship		
	HS or Less	Some College	Bachelor's Degree	Grad. Degree	Seldom or Never	1–2 times/ mon.* or yr.	Weekly or more	Dem.	Ind.	Rep.
Sex change operations are morally wrong.										
• Agree	43.8	28.1	24.4	14.0	19.4	34.4	54.2	20.2	36.7	46.3
• Neutral	30.0	37.7	27.6	24.1	31.2	34.3	26.5	29.9	42.3	31.3
• Disagree	26.3	34.3	48.1	61.9	49.4	31.3	19.3	49.9	21.0	22.4
It is morally wrong for a woman to present herself as a man in public.										
• Agree	35.3	28.8	23.4	16.2	16.5	31.5	50.5	18.9	40.2	40.0
• Neutral	35.7	33.7	26.3	23.8	30.3	38.8	28.4	29.7	36.7	33.9
• Disagree	29.0	37.5	50.3	60.0	53.2	29.8	21.1	51.4	23.1	26.1
God made two sexes and two sexes only.										
• Agree	58.2	49.4	48.5	30.5	34.8	59.6	71.7	36.3	51.2	67.3
• Neutral	24.5	31.4	29.5	20.8	30.9	25.9	20.0	31.5	33.9	21.1
• Disagree	17.2	19.2	21.9	48.8	34.3	14.5	8.3	32.2	14.9	11.7
It is possible to for a person to be born one sex, but feel like the other sex.										
• Agree	54.0	55.9	63.7	70.3	65.9	54.2	46.8	67.1	45.9	48.6
• Neutral	28.0	30.5	21.5	15.8	25.5	30.0	24.1	23.3	34.3	28.8
• Disagree	18.1	13.6	14.9	13.9	8.5	15.9	29.1	9.5	19.8	22.5
Parents should let their children express their transgender identity.										
• Agree	33.5	39.6	42.3	56.5	49.1	39.0	23.7	52.6	26.7	25.0
• Neutral	36.9	37.1	31.3	22.7	34.6	36.9	29.7	31.9	50.0	35.2
• Disagree	29.6	23.2	26.3	20.9	16.3	24.2	46.6	15.5	23.3	39.8
Parents should assist their child in expressing a transgender identity [with hormone blockers to delay puberty].										
• Agree	21.5	17.6	13.8	18.4	20.2	23.8	11.8	24.6	9.2	12.3
• Neutral	36.8	41.6	41.3	39.0	44.9	37.4	30.1	43.3	51.1	32.7
• Disagree	41.8	40.8	45.0	42.6	35.0	38.9	58.2	32.1	39.7	55.0

Source: GfK Survey, October 9–11, 2015

Notes: Entries are percentages. Both partisan categories include independents that lean toward that party. "Agree" category includes respondents that "strongly agree," "agree," and "somewhat agree." "Disagree category includes respondents that "strongly disagree," "disagree," and "somewhat disagree." Neutral responses are "neither agree nor disagree."

larger portions of each demographic group opting for a neutral response. A similar pattern is evident when examining ideology (results not shown). Interestingly, other demographic factors, such as age and race, do not show consistent relationships with these attitudes. In all, these cross-tabulations reveal general patterns that more educated respondents, less religious respondents, liberals, and those who identify with or lean toward the Democratic Party tend to be more accepting of transgender people and concepts.

Another way to gauge general attitudes toward transgender people is to ask survey respondents about transgender individuals serving in various public roles. In particular, we asked respondents about hiring a transgender person as an elementary school teacher and a clergy member. We also asked whether respondents would vote for a transgender candidate who shared their political views. In the June 2015 CVR survey, Americans favored allowing a transgender person to be hired as an elementary school teacher, 55 to 42 percent. This gap narrows, 49 to 46 percent, when considering whether a transgender person should be a member of the clergy. For comparison purposes, we also asked whether a gay person should be hired in these two professions. For elementary teachers and clergy, 68 and 55 percent, respectively, of respondents said that a gay person should be allowed in those professions. There has been an increase in support for gay people in these professions compared to a Gallup survey conducted in 2005 (Gallup 2017a).

When considering hypothetical political candidates, a majority of Americans would vote for a transgender candidate if they shared their political views, 54 to 56 percent depending on the office in question.[8] At the same time, 41 percent of the public would not vote for these candidates even though they share political views. This level of support for transgender candidates is slightly lower than the support for gay or lesbian candidates, who garner support from about 60 percent of the public. This pattern is consistent with group thermometer ratings in which the public tends to have more positive feelings toward gay men and lesbians.

As a relatively new political and social issue for many Americans, these mixed, fluid, and sometimes contradictory attitudes may not be surprising—especially when considering how few Americans report personal interactions with transgender people. A long line of literature shows how interpersonal contact with out-groups can increase tolerance and positive feelings toward these groups (Allport 1954), including the LGBT community (Herek and Capitanio 1996; Flores 2015a; Tadlock et al. 2017). As such, we asked respondents in the October 2015 GfK and June 2016 CVR surveys whether they knew someone who is transgender: a family member, a close friend, or an acquaintance. Within the categories in the October 2015 survey, almost 3 percent of respondents reported a transgender family member, nearly 4 percent reported a close friend, and 10 percent reported an acquaintance such as a coworker or schoolmate. Overall, just 15 and 18 percent of Americans reported knowing a transgender person in any of these three categories in the two surveys, indicating that relatively few people are likely to be influenced by interpersonal contact. For comparison purposes, approximately 73 percent of respondents knew a gay or lesbian person in at least one of these three categories in the October 2015 survey. Within those categories of contact, 36 percent of respondents had a gay family member, 38 percent had a close friend who is gay, and 56 percent had a gay acquaintance from work or school.

Similar questions have been asked in other national surveys as well, as far back as 2002. However, surveys before 2015 only asked about close friends and family while later surveys tend to use more expansive questions of interpersonal contact—either adding a category of acquaintances or just asking whether respondents know someone who is transgender. Figure 2.5 shows that both types of questions reveal increases in interpersonal contact over time. The percentage of Americans that report knowing a close friend or family member who is transgender has nearly doubled, from about 11 percent in 2011 to 21 percent in August 2016. The growth in more casual forms of interpersonal contact has increased even more over time. In 2002, about 16 percent of Americans reported knowing someone who is transgender,[9] but by 2016 several surveys put this number at 39 percent. This rather sharp increase in knowing a transgender person is likely a result of the growing public attention to issues of transgender rights in recent years. However, it is not clear whether these increased rates are actually indicative of significant increases in meaningful interpersonal contact with transgender people or are just a result of people being relatively more aware of the concepts and issues related to the transgender community. As discussed in chapter 1, increased parasocial contact through the mass media may increase familiarity with transgender people (Garretson 2015). Some people may report contact with transgender people if they are familiar with transgender celebrities like the former Olympian Caitlyn Jenner or the television star Laverne Cox, despite not actually knowing them.

The overall picture of feelings and general attitudes toward transgender people is relatively negative. However, the surveys also revealed significant uncertainty about transgender people and ideas. When given the option to neither agree nor disagree with a statement, regardless of whether it was framed in a positive or negative manner toward transgender people, 20–30 percent of Americans declined to state an opinion. Although a plurality of the public tends to have somewhat negative attitudes on many of these topics, they usually do not constitute a clear majority. Further, the framing and

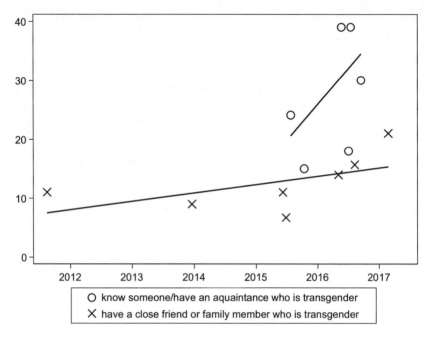

Figure 2.5. Personal Contact with Transgender People, 2011–2017

Notes: Data from various national surveys listed in appendix C (wording varies slightly across surveys); separate linear regression lines are plotted for each type of reported contact.

content of different statements regarding transgender people seems to have significant effects on whether responses are relatively more positive or more negative. From these survey items, it seems that many Americans have yet to solidify their attitudes on many different topics related to gender identity and transgender people.

Policy Attitudes

General feelings and attitudes toward out-groups tend to inform attitudes toward public policies that address those groups (Gilens 1999). However, Americans are also often supportive of policies that protect individual rights (e.g., McClosky and Brill 1983). Therefore, in addition to asking about general feelings and attitudes toward transgender people, our surveys also assessed public support or opposition to a range of public policies that affect the lives of transgender people. For comparison purposes, we also asked respondents about similar gay rights issues in our October 2015 and June 2015 surveys.

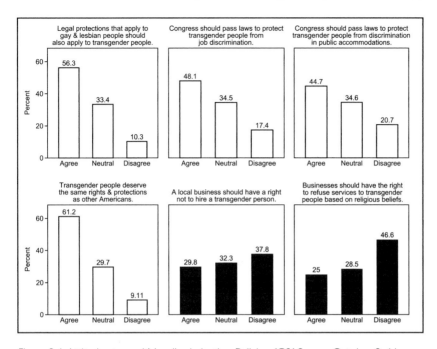

Figure 2.6. Attitudes toward Nondiscrimination Policies. (GfK Survey, October 9–11, 2015.)

Notes: Bars for negatively framed statements in black; bars for positively framed statements in white.

Among the earliest public policies that explicitly addressed gender identity are nondiscrimination policies. Though these policies vary significantly in their content, they most prominently provide protections against discrimination in employment, housing, and public accommodations (Taylor et al. 2012). Most Americans are broadly supportive of policies that emphasize equality, like protection against discrimination or the provision of basic civil rights (McClosky and Zaller 1984). As seen in figure 2.6, this pattern certainly holds for transgender rights. The four graphs with white bars plot the level of agreement with statements regarding nondiscrimination policies toward transgender people. In each case, a large plurality or a majority agrees that government should protect transgender people from discrimination. When respondents are asked about rights more generally, they were even more supportive, with over 60 percent agreeing that "transgender people deserve the same rights and protections as other Americans." Further, for each of the statements about legal rights and nondiscrimination, relatively few respondents reported opposition to these policies.

Although strong majority support for abstract concepts such as rights and

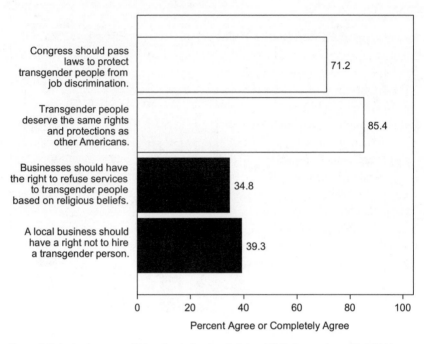

Figure 2.7. Attitudes toward Nondiscrimination Policies. (CVR Survey, June 29, 2016.)
Notes: Bars for negatively framed statements in black; bars for positively framed statements in white.

nondiscrimination is not particularly surprising, figure 2.6 also reveals that a significant portion of the public is not willing to state an opinion on these policies. Roughly 30 to 35 percent of respondents chose the neutral option of "neither agree nor disagree" when presented with these policy statements. By comparison, 29 percent and 31 percent of respondents, respectively, in our October 2015 survey were undecided on whether Congress should pass laws to protect gays or lesbians from employment or public accommodations discrimination. However, when respondents are not given the option to "neither agree nor disagree," as in our June 2016 survey, the percentage supporting transgender-inclusive employment nondiscrimination policies and legal rights increases to over 71 percent and 85 percent, respectively (see figure 2.7). These high levels of support are consistent with most surveys about transgender rights from 2011 to 2017, suggesting that these increases are not part of a temporal trend. Rather, it suggests that respondents that chose "neither agree nor disagree" will support these policies, but only if they are forced to pick a side. This reflects existing research demonstrating how survey results on these issues can be sensitive to response choices and question wording (Brewer 2003; Flores 2015b). Together, these questions show broad support for the protection of the rights of transgender people, but this support may not be as solid as it initially seems.

Figure 2.6 also shows the results from two statements regarding the specific implications of policies that provide discrimination protections in employment and public accommodations (presented in the graphs with black bars). Though 48 percent support the passage of laws to protect against job discrimination, nearly 38 percent oppose the idea of a local business discriminating against a transgender job candidate. Support for transgender protections is slightly less than the 53 percent of respondents who support these protections for gays and lesbians in the GfK poll. Meanwhile, 47 percent of respondents opposed the idea of a local business discriminating against a gay or lesbian job candidate. For public accommodations, support looks more consistent, even when introducing the strongly held value of religious freedom. Whereas about 45 percent of Americans supported discrimination protections for public accommodations, nearly 47 percent disagree with allowing businesses to refuse service to transgender people based on the businessperson's religious beliefs. For comparison purposes on public accommodations protections, 51 percent of respondents are supportive of inclusion for gay people and 46 percent oppose allowing businesses to refuse services to gay men and lesbians based on religious beliefs. As seen in figure 2.7, when respondents are forced to choose a side in our 2016 CVR poll, the percentage that opposes policies protecting transgender people from employment and public accommodations discrimination increases by roughly 10 points. The other 20 percent that likely would have chosen a neutral option, instead, opted to support these policies.

As expected, attitudes toward nondiscrimination policies are also associated with various demographic factors (see table 2.2). Large majorities support general job nondiscrimination laws across different education levels, but support for these policies does vary across religiosity and partisanship, with relatively smaller majorities of the most religious respondents and Republicans favoring job protections. Support for more general rights is even higher, with more than 80 percent agreeing with the statement across all demographic groups. Still, this support tops 88 percent among those with graduate degrees, the least religious respondents, and Democrats. The two statements regarding businesses and their right to not hire or refuse service to transgender people produce less support overall and show more variation across the demographic groups, particularly religious attendance and partisanship. Consistent with research on gay rights (Brewer 2008) and in our questions on gay rights issues, levels of support also vary by gender (not shown). Women tend to support nondiscrimination policies more than men by roughly 10 points ($p < 0.001$), depending on the statement.

In terms of broad nondiscrimination policy, the public is fairly supportive of transgender rights. Yet these laws are not the only policies that directly affect transgender people. Our surveys also asked about a range of more specifically tailored policies, ranging from adoption to health care and bathroom access. Figure 2.8 shows the results from questions relating to five of these more specific policies from our 2015 GfK study. As in the previously discussed survey results, a substantial portion of the public chose neutral positions, in three cases accounting for a plurality of the responses. Again, this likely reflects a relatively high degree of uncertainty and fluidity in public attitudes. Although 35 percent of the public agrees that transgender people should be allowed to adopt children, 37 percent neither agree nor disagree, and nearly 28 percent disagree with this statement. In comparison, 49 percent were supportive, 20 percent were opposed, and 29 percent were ambivalent about adoption rights for gays and lesbians. A similar distribution

TABLE 2.2. Attitudes toward Nondiscrimination Policies, by Various Characteristics

	Education				Religious Attendance			Partisanship		
	HS or Less	Some College	Bachelor's Degree	Grad. Degree	Yearly or Less	Occasionally	Weekly or More	Dem.	Ind.	Rep.
Congress should pass laws to protect transgender people from job discrimination.										
Agree	67.9	73.9	70.2	70.5	74.7	77.4	59.9	87.1	69.4	52.3
Disagree	32.1	26.1	29.8	29.5	25.3	22.6	40.1	12.9	30.6	47.7
Transgender people deserve the same rights and protections as other Americans.										
• Agree	80.9	85.9	85.5	90.2	88.1	84.9	80.4	88.6	86.0	80.9
• Disagree	19.1	14.1	14.5	9.8	11.9	15.1	19.6	11.4	14.0	19.2
Businesses should have the right to refuse services to transgender people based on their religious beliefs.										
• Agree	38.2	32.1	35.9	34.7	27.1	32.9	51.1	19.2	37.4	52.8
• Disagree	61.8	67.9	64.1	65.3	72.9	67.1	48.9	80.9	62.6	47.2
A local business should have the right not to hire a transgender person.										
• Agree	43.5	36.7	39.7	39.3	31.6	39.7	54.0	26.1	40.3	55.2
• Disagree	56.5	63.4	60.3	60.7	68.4	60.3	46.0	73.9	59.7	44.8

Source: CVR Survey, June 29, 2016.

Notes: Entries are percentages. Both partisan categories include independents that lean toward that party. "Agree" category includes respondents that "strongly agree," "agree," and "somewhat agree." "Disagree" category includes respondents that "strongly disagree," "disagree," and "somewhat disagree." Neutral responses are "neither agree nor disagree."

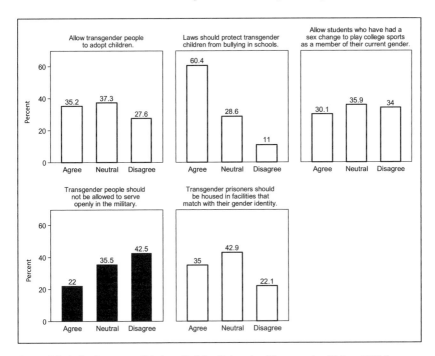

Figure 2.8. Attitudes toward Various Policies Related to Transgender Rights. (GfK Survey, October 9–11, 2015.)

Notes: Bars for negatively framed statements in black; bars for positively framed statements in white.

is evident for policies regarding prison facilities. More Americans agree with housing prisoners in facilities that match their gender identity than disagree (35 to 22 percent), but nearly 43 percent are neutral on this issue. When we asked about college sports, the public is almost evenly divided among the three response categories.

Two of the specific policy statements in figure 2.8 generated more clear-cut pluralities. Over 60 percent of the public agrees that laws should protect transgender children from bullying and only 11 percent disagreed with this statement. Similarly, 62 percent of respondents supported protections for gay or lesbian children. As with the broad support for nondiscrimination policies, most Americans are unwilling to oppose protections for basic rights. A clear plurality in opposition to banning transgender people from the military is also evident from the figure. Just 22 percent agree with such a ban, but a large proportion of the public (about 36 percent) is neutral on this policy.

In our June 2016 survey, we followed up on four of these specific policy statements, but did not allow a "neither agree nor disagree" option. Figure 2.9 shows a public that is more supportive of transgender rights. Only a third of the public agrees with barring transgender people from adopting children, leaving two-thirds in opposition to such a ban. A large majority of respondents agree with antibullying laws to protect transgender children, perhaps suggesting that respondents that would have opted for the "neither agree nor disagree" category chose to agree or somewhat agree with this policy. Opposition to allowing student athletes to play collegiate sports as a member of the gender that they identify with only increases from 35 percent in the previous survey to nearly 40 percent here, leaving about 60 percent supporting transgender athletes. Last, the percentage that agrees with allowing transgender people to serve in the military increases to over two-thirds.

With respect to attitudes about military service in the 2016 data, we subsequently used a statistical technique known as multilevel regression and poststratification to estimate state-level opinion on transgender military service. These findings were published in the *Washington Post* (Flores et al. 2017b). We found that majorities in every state favored allowing transgender people to engage in military service. The state where attitudes were least supportive of transgender military service was Wyoming where 55 percent of respondents were estimated to approve of it. Hawaii and Vermont were estimated to be the most supportive states with 75 percent approval. The mean level of support across the states for transgender military service was approximately 66 percent.[10]

The surveys also addressed policies that affect the ability of transgender people to navigate the transition process, including changing gender markers on government documents and accessing medical treatments. As displayed in figure 2.10, the public is divided on whether to allow gender marker changes on state identification cards. Although a small plurality supports allowing these changes, 35 percent "neither agree nor disagree" and another 29 percent oppose them. The Williams Institute sponsored a national survey in August 2016 that explores these attitudes in more detail (Flores, Brown, and Park 2016). It asked whether official gender marker changes should be allowed without restrictions, only with a doctor's approval, only after surgery so that their body matches their identity, only with approval from a government official, or should not be allowed, no matter what. Only 23 percent of respondents in the Williams Institute's survey believed that gender marker changes should be allowed without restrictions, but the study revealed relatively more support for changes under specific conditions. Consistent with many current state policies, 12.5 percent agreed with requiring a doctor's approval and 24 percent believed that gender confirmation surgery

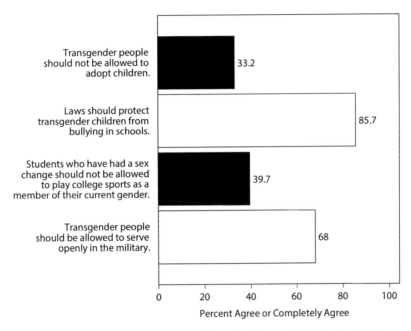

Figure 2.9. Attitudes toward Various Policies Related to Transgender Rights. (CVR Survey, June 29, 2016.)
Notes: Bars for negatively framed statements in black; bars for positively framed statements in white.

should be required for a gender marker change on a government identification document. Another 8 percent favored allowing gender marker changes with the approval of a government official. Together, just over two-thirds of the public agrees with allowing gender marker changes, but most supporters favor medical or governmental restrictions (Flores, Brown, and Park 2016).

Figure 2.10 also shows responses to questions about access to medical treatments in our 2015 GfK poll. A roughly even proportion of the public (about 36 percent) agrees that insurance companies should *not* be required to pay for medical treatments related to transgender identity or takes a neutral position on this policy. Just over 28 percent think that insurance companies should be required to cover these treatments. Opposition to insurance coverage for transgender medical treatments increases for Medicare, a publicly funded program. Opposition especially exists for publicly funded surgical treatments. However, since we fielded this survey in October 2015, two subsequent surveys in the summer of 2016 found more support for the idea of insurance companies covering transgender medical treatments. In our June 2016 survey, which lacked neutral response options, 50 percent dis-

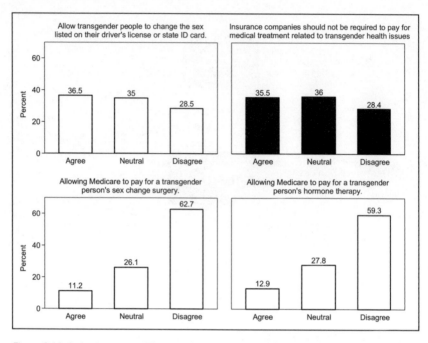

Figure 2.10. Attitudes toward Transgender Health and ID Policies. (GfK Survey, October 9–11, 2015.)

Notes: Bars for negatively framed statements in black; bars for positively framed statements in white.

agreed with the statement that insurance companies should be required to pay for medical treatment related to transgender health issues. An Associated Press/NORC national survey conducted in July 2016, using a split sample approach, found that over 67 percent of the eighteen to thirty year olds favored the coverage of transgender health issues generally, though this question did not address requirements for coverage (Associated Press 2016).[11] In the same survey, a half sample was asked the same question, but with specific examples of transgender medical treatments, including hormone treatments and sexual reassignment surgery. Sixty percent of this sample favored covering these treatments. Together, these questions about transgender health care suggest that the public is open to coverage of these treatments, but is hesitant to require coverage and is opposed to governmental programs, like Medicare, covering them.

Perhaps the most salient contemporary policy associated with transgender rights involves access to public restrooms. As seen in the discussion of recent popular referendum campaigns and state legislation, including North

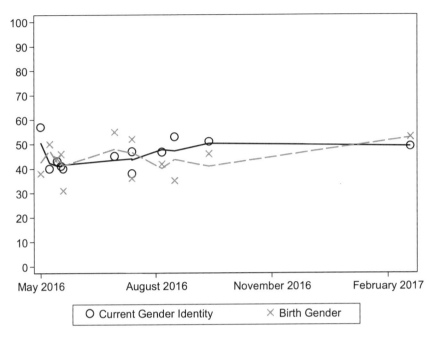

Figure 2.11. Attitudes toward Transgender Restroom Policies, 2016–2017
Notes: Data from various national surveys listed in appendix C (wording varies slightly across surveys); separate lowess lines are plotted for each response type.

Carolina's HB2, the bathroom issue has become a salient flashpoint in the debate over transgender rights. This issue has been used to oppose or repeal broader nondiscrimination policies for public accommodations (an issue that we discuss in chapter 7). Though majorities in most surveys tend to support public accommodations protections for transgender people, public support in the specific instance of bathroom access is less clear. In our June 2016 survey, 55 percent favored requiring transgender individuals to use restrooms that correspond with their birth gender, while just 45 percent preferred to allow transgender people to use the restroom that corresponds to their gender identity.[12] Other polls have found more support for policies that allow access to public restrooms based on gender identity, but there has been a fairly even split in public opinion since the issue began being included in surveys in 2015. As seen in figure 2.11, attitudes toward the bathroom issue have been consistently divided over time, even though there is substantial variation in the wording of these survey questions.[13] As such, survey results are likely sensitive to question wording and response choices.

Although the public is evenly divided on policies regarding access to public restrooms, as seen in table 2.3, the split varies across different demographic groups. Men are slightly more likely than women to support access requirements based on birth gender. Levels of educational attainment also seem to be associated with varying preferences for access based on birth gender versus gender identity. In particular, nearly two-thirds of respondents who have not attended college prefer birth gender restrictions, nearly 13 points higher than those that have attended at least some college. Religious attendance and partisanship show even starker differences. A majority of respondents who rarely, if ever, attend religious services prefer allowing access based on gender identity, but just 28 percent of respondents who attended services on a weekly basis or more frequently support this policy. Similarly, over three-quarters of Republicans prefer restrictions based on birth gender while over 62 percent of Democrats prefer allowing access based on gender identity.

TABLE 2.3. Attitudes toward Public Restroom Policies, by Various Characteristics

	These policies should require transgender individuals to use the restroom that corresponds with their birth gender.	These policies should allow transgender individuals to use the restroom that corresponds with their gender identity.
Total	55.1	44.9
Gender		
• Male	57.7	42.3
• Female	52.5	47.5
Education		
• High school	67.2	32.8
• Some college	54.5	45.6
• Bachelor's degree	50.1	49.9
• Graduate degree	48.0	52.0
Religious Attendance		
• Yearly or less	47.2	52.8
• Occasionally	52.0	48.0
• Weekly or more	72.2	27.8
Partisanship		
• Democrat	37.8	62.2
• Independent	53.6	46.4
• Republican	77.3	22.7

Source: CVR Survey, June 29, 2016.

Notes: Entries are percentages. Both partisan categories include independents that lean toward that party.

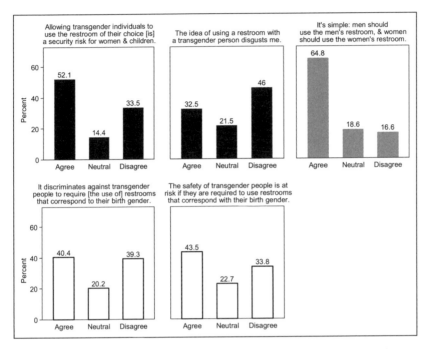

Figure 2.12. Attitudes toward Transgender Restroom Policies. (CVR Survey, June 29, 2016.)

Notes: Bars for negatively framed statements in black; bars for positively framed statements in white.

To explore why roughly half of Americans are opposed to allowing transgender people to use public restrooms that correspond with their gender identity, we asked respondents in our June 2016 survey whether they agreed or disagreed with a set of statements that provide justifications for opinions on both sides of the issue. Figure 2.12 shows the distribution of responses to these statements. One of the more common arguments used to oppose public accommodations protections has been the safety of women and children. In our survey, 52 percent of Americans agreed that allowing transgender people to use the restroom of their choice posed a security risk for women and children and only a third of the respondents disagreed. Interestingly, the neutral category attracted relatively fewer responses than in other questions on our surveys. Another factor that may underlie opposition to more open bathroom policies is disgust sensitivity; Miller et al. (2017) found that although about a third of the public agreed that the idea of using a restroom with a transgender person disgusts them, 46 percent disagreed.

The public is more evenly divided on whether restrictive bathroom policies are discriminatory, with about 40 percent agreeing that they are discriminatory and about 39 percent disagreeing. Interestingly, and despite relatively high levels of opposition to more open bathroom policies, nearly 44 percent of Americans agree that the safety of transgender people is at risk if they are required to use restrooms that correspond with their birth gender. So while a clear majority of Americans is concerned about the safety of cisgender women and children if transgender people are allowed to use restrooms that correspond with their gender identity, a substantial plurality is also concerned about the safety of transgender people under restrictive policies. Finally, respondents were presented with the argument regarding bathroom policies that stated, "It's simple: men should use the men's restroom and women should use the restroom"; here, 65 percent of the public agree with the statement. Even though this argument is clearly popular and seemingly simple, it can be interpreted as support for both sides of the issue depending on how one defines man and woman. For proponents of restrictive bathroom policies, the statement refers to men and women in terms of biological gender at birth. However, the statement could also be interpreted as referring to a person's current gender or gender identity, or both, particularly if their transition has included medical procedures or legal status changes. Our survey results suggest that the public has opinions that are more crystallized on bathroom policies than on other transgender related policies.

Further, the close divide on the issue seems to be associated with individually salient concerns over safety and civil rights. The debate over bathroom policies may also take on an added wrinkle when considered in the context of schools. In light of a high-profile court case about a transgender boy's access to restrooms at his high school (*G.G. v. Gloucester County School Board* 2016) and the Obama administration's guidance on Title IX (withdrawn by the Trump administration), the issue of bathroom and locker room access for transgender students entered the national spotlight. A July 2015 survey following California's adoption of a policy to allow transgender students to "participate in sex-segregated programs, activities, and facilities" based on their self-perception and regardless of their sex assigned at birth, found that 37 percent of the public supported the policy while 40 percent opposed it (University of Illinois, Springfield Survey Research Office 2015). The same poll asked respondents to which restroom/locker facilities transgender students should have access.[14] It found that 29 percent selected "restroom/locker room of their gender identity," 39 percent selected "restroom/locker room of their birth gender," 43 percent selected "a gender-neutral restroom/locker room," and 10 percent chose none of the listed facilities. Nearly a year later, following the Title IX guidance in May 2016, a national Quinnipiac poll found that just 36 percent of registered voters agreed with requiring schools to allow transgender students to use bathrooms and locker rooms consistent with their gender identity and 56 percent opposed the policy (Quinnipiac University Polling Institute 2016). However, a subsequent poll of registered voters in March 2017 found that the percentage favoring requiring student access to restrooms based on their gender identity had increased to 48 percent, with 45 percent opposed to this policy (Quinnipiac University Polling Institute 2017).

Conclusion

These three national surveys, combined with evidence from other national surveys, paint a complex and potentially fluid picture of public attitudes toward transgender people and transgender rights. Overall, attitudes tend to be fairly negative. On average, transgender people are on the colder side of feeling thermometer ratings, below gay men and lesbians and just above negatively viewed groups like atheists and Muslims. The majority of Americans report being comfortable around transgender people, but this percentage is far below other out-groups. Indeed, a significant portion of the public finds the concept of transgender identity as morally wrong and is not supportive of transgender expression. In terms of policy, the public tends to be supportive of general nondiscrimination policies; however, this support declines when presented with specific situations, such as a business owner's right to refuse to hire a transgender person. Further, there is a clear majority that opposes public assistance for medical treatments related to transgender identities, and most Americans believe that access to public restrooms should be based on a person's birth sex rather than a person's gender identity.

Our evidence that paints a negative picture of public opinion presents significant challenges for the transgender rights community, but there are some positive takeaways that can help explain the relatively remarkable success of the transgender right movement to date and point to opportunities in the future. First, and despite our analysis largely focusing on our polling data, that transgender issues are occasionally being included in national surveys performed by recognized polling organizations (see appendix C for examples) is a signal about the increasing salience of transgender issues in our political discourse. Symbolically, this speaks to the increasing legitimization of transgender rights claims (e.g., Herbst 1993). This is very different from the situation even a few short years ago. In addition, although the public is clearly not supportive of many issues related to transgender rights, there is strong support in some areas. For example, most people are supportive of nondiscrimination protections for employment and public accommodations, with overwhelming support evident when respondents are not given a neutral response option (see figure 2.7). Further, most people are in favor of antibullying laws, and a plurality of the public is open to allowing transgender people to serve in various roles, including as soldiers, teachers, and as elected officials. This support for trans rights, and its documentation via polling, is useful in the struggle for transgender rights. Advocacy groups, such as the Human Rights Campaign (2017b), strategically trumpet favorable polling results to policymakers and the public in an effort to establish the legitimacy of their claims as they attempt to build support for their policy goals (e.g., Stone 2012; Herbst 1993).[15]

Beyond these relatively positive attitudes, many of the survey items showed evidence of ambivalence and nonattitudes, which suggest a lack of exposure to or knowledge about transgender people. Indeed, on most transgender issues, a substantial portion of the public chose a neutral response if allowed, neither agreeing nor disagreeing with the survey statement. As a newer issue, this is not particularly surprising. In their 2011 survey, the Public Religion Research Institute (PRRI) found that only 70 percent of the public reported being familiar with the term "transgender" (Public Religion Research Institute 2011a). Despite the rise in the public prominence of the transgender issue, the level of familiarity in 2017 survey increased by only 10 percentage points, leaving nearly 20 percent of the public unfamiliar or somewhat familiar with the term (Public Religion Research Institute 2017). This corresponds with the public's lack of personal contact with transgender people. Most Americans still do not know anyone who is transgender and only about 15 to 20 percent report knowing a close friend or family member who is transgender. Thus, many people's opinions on these issues do not seem to be fully formed. There is clearly an opportunity for the transgender movement, as well as opponents of transgender rights, to sway public opinion. This fluidity is especially evident in a recent field experiment where canvassers were successfully able to reduce levels of transphobia by encouraging people to think about experiences where they felt judged negatively for being different and consider this experience in light of transgender people's perspectives (Broockman and Kalla 2016; see also Flores et al. 2017a). As such, the news we provide here should inspire both caution and hope for those desiring to shape attitudes. In the next chapter, we examine why individuals might hold these views.

CHAPTER 3

The Factors Underlying Public Opinion about Transgender Rights

with Andrew Flores, Patrick Miller, and Barry Tadlock

In this chapter, we further analyze the survey data introduced in chapter 2 to help us better understand public attitudes toward transgender people and transgender-related policy. The analyses examine attitudes toward transgender people, such as group affect ratings, as well as attitudes toward policies that affect the lives and rights of transgender people. In addition, we explore public attitudes toward transgender political candidates given the importance of descriptive representation in securing minority rights (Haider-Markel 2007, 2010; Reynolds 2013). Moving beyond the descriptive and bivariate relationships presented in the previous chapter, we employ multiple regression analyses to assess a wide range of factors that may underlie attitudes regarding transgender people and rights. These factors include individual demographics, such as age, gender, and race, and political orientations like partisanship and ideology. Our analyses also investigate the effects of individual values and personality traits, such as authoritarianism and egalitarianism. In addition, we assess the impact of interpersonal contact with LGBT individuals. Finally, where possible, we explore how the determinants of attitudes towards transgender rights compare to those factors that affect attitudes toward gay rights using seemingly unrelated regression (SUR) analysis.

Individual Characteristics and Political Orientation

A logical first place to begin our examination of the factors that shape public attitudes toward transgender people and rights is with individual characteristics and political orientations. We might expect that feelings toward transgender people and their rights would be shaped by the same individual characteristics that are also associated with feelings about other sexual minorities, such as gays and lesbians (Flores 2015a). Numerous studies have shown that attitudes toward gay people, tolerance of homosexuality, and support for gay civil rights are influenced by demographics like race, education, and gender (Herek 2002; Lewis 2003), religiosity (Olson et al. 2006; Mucciaroni 2008), partisanship, ideology (Brewer 2003, 2008), and attributions for homosexuality (Haider-Markel and Joslyn 2005, 2008, 2013; Lewis 2009).

Yet, as noted in the previous chapter, attitudes toward transgender people may differ from attitudes toward gays and lesbians. Further, Lewis et al. (2017) find that the factors underlying public attitudes toward these subgroups of the LGBT community may differ significantly. Indeed, there is a growing and distinct body of literature about attitudes toward transgender people (Flores 2015a; Flores, Herman, and Mallory 2015; Flores et al. 2017a; Haider-Markel et al. 2017; Jones et al. 2018; Miller et al. 2017; Nagoshi et al. 2008; Norton and Herek 2013; Tadlock et al. 2017).

Norton and Herek (2013) provided one of the first peer-reviewed journal articles to examine attitudes about trans people and their rights. Consistent with research on gays and lesbians, they find that women and the more educated are more likely to exhibit more positive feelings toward transgender people, while race mattered little. Religiosity and political conservatism were also associated with negative feelings. However, attitudes about transgender people are significantly more negative than attitudes about gays and lesbians (Norton and Herek 2013). Lewis et al. (2017) attribute this difference to three factors. The first of these is asymmetric contact levels with gay and transgender people. The second factor is cognitive consistency. This is due to constrained belief systems that might be attributed to ideology or religiosity (Converse 1964; Peffley and Hurwitz 1985; Wilcox 1990). The third factor that might explain the gap is elite cues on these issues. Cues by party elites can be important in shaping public opinion (Druckman, Peterson, and Slothuus 2013), and elite cues are more likely to be received and accepted by strong partisans (Zaller 1992). As such, strong partisans are likely more attitudinally consistent on gay and transgender rights.

Values, Personality Traits, and Experience

Beyond personal characteristics and political orientations, values and personality traits are known to shape attitudes toward sexual minorities and their rights. Values are the principles on which an individual places great importance in considering what is good for themselves and society. One important value is egalitarianism. It is a "belief that citizens should be equal regardless of their personal characteristics" (Clawson and Oxley 2013, 176). Egalitarianism is related to a person's views about policy issues (Feldman 1988). It predisposes individuals to support gay rights (Wilcox and Norrander 2002). Another important value is moral traditionalism. It reflects a person's "predisposition for traditional family and social structure" (Clawson and Oxley 2013, 178). Moral traditionalists favor married two-parent households where one parent is male and one female (Clawson and Oxley 2013). Unsurprisingly, moral traditionalism predisposes individuals to oppose a variety of gay rights issues (Wilcox and Norrander 2002; Brewer 2003; Egan, Persily, and Wallsten 2008). When individuals hold opposing core values, they might be ambivalent about gay rights issues (Craig et al. 2005).

In addition to values, personality traits also affect attitudes. Personality traits are habitual behavioral patterns, characteristics, and emotions that distinguish people from one another. Authoritarianism is a set of personality traits that involve submissiveness to authority, a preference for a strong leader, hostility and cynicism toward people, adherence to convention, and a belief that people should be punished for defying conventions (Clawson and Oxley 2013; Adorno et al. 1950). Authoritarians value conformity (Stenner 2005). When threat situations are perceived by authoritarians, they may become intolerant (Hetherington and Weiler 2009). Higher levels of authoritarianism are associated with antagonism toward the rights for minority groups, including gays and lesbians (Barker and Tinnick 2006; Hetherington and Weiler 2009; Laythe, Finkel, and Kirkpatrick 2001; Peterson, Doty, and Winter 1993). Recent research by Miller et al. (2017) extends the findings about authoritarianism to opposition of transgender rights.

Another personality trait that might affect responses to transgender rights and transgender people is disgust sensitivity (e.g., Casey 2016; Miller et al. 2017).[1] Schirmer (2013, 599) describes disgust as something "experienced in response to repulsive objects." Disgust is a protection mechanism that is activated by potentially harmful visual stimuli and by things that might be morally contaminating (Haidt, McCauley, and Rozin 1994; Hodson and Costello 2007; Horberg et al. 2009; Miller 1997; Rozin et al. 1999). Disgust sensitivity is part of the "behavioral immune system" (Schaller and

Duncan 2007). It is a relatively stable trait, and it predicts both disgust reactions to a myriad of aversive stimuli and a willingness to engage in activities that might be disgust-inducing (Haidt, McCauley, and Rozin 1994; Olatunji and Sawchuk 2005; Olatunji et al. 2007). When applied to social groups, the behavioral immune system generally elicits in-group favoritism and out-group bias (Faulkner et al. 2004; Navarette and Fessler 2006; Park, Faulkner, and Schaller 2003; Park, Schaller, and Crandall 2007; Schaller and Duncan 2007).

Individual experiences shape attitudes as well. Education is a form of experience, as is age, and both have been shown to influence attitudes toward sexual minorities (Brewer 2008). Educational experiences like attending college tend to increase social support for sexual minorities (Lottes and Kuriloff 1994). Indeed, education and cognitive sophistication have been related to political tolerance of unpopular groups (Bobo and Licari 1989). Age additionally defines different generational cohorts with a set of social and political experiences, which generally influence politics and policies (Carmines and Stimson 1981). However, the experience most powerfully shaping opinions toward out-groups is having contact with that group (Allport 1954; Pettigrew 1998; Pettigrew and Tropp 2008). This might include having a close friend, family member, or even an acquaintance such as a coworker who is a member of the group. It might also extend to parasocial contact with the out-group via the media (Schiappa, Gregg, and Hewes 2006). These types of interpersonal contact may increase knowledge, reduce anxiety, and increase empathy toward the out-group (Pettigrew and Tropp 2008).

Research on interpersonal contact has looked at its effect on prejudice reduction against racial minorities (Powers and Ellison 1995; Jackman and Crane 1986), immigrants (Schlueter and Scheepers 2010; Berg 2009), and people with disabilities (Cameron and Rutland 2006). The relationship between prejudice reduction and contact with gays and lesbians is very strong (Pettigrew and Tropp 2008; Flores 2015b; Garner 2013; Herek and Capitanio 1996; Herek and Glunt 1993; Brewer 2008; Overby and Barth 2002). However, prejudice reduction may not always translate into support for gay rights (Barth, Overby, and Huffmon 2009), partly because the effect of contact is conditioned by age (Becker and Scheufele 2011) and ideology (Bramlett 2012; Garner 2013; Skipworth, Garner, and Dettrey 2010). Parasocial contact has also been shown to facilitate positive attitudes toward gays and lesbians (Garretson 2015; Schiappa, Gregg, and Hewes 2006). In addition, Flores (2015a) and Norton and Herek (2013) find that contact with gays and lesbians has a positive secondary transfer effect on opinions about transgender issues.

Yet, the existing research on the effect of contact with transgender people is mixed. A study from Hong Kong found a weak relationship between knowing a transgender person and prejudice reduction (King, Winter, and Webster 2009). Meanwhile, a study of British college students failed to establish a link between transgender contact and prejudice reduction (Tee and Hegarty 2006). In a study of American adults, Flores (2015a) also failed to find a statistically significant relationship between contact with transgender people and attitudes on transgender equality. However, Tadlock et al. (2017) recently found that contact with transgender people generated a reduction in prejudice.

Methods and Data

To assess the impact of these factors on various attitudes related to transgender rights in a consistent and systematic manner, we analyze data from our nationally representative survey conducted via GfK's KnowledgePanel (n=1,020) on October 9–11, 2015. Additional details about the survey and instruments are described in chapter 2 and survey questions are listed in appendix F. Before analyzing the data, we impute missing values using Amelia II (King et al. 2001) to avoid systematic bias due to case-wise deletion from missing values.

Dependent Variables

The first set of dependent variables concern affect and comfort around transgender people. To assess general feelings (or group affect) toward transgender people, we employ a feeling thermometer scale, similar to the one presented in figure 2.1, which asks respondents to provide a temperature feeling toward a group. High ratings (above 50) indicate favorable or warm feelings toward the group and low ratings (below 50) indicate cold or unfavorable feelings. As noted previously, the public has, on average, relatively negative feelings toward transgender people. In the October 2015 survey, the mean rating for transgender people was just 43, significantly lower than the mean rating of gay men and lesbians at nearly 52.

Personal comfort with transgender people is gauged using an additive scale derived from responses to three items: "Are you, personally, comfortable or uncomfortable when you are around someone who is . . . transgender, a crossdresser, a transsexual?" The response categories to these questions were comfortable (3), somewhat comfortable (2), somewhat uncomfortable (1), uncomfortable (0) (see appendix F).[2] The resultant scale ranges from zero, for respondents who are uncomfortable with all three scenarios, to nine for respondents who are comfortable for all cases. The mean comfort score is about five.

As we move to examine more politically oriented attitudes, we assess the public's willingness to vote for transgender candidates as well as lesbian and gay candidates. We asked respondents how likely they would be to vote for a hypothetical transgender candidate who shared their views on political issues in races for city council, state legislature, governor, and the U.S House of Representatives. We combined responses to these questions into an additive scale, ranging from zero for respondents who would "definitely vote for someone else" in all four races to twelve for respondents who would "definitely vote for the transgender candidate."[3] For comparison purposes, we asked a similar set of questions about gay or lesbian candidates and constructed a corresponding additive scale.

We also analyze public attitudes toward a range of specific policies that affect the lives of transgender people. Respondents were presented with a series of policy statements and were asked how much they agreed or disagreed with those statements, generating a five-point response ranging from "strongly agree" to "strongly disagree" with a neutral midpoint:

- Legal protections that apply to gay and lesbian people should also apply to transgender people
- Congress should pass laws to protect transgender people from job discrimination
- Congress should pass laws to protect transgender people from discrimination in public accommodations like restaurants and movie theaters
- Laws should protect transgender children from bullying in schools
- Transgender people deserve the same rights and protections as other Americans
- Laws to prevent employment discrimination against transgender people[4]
- Allowing transgender people to serve openly in the military
- Insurance companies should **not** be required to pay for medical treatment related to transgender health issues
- Allowing transgender people to use public restrooms that are consistent with the way that they express their gender
- Allowing transgender people to adopt children

- Allowing transgender people to change the sex listed on their Driver's License or state ID card
- Allowing Medicare to pay for a transgender person's sex change surgery
- Allowing Medicare to pay for a transgender person's hormone therapy
- Allowing students who have had a sex change to play college sports as a member of their current gender.

To develop a policy attitude scale based on these items, we follow the approach of Miller et al. (2017) and use Principal Component Analysis to find two correlated, but distinct, attitudinal dimensions that these items tap. The latter seven items, addressing specific health care policies, societal roles, and sex segregation, all relate to issues dealing with bodies and gender presentation that Miller et al. (2017) term the "body-centric" dimension. The first seven items all deal with issues such as discrimination, bullying, and individual rights, constituting a "civil rights" dimension. Thus, we create two additive scales, coded so that higher values indicate more positive attitudes toward transgender rights.[5] For the body-centric dimension, 54 percent of respondents have negative scale values, 12 percent neutral, and 33 percent positive. On the civil rights scale, 22 percent of respondents have negative scores, 11 percent neutral, and 67 percent positive.

For a comparison to gay rights policies, we also constructed an additive scale of the following five survey items:

- Congress should pass laws to protect gay men and lesbians from job discrimination
- Congress should pass laws to protect gay men and lesbians from discrimination in public accommodations
- Laws should protect gay or lesbian children from bullying in schools
- Businesses should have the right to refuse services to gay men or lesbians based on religious beliefs
- Allowing gays and lesbians to adopt children

These items primarily address civil rights issues and are most comparable to the transgender civil rights scale. Higher values on the resultant scale indicate positive attitudes toward gay and lesbian rights. Twenty percent of respondents have negative scale values, 16 percent are neutral, and 64 percent have positive values. Since the values on this scale differ from the transgender policy scales, we standardize each scale with a mean of zero and a standard deviation of one before estimating the regression models.

Independent Variables

The independent variables follow from our literature review, along with a set of standard demographic control variables. The multivariate models include race (white = 0; nonwhite = 1), sex (female = 1; male = 0), age (in years), educational attainment (seven-point scale from less than high school [1] to professional or doctorate degree [7]), household income (19-point scale from less than $5,000 [1] to more than $175,000 [19]), sexuality (heterosexual = 0; gay/lesbian/bisexual = 1), ideology (seven-point scale from very liberal [1] to very conservative [7]), and partisan identification (seven-point scale from strong Republican [1] to strong Democrat [7]). We capture religiosity with a six-point scale of the frequency of religious service attendance, ranging from never (0) to more than once a week (5). The models also include dichotomous religious identification indicators for Protestants and Catholics (other religions serve as the reference category). The primary measure of interpersonal contact indicates whether respondents know a transgender person who is a family member, a close friend, or an acquaintance (no = 0; yes = 1).

Our measures of egalitarianism, moral traditionalism, and authoritarianism follow the construction of additive scales based on responses to a series of questions as utilized in the American National Election Study. Each of the series of questions was rescaled so that higher values are associated with egalitarianism, traditionalism, and authoritarianism. We also created an additive disgust sensitivity scale from a series of four questions asking about personal hygienic preferences, with higher values indicating more sensitivity (Haidt, McCauley, and Rozin 1994).[6] All items used to construct these scales are presented in appendix F.

Results

Group Affect and Personal Comfort

The analyses begin with a model of group affect, as gauged by feeling thermometer ratings. Since respondents issued ratings of both transgender people and gay men and lesbians, we estimate two models simultaneously as seemingly unrelated regressions (SUR). By linking the error terms of these equations, we can statistically test the equality of coefficients across equations and assess whether the effects of the various factors differ across the two groups.

The results are presented in table 3.1. For ratings of transgender people, only a few demographic and political variables are significant factors. Women tend to rate transgender people more than eight degrees warmer than do men. Older respondents, meanwhile, report slightly lower ratings. For every ten years of age, the average thermometer rating is about one degree lower. The household income coefficient is also statistically significant and shows that, for every two income categories, thermometer ratings increase by about one degree, on average. Surprisingly, party identification and ideology do not have significant effects once the models account for personality traits and values. While religious attendance is not a significant factor, we find that Catholic identifiers have significantly more negative feelings toward transgender people than other religions (including Protestants). This surprising finding is possibly an artifact of survey construction. Our respondents' religious choice responses included evangelical denominations and mainline Protestant denominations as a single response choice. Given

TABLE 3.1. SUR Model of Feeling Thermometer Ratings

	Transgender People		Gays and Lesbians	
	b_i	SE_b	b_i	SE_b
Nonwhite	−0.831	(1.917)	−2.390	(1.900)
Female	**8.181*****	**(1.673)**	**5.444****	**(1.658)**
Age	−0.092+	(0.050)	−0.054	(0.049)
Ideology (Liberal → Conservative)	−0.680	(0.726)	−0.947	(0.719)
Partisanship (R → D)	0.813	(0.536)	−0.441	(0.531)
Religious Attendance	**0.156**	**(0.552)**	**−1.428****	**(0.547)**
Gay, Lesbian, Bisexual	**0.638**	**(2.366)**	**6.011***	**(2.345)**
Protestant	−1.413	(2.127)	3.406	(2.108)
Catholic	**−7.197****	**(2.384)**	**−1.911**	**(2.363)**
Educational Attainment	**0.407**	**(0.582)**	**1.336***	**(0.577)**
Household Income	**0.620****	**(0.212)**	**0.996*****	**(0.210)**
Authoritarian	−1.119	(0.725)	−0.860	(0.719)
Egalitarian	**1.336*****	**(0.291)**	**1.142*****	**(0.288)**
Moral Traditionalism	**−2.624*****	**(0.327)**	**−2.819*****	**(0.324)**
Disgust Sensitivity	**−1.180*****	**(0.291)**	**−0.659***	**(0.288)**
Transgender Interpersonal Contact	**10.014*****	**(2.423)**	**4.292+**	**(2.401)**
Gay/Lesbian Interpersonal Contact	**6.905*****	**(1.915)**	**13.566*****	**(1.898)**
Constant	38.347***	(6.123)	38.079***	(6.068)
R^2	0.354		0.370	
N	1,020		1,020	

Notes: Results of Seemingly Unrelated Regressions (SUR analysis); dependent variables are thermometer ratings of transgender people and gays/lesbians; statistically significant differences in row coefficients are listed in bold (χ^2 tests, $p < 0.1$); data are from a national probability sample survey of 1,020 adults conducted for the authors by GfK on October 9–11, 2015.

+ $p < 0.1$; * $p < 0.05$; ** $p < 0.01$; *** $p < 0.001$; two-tailed tests

the heterogeneous views of Protestant denominations on matters of sexuality (Rayside and Wilcox 2011), we are cautious in our findings as they pertain to religious identification.

However, the results consistently show that personality traits, values, and experience variables are statistically significant predictors of group affect. As expected, respondents with more traditional values and those who have higher levels of disgust sensitivity report lower thermometer ratings, decreasing ratings by about 2.6 and 1.2 degrees for each unit increase in the respective scales. Respondents who are more egalitarian, meanwhile, tend to have positive feelings toward transgender people. Finally, contact, or knowing both transgender people and gays and lesbians, has large positive impacts on evaluations of transgender people. Interpersonal contact with a transgender person increases thermometer scores by ten degrees while contact with a gay or lesbian person increases these ratings by nearly seven degrees.

Table 3.1 also shows how the factors associated with thermometer ratings of gays and lesbians differ from those that underlie ratings of transgender people. Statistically significant differences as determined by Wald-χ^2 tests ($p < 0.1$) are indicated with bold font. For example, while women report higher ratings than men for gays and lesbians, this 5.4 degree difference is significantly smaller than the eight degree effect for transgender people. Consistent with Lewis et al. (2017), we also find that religious attendance is a significant factor in the ratings of gays and lesbians, but not transgender people. However, religious affiliation is not significant in the model of gay and lesbian ratings. Another difference that stands out is that disgust sensitivity has a smaller effect on ratings of gays and lesbians, which highlights the centrality of body issues in attitudes toward transgender people (Miller et al. 2017). Last, and not surprising, the models reveal how interpersonal contact with a member of that group has a larger effect than contact with a member of a related group. In other words, the gay/lesbian contact effect for ratings of gays and lesbians is larger than the secondary transgender contact effect is on respondent views about gay people. Similarly, the contact effect for transgender people on transgender ratings is also larger than the secondary gay/lesbian contact effect is for ratings of transgender people.

In addition to group affect, we also analyze the factors that underlie feelings of personal comfort or discomfort with transgender people, including crossdressers and transsexuals. As seen in table 3.2, the results largely mirror the group affect model. Women tend to be more comfortable than men around transgender people. Egalitarian values are also associated with higher levels of comfort. Meanwhile, both traditionalism and disgust sensitivity have negative impacts on personal comfort around transgender people. Interpersonal contact with both transgender people and gays and lesbians show large effects, suggesting that experience around someone from the LGBT community increases comfort with transgender people by nearly 1 percentage point. As with the previous models, political factors like ideology and partisanship are not significant predictors of these personal feelings when we account for other factors. Even the religious variables do not seem to have a significant effect. Instead, personal comfort seems to be driven primarily by personality traits, values, and experience.

Lesbian, Gay, and Transgender Candidates

Next, we examine more politically oriented attitudes by modeling the willingness of the public to vote for transgender and gay and lesbian candidates. Like the thermometer rating analysis, we estimate the models using SUR

TABLE 3.2. Regression Model of Personal Comfort

	b_i	SE_b
Nonwhite	0.212	(0.197)
Female	0.436*	(0.172)
Age	−0.004	(0.005)
Ideology (Liberal → Conservative)	−0.036	(0.075)
Partisanship (R → D)	0.045	(0.055)
Religious Attendance	−0.085	(0.057)
Gay, Lesbian, Bisexual	0.082	(0.243)
Protestant	0.050	(0.219)
Catholic	0.142	(0.245)
Educational Attainment	−0.053	(0.060)
Household Income	−0.011	(0.022)
Authoritarian	−0.067	(0.075)
Egalitarian	0.143***	(0.030)
Moral Traditionalism	−0.240***	(0.034)
Disgust Sensitivity	−0.080**	(0.030)
Transgender Interpersonal Contact	0.941***	(0.249)
Gay/Lesbian Interpersonal Contact	0.869***	(0.197)
Constant	5.048***	(0.630)
R^2	0.282	
N	1,020	

Notes: Results of OLS Regression; dependent variable is a scale of personal comfort around transgender people, cross-dressers, and transsexuals; data are from a national probability sample survey of 1,020 adults conducted for the authors by GfK on October 9–11, 2015.

* $p < 0.05$; ** $p < 0.01$; *** $p < 0.001$; two-tailed tests

to allow for comparisons between factors underlying willingness to vote for transgender candidates vs. gay/lesbian candidates. The results are presented in table 3.3.

The models show that several demographic characteristics are significantly related to a respondent's willingness to vote for a transgender candidate. Once again, women have more favorable attitudes toward transgender people and are more likely to support a transgender candidate. However, gender is not a factor in hypothetical support for gay and lesbian candidates. Religiosity, as indicated by religious service attendance, also affects vote choice, with more religious respondents less likely to support a transgender candidate. Religious attendance also negatively affects gay and lesbian candidates, but the magnitude of the effect is significantly larger. Interestingly gay, lesbian, and bisexual respondents are more likely to vote for a transgender candidate, but sexuality does not a have a statistically significant impact in

TABLE 3.3. SUR Model of Willingness to Vote for LGT Candidates

	Transgender Candidates		Gay/Lesbian Candidates	
	b_i	SE_b	b_i	SE_b
Nonwhite	−0.180	(0.234)	−0.074	(0.235)
Female	**0.487***	**(0.204)**	**0.117**	**(0.205)**
Age	0.010	(0.006)	0.013*	(0.006)
Ideology (Liberal → Conservative)	−0.126	(0.089)	0.021	(0.089)
Partisanship (R → D)	0.045	(0.065)	0.045	(0.066)
Religious Attendance	**−0.275***	**(0.067)**	**−0.351***	**(0.068)**
Gay, Lesbian, Bisexual	0.618*	(0.289)	0.448	(0.290)
Protestant	0.231	(0.260)	0.135	(0.261)
Catholic	0.411	(0.291)	0.309	(0.292)
Educational Attainment	**0.140***	**(0.071)**	**0.351***	**(0.071)**
Household Income	0.029	(0.026)	0.018	(0.026)
Authoritarian	−0.330***	(0.089)	−0.426***	(0.089)
Egalitarian	**0.198***	**(0.035)**	**0.148***	**(0.036)**
Moral Traditionalism	−0.325***	(0.040)	−0.288***	(0.040)
Disgust Sensitivity	−0.108**	(0.036)	−0.129***	(0.036)
Transgender Interpersonal Contact	**1.108***	**(0.296)**	**0.741***	**(0.297)**
Gay/Lesbian Interpersonal Contact	**1.050***	**(0.234)**	**1.937***	**(0.235)**
Constant	5.997***	(0.747)	5.304***	(0.751)
R^2	0.399		0.406	
N	1,020		1,020	

Notes: Results of Seemingly Unrelated Regressions (SUR analysis); dependent variables are scales of willingness to vote for transgender and gay/lesbian candidates; statistically significant differences in row coefficients are listed in bold (χ^2 tests, $p < 0.1$); data are from a national probability sample survey of 1,020 adults conducted for the authors by GfK on October 9–11, 2015.
* $p < 0.05$; ** $p < 0.01$; *** $p < 0.001$; two-tailed tests

the gay and lesbian candidate model. Last, educational attainment is associated with an increased willingness to support both types of candidates, but the effect is significantly larger for gay and lesbian candidates.

As with the previous analyses, personality traits, values, and experience are also significant underlying factors. Respondents who have authoritarian personalities, hold traditional moral values, and have high levels of disgust sensitivity are less likely to support both transgender and gay and lesbian candidates. Egalitarian values, meanwhile, are associated with an increased likelihood of voting for these candidates, though the effect is larger for transgender candidates. Knowing lesbian, gay, or transgender people also increases an individual's willingness to support lesbian, gay, or transgender candidates.[7] For transgender candidates, the effects are roughly of the same magnitude for transgender contacts and lesbian and gay contacts. However, for gay and lesbian candidates, knowing someone who is gay or lesbian has a much larger effect than knowing someone who is transgender ($p < 0.01$). The results in table 3.3 also show there are differences in the contact effect across the candidate types, with relatively larger effects for the corresponding type of contact in each case.

Policy Attitudes

The last set of analyses models support for various public policies affecting transgender people. As discussed above, attitudes toward these policies tend to fall along two related, but distinct, dimensions: body-centric policies and civil rights policies. To analyze the factors underlying these two attitudinal dimensions as well as attitudes toward gay rights policies, we estimate a SUR with three equations. The dependent variables are all transformed into standardized units in order to facilitate direct comparisons. The results of the three regression models are presented in table 3.4.

Beginning with the transgender policy models, it is apparent that demographics and political factors play a more substantial role than in the previous analyses. For both policy dimensions, race and gender have significant coefficients, indicating that nonwhite respondents are less supportive of both sets of transgender policies and women are relatively more supportive. Age, meanwhile, is a significant factor for body-centric policies only, with older respondents less supportive of these types of policies than younger respondents. Similarly, sexuality is only statistically significant in the body-centric policies equation, but not in the Civil Rights equation. Ideology and partisanship are also roughly equally associated with both policy dimensions.

Conservatives and Republicans hold significantly more negative attitudes than liberals and Democrats. Religiosity appears not to play a significant role in support for either of these transgender policy scales, though Protestants do tend to hold more negative attitudes on the body-centric policies scale.

As with the previous analyses, personality traits, values, and experiences are strong predictors of attitudes toward transgender rights, though there are some significant differences in these effects between the two policy dimensions. Authoritarianism is a significant predictor of opposition to transgender civil rights, but it is not statistically significant in the body-centric policies equation. Both policy dimensions are positively associated with Egalitarianism, but the relationship is significantly stronger on the civil rights dimen-

TABLE 3.4. SUR Model of Support for Various LGBT Policies

	Trans Body Policies		Trans Civil Rights		Gay/Lesbian Policies	
	b_i	SE_b	b_i	SE_b	b_i	SE_b
Nonwhite	−0.099*	(0.049)	−0.089+	(0.051)	−0.188***	(0.050)
Female	0.111**	(0.043)	0.074+	(0.045)	0.097*	(0.044)
Age	**-0.003***	**(0.001)**	**−0.001**	**(0.001)**	0.001	(0.001)
Ideology (Liberal → Conservative)	−0.058**	(0.018)	−0.053**	(0.019)	−0.057**	(0.019)
Partisanship (R → D)	0.034*	(0.014)	0.026+	(0.014)	0.033*	(0.014)
Religious Attendance	−0.016	(0.014)	0.004	(0.015)	−0.007	(0.014)
Gay, Lesbian, Bisexual	0.120*	(0.060)	0.081	(0.063)	0.102+	(0.062)
Protestant	**−0.099+**	**(0.054)**	**0.062**	**(0.057)**	−0.001	(0.056)
Catholic	−0.030	(0.061)	0.015	(0.064)	0.077	(0.062)
Educational Attainment	0.003	(0.015)	0.017	(0.016)	0.019	(0.015)
Household Income	−0.005	(0.005)	0.006	(0.006)	−0.002	(0.006)
Authoritarian	**−0.021**	**(0.018)**	*−0.068***	(0.019)*	−0.035+	(0.019)
Egalitarian	**0.045***	**(0.007)**	*0.069***	(0.008)*	0.057***	(0.008)
Moral Traditionalism	**−0.116***	**(0.008)**	*−0.091***	(0.009)*	−0.111***	(0.009)
Disgust Sensitivity	−0.019*	(0.007)	−0.012	(0.008)	−0.003	(0.008)
Transgender Interpersonal Contact	0.299***	(0.062)	*0.280***	(0.065)*	0.191**	(0.063)
Gay/Lesbian Interpersonal Contact	**0.079**	**(0.049)**	**0.333***	**(0.051)**	0.334***	(0.050)
Constant	0.350*	(0.156)	−0.157	(0.164)	−0.192	(0.160)
R^2	0.529		0.499		0.522	
N	1,020		1,020		1,020	

Notes: Results of Seemingly Unrelated Regressions (SUR analysis); dependent variables are scales of support for various LGBT policies; statistically significant differences in row coefficients between the two transgender policies are listed in bold (χ^2 tests, $p < 0.1$); statistically significant differences in row coefficients between transgender and gay/lesbian civil rights policies are listed in italics (χ^2 tests, $p < 0.1$); data are from a national probability sample survey of 1,020 adults conducted for the authors by GfK on October 9–11, 2015.

+ $p < 0.1$; * $p < 0.05$; ** $p < 0.01$; *** $p < 0.001$; two-tailed tests

sion (as might be expected). Moral Traditionalism, meanwhile, shows the opposite pattern. It is negatively associated with both policy scales, but has a stronger relationship with body-centric policies. Unsurprisingly, Disgust Sensitivity is negatively related to the body-centric policies attitudes, but it has no significant association with civil rights policy attitudes. Interestingly, while transgender interpersonal contact equally affects both transgender policy attitude scales, gay or lesbian contact only significantly affects civil rights related attitudes.

Turning to the Gay/Lesbian Policy equation, the results show some significant differences from the Trans Civil Rights equation (indicated by italics in table 3.4). First, race has a significantly larger negative effect in the Gay/Lesbian Policy equation. Next, while authoritarianism and egalitarianism both influence attitudes toward gay rights, these effects are significantly smaller than they are for transgender rights attitudes. Yet moral traditionalism has a stronger negative association with gay rights attitudes than with attitudes about transgender civil rights. This may reflect a stronger vein of morality politics evident in gay rights compared to transgender rights as noted in diffusion studies of nondiscrimination policies (e.g., Taylor et al. 2012) and the more direct treatment of homosexuality as a moral wrong in most major religions (Ishak and Haneef 2014). Last, transgender interpersonal contact has a significantly smaller coefficient in the Gay/Lesbian Policy equation. The political variables, however, are roughly the same as in both transgender policy equations. This may reflect the political nature of public policies more generally and the partisan and ideological linkages of the LGBT community in the U.S. political system.

Conclusion

In this chapter, we explored the determinants of attitudes toward transgender people and transgender related policies. We outlined a series of expectations based on existing literature about attitudes toward sexual minorities and a smaller set of studies about transgender people. Drawing on a range of public attitudes, ranging from group affect to support for specific policies, we were able to identify several patterns in the factors that shape attitudes toward transgender people and their rights. Further, using SUR analysis we were able to directly compare individual factors across different attitudes and attitudes toward gays and lesbians.

The most important demographic factor shaping attitudes was gender. In every analytical model, women held more favorable attitudes. This may reflect an increased sensitivity to issues related to gender and gender discrimination, even in cases of transgender identification. Other demographic factors seemed to have varying associations, depending on the specific attitude. Older Americans have relatively more negative attitudes in terms of group affect and body-centric transgender policies, but not on the other attitudes that we examined. Religious variables, meanwhile, seem largely unrelated to personal feelings like group affect and comfort, but they show more significant effects on policy attitudes. However, some of these contradictory findings may be driven by the inclusion of moral traditionalism, which tends to be correlated with religiosity (De Koster and Van der Waal 2007). In this survey, the two variables have a moderately strong correlation of 0.45.

Another interesting pattern that emerged from the analyses was the absence of political identification effects until specific policy attitudes were modeled. Despite strong partisan and ideological relationships that are evident when examining the behavior of political elites, such as legislators, governors, and party officials (see section III), the public does not seem to draw significantly on these identifications when evaluating transgender people. Rather, these political factors only seemed to play a role when respondents were asked about policies that involve government action.

Personality traits and values, however, tend to show consistent relationships with all the attitudes examined here. In particular, moral traditionalism and egalitarianism were statistically significant factors in every model. People who express concern about the changing world and the deterioration of moral values tend to have more negative attitudes toward transgender people and toward transgender related policies. People that place a high value on equality, however, tend to hold positive attitudes toward transgender people and their rights. Authoritarian personality traits were less consistently relevant, but were a negative factor in views of transgender candidates and transgender civil rights. Disgust sensitivity, meanwhile, was a significant negative factor in all attitudes toward transgender people except the civil rights policy dimension.

Finally, personal contact with LGBT individuals was a consistently important factor across the analyses. In particular, knowing a transgender person, whether it is a family member, a friend, or just an acquaintance, significantly increases support for transgender people and their rights. Further, interpersonal contact with gays or lesbians also had a positive, albeit smaller, effect on these attitudes. Again, inclusion in the LGBT community seems to pay dividends for transgender rights both from an advocacy capacity perspective and for public perceptions. This point may be crucial for the advancement of transgender rights due to asymmetric contact patterns.

Contact rates with gay men and lesbian women are much higher than contact with transgender people (Lewis et al. 2017; Tadlock et al. 2017).

We also see this connection between transgender rights and gay rights in the analytical comparisons with gay rights attitudes. Many factors showed very similar relationships with attitudes toward both groups. However, some key distinctions certainly emerged. Religious factors and education were more consistently related to attitudes toward gay and lesbian people and gay rights. Personality traits and values, especially disgust sensitivity, tend to have smaller associations with attitudes toward gays and lesbians compared to the associations with attitudes toward transgender people.

The Political Opportunity Structure and Transgender Rights

Section III Introduction

In chapter 1, we discussed the rise of a combined LGBT advocacy movement. This social movement fought to overturn widespread discriminatory treatment and policies, such as the prohibitions against same-sex marriage and those that have limited the ability of LGBT identified individuals to serve in the military (Rimmerman 2015; Chauncey 2005). The movement has also challenged laws criminalizing acts associated with LGBT identified people, such as same-sex sexual relations and crossdressing. In addition, there have been enhanced movement efforts to multiply civil rights laws to prohibit discrimination based on sexual orientation and gender identity. These discrimination protections are critical to securing LGBT rights because public policy has historically reinforced heteronormative institutions and reified traditional views of masculinity and femininity (Barclay, Bernstein, and Marshall 2009).

Since the goals of the LGBT rights movement tend to require changes to the status quo, including advocating for brand-new policies, the expansion of existing ones, and the overturning of policies, the movement generally faces significant challenges in meeting its policy objectives. The U.S. federal system of separated powers and checks and balances serves to advantage the status quo. In other words, policy change is typically slow and difficult. For example, most introduced legislation does not pass. In order to become law, bills must clear many legislative hurdles, such as committees, identical passage in separate chambers, and usually gain the assent of the executive. Those seeking to thwart legislative change only have to win at one of these steps to block pro-LGBT policies. Due to this "defensive advantage" (e.g., Wiggins and Browne 1982; Wright 2003), opponents of LGBT rights, with some exceptions, have generally held the policymaking advantage over LGBT activists. Policy gridlock is difficult to break, and long periods where the status quo remains relatively unchanged are common (Baumgartner and Jones 1993). While the courts can offer relief to oppressed groups, there are significant challenges to viewing the courts as agents of social change (Rosenberg 2008). In addition, courts generally have rules that favor powerful interests and repeat players (e.g., Galanter 1974). Even rule changes initiated by the executive branch can be slow and difficult, with the Administrative Procedures Act requiring hearings, public comments, and agency responses. Such changes might be reversed a future executive as well. Given that policy in the states is often responsive to public opinion (Erikson, Wright, and McIver 1993), and with public opinion toward transgender people and their rights being somewhat negative (see chapter 2), the states might also serve as a brake on transgender rights. This might be particularly true in the South where the political culture has long favored the maintenance of traditional social patterns (Elazar 1984).

Conversely, the federal system offers policymaking opportunities for those marginalized by existing policy. Indeed, Alexander Hamilton hints at the counterbalancing powers of states and the national government in Federalist 28: "If their rights are invaded by either, they can make use of the other as the instrument of redress." Madison's entire Federalist 10 is concerned with the protection of minority interests in a federal system. Of course, Justice Louis Brandeis, in an often-cited dissenting opinion in *New State Ice Co. v. Liebmann* (1932), noted:

> To stay experimentation in things social and economic is a grave responsibility. Denial of the right to experiment may be fraught with serious consequences to the nation. It is one of the happy incidents of the federal system that a single courageous State may, if its citizens choose, serve as a laboratory; and try novel social and economic experiments without risk to the rest of the country.

Thus, our federalist system offers opportunities to innovate and experiment. States and localities are laboratories of democracy. There are, have been, and will be chances to advance transgender-inclusive policies via the states or their localities when political conditions are favorable in these jurisdictions (Sharp 1999; Taylor et al. 2012; Taylor and Haider-Markel 2014).

Organizing for Advocacy

Despite the challenges faced by the LGBT movement in advancing transgender rights, the American political system is nonetheless highly permeable to organized interests. Its federal system, with each level having some degree of separation of powers, plus thousands of local jurisdictions, offers many opportunities for policy change. Indeed, our federal system spurs interest group formation by giving organized interests a myriad of venues and advocacy opportunities to pursue their policy goals (Gray and Lowery 1996). As such, it is not surprising that there are many LGBT interest groups in this social movement. The structure of the LGBT movement in some respects mirrors our federal system. It includes large nationally focused organizations like the Human Rights Campaign and the National Gay and Lesbian Task Force. There are state-level groups like Equality North Carolina, Basic Rights Oregon, and Equality California. There are local groups like Equality Toledo or the Kalamazoo Alliance for Equality. A few organizations have a regional focus, such as GLBTQ Legal Advocates & Defenders (GLAD) in New England. Some of these organizations operate primarily via the courts, such as Lambda Legal, GLAD, and the National Center for Lesbian Rights. Others specialize in one part of the LGBT community, such as the transgender advocacy done by the National Center for Transgender Equality, the Transgender Law Center, or the Sylvia Rivera Law Project. Some LGBT rights groups, such as PFLAG, have a support function as well as an advocacy component. There are also LGBT community centers, health centers, pride festivals, LGBT cultural and sporting organizations, groups centered on LGBT individuals in particular professions, and LGBT religious groups. Many of these organizations intersect with advocacy efforts and with building a sense of shared identity that facilitates advocacy (Taylor and Whittier 1992). In addition, there are issue-focused LGBT advocacy groups that have concentrated on policies related to service in the military (e.g., OutServe-Service Legal Defense Network and the Palm Center), same-sex marriage (e.g., Freedom to Marry),[1] and HIV/AIDS (e.g., AIDS Coalition to Unleash Power). Others focus on specialized tactics, such as the Victory Fund that works on LGBT candidate recruitment and training in an effort to increase descriptive representation. Similarly, GLAAD focuses its advocacy efforts on the media. Others, such as the Gill Foundation, Arcus Foundation, or the Equality Federation, exist to build the capacity of other LGBT advocacy organizations through grant funding or information sharing and training. There are grassroots-focused direct action organizations such as GetEQUAL, which can pressure policymakers when insider advocacy tactics have failed. Table III.1 provides revenue and asset information for some well-known national LGBT organizations.[2]

The structure of the LGBT advocacy community is in large part determined by its environment. Indeed, some LGBT groups set up multiple entities because of restrictions on what types of advocacy different types of organizations are allowed to do under the tax code and under campaign finance laws. For instance, the Human Rights Campaign has a 501(c)(4) organization, Human Rights Campaign, Inc.; a 501(c)(3) organization, the Human Rights Campaign Foundation; and a political action committee, Human Rights Campaign PAC. What types of political and legislative activities these organizations may or may not engage in is related to the section of the tax code that it is organized under, the type of activity, and the amount of the activity in question (Internal Revenue Service 2017). For example, a 501(c)(3) organization has greater restrictions on legislative lobbying than does a 501(c)(4) organization. Many state-level groups, such as Equality North Carolina, have created similar structures of affiliated but legally separate entities so that they can engage in lobbying, education campaigns, and electioneering activities like endorsing candidates and contributing to their campaigns. In 2017, one of the nation's largest transgender rights organizations, the National Center for Transgender Equality, a 501(c)(3) organization, announced that it was setting up a 501(c)(4) affiliate, the National Center for Transgender Equality Action Fund (2017), so that it could better engage with lawmakers and candidates.

To survive, LGBT rights organizations must have a niche within the environment (e.g., Gray and Lowery 1996; Haider-Markel 1997). While they are all largely tied together by similar belief systems and overall goals within an

TABLE III.1. Income and Assets of Selected Large LGBT Organizations

Organization	Income	Assets
Human Rights Campaign Inc.	$41,364,760	$16,049,078
Lambda Legal Defense and Education Fund Inc.	$29,654,304	$21,902,360
Human Rights Campaign Foundation	$15,075,163	$32,859,570
National LGBTQ Task Force	$9,482,051	$5,152,314
Freedom To Marry Inc.	$7,717,006	$2,426,823
GLSEN Inc.	$6,810,331	$5,505,278
Gay & Lesbian Alliance Against Defamation Inc.	$6,349,007	$6,351,178
Out & Equal	$5,345,610	$1,762,338
Trevor Project Inc.	$5,165,911	$3,271,924
National Center for Lesbian Rights	$4,819,992	$1,695,003
Freedom To Marry Action Inc.	$4,089,389	$1,376,224
Gay & Lesbian Advocates & Defenders Inc.	$3,861,544	$2,744,237
Gay & Lesbian Leadership Institute Inc.	$2,266,244	$711,207
Transgender Law Center	$1,285,591	$1,512,630
National Center for Transgender Equality	$1,113,303	$787,329

Source: IRS Business Master File for December 2014 obtained from the National Center for Charitable Statistics.

LGBT rights advocacy coalition (e.g., Sabatier and Weible 2007), the organizations have to differentiate themselves from other organizations within the LGBT movement (Haider-Markel 1997). This is important as they each struggle to attract the resources (e.g., financial, managerial, political) necessary for organizational survival. Differentiation allows them to justify their existence to stakeholders who could provide resources to any number of organizations. Differentiation is also a statement of organizational identity that affects which issues the organization works on, in which policymaking venues, and how they engage in their advocacy work (Engel 2007). Interest groups work to construct clear identities through those they represent, their ideology, and their advocacy techniques (Heaney 2004). For instance, the Human Rights Campaign, the largest LGBT rights organization, is described by Eleveld (2015, 9) as about as "mainstream as gays could get" but could be criticized for not representing the diversity in the LGBT community. To establish itself as further to the left politically than HRC, the National Gay and Lesbian Task often takes contrasting positions (Eleveld 2015). LGBT organizations are at once allies within the social movement and competitors for resources.

The LGBT movement's network of interest groups is quite decentralized. While large LGBT advocacy organizations sometimes meet to discuss issues (Keisling 2017), coordination between groups is not always present (e.g., Engel 2007). The organizations may also differ on tactics. For example, in 2016 a rift developed between groups that believed that dropping gender-identity-inclusive public accommodations protections from state-level nondiscrimination bills could offer incremental opportunities for progress versus those that would only accept truly comprehensive nondiscrimination legislation (Johnson 2016b). The Gill Foundation and some of the organizations that it funds, such as the National Center for Transgender Equality and Freedom for All Americans, viewed postponing public accommodations protections as acceptable while the Human Rights Campaign, Lambda Legal, and the American Civil Liberties Union (ACLU) opposed this strategy. Similarly, Engel (2007) described the rift between the National Gay and Lesbian Task Force and the Human Rights Campaign over transgender inclusion in the Employment Nondiscrimination Act in 1996. As an organization rooted in grassroots and intersectional work, the Task Force raised alarms about the Human Rights Campaign's actions. Similarly, GetEqual, a direct action organization, took a far more aggressive approach than the insider-focused Human Rights Campaign during the fight for repeal of the Don't Ask Don't Tell policy that restricted military service by gays and lesbians (Eleveld 2015). Their activists heckled President Obama, protested his fundraisers, sharply criticized him on blogs, and chained themselves to the White House fence.

Regardless of their coordination issues, LGBT groups share significant amounts of information. They learn of each other's successes and failures. They share political information and best practices. Successes can be used by policy entrepreneurs to demonstrate the lack of risk in passing LGBT-inclusive policies (Mintrom and Norman 2009). Indeed, the Equality Federation exists to develop the capacity of state-level groups and to share this type of information. The National Gay and Lesbian Task Force sponsors a conference, Creating Change, where activists from all over the nation learn about tactics and share insights. Individual groups consult with each other as well. For instance, during Jami Taylor's time on the board of directors of Equality North Carolina, she e-mailed Shannon Minter of the National Center for Lesbian Rights for technical advice about the wording in a transgender-inclusive bill that was before the state legislature.[3] As noted in our chapter on the rise of LGBT advocacy, activists also move between organizations and enable the diffusion of knowledge between groups. In accordance with Boushey's (2010) policy diffusion work, LGBT groups are an important vector that spreads LGBT policy ideas between jurisdictions.

Advocacy and the Political Opportunity Structure

LGBT interest groups look to advance their favored policies when opportunities arise in policymaking venues (Baumgartner and Jones 1993; Haider-Markel and Meier 2003). They engage in agenda setting by publicizing focusing events (such as violence or discrimination) and attempt to collect data about the scope and magnitude of these problems (Kingdon 1984; see James et al. 2016 for a transgender related example). Advocacy organizations also try to obtain access to decision-making arenas and get access to decision makers (Andrews and Edwards 2004). Typically, LGBT advocacy organizations and LGBT activists tend to have more access to Democratic elected officials. This is in part because gays and lesbians are an important voting bloc for Democrats nationwide. While gay voters are approximately 5 percent of the voting public, they are overwhelmingly Democratic. Indeed, 82 percent of gay and lesbian registered voters lean Democratic (Kiley and Maniam 2016). In addition, the vast majority of openly gay and lesbian state and federal elected officials are Democrats, and they often strategically run in liberal leaning districts where they can be elected and shape party politics (Haider-Markel 2010). These openly gay and lesbian legislators play an important role in advancing LGBT rights by increasing the familiarity of other legislators with these issues (Haider-Markel 2010; Reynolds 2013).

During lobbying campaigns for or against legislation, LGBT groups educate the public, mobilize their constituents to contact legislators, and use inside lobbying tactics (Wright 2003). Further, they try to shape the implementation of existing policies and monitor the performance of those policies (Andrews and Edwards 2004). Because policymaking is a cycle, feedback about existing policies facilitates future agenda-setting attempts (Theodoulou 2013). Over the long term, advocacy organizations attempt to shift government resources and priorities in their favored direction (Andrews and Edwards 2004).

LGBT rights groups do not directly control which issues will be on the governmental agenda. They must also attempt to thwart a countermovement, the Christian Right, which has sometimes attempted to roll back gains via direct democracy institutions or the executive branch, challenge such policies in the courts, or enact discriminatory legislation (Fetner 2008; Haider-Markel 2001). Examples include the bans on same-sex marriage enacted during the 1990s through the early 2010s, and North Carolina's HB2. This has occurred at the local, state, and national level. Thus, LGBT advocacy is both proactive and reactive. The LGBT movement and the Christian Right have a symbiotic relationship where the two movements affect each other's development (Bull and Gallagher 1996; Fetner 2008). They react to each other's tactics and to their advances. Indeed, opposition groups, such as the Family Policy Network, Alliance Defending Freedom, and the Family Research Council, are engaged in their own agenda setting efforts. The Christian Right also contains groups that focus on litigation, such as Liberty Counsel. Burack (2008) notes that Christian Right organizations have become more adroit at tailoring their messages to specific audiences. They also tend to have more access to the Republican Party and have made common cause with economic conservatives to advance their interests (Wilson and Burack 2012).

Rather than describing the work of LGBT rights organizations as venue shopping, it is likely more accurate to say that organizations take advantage of opportunities and respond to threats that arise within the venues they specialize in. For instance, when President Obama took office, the Human Rights Campaign provided his administration with a document, *Blueprint for Positive Change*, outlining ways that the administration could advance LGBT rights via executive action (Maril 2016). However, it did not stop lobbying members of Congress on legislation. Further, HRC did not switch its venue to the courts or states when Republicans took control of the House of Representatives in 2011 or complete control of Congress in 2015, but rather focused on stymieing potential progress by their opposition in that venue.

Similarly, Lambda Legal did not give up legal advocacy when the Supreme Court upheld sodomy restrictions in *Bowers v. Hardwick* (1986). The organization continued its legal advocacy and its attorneys eventually ligated the case that overturned *Bowers*, *Lawrence v. Texas* (2003).

Nationally focused LGBT rights groups might provide some resources to state or local efforts when opportunities or needs arise (Wisneski 2016). For instance, the Human Rights Campaign provided Equality North Carolina a grant in 2011 to fight a proposed constitutional referendum on same-sex marriage (Comer 2011). The National Center for Transgender Equality sent its executive director, Mara Keisling, to North Carolina to help combat HB2. Subsequently, she was arrested at a protest (Ring 2016b). In these local-national partnerships, the local group might lead the messaging and member mobilization while the national organization leverages its media access (Wisneski 2016). This strategy was successful in convincing South Dakota's Republican governor to veto an antitransgender bill (Wisneski 2016). Of course, large LGBT funders, such as the Gill Foundation, also strategically fund movement organizations via grants (Callahan 2015). Mara Keisling (2017) notes that the National Center for Transgender Equality, one of the largest transgender focused organizations, is heavily funded by these sources.

Further, the LGBT movement is not self-contained. It works in coalition with other social movements. These movements learn from each other through these coalitions and via the overlapping social movement memberships that individuals may have (e.g., Meyer and Whittier 1994). In their advocacy, LGBT groups may join with like-minded organizations, such as the American Civil Liberties Union, in litigation or lobbying efforts (Wisneski 2016). LGBT legal groups also collaborate with private sector lawyers at firms like Jenner & Block on impact litigation. These large law firms have resources that the LGBT movement organizations often lack. Often, this work is done pro bono and is part of a strategic process of precedent building that draws on the legal advocacy of Justice Ruth Bader Ginsburg, who prior to becoming a judge, worked to change the standard under which sex-based classifications were viewed under the equal protection clause of the Fourteenth Amendment (Gaber 2016; Campbell 2002).

Over the next several chapters, we look at the fight for transgender rights in executive, legislative, and judicial venues at all levels in the federal system. We also address direct democracy and battles over gender-identity-inclusive laws. Our goal is to highlight the factors that lead to the adoption of transgender-inclusive policies in these venues. This will help us understand how transgender rights have advanced so rapidly over the past few decades.

CHAPTER 4

Transgender Rights and Legislative Bodies

A significant portion of the policy success of the transgender movement has occurred through the actions of legislative bodies at every level of government in the United States. In this chapter, we explore how this progress occurred by examining what we know about the adoption of transgender-inclusive policies. We begin with a brief overview of the increased salience of transgender issues in state legislatures. Next, we review existing research on the adoption of transgender-inclusive nondiscrimination laws by states (e.g., Lewis et al. 2014) and similar ordinances by localities (Colvin 2007; Taylor, Tadlock, and Poggione 2014). We also provide new analysis of state adoption of hate crime laws that include gender identity or otherwise provide protections for trans people. In addition, we add insights from research (Taylor, Tadlock, and Poggione 2013) about the passage of transgender inclusive birth certificate amendment laws by states. Grounded in the literature summarized earlier in the chapter, we include a new case study that addresses passage of the transgender inclusive hate crimes law by Congress in 2009. A case study approach is necessary to investigate passage of this law, commonly known as the Matthew Shepard and James Byrd Jr. Hate Crimes Prevention Act, because it is the primary piece of transgender positive legislation passed by Congress.

Transgender Issues in Legislatures

To provide a sense of how much attention has increased for transgender issues in state legislatures we conducted a search on state legislation covering transgender-related issues in the *LexisNexis State Capitals* database.[1] The results for the total number of bills, nondiscrimination bills, hate crime bills,

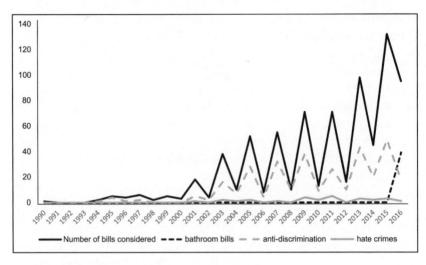

Figure 4.1. State Legislation on Transgender Issues, 1995–2016

Notes: Compiled by the authors based on transgender related search terms in LexisNexis *State Capitals* database; searches conducted in September 2016.

and public accommodations (bathrooms) from 1990 to 2016 are displayed in figure 4.1. The pattern clearly shows that there were few transgender-related bills introduced in state legislatures before 2000, but the number grows dramatically beginning in 2001. Significant valleys result in the pattern because some state legislatures, including the Texas legislature, only meet every other year. Most legislation through 2014 has actually been supportive of trans rights. It has often focused on topics like gender identity inclusive nondiscrimination laws or hate crimes policy. However, beginning in 2015 there was an influx of bills promoting discrimination against transgender people in public accommodations, primarily focused on policing bathroom use. This negative pattern continued into 2017, with the National Conference of State Legislatures reporting that bathroom bills were introduced in sixteen states, six states considered bills that would preempt local nondiscrimination laws, and fourteen states considered limiting the rights of transgender students in public schools (Kralik 2017).

Likewise, in Congress the salience of transgender issues has increased sharply. Because Congress has considered relatively few bills that address transgender issues, it makes more sense to examine the use of transgender-relevant terms in the Congressional Record. In table 4.1, we summarize the results of a keyword search of the Congressional Record from 1995 to 2014, encompassing the 104th through 113th Congresses.[2] We used the following search terms: transgender (472 hits), gender identity (386 hits), transsexual (32 hits), transvestite (21 hits), sex change (15 hits), crossdresser (2 hits), drag queen (2 hits), transexual (0 hits), gender queer (0 hits). Derivations of the terms, such as transgendered, transsexualism, crossdressing, or transsexuals, were also used, but these yielded the same search results as did queries using the above terms.[3] A total of 930 documents were downloaded from Congress.gov. Of these documents, 173 files used multiple search terms, such as denoting transgender and gender identity. Table 4.1 shows the distribution of the overall term usage in the documents by year.

As observed in state legislatures, the pattern in table 4.1 reveals that attention to transgender issues has seen a significant uptick in the past twenty years, especially in the usage of "transgender" and "gender identity." While some of this attention was certainly negative, rapid increases in attention typically serve as a precursor to significant policy change (Baumgartner and Jones 1993), which is certainly positive for transgender rights.

Local Nondiscrimination Policy

As noted in section IV of this volume, a number of localities and states have considered and adopted laws that prohibit discrimination based on gender identity or transgender status, or both, typically in employment. At the local level, the first city to adopt a nondiscrimination policy that offered protections to transgender people was Minneapolis in 1975 (Colvin 2007). At this level, policy adoption is often viewed as a function of the political opportunity structure, which includes the resources and mobilization of activists

TABLE 4.1. Number of Search Term Hits by Congress, 1995–2014

Search Term	104th (95– 96)	105th (97– 98)	106th (99– 00)	107th (01– 02)	108th (03– 04)	109th (05– 06)	110th (07– 08)	111th (09– 10)	112th (11– 12)	113th (13– 14)	Total
Transgender	2	4	20	38	58	51	50	78	69	102	472
Gender Identity	2	8	1	4	11	14	44	90	74	138	386
Transsexual	4	10	0	2	4	1	6	2	2	1	32
Transvestite	4	0	1	3	3	1	7	2	0	0	21
Sex change	4	1	1	0	1	4	2	1	0	1	15
Crossdresser	0	0	0	0	0	1	1	0	0	0	2
Drag queen	0	0	0	1	1	0	0	0	0	0	2
Total	16	23	23	48	78	72	110	173	145	242	930

Note: Compiled by the authors from searches of the *Congressional Record* at Congress.gov.

and opponents, the receptivity of government officials, and the structure and openness of government institutions (Button, Rienzo, and Wald 1997). In their examination of local legislative adoption of transgender-inclusive nondiscrimination laws, Taylor et al. (2014) employ a similar framework, but supplement it with a policy diffusion perspective. In the diffusion framework, policy adoption is a function of political, economic, and social forces internal to a jurisdiction, but also forces external to a jurisdiction, such as decisions by higher levels of government and neighboring jurisdictions (Berry and Berry 2014). External forces are sometimes classified as horizontal (pressure from jurisdictions at the same level) or vertical forces (pressure from different levels of government in the federal system) that can make it more or less likely that a locality will feel pressure to adopt a given policy (Shipan and Volden 2008).

Colvin's (2007) review of the local laws that ban gender-identity discrimination suggests that internal forces, such as the education levels of the population, racial diversity, city size, and same-sex households tend to explain which cities have these policies. Cities that are larger, more diverse, and more educated tend to have more completely implemented transgender-inclusive policies. Likewise, Taylor et al.'s (2014) investigation of local transgender-inclusive nondiscrimination laws included the consideration of internal locality characteristics, including diversity and unconventional political subculture, the presence of a mobilized LGBT advocacy community, and the type of city government. In addition, Taylor et al. (2014) consider external factors that might drive policy adoption—in this case hypothesizing that the lack of statewide transgender protections might motivate cities to adopt compensatory local policies in the face of state indifference (Sharp 2005).

Their analysis only addresses cities with a population of 100,000 or more and covers the years 1990 to 2011. It accounts for a range of factors based on the political subculture, institutional elements, and horizontal diffusion factors.[4] The analysis in Taylor et al. (2014) suggests that the sociopolitical subculture of localities, type of government, and the presence of a state transgender-inclusive nondiscrimination policy are the largest drivers of local policy adoption. In particular, cities were more likely to adopt the policy if they had a greater portion of the population in the "creative class" (working in creative and white-collar sectors), but less likely to adopt the policy if the state already had a similar policy. Interestingly, the type of local government also played a role, but only if the LGBT population was mobilized. In cities with a mobilized LGBT population, the policy was more likely to be adopted if there was a mayor-council (nonreformed) form of government. This suggests that a more politically open government structure is more responsive, but only if the LGBT population is mobilized. This discovery is consistent with Colvin's (2007) finding that mayor-council forms implement transgender policy provisions at a faster rate.

Taylor et al. (2014) also provide descriptive case studies of policy consideration in three cities, which largely confirms the systematic analysis—political subcultures, political mobilization, governmental form, and state policy action are the most important influences on the adoption of transgender-inclusive nondiscrimination laws. However, the case studies also highlight the role of home rule for cities. Cities are creatures of the state and in states where home rule is restricted, localities are likely to have a difficult time enacting policies that are not consistent with state policy (Gossett 1999). Indeed, Tennessee preempted localities from passing nondiscrimination policies that are more expansive than the state's in 2011. Arkansas passed a similar restriction in 2015 (Eidelson 2017). In addition, North Carolina's HB2 preempted localities in that state, but this was reduced to a temporary moratorium for employment or public accommodations nondiscrimination policies through December 2020 once legislation (HB 142) was passed to repeal the law in 2017. However, HB 142 also preempted North Carolina's localities, and barred its public universities and government agencies from addressing access to multioccupancy restrooms, showers, or changing facilities unless it is in accordance with an act of the General Assembly, thwarting LGBT activists seeking less restrictive policies in those areas (Berman and Phillips 2017). Given the recent battles in Arkansas, North Carolina, and Texas over local transgender rights policies, home rule will likely be a key component of transgender-related policymaking at the subnational level going forward.

Sellers and Colvin (2014) also examine local adoption of transgender-inclusive antidiscrimination policies in employment, but approach the topic through the lens of policy learning and reinvention of innovative policies. As such, they examine how the language of transgender inclusion changed over time. They address how policies became more explicitly transgender inclusive, how protections were broadened, and how implementation standards were made more precise. For example, they argue that prior to 2000 many antidiscrimination policies used a variety of terms to cover transgender people. It was around the year 2000 that the terms gender identity or gender expression began to be included in new policies.

Sellers and Colvin (2014) conduct an analysis similar to that of Taylor et al. (2014), and they find that political subculture plays a significant role in the adoption of these policies. Additionally, their evidence strongly suggests that policy learning occurred over time. Cities that adopted transgender-inclusive antidiscrimination policies after 2000 were more likely to use more precise language, provide greater protections, and contain a more complete implementation plan that provided less discretion to bureaucrats. Whether it was transgender activists or city officials who learned from past policies is not clear, but it was likely a combination of these forces (Sellers and Colvin 2014, 223).

Two missing factors in the analysis of local adoption of transgender-inclusive antidiscrimination have been direct measures of public preferences and measures of LGBT representation, both of which have been shown to influence the adoption of sexual orientation policies (Haider-Markel 2010; Haider-Markel, Joslyn, and Kniss 2000). However, there have been few transgender elected officials up to this point (Taylor and Haider-Markel 2014).[5] In addition, public opinion measures at the local level have been developed only recently and are limited to general measures of citizen ideology (Tausanovitch and Warshaw 2014).

Although the lack of local transgender officials is troubling for transgender rights, it is plausible that gay or lesbian local officials might act as surrogates for the transgender community. Indeed, we interviewed Mark Kleinschmidt (2017), an openly gay former mayor of Chapel Hill, North Carolina. During his time on the city council, Kleinschmidt pioneered that city's inclusive nondiscrimination policies that cover city employees and address discrimination in the provision of services. He stated that the origin of these policies was a reaction to a discriminatory incident that targeted a transgender person on a city bus in the early 2000s. Not long after the incident, gay and transgender community members approached Kleinschmidt to take action. As he considered his response, he thought, "if I would not do it, who would?" Kleinschmidt educated other council members about transgender identities and the problems faced by transgender people. Council members looked to him for guidance on transgender issues. They did so even though he was not a member of the affected group. It was because he was an openly gay man and thus a member of the broader LGBT community. Kleinschmidt noted that gay and lesbian elected officials could be helpful in securing transgender-inclusive policies. However, he stated:

> We need to get transgender people elected. When you are an elected official, you get peer-to-peer respect. You are not an activist. They know you have press access. They know that you have done what it takes to get elected. It is easier to make "asks" then. Gay and lesbian elected officials are surrogates for the transgender community. It is the next best thing, but it is not good enough.

State Nondiscrimination Policy

State-level studies of nondiscrimination policies that include transgender people have also approached the topic from a diffusion of innovation policy perspective (e.g., Lewis et al. 2014), which models political opportunity structure based on characteristics internal and external to a state (Berry and Berry 2014). One such study by Taylor and her coauthors (2012) specifically examined the context and complexity of these laws in reference to similar laws that included sexual orientation. They argued that the forces predicting passage of nondiscrimination laws would vary based on the scope and content of the policies, and be distinct from the forces predicting the passage of sexual-orientation-inclusive antidiscrimination laws. In short, they focus attention on explaining what and who is protected by these laws.

The findings in Taylor et al. (2012) suggest that although the adoption of sexual-orientation-inclusive antidiscrimination policies is largely due to the internal political opportunity structure of a state, internal state factors play less of a role in the adoption of gender-identity-inclusive nondiscrimination policies. Regional diffusion plays a larger role. Indeed, states were more likely to adopt a transgender-inclusive antidiscrimination policy if other states in their region had done so. The authors suggest that this indicates that policymakers might not view transgender policy as morality policy, and therefore may be inclined to see this as a simple incremental step in antidiscrimination law. If lawmakers are already considering a sexual orientation policy, they follow the lead of neighboring states (Taylor et al. 2012, 89–90). However, it is important to note that their study only tracked laws through 2011, well before the current wave of transgender backlash.

Additionally, Taylor et al. (2012) suggest that the regional diffusion influence on adoption of a trans-inclusive policy might be an example of policy learning because this is a policy area that many lawmakers knew little about for much of the period under analysis. Indeed, most of our interviews, particularly in our earlier interview periods, revealed that legislators were often unaware of the distinctions between gay and transgender people. Earlier on, LGBT activists could be strategically ambiguous in their advocacy (Stone 2012). This likely helped passage of legislation in the late 1990s and 2000s. For example, in 2012 a former Equality Ohio staffer told us that they intentionally avoided using the word "transgender" when lobbying. Instead, they talked about gender identity. Multiple activists also discussed the problems associated with advocating for the gender queer. That was a topic best avoided. Respondents were much more comfortable discussing binary gendered trans people when lobbying. However, longtime transgender activist

Gunner Scott (2016) notes that the use of gender identity and expression is intentionally broad enough to encompass gender queer individuals as well.

Over time, though, the awareness of legislators has grown. Scott (2016) reflected on this change, saying that legislators are now "increasingly respectful and scared of offending . . . even if they do not always get all of the intricacies." However, awareness creates hurdles as well. Indeed, our interview with Representative Paul Stam (2016), one of the architects of HB2, revealed him as quite knowledgeable about transgender identities. He was well versed in different identities under the transgender umbrella. He expressed great reservations about accommodating people who have a gender identification that is different from their birth sex, but who have not undergone surgical medical procedures to address that. From a policy perspective, he was not at all bothered by transgender people who undergo sex reassignment.[6] In addition, our interviews with multiple activists at Equality Ohio noted that Republicans who control that state have great discomfort with transgender people. Indeed, they found that legislator discomfort was so great that parents of transgender people often made better advocates on these issues than transgender people themselves. Similar concerns came from other activists in other states.

The regional diffusion influence suggests that national policy networks of LGBT activists and interest groups might be learning how to pursue inclusive laws, or they may also be educating state legislators, or both. Nevertheless, the pattern of policy adoption also supports a point of view that bundling gay and transgender protections together in the same legislation might be more effective for getting trans protections through the legislature. Here, ignorance about transgender identities might be an advantage, as suggested by a Georgia Equality staff member in 2012: "Our allies are all over the board. There is ignorance about trans; they are just doing this [supporting gender identity inclusion] because Georgia Equality says it is right" (Taylor and Lewis 2014).

In Lewis et al. (2014), the authors provide a similar analysis of state-level transgender-inclusive antidiscrimination policy adoption, but they also include case studies of the process of policy consideration in several states. The three states studied, Maryland, Massachusetts, and Hawaii, adopted transgender-inclusive protections only after having provided sexual-orientation-inclusive protections at an earlier date.[7] The findings of the multivariate analysis and case studies suggest that Democratic control of state legislative chambers plays an important role in the adoption of both sexual orientation and gender identity policies, but other factors internal to a state are more inconsistent. For example, LGBT interest group capacity had a strong influence on the adoption of sexual orientation protections, but not on gender identity protections. Partisan competition in elections also played an important role in the models predicting the adoption of transgender protections, but not in the sexual orientation models. The authors conclude that "gay rights anti-discrimination policy seems much more driven by typical morality policy explanations whereas transgender policy is, in part, driven by reinvention pressures" (Lewis et al. 2014, 179). In sum, they conclude that, for states that adopted sexual orientation protections before 2003, those that came back to the transgender issue later found it more difficult to adopt expansive protections for transgender people, especially in the area of public accommodations. As demonstrated with Hawaii's sexual-orientation and gender-identity-inclusive housing (2005) and public accommodations bills (2006), transgender-inclusive protections generally fare better when they can be simultaneously packaged with similar protections for gays and lesbians. Largely because of concerns about the restroom issue (Lewis et al. 2014), Massachusetts would not a pass transgender-inclusive public accommodations law until 2016, five years after the passage of stand-alone gender-identity-inclusive protections in employment and housing. As has been observed in local politics and local-state conflicts in states such as North Carolina, public accommodations will likely be an area where antidiscrimination protections continue to lag behind protections in areas such as public or private employment. Indeed, some leading LGBT activist groups, including the National Center for Transgender Equality, are controversially willing to countenance dropping public accommodations protections in order to pass policies in some states (Johnson 2016b). It is also important to note that activists in Massachusetts eventually settled on this compromise to help advance legislation employment and housing protections in 2011. At the time, opponents were dubbing the public accommodations aspect the "bathroom bill" (Fleming 2012). Similarly, Utah's 2015 gay and transgender-inclusive nondiscrimination policies also dropped public accommodations protections (Ford 2015).

A final study on antidiscrimination policy for transgender people focused on the influence of public opinion on policy adoption. Flores, Herman, and Mallory (2015) use a method called multilevel regression and poststratification to estimate state support for antidiscrimination protections for transgender people; their technique mirrors that of Lax and Phillips (2009) in their examination of state adoption of gay rights policies. Flores et al. (2015) examine the likelihood of a transgender-inclusive antidiscrimination law being adopted only through 2010 (given the limits of their public opinion measure) and proceed to examine whether state policy is congruent with public attitudes on transgender rights. In addition, their multivariate model accounts for additional factors internal to a state, such as Democratic control in state government, legislative ideology, voter ideology, and legislative professionalism. Given that policy–public opinion congruence would be met if state policy were consistent with majority opinion, they find that states have a "democratic deficit" on transgender policy. In other words, transgender policies in the states do not reflect majority opinions. Indeed, their analysis indicates that, on average, public support for transgender rights must reach 81 percent before a state adopts a transgender-inclusive antidiscrimination policy.

Although this finding might be disheartening to advocates, Lax and Phillips (2009) uncovered similar, though somewhat smaller, gaps between public preferences and policy on gay rights issues. Moreover, the findings mask the fact that some states do adopt these policies without supermajority support in public preferences. Further, as seen in chapter 2, levels of public support for broad nondiscrimination policies often far outstrip support for specific implications of those policies, such as a bathroom access, and general feelings toward transgender people. Thus, stated public support for nondiscrimination may not be an accurate reflection of public preferences on these issues given the negative attitudes they tend to hold on other aspects of transgender rights.

Although the Flores et al. (2015) analysis improves on local-level studies by including a more specific measure of public preferences, this study and the others do not consider the role of symbolic and substantive representation in the policymaking process. In particular, none of these studies include a direct measure of LGBT officials or officials who may serve as advocates for the transgender community. Although there have been few transgender officeholders, we do know that gay and lesbian officials have advocated for transgender issues (Haider-Markel 2010), and cisgender officials have sometimes stood up as well (Taylor and Lewis 2014). Openly gay legislators often become the primary legislative champions of state-level transgender-inclusive legislation. Indeed, during the recent fight for public accommodations protections in Massachusetts, Mason Dunn (2016), the executive director of the Massachusetts Transgender Political Coalition, talked about the role of the openly gay Senate president, Stanley Rosenberg. He was a "standout champion" whose words during the floor debate mattered and who provided necessary leadership in the chamber. Another openly gay representative in Massachusetts, Carl Sciortino, was extremely influential in the long fight to achieve the state's earlier transgender-inclusive employment and housing nondiscrimination law (Firestone 2012). Similarly, Maryland state senator Rich Madeleno was the driving force behind Maryland's transgender-inclusive law that was passed in 2014 (Dresser and Cox 2014). Delaware state senator Karen Peterson (2016) talked with us about her role during the fight for a transgender-inclusive bill in 2013. As an out lesbian, she could not be the public face of the bill given that parts of Delaware are "a southern state." However, she was a passionate defender in the Democratic legislative caucus. Further, in Utah, openly gay state legislator Jim Dabakis was part of a bipartisan working group that negotiated and drafted the state's nondiscrimination bill that included transgender protections (Romboy 2015).

As more transgender candidates seek and win public office, assessing the influence of these symbolic representatives and substantive policy entrepreneurs will likely become more important for understanding the adoption of transgender protections (Haider-Markel et al. 2017). In one recent example, a transgender candidate in Virginia, Danica Roem, sought to unseat an archconservative state delegate, Robert Marshall (R-Prince William), who had introduced a "bathroom bill" similar to North Carolina's HB2 and had authored the state's ban on same-sex marriage (Nirappil 2017). Roem made history in 2017 by becoming the first transgender candidate to win a primary election in the state (Dvorak 2017), and then won the general election in November by a significant margin (Olivo 2017). When Roem was sworn into office in January 2018, she became the first transgender state legislator who was out at the time of election.[8] On the same election night that Roem shocked Virginia, Andrea Jenkins also made history by becoming the first openly transgender African American woman elected to any office in the country when she won a seat on the Minneapolis City Council (Eltagouri 2017a). Jenkins's victory was followed the next day by the revelation that Phillipe Cunningham, a transgender man, had also won a seat on the Minneapolis City Council. Notably, their city council elections occurred in the city that passed the first transgender-inclusive nondiscrimination ordinance in the country. In 2018 as we were going to press, Christine Hallquist won Vermont's Democratic gubernatorial primary. She became the first transgender nominee for governor from either major party (Stack 2018).

Birth Certificate Laws

Distinct from the broader LGBT movement, one priority of the trans community has been changing policies and administrative rules concerning official government documents, especially birth certificates. Sex classification on birth certificates determines a set of responsibilities and benefits for individuals as they interact with the state and society. In addition, it turns out that the politics surrounding policy change and official documents has not been completely embedded in the same morality policy framework that is found in much LGBT policymaking.

Taylor, Tadlock, and Poggione (2013) examined the adoption of laws that make it easier for some transgender people to amend their birth certificates. Using a policy diffusion approach, they contend that prior to the 1990s policy adoption in this area was driven in part by vertical diffusion of best practices. However, once transgender issues were incorporated into the LGBT movement in the 1990s, the adoption of these policies began to look like morality politics and subject to the political opportunity structures internal to each state. Since 1962, half of the states have adopted statutes that specifically allow individuals to change their sex classification on their birth certificate, typically after undergoing a series of medical procedures. Interestingly, this list of states, ranging from Illinois, to North Carolina, to Arizona, includes about half of the states from the South.[9] Only Tennessee statutorily bans changing birth certificate sex classification.

Taylor et al. (2013) point out that in 1977 and 1992 the Centers for Disease Control and Prevention issued model vital record statutes that were meant to modernize relevant state law. The model statutes included guidelines for changing birth certificates for individuals that had undergone sex reassignment surgery. Such guidelines can serve as a vertical diffusion pressure to state policymakers, and a similar process was observed in state repeal of antisodomy laws based on Model Penal Code guidelines (Kane 2007). But Taylor et al. (2013, 252) argue that the pressure to follow the CDC would likely only be strong in states with more professionalized bureaucracies where there would be a greater desire to follow best practices.

In their multivariate analysis of state adoption of transsexual birth certificate laws, they account for the CDC vertical diffusion pressure with a time code variable. To test their argument about professionalization, they interact the vertical diffusion variable with a measure of bureaucratic professionalization. The model also accounts for state internal political opportunity structure factors, including citizen ideology, legislative ideology, historical policy innovation, being in the South, education levels, opposition Christian conservatives, and the mobilization of the LGBT community. Their findings suggest that vertical diffusion pressure and state bureaucratic professionalization significantly increase the likelihood of policy adoption, and this was especially true in the South. In short, the adoption of these policies prior to the 1990s, before the full inclusion of trans issues into gay politics, was largely a bureaucratic affair, shaped in part by a state's history of policy innovation. Once the LGBT movement really included the T, political forces such as citizen ideology and legislature ideology factored into the policy process to a greater degree. However, it is also notable that the results do not show an independent influence by a mobilized LGBT community or their Christian conservative opponents.

Finally, in a follow-up study Taylor, Tadlock, and Poggione (2014) expanded their 2013 analysis of birth certificate amendment laws to account for additional factors in state internal political opportunity structure, including legislative professionalism, state political culture, and an updated measure of state historical policy innovation. Their findings are substantively the same: adoption of birth certificate amendment laws has been driven by citizen and legislative ideology, as well as by vertical pressures interacting with state bureaucratic professionalization.

One limitation in the Taylor, Tadlock, and Poggione (2013, 2014) research is that they used a dichotomous indicator for birth certificate laws in their modeling. This ignores the considerable variation in the content of those laws (see chapter 8). States that have birth certificate amendment laws might have burdensome restrictions like requirements for specific surgeries. They might also have requirements for a court order. At this time, some states are modernizing their approaches to birth certificate amendment by trans people, but the legislative push for these changes will likely resemble traditional LGBT policy battles in the states.

Forces Driving Policy Adoption: State Hate Crime Laws

One element of the political opportunity structure suggested by our review of research on the adoption of local and state transgender-inclusive policies has been partisanship and ideology. Democrats and liberals tend to be more supportive of these policies than Republicans and conservatives. However, when it comes to combatting crime, we would typically expect Republicans to take the lead since the party tends to "own" the crime issue (Holian 2004). Moreover, even though data on hate crime violence against transgender people is problematic and underreported (see chapter 12), it is clear that hate crimes have disproportionately affected the transgender community (James et al. 2016). This raises a question given the police powers that states have to ensure public safety. Why have some states chosen to adopt hate crime laws that cover gender identity while others have not?

Existing literature on the adoption of hate crime laws suggests that political parties, ideology, and mobilized groups tend to drive the adoption of hate crime laws in the states (Allen et al. 2004; Jenness and Broad 1997;

Jenness and Grattet 2001; Soule and Earl 2001). This seems especially true of hate crime laws that include sexual orientation (Haider-Markel 1998; Lewis 2013). However, to date few studies have explored the protection of transgender people in state-level hate crime laws.

Here, we model the likelihood that a state will adopt a transgender-inclusive hate crime law using event history analysis with logistic regression estimation. The dataset is structured by state-years and it begins with the first state-year that any state adopted a transgender -inclusive hate crime law, which was Minnesota in 1993. All state-years are coded zero unless a state adopts the policy. In that state-year, the dependent variable is coded as 1 and no additional state-years appear in the dataset for that state following the year of adoption.[10]

Based on previous studies, we expect that citizen and legislative ideology (Berry et al. 1998, 2010) should play a role; in states with a more liberal populace or a more liberal legislature, or both, the likelihood of adopting these policies should be higher.[11] Previous studies have also indicated that high levels of party competition should increase the number of groups covered in state hate crime laws (Allen et al. 2004; Haider-Markel 1998). Here we account for party competition with a version of the Holbrook and Van Dunk (1993) measure that employs data from state legislative election outcomes.[12]

LGBT interest groups have strongly advocated for hate crime laws while religious conservatives have consistently opposed including sexual orientation and gender identity in these policies (Haider-Markel 1998; Jenness and Broad 1997; Soule and Earl 2001). We account for these mobilized groups in two ways. First, we measure the strength of state LGBT interest groups by creating a measure of LGBT interest group assets per capita as derived from IRS Business Master File data obtained from the National Center for Charitable Statistics (see appendix A for further information).[13] Second, we measure the percentage of a state's population that identifies with evangelical congregations with data obtained from the Association of Religion Data Archives.[14] We measure the salience of transgender issues using the *New York Times* coverage of transgender issues in each year (as explained in chapter 1). Following Haider-Markel (1998), our expectation is that the higher salience of transgender issues will increase the likelihood of policy adoption.

The policy diffusion literature suggests that one of the external forces to a state that can motivate policy adoption is the adoption of the same policy or a similar policy by neighboring states (Berry and Berry 2014). Thus, we account for the potential for policy diffusion by including a variable that captures the percentage of contiguous states that have adopted a gender-identity-inclusive hate crime law for each state year.[15] In addition, we know that policymaking is often incremental in nature, such that officials are more likely to consider and adopt policies that are similar to past policies or that only modestly adjust existing policies (Baumgartner and Jones 1993; Boushey 2010; Haider-Markel and O'Brien 1997). Given that no state has adopted a gender-identity-inclusive hate crime law before adopting a sexual-orientation-inclusive hate crime law, we treat the adoption of gender identity in state hate crime policy as an incremental change to a sexual-orientation-inclusive policy. Also note that this pattern is consistent with our earlier discussion of how state and local government have often "come back for the T" in antidiscrimination policy. Our measure is coded as one for every year that the state has a sexual-orientation-inclusive hate crime law.

The logistic regression results reported in table 4.2 strongly suggest that LGBT interest groups and legislative ideology are driving the adoption on transgender-inclusive hate crime laws in the states. LGBT interest groups with more resources increase the likelihood of policy adoption and so too does a more liberal legislature. These findings are consistent with the existing literature on hate crime policy and transgender-inclusive policy more generally. The signs of the coefficients on most of the other variables are in the expected directions, but none of them achieve standard levels of statistical significance.[16]

Given collinearity issues in the model, and the fact that the incrementalism variable is such a powerful predictor in Lewis et al. (2014), we estimated a separate model that includes the incrementalism variable capturing state adoption of a sexual-orientation-inclusive hate crime law. Table 4.3 displays the results for this model. We observe similar results to what we saw in table

TABLE 4.2. Adoption of Transgender-Inclusive State Hate Crime Laws, 1993–2017

	b_i	SE_b
Legislative Ideology (Conservative →Liberal)	.043*	(.018)
Citizen Ideology (Conservative →Liberal)	.039	(.029)
LGBT Assets	.098**	(.033)
New York Times Coverage	.001	(.001)
Evangelical Population (% in State)	.005	(.041)
Party Competition	.065	(.041)
Diffusion: Neighbor Adoption	.016	(.010)
Constant	−4.807	(3.051)
Total Observations	1,030	
χ^2	36.77**	
Pseudo R^2	.21	

Notes: Results are from an event history analysis estimated with a logistic regression model. Dependent variable is coded 0 if transgender-inclusive hate crime law was not adopted and 1 if a law was adopted. *$p < 0.05$, **$p < 0.01$.

4.2. However, because the adoption of transgender policies is closely linked to the same factors that drive the adoption of sexual-orientation-inclusive hate crime policies, the inclusion of the incrementalism variable reduces the predictive performance of some of the other variables in the model. Including the incrementalism variable significantly improves the overall fit of the model and powerfully predicts the likelihood of adopting a gender-identity-inclusive hate crime law.

The performance of the incrementalism variable should not be too surprising. No state has adopted a gender-identity-inclusive hate crime law without either first adopting a sexual-orientation-inclusive hate crime law or adopting both simultaneously. As with antidiscrimination policy, the pattern has often been to "come back for the T" later. Additionally, the majority of states that have adopted a sexual-orientation-inclusive hate crime law have also adopted a gender-identity-inclusive hate crime law (seventeen of the twenty-nine states). Overall, the pattern suggests that state adoption of gender identity in hate crime law is similar to the adoption of sexual orientation, with comparable forces at play; it has simply taken a bit more time.

TABLE 4.3. Adoption of Transgender-Inclusive State Hate Crime Laws, 1993–2017

	b_i	SE_b
Legislative Ideology (Conservative →Liberal)	.033#	(.018)
Citizen Ideology (Conservative →Liberal)	.040	(.029)
LGBT Assets	.099**	(.038)
New York Times Coverage	−.000	(.001)
Evangelical Population (% in State)	.028	(.045)
Party Competition	.063#	(.038)
Diffusion: Neighbor Adoption	−.001	(.012)
Incremental Policy: SO Law	3.366**	(1.087)
Constant	−9.994**	(2.391)
Total Observations	1,030	
χ^2	55.43**	
Pseudo R2	.32	

Notes: Results are from an event history analysis estimated with a logistic regression model. Dependent variable is coded 0 if transgender inclusive hate crime law was not adopted and 1 if a law was adopted. #p <0.10, *p < 0.05, **p < 0.01.

Congress and the Adoption of the Matthew Shepard and James Byrd Jr. Hate Crimes Prevention Act

Given the historic nature of gender identity being included in the federal hate crime law in 2009, we explore in greater detail how this was enacted and its implications. The Matthew Shepard and James Byrd Jr. Hate Crimes Prevention Act (18 U.S.C. § 249), also known as the Matthew Shepard Act, became law after being signed by President Obama on October 28, 2009 (Public Law No. 111–84) as a rider to the National Defense Authorization Act of 2010. The Hate Crimes Prevention Act (HCPA) expanded existing federal law so that bias motivated crimes based on perceived or actual victim gender, gender identity, disability, or sexual orientation could be prosecuted as hate crimes. The act also removed a previous element of hate crime law that required that a victim be engaged in a federally protected activity, such as voting. In addition, it expanded hate crimes statistics collection to include crimes based on gender identity and gender, enhanced the FBI's ability to investigate hate crimes, and enhanced funding for local and state agencies to investigate and prosecute hate crimes.

So how did this historic law, which is the first federal law to list gender identity as an enumerated category, come to be? Since the passage of the Hate Crimes Statistics Act of 1990 (see chapter 12), advocates had attempted to expand the law beyond statistics collection and cover additional groups. However, the main content of what became the HCPA was not introduced until 2001 by Representative John Conyers (D-MI) and did not include gender identity as a category. The measure failed in committee, and similar bills failed in 2004 and 2005 after facing continued Republican opposition. A similar measure passed the Democrat-controlled Senate, 65–33, in 2004 as an amendment to the Defense Authorization Act of 2005, but the relevant language of the amendment was removed in conference committee.[17]

In 2007, Rep. Conyers reintroduced the bill (H.R. 1592, Local Law Enforcement Hate Crimes Prevention Act) to a Democratic-controlled House, but this time it included gender identity. In the House, the Subcommittee on Crime, Terrorism and Homeland Security reviewed the bill first and passed it on to the House Judiciary Committee on a voice vote. The bill had significant support in the committee and passed by a 20–14 vote. On May 3, 2007, with Representative Barney Frank (D-MA) presiding over the House, the measure passed 237–180 (Simon 2007). Most Democrats supported the measure, while most Republicans opposed it. James Dobson, the founder of a conservative Christian group Focus on the Family, said the purpose of the bill was "to muzzle people of faith who dare express their moral and biblical concerns about homosexuality" (Stout 2007).

In the Senate, the measure (S.1105) was sponsored by Senators Ted Kennedy (D-MA) and Gordon Smith (R-OR). In the Senate Judiciary Committee, the bill stalled without a vote. Senator Kennedy then reintroduced the measure as an amendment to the National Defense Reauthorization bill (H.R. 1585), along with forty-three other cosponsors, including four Republicans (Wooten 2008). Voting on H.R. 1585 was delayed due to Republican concerns about an amendment on troop withdrawals in Iraq. The reauthorization bill did finally pass in September, and the hate crime amendment was approved by voice vote. However, the Bush administration signaled that the reauthorization bill might be vetoed if it arrived with the hate crime language attached (Pink News 2007). The veto threat and divisions among Democrats led to the withdrawal of the amendment by party leadership (Wooten 2008).

With the election of Barack Obama to the presidency in 2008, the political opportunity structure for a transgender-inclusive hate crimes law brightened. Coming into office, President Obama had said that his administration would work to pass a hate crime law (Ferraro 2009). As a senator, he had been a cosponsor of that chamber's 2005 and 2007 versions of the hate crime bill. The new 111th Congress, now completely controlled by Democrats after the 2008 election, appeared to be quite willing to work with the president. A version of what would be known the HCPA was again introduced in the House by Representative Conyers, along with Mark Kirk (R-IL), as the Local Law Enforcement Hate Crimes Prevention Act (H.R. 1913). The measure was "endorsed by more than 300 law enforcement, civil rights, and civic and religious organizations, including the International Association of Chiefs of Police, National District Attorneys Association, Presbyterian Church, Episcopal Church, National Association for the Advancement of Colored People, Young Women's Christian Association, and the National Disability Rights Network" (Human Rights Campaign 2010a). In the Senate, the primary sponsors of the bill (S. 909) were Senators Edward Kennedy (D-MA), Patrick Leahy (D-VT), Arlen Specter (D-PA), Susan Collins (R-ME), and Olympia Snowe (R-ME) (Human Rights Campaign 2010a).

The House bill passed out of the Judiciary Committee on a narrow margin of 15 to 12. As the measure was being debated on the House floor, Rep. Janice Schakowsky (D-IL) spoke in favor of the bill and thanked Representative Tammy Baldwin (D-WI) "and the entire LGBT Equality Caucus for their tireless work to get this bill passed." (Congressional Record 2009, E1035). The full House approved the bill 249–179 on April 29, 2009; only eighteen Republicans supported the measure. In discussing his support of the legislation, Representative Mike Honda (D-CA) raised the murder of Angie Zapata, a young transgender woman, in Colorado (Congressional Record 2009, E1004). In contrast, Representative Steve King (R-IA) argued:

> Liberals in Congress want to create new laws to protect classes of people that have never been defined or identified as a class before.

This unconstitutional bill aims to protect new classes of people based on "gender identity" and "sexual orientation." These are classifications of people that are based on their inner feelings—their thoughts. Punishing "thought crimes" will infringe on freedom of speech and religious expression, rights endowed to all Americans in the Constitution. Under this legislation, justice will no longer be equal. Instead, justice will depend on the race, sex, sexual orientation or protected status of the victim, setting up different penalties for the same crime. I support continuing the American tradition of equal justice under the law, and I oppose this unconstitutional "thought crimes" bill. (IowaPolitics.com 2009)

The original Senate version of the bill was again introduced by Senator Kennedy (S.909) and had thirty-three original cosponsors (Congress.gov 2009). During June hearings in the Senate Judiciary Committee, Attorney General Eric Holder testified in strong support of the bill:

Hate crimes victimize not only individuals but entire communities. . . . Perpetrators of hate crimes seek to deny the humanity that we all share, regardless of the color of our skin, the God to whom we pray, or the person who we choose to love. . . . The time is now to provide justice to victims of bias-motivated violence and to re-double our efforts to protect our communities from violence based on bigotry and prejudice. (CNN 2009)

S.909 was converted to an amendment (S. Amdt. 1511) to the Defense Authorization Bill (S. 1390). The amendment was adopted on July 16, 2009 by a 63–28 vote, including the support of five Republicans. The Defense Authorization Bill did not pass until July 23, 2009.

Even though earlier versions of the bill had been inspired by two brutal bias crime attacks, little testimony addressed these attacks in 2009 until versions of the measure had passed both chambers.[18] The differences between the House and Senate version of the measure had to be ironed out in conference committee, which is a special committee composed of both House and Senate members. The conference committee renamed the hate crime provision of the Defense Reauthorization Act the Matthew Shepard and James Byrd Jr. Hate Crimes Prevention Act in the memory of these two men. Matthew Shepard was a gay student at the University of Wyoming who had been brutally killed in a hate crime attack by two men in 1998. James Byrd Jr. was an African American man who was attacked by three white supremacists and dragged behind a truck for at least three miles before he died in 1998. Diego Sanchez (2016), who was a senior policy advisor to Rep. Barney Frank during this period, told us that the inclusion of James Byrd in the title of the bill was important in getting full buy-in from the entire Democratic caucus. The HCPA passed the House as part of the Defense Reauthorization Bill on October 8, 2009, with the support of forty-four Republicans, and it passed the Senate on October 22, 2009. President Obama later signed the measure into law.

Although the passage of the HCPA was historic, and its use to pursue gender-identity-related hate crime marked an important milestone, the attorney general in the Trump administration is Jeff Sessions. As a senator, Sessions opposed the HCPA in impassioned chamber speeches (Patterson 2016), and it seems unlikely that as attorney general he will pursue aggressive enforcement of the HCPA for LGBT victims. However, in a surprising move, Sessions appears open to vigorously enforcing hate crimes policy as it concerns transgender people. He approved of the handling of a transgender hate crimes case that was opened under the Obama administration.[19] At a Justice Department gathering, Sessions noted, "We have and will continue to enforce hate crime laws aggressively and appropriately where transgendered individuals are victims" (Gerstein 2017). Nonetheless, LGBT rights advocates remain skeptical about Sessions's commitment given his history on transgender rights (NBC News 2017b).

Gay and lesbian legislators were central figures in the passage of the trans-inclusive HCPA, but that has not always been the case on transgender related legislation. Although openly gay Representative Barney Frank (D-MA) had supported the inclusion of gender identity in the 2007 and 2009 versions of the HCPA, and strongly advocated for both bills, Frank had been accused of caving to pressure on pre-2009 versions of the Employment Nondiscrimination Act that he had consistently introduced in the House without including gender identity. In addition, when the 2007 version of ENDA (H.R. 2015) died in committee, Representative Frank removed gender identity and reintroduced the bill (H.R. 3685).[20] On this, he received considerable push-back from the United ENDA coalition (e.g., Molloy 2014; Johnson 2017). He also received criticism from openly lesbian Representative Tammy Baldwin (D-WI), who was also a key advocate for the transgender-inclusive HCPA bill (Rosky 2016, 88–90). Over the years, Frank has defended his decision to move forward with the sexual orientation only bill, despite the consternation it caused in the LGBT movement, because it got many members of the House on record as supporting gay rights and nobody lost their reelection because of it. He argues that this was important in later legislative successes, such as the HCPA and the repeal of Don't Ask Don't Tell. Frank stated (Johnson 2017):

> "One of the problems we've had historically—we don't have it anymore—is members being afraid to vote for us because they thought they could be defeated, that it would be a tough vote," Frank said. "So, here we had members voting for a bill that was a broad protections for LGB people and nobody lost because of it. That was very helpful in setting the foundation."

Conclusion

Legislative bodies are fundamental representative policymaking institutions in the American system, at every level of government. For transgender rights advocates, they present a permeable access point to pursue policy goals. However, as majoritarian institutions, legislatures also can present roadblocks, deferring to the intense preferences of constituents and bargaining away rights through negotiation and compromise. Institutional rules, such the requirements in some legislative bodies for a supermajority, may also produce a hurdle.

The policymaking examples presented here, including research published elsewhere, suggests that transgender-inclusive policies are sometimes subject to the political opportunity structures available based on time and place, but at other times may follow a more routinized, bureaucratic process. When dependent on political opportunity structure, transgender-inclusive policymaking looks more like gay rights policymaking, following the patterns of morality policy. In these cases, majoritarian pressures in many parts of the country have defeated transgender interests. However, in other parts of the country with more favorable opportunity structures, transgender activists have stacked up victories over time. In addition, as the case study of the HCPA in Congress suggests, even the national government can be responsive to transgender interests under the right conditions, such as Democratic control of Congress and having a Democrat ensconced in the White House.

CHAPTER 5

Transgender Rights and the Judiciary

with Jason Pierceson

Joining us on this chapter is Jason Pierceson, an expert on LGBT rights and judicial politics. Together, we examine transgender rights in the courts. Despite criticism of litigation-based strategies of social and political change (e.g., Rosenberg 2008), courts have been central to the success of the LGBT rights movement, especially the LGB movement, as represented by the judicial elimination of sodomy laws, the striking down of discriminatory policies, and the legalization of marriage equality. Critics of litigation to date, despite this success, have argued that the litigation strategy of the past several decades has focused mostly on more privileged elements of the movement, to the clear detriment of more marginalized groups, such as transgender individuals. Another line of critique is that litigation strategies cause backlash (Flores and Barclay 2016; Klarman 2013; Kreitzer, Hamilton, and Tolbert 2014; Ura 2014), and discourage and marginalize more effective grassroots approaches (Haider-Markel and Taylor 2016).

Any social movement faces limited resources and the "crowding out" of other issues and tactics is often inevitable, but we argue that these critiques are overdrawn. First, the transgender movement has benefited from the legal infrastructure (financial and jurisprudential) of previous movements that have employed litigation (e.g., LGB movement, civil liberties, civil rights, women's movement), demonstrated by the turn of "mainstream" litigation organizations to transgender rights litigation and the use of the previous jurisprudential shift as a partial foundation for the newer litigation. This legal foundation and the consequent higher salience of LGBT rights has also led to important bureaucratic policy change in favor of transgender rights, though those bureaucratic policy gains are at risk given actions by the Trump administration. Second, with some exceptions, the transgender movement generally developed and engaged the policy and legal arenas later than the lesbian and gay rights movement.[1] Finally, the transgender rights movement encounters a somewhat different legal and political environment. As discussed in chapter 2, transgender rights have relatively lower levels of public support and arguably face stronger forms of political and social resistance. The legal and policy setting can be more favorable, but the rigidity of the gender binary in society and the law makes the political advocacy of a range of transgender rights claims more difficult, requiring an aggressive court-based strategy.

This chapter introduces the primary actors engaged in transgender rights litigation and addresses some of their favored tactics. We also examine recent and ongoing litigation in the transgender rights movement in the areas of employment discrimination, inmate rights to gender affirming health care, student rights, marriage, the right to accurate identity documents, and other areas. Ultimately, we contend that litigation campaigns are vital for the advancement of transgender rights and the rights of other marginalized groups, that these campaigns are much more helpful than harmful, and that the transgender movement has benefitted from prior LGB litigation.

Key Actors in Transgender Litigation

Several key actors are involved in transgender rights advocacy via the state and federal court systems. Among these are prominent LGBT rights groups like the National Center for Lesbian Rights (NCLR), Lambda Legal, and GLBTQ Legal Advocates & Defenders (GLAD). In addition, allied groups, such as the American Civil Liberties Union (ACLU), like-minded law firms, and occasionally other social movements (e.g., women's rights), work closely with LGBT rights organizations on litigation and advocacy (Thompson 2016). There are networks of cooperating attorneys such as the National Center for Transgender Equality's Transgender Legal Services Network (2016b). Finally, the transgender movement itself has more narrowly tailored trans legal specialists that reside with the California-based Transgender Law Center and two New York-based groups, the Sylvia Rivera Law Project and the Transgender Legal Defense & Education Fund. Other small firms exist as well. The most prominent of the trans specific firms is the Transgender Law Center.

The networks of cooperating attorneys are vital to the movement. For instance, Ohio-based attorney Randi A. Barnabee was the lead lawyer on a seminal Title VII transgender rights case, *Smith v. City of Salem* (2004). In part, the use of local lawyers is necessary because attorneys must be licensed and authorized to practice law in a jurisdiction or they must request *pro hac vice* admission from the court to be the attorney of record for a case. Perhaps as importantly, and as noted by Gash (2015) in her study of same-sex parenting litigation, local attorneys have knowledge of the legal frameworks and arguments that are most likely to work with local judges and in local communities. National or regional advocacy organizations may coordinate with these local lawyers to serve as lead attorneys in the case and thereby lower the profile of cases, and to conserve their own limited resources (Gash 2015).

Shannon Minter (2016), a longtime LGBT rights attorney with the National Center for Lesbian Rights, contends that money is centrally important to the work of gay and transgender rights litigation. Legal advocacy is expensive. Following Andersen (2009), we look at revenues as a guide to group resources. Table 5.1 shows the financial resources available to select nonprofit organizations that address transgender rights. Lambda Legal is by far the largest LGBT litigation-based advocacy organization in terms of mean real income and mean real assets (1995–2015). Other umbrella LGBT organizations are also at the top of the list in terms of resources. Transgender-specific organizations, which were founded more recently, have significantly fewer organizational resources than the broader LGBT rights organizations. Of the transgender-focused organizations, the Transgender Law Center is the largest in terms of mean real income and mean real assets. Yet even their substantial resources are dwarfed by the LGBT organizations. The combined resources of the three transgender-focused organizations listed here are still less than the smallest LGBT organization that we examined (Gay & Les-

TABLE 5.1. Select Organization Resources in LGBT Law

Organization	Mean Real Income	Mean Real Assets	IRS Rule Date
Lambda Legal Defense and Education Fund	$12,829,033	$8,678,546	1974
National Center for Lesbian Rights	$3,040,784	$1,481,521	1993
Gay & Lesbian Advocates & Defenders	$2,265,844	$1,482,994	1980
Transgender Law Center	$789,686	$771,288	2005
Sylvia Rivera Law Project	$476,843	$495,281	2004
Transgender Legal Defense and Education Fund	$139,231	$98,609	2003

Sources: National Center for Charitable Statistics; compiled IRS Business Master Files 1995–2015.
Notes: Amounts are in 2009 dollars and reflect the mean for the years appearing in the dataset. IRS rule dates are for the achievement of tax-exempt status. This may not reflect the actual founding date.

bian Advocates & Defenders). As Minter (2016) stated, without gay rights money, transgender legal advocacy "would be sunk."

The Work of Transgender Rights Legal Groups

Legal advocacy can take several forms. Advocacy organizations can choose to engage in impact litigation. This type of work involves the filing of lawsuits on behalf of clients to challenge or change laws to advance rights on behalf of a group of people. We see an example of this in *Carcaño v. McCrory* (2016). In this case, the ACLU, working with Equality North Carolina, on behalf of several plaintiffs, filed suit to block North Carolina's infamous HB2 law that restricted restroom use in public buildings by most transgender individuals.[2] This type of legal advocacy might also target instances of bias that affect individuals (as opposed to directly challenging a policy). An example of this occurred in *Glenn v. Brumby* (2011) when Lambda Legal served as the lead attorney for a client that was discriminated against in an employment context. In addition to addressing that individual's claim, Lambda Legal was attempting to create a binding legal precedent that would offer protections to the transgender community.

When it comes to representing clients, legal advocates have learned much from the gay and lesbian movement. They saw that success was not just about the facts of the case and legal arguments, but it also depended on persuasion by invoking empathy. Indeed, Shannon Minter (2016) notes the need to humanize transgender issues for the court. Of course, this is easier to do at the trial level because a transgender client can be in the courtroom. The appellate levels are different because they rely on written briefs to convey the core arguments rather than in-person testimony. To mitigate this problem, Minter said that preeminent LGBT rights attorney Jennifer Levi (GLAD) started adding photos of the transgender clients in appellate level case briefs.[3]

On some occasions, if the organization itself can prove sufficient connection to the law or action in question, they might have standing to file suit themselves and not just as a representative of a client. They could also serve as intervenor to protect an existing law from challenge by hostile advocacy groups. For example, the ACLU represented an intervening LGBT rights group, the Fairness Campaign, to protect the City of Louisville's nondiscrimination ordinance in *Hyman v. City of Louisville* (2001). Often, impact litigation organizations, like the ACLU, lobby the legislative and executive branches as well. For example, the ACLU's legislative representative, Ian Thompson (2016), emphasized the connection between his organization's legal and policy advocacy on LGBT rights.

Another legal technique that advocacy organizations use are cease and desist letters issued to individuals, businesses, or governments that are engaged in unlawful or potentially unlawful conduct. As noted by Thompson (2016), these tools often spare participants the expense of litigation. The ACLU attempted to use this technique, albeit unsuccessfully, in Gavin Grimm's dispute over restroom access at his high school in Virginia. Subsequently, this case would become *G.G. v. Gloucester County School Board* (2016).

Yet another tool, amicus curiae (friend of the court) briefs, are used when advocacy organizations are interested third parties to a case. This is one of the most common tools for LGBT legal advocacy groups to use. For instance, Lambda Legal filed an amicus brief in a Kansas case that involved the marriage of a transgender woman, *In re: the Estate of Gardiner* (2002) and in a case about whether a local nondiscrimination ordinance was preempted in *Air Transport Association of America v. City and County of San Francisco* (2001). Shannon Minter (2016) notes that friend of the court briefs are used to tell courts "our side of the issue." As Andersen (2009) observed, filing an amicus brief is a cost-effective way to spread a group's resources among many cases and issues.

To explore the legal work of LGBT advocacy organizations on transgender rights, we used LexisNexis Academic to search for cases using the following key words: gender identity, transgender, transsexual, and transvestite, along with derivations of those words. This yielded 112 possible trans-related cases that appeared at the appellate level in the federal system or in state supreme courts. Since LexisNexis does not search below the appellate level for federal cases or the state supreme courts during keywords searches, we supplemented this data with searches of online sources, including LGBT advocacy groups' websites. We also included ongoing litigation efforts found on LGBT advocacy group websites and in the media. Information from these sources increased our total to 167 cases from 1971 to September 2016.[4] While we may miss cases that were solely addressed at lower levels, or that garnered little attention, our dataset has the overwhelming majority of frequently cited transgender rights cases.

LGBT rights organizations, transgender focused organizations, or the ACLU served as the lead attorney in thirty-six of the 167 cases (21.56 percent).[5] They filed briefs (either as lead attorney or amicus) in fifty-five of the 167 cases (32.93 percent). The most active advocacy organizations in our

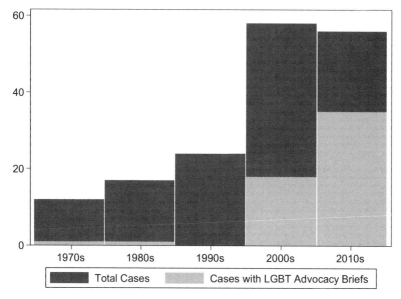

Figure 5.1. Advocacy Group Involvement in Trans Cases by Decade
Source: Data compiled from LexisNexis Academic and LGBT advocacy group websites.

dataset are the ACLU (twenty-six briefs), Lambda Legal (seventeen briefs), Transgender Law Center (sixteen briefs), the National Center for Lesbian Rights (twelve briefs), and Gay & Lesbian Advocates & Defenders (ten briefs).

The involvement of these organizations in transgender-related legal cases, however, has not been consistent over time. Table 5.2 shows that advocacy organizations have been far more likely to intervene in cases in the past two decades. Importantly, Minter (2016) notes the important impact of the marriage cases on LGBT legal advocacy. For a while, marriage litigation drew significant time and energy from LGBT advocacy organizations. However, it also increased their capacity because it brought in new resources, and advocacy groups were able to learn from the experience (Minter 2016). With marriage equality achieved in 2015, it appears that there has been a shift in interest to transgender issues. There were more cases with amicus briefs filed by LGBT or trans specific legal groups between January and September 2016 than in any year in our database (twelve for the partial year). This follows on the heels of another banner year of ten cases filed in 2015. While the use of advocacy group websites and other online sources to find cases could bias the number of cases upward for later years of the dataset, the findings are consistent with a shift in LGBT group resources toward transgender rights litigation. Minter (2016) said that "[t]his is safe now. . . . All the advocacy groups want to be seen as leaders on this."

While figure 5.1 reveals an important temporal trend toward increased involvement in transgender rights litigation, it is not clear why organizations have increased these tactics in recent years. So far, we have emphasized the importance of group resources and the changes in the policy agenda over time as primary explanations for these trends. In order to systematically examine these factors, and others, that contribute to whether an advocacy group becomes involved in a legal case, we turn to multivariate analysis. The dependent variable in our model is a binary indicator of whether a LGBT group has filed a brief. The primary explanatory variables measure LGBT group legal resources and issue salience. Legal resources are measured as the total annual mean revenue from 1995 to 2015 (in millions) for the six LGBT rights groups listed in table 5.1.[6] Issue salience is gauged using a count of the number of stories in the *New York Times* from 1970 to 2015 that mention "transgender" and related terms (Gash 2015).[7] Additionally, we include several binary indicators related to factors about the parties involved in a case: we control for whether a government actor was involved in a discriminatory action or policy that is being challenged/defended. We separately account for prisoner or immigrant rights cases. While these cases also involve government action, they should be treated as a distinct category because they involve unpopular groups often classified as deviants (Schneider and Ingram 1993) and because prisoners file significant numbers of *pro se* cases to argue on their own behalf. Last, discriminatory action by nongovernmental actors provides a third case type related to the parties. The omitted reference category is cases where the parties are individuals not pitted against government or nongovernmental organizations, such as in marriage, divorce, or custody cases.

Data limitations for the salience and financial resources variables restrict the period of analysis for the logistic regression to cases between 1995 and 2015. Given the strong correlation between financial resources and the year ($r = 0.95$), we also specified two additional logistic regression models that replaced financial resources with the year of the case, resulting in 149 cases. Since our measure of issue salience ends in 2015, the third model omits this variable to allow all 167 cases to be included. The results from all three models are shown in table 5.2.

Model 1 reveals that LGBT group resources are, indeed, significantly related to the likelihood of LGBT group involvement in a transgender-related case. This effect, however, is not very large. Increasing LGBT group resources by one million dollars increases the odds of case involvement by just 6 percent. Still, as LGBT group resources have grown from less than five million dollars in the mid-1990s to more than thirty-five million dollars in the 2010s, their propensity to be involved with transgender litigation has risen significantly. A substantively larger effect is driven by the nature of the case. Cases with government actors are significantly more likely than any other case type to involve action by LGBT organizations. Compared to the other three case types, the odds of LGBT advocacy group involvement is 4.7 to 12.9 times greater when a governmental actor is involved.

Model 2 replaces the LGBT resources measure with a year variable, allowing for an additional thirty-nine cases from before 1995. The results remain consistent with the first model. Unsurprisingly, the year variable is positively related to LGBT group involvement, not only reflecting the increased group resources over time but also the temporal trends we discussed earlier. On average, each year increased the odds of LGBT group involvement by 11 percent. This effect is significant despite also controlling for issue salience, which tends to increase over time. Although it is difficult to disentangle the temporal patterns from changes in LGBT group resources, the growth of LGBT group budgets is clearly associated with increased involvement in transgender cases. Since we controlled for issue salience, the temporal effects evident in Models 2 are more likely tied to resource changes rather than changes in public attention to transgender issues. As with Model 1, having a government actor involved in the case continued to be a statistically signifi-

TABLE 5.2. Logistic Regressions of LGBT Group Briefs Filed

	(1)		(2)		(3)	
	OR	SE	OR	SE	OR	SE
LGBT Resources	1.060*	(0.036)	—	—	—	—
Year	—	—	1.110*	(0.045)	1.133*	(0.029)
Issue Salience	1.002	(0.002)	1.001	(0.002)	—	—
Governmental Actor	4.743*	(3.611)	5.263*	(3.738)	5.155*	(3.531)
Prisoner/Immigrant	0.368	(0.284)	0.497	(0.359)	0.357	(0.255)
Nongovernmental Actor	0.827	(0.652)	0.851	(0.636)	1.006	(0.709)
Constant	0.082*	(0.070)	0.000*	(0.000)	0.000*	(0.000)
N	110		149		167	
Pseudo R^2	0.255		0.300		0.336	

Notes: Results are from logistic regression models. Dependent variables indicate whether an LGBT group filed an amicus curiae brief.

* p <0.05 (directional tests)

cant variable. The presence of a government actor increased the likelihood of a brief being filed by a LGBT rights group by factors of 5.26, 6.19, and 10.60, depending on the comparison case.

The third model, which includes cases from 1970 to 2016 and omits the issue salience variable, produces similar results. The year variable remains statistically significant, with each additional year increasing the odds of a brief being filed by a factor of 1.13. The increase in odds associated with governmental actors ranges from 5.12 to 14.44.

LGBT rights organizations are likely to favor cases involving government actors because of the policy dimension often involved. As Shannon Minter (2016) notes, the National Center for Lesbian Rights is focused on "advancing rights for the most people." Given limited resources, they strategically prioritize Title IX and Title VII cases. Changing the interpretation of sex in these statutes to be inclusive of gender identity and gender expression offers benefits for the greatest number of trans persons (and for the broader LGBT community) since nearly all people need discrimination-free education and jobs. There are numerous Title VII and Title IX cases that we will discuss in greater detail in our chapters on nondiscrimination law and education.

It should also be pointed out that defending already inclusive government policies also benefits a large number of people. LGBT rights organizations were involved in the defense of California (*Welch v. Brown* 2016) and New Jersey (*King v. Governor of New Jersey* 2014) laws banning sexual orientation and gender identity change therapies on minors. Challenging discriminatory policy is an important way to benefit trans individuals as well. The ACLU successfully challenged a Chicago law that banned cross-dressing (*City of Chicago v. Wilson*, 1978) and GLAD forced the Internal Revenue Service to allow medical deductions related to a transgender person's transition (*O'Donnabhain v. Commissioner of Internal Revenue*, 2010). These types of cases generally offer greater potential gains for more trans people than intervening in private matters. We expect to see a significant rise in such litigation given the increased resources in the LGBT advocacy community and due to governmental policy changes with discriminatory impacts against transgender people. Indeed, as this book was in the final stages of preparation in 2017, the National Center for Lesbian Rights and GLAD filed suit on behalf of five anonymous plaintiffs against the Trump administration over the president's "tweeted" ban on transgender military service (Savage 2017a). After President Trump directed the Department of Defense to stop accepting transgender recruits, Lambda Legal, Outserve, and the ACLU followed with lawsuits against the administration (Wheeler

2017). A Washington, DC District Court judge responded to these suits by issuing an injunction on the ban, ruling that the plaintiffs had a strong possibility of prevailing in the case (Jouvenal 2017). In response to court rulings on the lawsuits, the Department of the Defense adopted a policy that allowed transgender recruits to enlist (Vanden Brook 2018). However, in March 2018, the Trump administration instituted a new ban on those with a history of gender dysphoria. As of this writing, court injunctions have contined to block implementation of that directive (Kilmas and Bender 2018).

Legal Advocacy

As discussed earlier, organized litigation for transgender rights has been relatively slow to form, but is now expanding. In an earlier phase of litigation during the 1970s and 1980s, transgender litigants sued without the support of regional or national organizations, and generally were not successful. Examples include *Holloway v. Arthur Anderson* (1977) and *Ulane v. Eastern Airlines* (1984), both cases involving Title VII and the dismissal of transsexual women from jobs.[8] Indeed, with a few exceptions, courts have not always been good venues for the movement. But as discussed below, this seems to be changing as we increasingly see a more liberal federal judiciary open to constitutional rights claims (Ura 2014). Indeed, unlike the LGB litigation movement, much transgender-related litigation has involved federal, rather than state, courts.

The focus on federal litigation stems from stronger statutory and constitutional protection for sex and gender than for sexual orientation. For instance, sex-based discrimination triggers a higher level of scrutiny under the equal protection clause than does sexual orientation, and Title VII of the Civil Rights Act of 1964 covers sex but not sexual orientation.[9] In addition, the Eighth Amendment's prohibition on cruel and unusual punishment has been used to protect the right to health care for transgender inmates. Thus, despite higher levels of social and political marginalization, the legal framework is potentially more supportive of a range of transgender rights claims than claims based upon sexual orientation. Recent transgender rights litigation has also built upon the successes of the LGB rights movement. We discuss below how current litigation utilizes important precedents relating to sexual orientation, such as *Lawrence v. Texas* (2003). Thus, transgender rights litigation is grounded in a potentially rich legal milieu, some from outside the sexual orientation framework but also some relying heavily on the relatively new case law.

Litigation Critiques

Using courts to achieve policy and social change is empirically and nor-
matively contested. Gerald Rosenberg (2008) has most prominently developed the empirical critique, drawing upon the insights of Robert Dahl in
a classic 1957 essay about the limits on the Supreme Court's power and on
scholarship from the 1970s and 1980s about the inefficacy of rights claiming (see Scheingold 1974, 2004). In two editions of his book, *The Hollow
Hope*, Rosenberg argued that the Supreme Court is merely a reactive institution and social change comes only from the political arena, usually through
grassroots activism. Advocates turning to the courts will be disappointed,
and, more dangerously, they will provoke a backlash that will harm the
movement. However, a strong line of scholarship has disputed these claims,
particularly in the area of LGBT rights (Keck 2009; Mezey 2007, 2009;
Pierceson 2005, 2013; Bishin et al. 2015). Independent judicial policymaking
is real and deeply embedded in the U.S. policymaking system (Howard and
Steigerwalt 2012; Grossman and Swedlow 2015).

A normative critique of litigation-based liberation strategies stems from
the influence of critical theory and queer/radical gender critiques of the
LGBT movement, especially the mainstream gay and lesbian movement.
While these critiques have been effective in unmasking hidden power dynamics, they tend to overemphasize the lack of utility of rights-based litigation and argue that this litigation is harmful in two important ways. First,
it has a normalizing effect on sexual and gender minorities by demanding
inclusion into oppressive power structures. Second, it crowds out resources
that could be devoted to more marginalized elements of the movement in
favor of educated, upper-middle class (mostly white cisgender male) goals,
such as marriage equality. Many transgender theorists, such as Dean Spade,
argue against utilizing a liberal, rights-claiming approach in the movement for transgender liberation. According to Spade, a liberal approach
"merely tinkers with systems while leaving their most violent operations in-
tact" (Spade 2011, 91). Further, as Spade bluntly states, "The standard law
reform strategies most often employed to remedy the problems faced by
trans people fundamentally misunderstand the nature of power and control
and the role of the law in both" (Spade 2011, 101). It should be noted that
similar arguments have been used in the past to oppose the use of litigation to achieve lesbian and gay rights, especially marriage equality litigation
(D'Emilio 2007).

Certainly, courts are imperfect vehicles for the protection of the rights of
marginalized groups, as are most public institutions. Indeed, courts have only
recently begun to protect transgender individuals (Levasseur 2015). However,

they may prove to be a necessary antidote to hostile public opinion. Furthermore, courts potentially can play an important antimajoritarian, safety net role to counter the majoritarian tendencies of the other branches of government. Finally, objection to rights-based litigation is largely grounded in normative opposition to the approach, rather than empirical assessments of it. The objections often deny most real and potential change stemming from legal liberal reform strategies. As Pierceson (2005, 2013) argues, rights-claiming can work quite well. In addition, Karen Zivi (2012) provides an effective counterargument to critical theorists in her important book *Making Rights Claims: A Practice of Democratic Citizenship*. According to Zivi, rights-claiming by marginalized groups is "a rule-breaking practice that opens up the possibilities of the new, and this is precisely what makes it suitable for democratic politics" (Zivi 2012, 19). The cases below demonstrate this potential.

Constraints of Public Opinion on Transgender Rights Policy

Although polling (see chapter 2) indicates public disapproval of discrimination toward transgender individuals, the public tends to hold negative attitudes toward transgender people and is generally not supportive of many policies required to achieve transgender equality and full integration into society. Additionally, while there are varying levels of support for transgender rights across states, a "democratic deficit" exists between public opinion and transgender-supportive policies, as it may take much more than simple majority support to enact these policies (Flores, Herman, and Mallory 2015). Moreover, positive policy change that has occurred in states is in part the result of policy diffusion from other progressive states, not internal state politics. In more conservative regions of the country, this is not as much of a factor, leaving many states outside the possibility of positive policy change (Taylor et al. 2012). With estimates of the transgender population at 0.6 percent of the total U.S. population (Flores et al. 2016), this is clearly a "discrete and insular minority" (*United States v. Carolene Products Company* 1938, footnote 4) needing significant support from the judiciary.

Transgender Rights Cases

Transgender Employment Discrimination

In response to the disproportionately high levels of employment discrimination faced by transgender and gender nonconforming individuals, legal challenges to this type of bias began to appear by the 1970s, not as an orchestrated strategy but through individuals bringing claims with local attorneys. Initially, courts were not receptive to these claims, as there were no explicit statutory protections in state or federal law. While a handful of localities had adopted trans-inclusive ordinances, Minnesota became the first state to pass a trans-inclusive nondiscrimination law in 1993. As of June 2018, twenty states offer comprehensive discrimination protections based on gender identity.[10] However, such protections do not explicitly exist in federal statutes.

In addition, judges were not initially receptive to the arguments that sex-based prohibitions covered transgender and gender nonconforming persons and that external organs alone do not define gender or sex. Levasseur (2015) notes that the type of reasoning employed by an English court in 1970, *Corbett v. Corbett*, was adopted and utilized by U.S. judges in a variety of legal contexts. According to that court, "the biological sexual constitution of an individual is fixed at birth (at the latest), and cannot be changed, either by the natural development of organs of the opposite sex, or by medical or surgical means" (Levasseur 2015, 968). Typical of this approach was the Seventh Circuit decision in *Ulane v. Eastern Airlines* (1984): "[I]f Eastern did discriminate against Ulane it was not because she is female, but because Ulane is a transsexual—a biological male who takes female hormones, cross-dresses, and had surgically altered parts of her body to make it appear female" (1087). Thus, biological and gender essentialism was deeply embedded in the judiciary.

However, a legal breakthrough occurred in 1989 in the case of *Price Waterhouse v. Hopkins*. In that case, the U.S. Supreme Court held that sex stereotyping could be seen as discrimination under Title VII. Ann Hopkins, a cisgender woman, was fired because she was seen as being too "masculine." The Court later affirmed this stereotyping approach in the same-sex sexual harassment case of *Oncale v. Sundowner* (1998). While this innovation did not create full legal protections for gender identity, there was at least a hook from which to hang sex-based discrimination arguments for this protection. After a few years, some federal appellate courts began to use this reasoning to find in favor of transgender individuals claiming discrimination under Title VII in such cases as *Schwenk v. Hartford* (2000) from the Ninth Circuit, *Rosa v. Park West Bank* (2000) from the First Circuit, *Smith v. City of Salem* (2004) and *Barnes v. Cincinnati* (2005) from the Sixth Circuit, and *Glenn v. Brumby* (2011) from the Eleventh Circuit. GLAD was involved in the *Rosa* litigation, a case decided three years before GLAD's landmark marriage equality victory in *Goodridge v. Department of Public Health* in 2003.

Building on this jurisprudence, the Equal Employment Opportunity

Commission (EEOC) issued a groundbreaking ruling in 2012, holding that the Commission viewed Title VII as prohibiting discrimination based on gender identity (*Macy v. Holder* 2012). While the EEOC's rulings are not binding on federal courts, many federal judges make use of their findings, and the agency can be an important ally in combating discrimination, especially when joined by a supportive presidential administration. The Obama administration filed several briefs supporting the EEOC's position.[11] Interestingly, the EEOC later ruled that Title VII also prohibits discrimination based on sexual orientation (*Baldwin v. Department of Transportation* 2015). This was an inversion of the typical pattern of legal innovations where sexual orientation inclusion normally comes before gender identity inclusion. It is quite plausible that the federal courts will enshrine a gender identity protection in Title VII before Congress enacts such protections, especially given unified Republican control of the elected branches of the national government as of 2018 and that party's hostility toward LGBT rights. As evidence of this hostility, the Equality Act (a bill proposing to add sexual orientation and gender identity to the 1964 Civil Rights Act) had 176 Democratic cosponsors and two Republican cosponsors in the House during the 114th Congress.[12]

The emerging approach of federal courts can be seen in *Glenn v. Brumby* (2011), a case involving Lambda Legal that was cited by the EEOC. Vandiver Elizabeth Glenn was fired from a job with the Georgia Legislature's Office of Legal Counsel after transitioning. A district court sided with her, and this was upheld on appeal. The unanimous Eleventh Circuit panel found this discrimination to be a violation of both Title VII and the equal protection clause. The court invoked heightened scrutiny as required by sex discrimination under the clause. The decision also cited law review articles calling for the expansion of transgender rights under sex discrimination frameworks. Of the four judges involved in the litigation, three were Democratic appointees, including the trial judge, and one was a Republican appointee.

Of the policy areas discussed in this chapter, employment discrimination is the most advanced from a legal and policy perspective. Not only is this form of discrimination actionable under some state (and many local) laws, federal law concerning sex-based discrimination was increasingly being used by judges and administrative actors during the Obama administration to prohibit discrimination based upon gender identity. Of course, this policy area is arguably the least politically controversial, given the high levels of support for nondiscrimination laws shown in chapter 2. However, it is clear that action by legal policymakers has been required to expand the policy, given the democratic deficit discussed above (see also Lax and Phillips 2012).

Transgender Prisoner Rights

Transgender individuals, especially transgender women of color, encounter the criminal justice system at disproportionately high rates, due to social marginalization and discrimination (James et al. 2016). If incarcerated, transgender individuals are typically housed in facilities based on their biological sex, rather than their gender identity. This exposes them to high rates of violence. In addition, access to necessary health care is not guaranteed (Grant, Mottet, and Tanis 2011). As the discussion below indicates, only recently have corrections systems begun to allow hormone therapy for transgender inmates, and surgical treatment is rare. However, both forms of treatment are becoming more common in some jurisdictions due to litigation commenced by transgender inmates, at first on their own but now supported by advocacy organizations. As evidenced by the public opinion data presented in chapter 2, providing publicly funded transition-related health care to transgender inmates is a politically charged issue. Corrections officials are reluctant to provide services supported by public funds, and they are often supported in this position by elected officials.

Despite this political opposition, transgender inmates have a powerful legal tool in the Eighth Amendment's prohibition on cruel and unusual punishment. In particular, the Supreme Court case of *Estelle v. Gamble* (1976) held that the amendment is violated when corrections officials exhibit "deliberate indifference" to the medical needs of inmates. In addition, federal judges have been extensively involved in setting corrections policy over the past several decades (Feeley and Rubin 1998). In the past decade, federal judges have found that the refusal to provide hormone therapy violates this precedent, but judges are more divided on the question of surgical intervention.

A case from Wisconsin illustrates the mix of politics and law at play with this issue. After being provided hormone therapy for several years, an inmate sued over the state's denial of surgical treatment. As the suit was moving forward in 2005, the Republican-controlled legislature enacted the Inmate Sex Change Prevention Act with significant support from Democrats. The bill passed the Assembly 82 to 15 and by unanimous consent in the Senate, with a leading legislator calling the idea of taxpayer-supported surgical treatment "absurd" (Barton 2005). Despite the political emphasis on surgery, the law also banned hormone therapy.

Through coordinated litigation, the law was invalidated by a federal district judge (a Clinton appointee) and by a unanimous panel of the Seventh Circuit (with one George H. W. Bush and two Clinton appointees). Lambda Legal and the ACLU were directly involved in the litigation, including Lambda Legal's transgender rights project director, Dru Levasseur. The lead attorney for the ACLU, Lawrence Dupuis, had been active in marriage-equality-related litigation in the state. The Seventh Circuit decision equated the treatment of transgender inmates with other medical treatments. As the opinion stated, "Surely, had the Wisconsin legislature passed a law that DOC [Department of Corrections] inmates with cancer must be treated only with [mental health] therapy and pain killers, this court would have no trouble concluding that the law was unconstitutional" (*Fields v. Smith* 2011, 557). Thus, the court fully supported the Eighth Amendment arguments of the inmates and viewed the law in terms of both cruelty and inequality.

A long-running Massachusetts case demonstrates both the power and potential limits of inmate-based litigation. Michelle Kosilek challenged the Massachusetts DOC denial of surgical treatment for her gender dysphoria. In 2012, a federal district court judge found in favor of Kosilek, twenty years after she first requested treatment via a lawsuit. Kosilek initially commenced this litigation *pro se* and without the support of regional or national groups. However, by the time of the most recent litigation, these groups were involved, particularly GLAD. Judge Mark Wolf, a Reagan appointee, found prison officials to have been politically motivated in their deliberate indifference (the legal standard to find a violation of the Eighth Amendment) to Kosilek's medical needs through their repeated stalling tactics, false claims about security concerns, and picking medical experts favorable to their position (*Kosilek v. Spencer* 2012).

A divided (2 to 1) panel of the First Circuit upheld Wolf's decision, largely agreeing with his conclusions. The judges in the majority, Rogeriee Thompson and William Kayatta, were Obama appointees. The dissenting judge, Juan Torruella, was a Reagan appointee. Rejecting the influence of politics and public outcry, he viewed the officials' actions as reasonable under the Eighth Amendment. As he stated, "Its boundary simply does not reach . . . to instances of care that, although not ideal, illustrate neither an intent to harm nor the obstinate and unwarranted application of clearly imprudent care" (*Kosilek v. O'Brien* 2014, 117).

However, after an en banc appeal by the DOC, the positions were reversed, with Torruella writing the majority opinion denying Kosilek's request, Thompson and Kayatta in dissent. Joining Torruella in the majority were Sandra Lea Lynch (Clinton appointee) and Jeffrey Howard (George W. Bush appointee). In a scathing dissent, Thompson compared the decision to the legal mistakes of *Plessy v. Ferguson* (1896) and *Korematsu v. U.S.* (1944) and asserted that the decision "enables correctional systems to further postpone their adjustment to the crumbling gender binary" (*Kosilek v. Spencer*

2014, 112). An appeal to the U.S. Supreme Court was denied, thus ending Kosilek's decades-long attempt to gain proper medical treatment. The U.S. Supreme Court also denied an appeal in *Fields*, perhaps indicating a Court waiting for the issue to develop more fully, or a Court concerned about the countermajoritarian implications, thus leaving the legal landscape in a bit of chaos.

Despite *Kosilek*, inmates have found success in other circuits, and their suits have resulted in policy change. Like Michelle Kosilek, Ophelia De'lonta began a *pro se* effort to receive transition-related medical treatment in a Virginia prison in 1999. She won a victory with court-ordered hormone therapy in 2004, but she continued to struggle with gender dysphoria, including an attempted self-castration in 2010 after being denied surgical treatment by prison officials. In 2011, she sued to receive this treatment (Spies 2015). Nixon appointee Judge James Turk sided with the state, but his decision was overturned unanimously on appeal on a panel made up of two Clinton and one Obama appointee. That court did not order surgical treatment but it held that De'lonta had demonstrated a valid legal claim of deliberate indifference, analogizing the denial of care to the denial of surgical treatment for an inmate suffering a serious injury from a fall (*De'lonta v. Johnson* 2013, 525–26). By the time of this phase of the litigation, the ACLU was involved. Ultimately, the state avoided the expense of further treatment when it granted parole to De'lonta in 2014 (Spies 2015).

A similar situation played out more recently in California. The state paroled a transgender inmate after a federal court sided with the inmate's request for surgical treatment, but this litigation also resulted in tangible policy change in the California correctional system. Interestingly, Michelle-Lael Norsworthy was resigned to the fact that she would never receive surgical treatment while incarcerated due to the policy. However, she was inspired to challenge the policy when she learned of Kosilek's victory in the federal district court in 2012, because, in her words, "it was the first time that an opportunity was provided to transgenders [*sic*] that said the State had to listen to me" (*Norsworthy v. Beard* 2015, 7). Judge Jon Tigar, an Obama appointee, ruled that Norsworthy was likely to succeed on her Eighth Amendment claim, having provided extensive evidence of deliberate indifference by prison officials, which was not justified by security concerns. Thus, the decision followed the approach of other judges finding Eighth Amendment problems with the denial of surgical treatment.[13] While the state appealed, Norsworthy was paroled in 2016, having been recommended for parole in 2015 for the first time in six opportunities (St. John 2015a; Allen 2016). Ultimately, in response to this and another case, the state changed its policy to include the possibility of surgical treatment (Pérez-Peña 2015). Judge Tigar also presided over litigation from another transgender inmate, Shiloh Quine. He appointed the Transgender Law Center to represent her. This has resulted in a settlement in which the state will pay for gender confirmation surgery for Quine. Approximately 400 California inmates were receiving hormone therapy as of 2015 (St. John 2015b).

Transgender Student Rights

As trans students have come out in recent years, they have begun to demand accommodations. Some refusals by school districts have resulted in litigation or complaints filed with the Department of Education (DOE). Successful intervention by the government in high-profile cases has triggered legislation in several states prohibiting the use of facilities based upon gender identity and mandating segregation based upon sex assigned at birth. A bill in South Dakota was vetoed by the state's Republican governor, but more bills are in the pipeline (Stuart 2016). As seen in chapter 2, public opinion is currently divided on the issue.

Defiance by local parents, school boards, and administrators against the Obama administration's interpretation of Title IX of the Educational Amendments of 1972 as protecting transgender students from discrimination became increasingly common toward the end of his term. One such dispute in suburban Palatine, Illinois garnered national headlines when a transgender female obtained restroom and locker room accommodations in accordance with her gender identity (Hartocollis 2017). In addition, after internal administrative deliberations and pressure from transgender activists, the Obama administration sent an advisory guidance letter in May 2016 to all school districts. It asserted that Title IX applies to transgender students and advised school districts to allow transgender students to use the facilities of their choice (Stolberg et al. 2016). This provoked North Carolina to sue the administration over this policy, while the administration sued North Carolina over its law (HB2) mandating that restroom use in public facilities be guided by biological sex as indicated on birth certificates.[14] Social conservatives clearly see the bathroom issue as useful to their cause of opposing LGBT rights, especially after the 2015 voter defeat of Houston's HERO ordinance (a broad antidiscrimination ordinance) in a referendum in which opponents focused almost exclusively on the "threat" to women and girls from predatory sex offenders "masquerading" as trans women.

Social conservatives also filed challenges to the Obama administration policy in the friendly venues of the Fifth and Eighth Circuits. At the time, other circuits either were controlled by a majority of Democratic appointees or have circuit court opinions finding that gender-identity-based discrimination is a form of sex discrimination under federal civil rights law. Opponents found remarkable success with this forum shopping through a Texas district court's nationwide injunction against enforcement of the Obama administration's Title IX policy. Thus, they delayed the policy via the courts until the Trump administration could reverse course in February 2017 (Peters, Becker, and Davis 2017).[15]

Yet federal judges have not taken a uniform approach to Title IX as it applies to transgender students. The Fourth Circuit ruled in favor of the Obama administration's transgender-inclusive interpretation in a case from Virginia (*G.G. v. Gloucester County School Board* 2016). Our initial analysis indicates that the partisan affiliation of federal judges or longevity on the bench (with more recent judges being more open to an expansive interpretation of sex), or both, is playing a role in the differential outcomes. The trial judge in the Virginia case took a retrograde approach to adjudicating the claims of Gavin Grimm, a transgender male student suing to use the male restrooms at his school. Grimm was initially allowed to use the boys' room, but the school board reversed this decision of the school administration after public outcry. Reagan-appointee Senior District Judge Robert Doumar struggled with the concept of gender dysphoria and repeatedly used dated language and old case law (he mostly ignored the employment cases discussed above) when discussing the case, viewing the case through the lens of cisgender privilege. He refused to give any standing to the DOE's position, because it was not a regulation, and favored the right to privacy of cisgender students over Grimm's equality rights. While discussing Grimm's claims, he bizarrely stated, "He fails to recognize that no amount of improvements to the urinals can make them completely private because people sometimes turn while closing their pants" (*G.G. v Gloucester County School Board* 2015, 24).

From the oral argument in the Fourth Circuit, the outcome looked a bit more promising for Grimm and other transgender students. The Obama administration submitted an amicus brief in support of Grimm, reflecting the administration's strong stance on transgender rights generally and transgender student rights in particular (Holden 2016a). The three-judge panel hearing the case was composed of a George H. W. Bush appointee (Paul Niemeyer) and two Barack Obama appointees (Henry Floyd and Andre Davis). Following the tenor of the oral argument, the Obama judges overturned Doumar's decision, while the longer-serving judge dissented. Niemeyer was also the only dissenting judge from the en banc denial of a rehearing of the case. The Fourth Circuit currently is composed of ten Democratic and five Republican appointees. Of the five Republican appointees, three were appointed by George W. Bush. It is clearly a Democratic and "newer" court.

The opinion by Floyd was much more sympathetic to Grimm. It noted the public hostility toward him at public meetings that drove the school board policy, and it noted the health complications encountered by Grimm because of the school's restrictive policy. Floyd found that the definition of sex as it applies to transgender individuals was sufficiently ambiguous to allow for deference to agency interpretation, citing the case of *Auer v. Robbins* (1997). He also invoked the famous *Chevron* (1984) precedent to reinforce the need for courts to defer to agency interpretations. In addition, Floyd clearly rejected the sex binary approach of opponents in favor of a broader interpretation of the definition of sex under federal law. As he stated, "Which restroom would a transgender individual who had undergone sex-reassignment surgery use? What about an intersex individual? What about an individual born with X-X-Y sex chromosomes? What about an individual who lost external genitalia in an accident?" (*G. G. v. Gloucester County School Board* 2016, 20). Clearly, the majority was invoking a more expansive and sophisticated interpretation of the statutory definition of sex, reflecting advances in thinking about sex and gender since the 1970s.

In August 2016, the U.S. Supreme Court stayed an order from the district court, following the Fourth Circuit opinion, that Grimm be allowed to use restrooms based upon his gender identity. Justice Steven Breyer stated that this stay was a "courtesy" pending appeal (Epps 2016). In October 2016, the Court granted review of the appeal on the questions of whether the administration was entitled to deference (not the larger question of the wisdom of *Auer* itself) on its interpretation of "sex" under Title IX and, more broadly, whether gender identity is included in the category of sex in Title IX. However, as noted previously, the new Trump administration quickly withdrew the Department of Education instructions that underpinned much of the appellate decision (Peters, Becker, and Davis 2017). Subsequently, the Supreme Court vacated the Fourth Circuit's decision and sent the case back to the lower courts for further consideration (Liptak 2017). In turn, the Fourth Circuit remanded the case back to the district court level to determine whether the issue was moot now that Grimm has graduated from high school (Marimow 2017). In May 2018, Grimm saw some measure of satisfaction as federal district judge Arenda L. Wright Allen denied the school board's attempt to have the Title IX case dismissed and she encouraged the parties to reach a settlement (Stevens 2018). However, the school board has stated that it will appeal the decision (Balingit

2018).

In the consolidated North Carolina cases involving HB2, district judge Thomas Schroeder (a George W. Bush appointee) issued an injunction against the state for two plaintiffs challenging the law's legality. Schroeder followed the Fourth Circuit on the administrative law issues, but his discussion of their constitutional claims (equal protection and due process) was dismissive of the notion that the Constitution protects transgender access to facilities based upon gender identity. Even under high levels of review (heightened scrutiny for sex-based discrimination and strict scrutiny for fundamental rights), he argued that the state's interest in protecting the privacy of cisgender persons under its jurisdiction was sufficient to trump discrimination or violation of fundamental rights (*Carcaño v. McCrory* 2016). Thus, this was a short-term victory for transgender rights advocates because the judge did not side with most of their substantive arguments. Overall, it was an opinion that matched conservative political and legal views on the question. The case against HB2 was later rendered a moot legal question after the law was repealed in 2017. However, plaintiffs continued to argue that the repeal measure, HB142, left discriminatory structures in place (Lambda Legal 2017a). The case was renamed *Carcaño v. Cooper*, reflecting the change in administrations with Roy Cooper's election in 2016 and given the continued legal maneuvering.[16]

As further evidence of the organizational link to marriage equality litigation, leading national LGBT rights groups were involved in the challenge to North Carolina's HB2 law. Among the organizations in this effort were the ACLU and Lambda Legal. Paul Smith, the Jenner & Block attorney who argued *Lawrence v. Texas* and *Obergefell* before the Supreme Court and is considered one of the leading LGBT rights attorneys in the country, was also involved. These and other organizations have moved aggressively to protect transgender rights post-*Obergefell*.

Texas district court judge Reed O'Connor (a George W. Bush appointee) took the opposite approach of the Fourth Circuit on deference and the definition of sex under federal law. In addition, he took the unusual step of granting a nationwide injunction against the Obama administration's policy. Typically, district court decisions apply only to the state in which the court sits, and judges commonly stay their orders pending appeal. It was also unusual given that many other circuits have interpreted the sex provisions more broadly. Judge O'Connor has a history of being out of step with federal judicial trends on LGBT rights. In 2015 and in the wake of *U.S. v. Windsor* (2013), when there was clear momentum from federal courts that bans on same-sex marriage were unconstitutional, he halted a rule from the Department of Labor applying the Family and Medical Leave Act to some same-sex couples, depending on where their marriage was performed. He was overruled by the Supreme Court ruling in *Obergefell v. Hodges* a few months later. When Texas attorney general Ken Paxton (a strong opponent of LGBT rights) decided to bring an action against the Obama administration over Title IX, he chose the Northern District of Texas in Wichita Falls where only one judge sits: Reed O'Connor (Council 2016). Paxton received the result he desired, and the decision created great uncertainty about the Obama administration's Title IX policy just as the 2016 school year was beginning. Completely ignoring the Fourth Circuit, O'Connor stated that sex in federal law strictly means "biological" sex and there was no authority or justification for the DOE's interpretation of Title IX (*Texas v. U.S.* 2016).

Cases originating in other jurisdictions have had more success. A Wisconsin case supported by the Transgender Law Center resulted in victories for a transgender student seeking to use the school facilities of his choice. Kenosha school officials required Ashton Whitaker to use girls' facilities and even allegedly proposed a policy of requiring transgender students to wear green wristbands to police their restroom usage more effectively. Whitaker was inspired by Gavin Grimm's case, and filed a federal suit in 2016. Judge Pamela Pepper, an Obama appointee, citing supportive employment discrimination precedents and other case law utilizing an expansive interpretation of sex, denied a motion to dismiss the case. She ordered the school district to allow Whitaker to use the boy's restrooms in the school (Barbash 2016; Vielmetti 2016). Subsequently, a unanimous three-judge panel of the Seventh Circuit upheld the district court's injunction and denied an attempt by Kenosha officials to have the case dismissed, finding the district's policy in violation of Title IX and the federal equal protection clause (*Whitaker v. Kenosha Unified School District* 2017).

An Ohio case, supported by the Transgender Law Center, provided another victory for transgender rights proponents (*Highland Local School District v. U.S. Dept. of Education* 2016). In that case, Clinton-appointee Algenon Marbley largely followed the reasoning and approach of the Fourth Circuit, but he also went further by ruling that classifications based upon transgender status are subject to heightened scrutiny under the federal equal protection clause.

In a higher education setting, a district judge (a George W. Bush appointee) found in favor of the University of Pittsburgh in its refusal to allow a transgender male student access to male restrooms and locker facilities (*Johnston v. University of Pittsburgh* 2016; Niland 2015). During the appeal, a settlement was reached with the university allowing access to facilities to students based upon gender identity. Transgender Law Center lawyer Ilona Turner called the settlement a victory (Holden 2016b). However, as this case reflects, some federal judges, especially Republican appointees, appear to be struggling with the novel nature of these cases. While there is evolving jurisprudence in this area, and the Obama administration took a strong position in favor of transgender equality, the Trump administration has changed direction. There is no question that the policy terrain is muddled and uncertain. As an attorney representing Illinois school districts stated about her clients: "They look at the Pittsburgh case, they look at what the OCR has said, they look at state and local laws, and it's really gray" (Leff 2016). The extent to which the U.S. Supreme Court can add clarity to this policy remains to be seen.

Marriage, Documents, and the Right to Privacy

The expansion and enriching of the right to privacy is one of the hallmark accomplishments of the lesbian and gay litigation movement, as reflected in the opinions of Justice Kennedy in *Lawrence v. Texas* (2003), *United States v. Windsor* (2013), and *Obergefell v. Hodges* (2015). These decisions provided vital protections for the entire LGBT community with respect to sexual relations in *Lawrence* and marriage in *Windsor* and *Obergefell*. Important for the transgender community, the latter decision ended the confusing and contradictory set of state laws and court decisions that challenged the marriage rights of transgender individuals who had undergone sex reassignment. Such individuals had marriages invalidated or blocked in Texas, Kansas, Florida, and Ohio (Taylor, Tadlock, and Poggione 2014). In a series of decisions, those states' courts had refused to respect the sex reassignment of trans individuals and had blocked or invalidated marriages to individuals of the same birth sex.[17] Even where their marriages might find legal shelter (e.g., *M. T. v. J. T.* 1976) some trans people risked having other states challenge the legality of marriage when crossing state lines (Greenberg and Herald 2005). In 2015, the Supreme Court ended this confusing and contradictory legal regime for transgender people and while doing so expanded their marriage rights. The right to privacy played an important role.

Privacy rights have also been successfully invoked in transgender rights litigation concerning state laws with burdensome requirements to change gender markers on government-issued identification documents, such as birth certificates. Many states require proof of surgical transition before a birth certificate can be amended and four states do not allow them to be amended at all (Lambda Legal 2015). Of course, many transgender individuals do not undergo this treatment. Reflecting the political power of the gender binary, only 41 percent of respondents in a recent survey supported gender marker changes without medical permission (Pierceson and Kirzinger 2015). There is still a strong political perception that one must be one gender or another, as reflected by the appearance of genitalia or approval by medical authorities, or both. A political movement exists to relax these policies, but to date the results have been limited, mostly to relaxing the requirement for gender confirmation surgery to a certification of some form of medical treatment. The federal government relaxed the requirement for confirmation surgery for passports in 2010.

Privacy-based (among other constitutional claims) litigation has also been used to challenge restrictive policies. In 2015, the ACLU filed suit against Michigan's restrictive policy of allowing gender marker changes on driver licenses or state ID cards only with a birth certificate matching the gender marker. Of course, Michigan also requires gender confirmation surgery for changing the gender marker on a state-issued birth certificate. Judge Nancy Edmunds (a George H. W. Bush appointee) agreed with the ACLU that the transgender plaintiffs' privacy rights were violated by the potential disclosure of their transgender status when their appearance did not match their state identification gender marker. As she declared, "the Court finds that by requiring Plaintiffs to disclose their transgender status, the Policy directly implicates their fundamental right to privacy" (*Love v. Johnson* 2015, 856). In response, the secretary of state amended the policy to include passports as evidence of gender, but the ACLU continued with the litigation to further narrow the restrictive policy. As the lead attorney in the case stated, "It's still not a model policy. It's still not a policy that other states have adopted to make sure transgender individuals can obtain ID. We are continuing with our lawsuit" (Chambers 2016). However, Judge Edmunds later declared the issue moot (Baldas 2016). This lawsuit followed ACLU litigation commenced in 2011 (well before same-sex marriage litigation was finished) in Illinois that resulted in an administrative policy change removing the confirmation surgery requirement (American Civil Liberties Union 2012a).

In 2012, an Alaska judge forced the elimination of the confirmation surgery requirement in that state, relying on the strong tradition of privacy rights in that state's constitutional jurisprudence (*K.L v. Alaska Dept. of Admin* 2012*)*. Indeed, judges in Alaska have long invoked the uniquely powerful right to privacy in the state on a range of LGBT rights issues, including a 1997 decision challenging the state's ban on same-sex marriage (Pierceson 2005, 2013). The ACLU spearheaded this legal challenge (American Civil Liberties Union 2012b).

Conclusion

Although the use of litigation to pursue transgender rights claims are in relatively early stages, litigation has already begun shaping policy in many instances. These legal advocacy strategies are particularly important in the context of sometimes hostile public opinion or hostile governmental action. LGBT movement lawyers have begun to engage this realm of litigation, often drawing from existing resources. Though more work needs to be done, it appears that litigation for transgender rights holds significant promise due to the previous experience with LGB litigation and its institution- and jurisprudence-building, as well as the more favorable federal legal setting. Overall, LGBT group-backed litigation is more successful than the more random and unsupported litigation of the past. Although not a perfect trend, it appears that more recent Democratic appointees to the federal bench are more receptive to the arguments of transgender litigants. Given their relative insulation from politics, federal courts may be a good place to help to deconstruct the gender binary that continues to drive majoritarian politics in the United States. At the very least, many trans activist lawyers see this potential, despite the criticism of rights-based litigation strategies.

However, the ability of the Trump administration to reshape the judiciary, from the Supreme Court level on down, should give advocates pause for concern. Indeed, this process has already begun with the confirmation of Justice Neil Gorsuch to the Supreme Court and the additional nomination that will replace retiring Justice Anthony Kennedy, who often provided the key vote on major LGBT rights cases. Despite what is likely to be a sharp right turn in the federal judiciary, LGBT advocates will be able to follow the model of their opponents and possibly delay some egregious actions by the Trump administration by venue shopping for favorable judges until more favorable political winds blow.

CHAPTER 6

Executive Branch Treatments of Transgender Rights

with Mitchell Sellers

This chapter explores the role of the executive branch and the bureaucracy in the development of transgender rights. Joining us is Mitchell Sellers, an expert on the intersection of executive branch politics and transgender rights. This chapter explores the role of the executive branch and the bureaucracy in the development of transgender rights. As noted in our introductory chapter, one of the key challenges facing transgender rights advocates is how to secure public policy for a small minority group in a majoritarian democratic system. Building the majority coalitions necessary for success in the legislative and electoral arenas can be daunting. However, the transgender rights movement has sometimes been able to secure policy victories through the executive branch, a venue in which presidents, governors, mayors, and bureaucratic officials can often shape policy unilaterally and in less publicly prominent ways. In this way, policymaking in the executive branch has sometimes been a fruitful avenue to explain the remarkable rise of transgender rights. Yet, as we discuss below, there are also limits to an advocacy strategy built on executive policymaking.

We start by briefly addressing the ways that the bureaucracy affects the lives of transgender people. Subsequently, we look at the ways that the upper echelons of the executive branches of the national, state, and local governments affect transgender rights through their various powers and in their role as chief executives. Subsequently, we explore the factors shaping executive policymaking on transgender rights by presenting a model of gubernatorial issuance of executive orders.

Bureaucracy

Bureaucracy is a system of organizational administration that is based on the specialization of job functions, hierarchical authority, and adherence to fixed rules. The U.S. federal, state, and local governments are organized in this fashion. In the face of often vague statutes that delegate authority, but often lack policy direction from elected officials (e.g., Epstein and O'Halloran 1999), bureaucracies have grappled with the complexities of trans identities for decades (Taylor 2007). They have done so by implementing existing policies with varying degrees of discretion, creating standard operating procedures to deal with transgender people and related issues, and by promulgating regulations. Depending on the delegated authority, agencies in some states have created nondiscrimination policies that apply only to public sector jobs, while other states have granted agencies even greater power to regulate the public and private sectors. Due to specialization, bureaucrats are experts in their competence area and can offer guidance to elected policymakers. As Svara (1999) notes, the complementarity between politics and administration allows public administrators to shape policymaking rather just carry out the policies set by elected officials.

The public encounters the bureaucracy directly through their interactions with street-level bureaucrats (Lipsky 1980). This includes police officers, firefighters, rescue workers, teachers, librarians, and other government bureaucrats who directly serve the public. They are important because they provide critical public services and they have discretion, to varying degrees, in how they carry out the policies of the jurisdiction that employs them. For instance, police discretion was used to enforce a law barring disguises used for the purpose of not being recognized on public roads and in fields (an old New York statute used to protect law enforcement from farmers disguised as Native Americans) to arrest transsexual individuals who were dressed appropriate to their gender identification (Sherwin 1969). Similarly, a South Carolina Division of Motor Vehicles office used its discretion, under a policy that forbade license pictures where an individual was altering his or her appearance, to bar an androgynous male-born teen from wearing makeup when attempting to get a driver's license (Kinnard 2014).

Additional examples of how street-level bureaucrats and higher-ranking administrators might engage in discriminatory treatment of transgender people who might or might not have protection under the law are easily found (Namaste 2000). For instance, a hiring official at the Library of Congress denied a highly qualified transgender person a job (unlawfully) after learning that individual was transitioning to a female identity (*Schroer v.*

Billington 2008). School officials nationwide, such as those in Gloucester County, Virginia (*G.G. v. Gloucester County School Board* 2016), have struggled with how to incorporate transgender students in terms of restroom and locker room access, identity recognition in school records, participation in sex-segregated activities, and in preventing bullying.

Likewise, technical expertise and familiarity with issues through casework might influence the recommendations of bureaucrats as it relates to transgender rights. For example, in 1977 the Centers for Disease Control and Prevention issued a model vital records act that recommended that individuals be allowed to amend their birth certificates in the event of sex reassignment surgery and a subsequent court order noting a change of sex (Centers for Disease Control and Prevention 1977, 17). The goals of these technical recommendations, which replaced an earlier model vital records act from 1959, were to "incorporate current social customs and practices," promote uniformity and comparability, and increase efficiency (CDC 1977, 1). They were developed with input from stakeholders such as the Association of State and Territorial Health Officials, the American Association for Vital Records and Public Health Statistics, and the United States Public Health Service. Subsequently, many state legislatures adopted the model legislation (Taylor, Tadlock, and Poggione 2014). Conversely, organized opposition by bureaucrats might derail a proposed regulation. In one such instance, a 2006 New York City Board of Health proposal to relax its birth certificate amendment policy was blocked when bureaucrats representing agencies (e.g., schools and jails) that commonly rely on an individual's legal sex in their work raised concerns about the consequences of the proposal (Yoshino 2006).

The intersection of administrative bias and bureaucratic discretion is well illustrated in the tax law case of Rhiannon O'Donnabhain, a transgender woman. The Internal Revenue Code allows medical expenses to be deducted for the costs to cure, mitigate, prevent, or diagnose physical or mental illness/defects. Cosmetic surgeries are specifically disallowed, and there has been debate about whether sex reassignment related procedures are cosmetic. O'Donnabhain underwent sex reassignment surgery and attempted to deduct these expenses on her taxes. The Internal Revenue Service disagreed. Thomas Moffitt of the IRS Office of Chief Counsel used his administrative discretion to outline the agency's position that sex reassignment surgery was not a deductible medical expense (Internal Revenue Service 2005). Moffitt's opinion had legal grounding, as he cited a lack of explicit statutory guidance in interpreting the tax law. However, he also referenced an editorial that was critical of sex reassignment and transsexualism from the religiously oriented opinion magazine *First Things*. Further, Moffitt failed to mention any of the scientific literature that supports sex reassignment surgery for treatment of gender dysphoria, raising significant concerns about possible bias in his decision-making. Despite this ruling by Moffitt, the Internal Revenue Service later lost the case on appeal (*O'Donnabhain v. Commissioner of Internal Revenue* 2010).

As in the preceding tax case, policies that ignore transgender identities might create obstacles to transgender equality because of bureaucratic discretion, a lack of information about trans people, and discriminatory treatment by street-level bureaucrats (e.g., Namaste 2000). Transgender people face a "thin, heterogeneous and ad hoc" policy framework (Dasti 2002). This incoherent policy framework results, in part, from the fragmented nature of the federal system in the United States. Additionally, the historic avoidance of clear policymaking on these issues by legislatures, combined with questions about the legitimacy of bureaucratic and judicial policymaking in controversial matters, has promoted a lack of coherence (Taylor 2007).

However, the lack of coherence and the fragmented nature of decision-making might also help LGBT activists gain support for transgender-inclusive policy change in some circumstances. For instance, in 2009, upon President Obama's inauguration, the Human Rights Campaign provided his administration with a document, *Blueprint for Positive Change*, that outlined agency level actions that the administration could take to make the lives of LGBT people better (Human Rights Campaign 2014). Often, as Robin Maril (2016), associate legal director for the Human Rights Campaign, notes, the goal is to get subregulatory guidance to protect people based on sexual orientation and gender identity. According to ACLU lobbyist Ian Thompson (2016), LGBT movement lobbyists commonly advocated on these issues with agency level staff, who were often appointees, and these conversations "percolated upwards." The White House could and would "tap the brakes or put pressure on the agency" in terms of the proposals. Some agencies, particularly the Departments of Justice, Education, Health and Human Services, and Housing and Urban Development were more aggressive in promoting transgender-inclusive policies than others during the Obama administration (Thompson 2016).[1]

Some of the agencies used court decisions, even if they were nonbinding on their agency, as legal cover for their transgender-inclusive policy changes. Generally, these decisions (e.g., *Smith v. City of Salem* 2004) found that gender identity discrimination is forbidden under the gender stereotyping prohibitions inherent under the protected class of sex in Title VII. This sort of cover to advance rights, through the discretionary use of nonbinding court precedent, is displayed in the Equal Employment Opportunity Commission's decision that Title VII prohibits gender-identity-based discrimination (*Macy v. Holder* 2012). We also see it in the Commission's *Lusardi v. Dept. of the Army* (2015) ruling that intentional misgendering of a transgender person and disregard for their new name constitutes sex-based discrimination and harassment. Similarly, the Department of Health and Human Services expansively interpreted the protected class of sex in Section 1557 of the Affordable Care Act to encompass gender identity in its rulemaking. In its final rule implementing Section 1557, the agency stated, "we noted that the approach taken in the proposed definition is consistent with the approach taken by the Federal government in similar matters" (Department of Health and Human Services 2016, 31384).[2]

Additionally, policies often have implications for transgender people even though they were not designed with regard to how they would affect transgender individuals. For example, many policies rely on a binary classification of sex in humans. For instance, men are required to register for the Selective Service while women are not. Multiuser restrooms and locker rooms are commonly divided by sex, as North Carolina legislated in HB2. There are separate prisons for men and for women. Birth certificates are required to register the sex of an individual at birth. Identification documents such as a passport or driver's license have a sex marker. Transgender people who try to fit into this binary system must deal with rules that govern when and if they might be able to switch from the male classification to the female classification or vice versa. For instance, when can a female-to-male transgender person legally change his identity to male and what is required to do that? What specific medical interventions are required and do you need a court order to approve this? Are the surgical requirements for female-to-male individuals more burdensome than those for male-to-female individuals given that surgeons can more easily construct a neovagina than create a phallus (Flynn 2006)?

Davis (2014) argues that sex classification policies, given the lack of consensus on how to define sex, subjectively allow government officials to deny public accommodations to people perceived to be transgender. Further, Namaste (2000, 187) notes that the judgment of transgender people based on their physical appearance, even if they attempt to conform to a binary sex classification system, can lead to bias. For the many transgender people that eschew or cannot, for reasons possibly beyond their control, conform to the rules of our binary gender system, interactions with government officials are particularly fraught (e.g., Spade 2015). People react negatively when individuals' appearances do not conform to binary gender expectations (e.g.,

Miller and Grollman 2015). Unfortunately, these subtle cues may trigger biased responses from government officials who have little knowledge of transgender issues and may not be sympathetic to transgender rights. It is well documented that transgender people of color face many more dangers than their white counterparts, such as higher rates of bullying (Daley et al. 2007), hate crimes (Witten and Eyler 1999), and murder (Grant, Mottet, and Tanis 2011). Factors such as racial, ethnic, or social class differences exacerbate bias and can further disadvantage individuals, especially when trying to navigate unclear administrative waters. Administrators might subtly move away from assisting or investing time to resolve problems faced by transgender individuals based on stereotypes about marginalized groups.

For those with nonbinary gender identities, such as gender queer individuals, nonconforming gender expressions may create even larger obstacles. Robin Maril (2016) notes that advocacy for those with nonbinary identities is especially difficult. Multiple interview respondents reported that gender queer is simply not understood by people and policymakers. North Carolina House majority leader Paul Stam (2016) referred to it as "nuts." Despite this, the movement continues to advocate for gender stereotyping protections. As Maril (2016) warns, "it is not a win to funnel people who don't want to be in a box into a box."

Executive Branch Leadership and Informal Power

Most government bureaucracy is wholly part of the executive branch. However, when talking about the executive branch, we normally think of its leadership—presidents, governors, additional state executives (e.g., state attorney generals), and mayors/city managers. The leadership in the executive branches of the national government, state governments, and localities has had an enormous effect on transgender rights. They can accomplish this because of the formal, indirect, and personal powers that elected executives have (Beyle and Ferguson 2008), such as high approval from the public, access to the media, and personal negotiation skills.[3]

Executive power is especially formidable in the U.S. presidency. Since the birth of the modern transgender rights movement in the late 1980s and early 1990s, the United States has witnessed four complete presidencies (George H. W. Bush, Bill Clinton, George W. Bush, Barack Obama) and the start of a fifth presidency under Donald Trump. These presidents have all grappled with various LGBT rights issues. High-profile battles have included the fight for HIV/AIDS policy and funding during the George H. W. Bush administration, the dashed hopes of gay service members under Bill Clinton's Don't Ask Don't Tell policy, and the fight over same-sex marriage that raged during the presidencies of Bill Clinton, George W. Bush, and Barack Obama.

Although some of these issues, most notably HIV/AIDS funding and same-sex marriage, affect the all of the LGBT community, the national executive branch rarely addressed transgender people and their policy concerns until recently. Indeed, prior to the Obama administration, the only attention given to gender identity was George W. Bush's veto threat of a gay and transgender-inclusive hate crimes bill (White House 2007) and President George H. W. Bush's signing of the Americans with Disabilities Act of 1990 that explicitly denied coverage based on transvestitism, transsexualism, and gender-identity-related disorders.[4] According to Deborah Sontag (2015) of the *New York Times*, no openly transgender person had ever visited the White House as an official guest prior to 2003 when George W. Bush graciously welcomed his former classmate, a transgender woman, Petra Leilani Akwai, to the White House.[5]

President Obama had, by far, the single largest impact on gay and transgender rights of any federal, state, or local executive prior to January 2017. His administration's attention to transgender rights was particularly striking because these issues were not even on the political radar for most his predecessors. They also did not receive much attention in either of his campaigns for the office. In his 2015 State of the Union Address, President Obama said:

> As Americans, we respect human dignity, even when we're threatened, which is why I have prohibited torture, and worked to make sure our use of new technology like drones is properly constrained. (Applause.) It's why we speak out against the deplorable anti-Semitism that has resurfaced in certain parts of the world. (Applause.) It's why we continue to reject offensive stereotypes of Muslims, the vast majority of whom share our commitment to peace. That's why we defend free speech, and advocate for political prisoners, and condemn the persecution of women, or religious minorities, or people who are lesbian, gay, bisexual or transgender. We do these things not only because they are the right thing to do, but because ultimately they will make us safer. (White House 2015)

With those words, President Obama became the first president to utter the word "transgender" in a State of the Union Address (Steinmetz 2015). While this was not the president's first time publicly saying the word "transgender" or the first time that he used the word in official communication, it was important for symbolic reasons. This was a high-profile speech and a constitutionally required message that occurred in front of a national audience. The usage of this single word was celebrated by the transgender community. As transgender activist Janet Mock said, "By speaking our community's name, the President pushes us all to recognize the existence and validity of trans people as Americans worthy of protection and our nation's resources" (Steinmetz 2015).

President Obama did not just give the transgender community symbolic victories, he and his administration changed policies as well. By the end of his term in January 2017, his administration had taken many policy actions to advance transgender rights, including, but not limited to, the following major policy changes (Human Rights Campaign 2016c):

- The Office of Personnel Management added gender identity to the equal opportunity employment policy for all federal jobs (2010).
- The Department of State eased standards for changing a gender marker on a passport (2010).
- The Social Security Administration stopped issuing "gender no match" letters to keep from unnecessarily outing prospective transgender employees (2011). It also made it easier to change the gender marker in agency records in 2013.
- The Equal Employment Opportunity Commission found that gender identity discrimination is a prohibited form of sex discrimination under Title VII (2012).
- The Department of Health and Human Services prohibited sexual orientation and gender identity discrimination under the Affordable Care Act (2013).
- President Obama signed an executive order prohibiting gender-identity-based discrimination (2014).
- The Departments of Education and Justice issued a guidance letter that protected transgender students under Title IX (2016).
- The Department of Defense lifted regulations barring transgender people from military service (2016).

Although these formal rules and executive guidances are critical in shaping the implementation of public policy, the informal power of executive leadership that is embedded in these actions is also important in influencing policy (Neustadt 1960). For example, in 2009 President Obama directed agencies to review what could be done to eliminate disparities between same-sex couples and married straight couples. Mara Keisling, executive director of the National Center for Transgender Equality, was frustrated at the time by the omission of transgender people in the executive memo, but later said "that memo turned out to be one of the most important things the president ever did" (Eilperin 2015). This memorandum and follow-up memos in 2010 and 2013 were important because they were interpreted by the agencies broadly as being pro-LGBT. As such, agencies reviewed over 1,000 statutes and hundreds of regulations for how they affected the lives of LGBT individuals (Eilperin 2015).

Many of the transgender rights advances happened with little public attention. The Obama administration was able to quietly advance many transgender rights policies in part because of the attention given to same-sex marriage. Most obviously, the decisions in the same-sex marriage cases of *United States v. Windsor* (2013), *Hollingsworth v. Perry* (2013), and *Obergefell v. Hodges* (2015) provided space for transgender rights. During the battle for same-sex marriage, advocates for transgender rights could educate members of the administration about the issues faced by transgender people and push for lower-profile policy changes (e.g., ending Social Security Administration gender no match letters in 2011). After marriage equality was achieved, there was less competition in the policy space. There were also few other major and achievable gay rights measures that the administration could work on after *Obergefell*. Transgender rights offered opportunities. Also important were the series of appellate court and EEOC decisions that interpreted the sex discrimination prohibition in Title VII of the Civil Rights Act of 1964 as protecting transgender people from gender based discrimination. These decisions emboldened the administration to take new executive actions by providing a legal rationale to justify policy changes.

Since President Obama faced a hostile Congress, with at least one chamber controlled by Republicans during the last six of his eight years in office, it is not surprising that he often relied on unilateral action to advance many of his policy initiatives. Of the major LGBT rights advances during his administration, with the notable exceptions of the sexual-orientation and gender-identity-inclusive Matthew Shepard and James Byrd Jr. Hate Crimes Prevention Act (2009), the Don't Ask, Don't Tell Repeal Act of 2010 (which was not transgender inclusive), and the Violence Against Women Reauthorization Act of 2013 (which included protections based on sexual orientation and gender identity), few gay and transgender rights advances came through the legislative process.

The Obama administration was forced to use the policy tools available to the president in his role as chief executive to advance his policy priorities during both of his terms. As Robin Maril (2016) noted, much of the Obama administration's executive action on LGBT rights started moving in 2011, after the Republican takeover of the House of Representatives. Dan Gurley, the Republican National Committee's deputy political director and national field director during the 2004 campaign, explained (2016) that intense Republican opposition to Obama's policies forced him to pursue unilateral action. Yet even through unilateral action, President Obama could rarely act alone. He had to persuade the executive branch to carry out his policy goals (Neustadt 1960). Gurley (2016) noted that

> [t]he President can set the tone from the top in a forceful way. Compliance is expected. There is an expectation that agencies will carry out policy—quietly or with a bang. If it is with a bang at the top, there is an expectation that it will be in agencies as well. The White House communicates to secretaries and their deputies. However, agencies can get out in front without guidance.

During his first term, Obama had been excoriated by gay supporters such as Andrew Sullivan (2009), who chided him for a "fierce urgency of whenever" on key LGBT rights issues ranging from the HIV travel ban, marriage equality, and Don't Ask Don't Tell. GetEQUAL activists such as Dan Choi and Autumn Sandeen even chained themselves to the White House fence (Montopoli 2010). Despite directing the Justice Department to stop defending the constitutionality of the Defense of Marriage Act (Savage and Stolberg 2011), Obama had also taken sharp criticism from gay rights advocates for his unwillingness to publicly back marriage equality (Curry 2012). However, as the tight reelection campaign of 2012 drew near, and as support for same-sex marriage grew, Obama "evolved" publicly on marriage (ABC News 2012). As a result, campaign contributions soared, particularly from the LGBT community, which became an important part of his political and financial base of support (Eggen 2012). Using the language of civil rights to justify his evolution on these issues, he was also able to persuade some laggard segments of the Democratic Party, particularly the NAACP and his African American supporters to back marriage equality and LGBT rights (Capehart 2012). At his Second Inaugural Address, President Obama said:

> We, the people, declare today that the most evident of truths—that all of us are created equal—is the star that guides us still; just as it guided our forebears through Seneca Falls, and Selma, and Stonewall; just as it guided all those men and women, sung and unsung, who left

footprints along this great Mall, to hear a preacher say that we cannot walk alone; to hear a King proclaim that our individual freedom is inextricably bound to the freedom of every soul on Earth. (Applause.)

It is now our generation's task to carry on what those pioneers began. For our journey is not complete until our wives, our mothers and daughters can earn a living equal to their efforts. (Applause.) Our journey is not complete until our gay brothers and sisters are treated like anyone else under the law—(applause)—for if we are truly created equal, then surely the love we commit to one another must be equal as well. (White House 2013)

Although he did not mention the word transgender in his Second Inaugural Address, President Obama's speech was a sharp departure from his First Inaugural Address where there was no mention of LGBT rights whatsoever (White House 2009).[6] After an uneven performance on LGBT issues during a first term, he strongly and eloquently connected the LGBT movement and the push for marriage equality to the other historic civil rights movements.[7]

Beyond his rhetorical flourishes, the Obama administration also aggressively moved to advance LGBT rights during his second term. From filing amicus briefs supporting same-sex marriage with the Supreme Court to the executive actions protecting transgender rights already alluded to in this chapter, the administration built an impressive legacy. However, until late in his administration much of the change on transgender rights was accomplished through very low-profile administrative action that lessened the likelihood for conflict expansion (Eilperin 2015). It was primarily in the latter years of his second term that Obama became more forceful on transgender rights. Indeed, it was on May 13, 2016 that his Department of Education, joined by the Department of Justice's Civil Rights Division, issued its bold and highly controversial guidance letter on school district obligations under Title IX.[8] Additionally, in perhaps one of the most high-profile actions taken by the administration, as Dan Gurley (2016) humorously noted, Obama "parachuted his Attorney General" into North Carolina in 2016 to combat the antitransgender legislation known as HB2. That much of the presidential action on transgender rights came late in his administration was not an issue. Even toward the very end of a presidency and with their powers diminished, presidents typically use their unilateral powers to affect policy change going forward (Howell and Mayer 2005). The Obama administration adhered to this strategy in its final days as it fought challenges to transgender inclusion under the Affordable Care Act (Dresden 2017). The president also spoke about transgender rights in his Farewell Address (White House 2017d), and he even appointed two transgender people to government posts on January 17, 2017 (Sopelsa 2017).

As Matt Foreman (2016) noted, President Obama's executive branch rule and policy changes affected gay and transgender people's lives. His changes moved beyond the policy realm. President Obama also advanced the cause of gay and transgender rights politically. Robin Maril (2016) stated that "Obama's actions have made it harder [for Democrats] to be anti-transgender." The fierce reaction in some states to the Department of Education's guidance on Title IX provided an opportunity for public opinion leadership and public education about transgender identities (e.g., Geer 1996). The president, at a town hall meeting in Elkhart, Indiana, defended his administration's actions on transgender people and bathrooms at length (White House 2016b):

> Q My question to you, Mr. President—I'm a strong believer in equal rights for everyone—a very strong believer in that. I was wondering, though, with all the pressing issues that you have before you right now, why is the issue of which bathroom a person uses such an issue?
>
> THE PRESIDENT: Well, you know what, it's a great question. Somehow people think I made it an issue. I didn't make it an issue. There are a lot of things that are more pressing, you're absolutely right. What happened, and what continues to happen, is you have transgender kids in schools, and they get bullied, and they get ostracized, and it's tough for them. And we're of a generation where that stuff was all out of sight and out of mind, and so people suffered silently. But now they're out in the open.
>
> And the question then is, schools are asking us, the Department of Education, for guidance, how should we deal with this? And my answer is that we should deal with this issue the same way we'd want it dealt with if it was our child. And that is to try to create an environment of some dignity and kindness for these kids. And that's sort of the bottom line. I have to just say what's in my heart, but I also have to look at what's the law. And my best interpretation of what our laws and our obligations are is that we should try to accommodate these kids so that they are not in a vulnerable situation.
>
> Now, I understand that people, for religious beliefs or just general discomfort, might disagree. And I'm not the one who's making a big issue of it, but if the school districts around the country

ask me, what do you think we should do, then what we're going
to do is tell them, let's find a way to accommodate them in a way
that makes sure that these kids are not excluded and ostracized.

Through the president's public statements, and actions by the attorney general, the administration was able to make its position on transgender rights
known to a public whose attitudes on the topic were ambiguous. His positions appear to be influencing public opinion, especially among Democrats
(e.g., Lenz 2009). In our June 2015 national survey, we observed that 46
percent of Democrats and 36 percent of independents disagreed with the
statement, "Transgender people should only be allowed to use public restrooms that are consistent with the sex listed on their driver's license/state ID
card." A year later, following the publicity over North Carolina's HB2 and
the administration's strong response, we found that 62 percent of Democrats
and 47 percent of independents supported policies to "allow transgender
individuals to use the restroom that corresponds with their gender identity,"
as opposed to restroom access policies based on birth gender. Based on our
polling results and the high-profile actions of the administration, we believe
that President Obama provided important opinion leadership on transgender rights.

President Obama's concern with his legacy, like many presidents (Light
1999), may have been an important motivating factor for his administration's actions on gay and transgender rights. While presidential legacies are
dependent on resources and opportunities available to a president, historians
have looked favorably on advancements in civil rights (Light 1984; Shull
1999). Indeed, many of our interview respondents and the White House
itself confirmed the importance of LGBT rights as a central component of
Obama's legacy building efforts (White House 2016a). After 2010, President
Obama faced a Congress intent on denying him legislative victories, leaving
him few opportunities to pursue items requiring legislative action. In his
second term and no longer facing short-term reelection concerns, he was
liberated to pursue policy goals related to his legacy (Cohen 1997). Though
it is fair to say that LGBT rights have roiled American politics for decades,
it is also accurate to note that public opinion on most LGBT issues has
become far more positive over time (e.g., Brewer 2008). This made it easier
for President Obama to support LGBT rights, in the broad sense, because
presidents have an incentive to be responsive to longer-term trends in public
opinion (e.g., Cohen 1997). Attitudes on transgender rights are more uncertain than most LGBT rights issues (as we discuss in earlier chapters), but
the president had greater latitude after 2012 to engage in opinion leadership
(e.g., Brewer 2008; Geer 1996) and let history judge him. For an issue that

had just reached a "tipping point" (Steinmetz 2014), the president could follow Lyndon Johnson's example on civil rights.

We also think that President Obama's motivations were not just about his legacy or rewarding supporters or even spending what political capital he had where he could. As our interview respondent Dan Gurley (2016) noted, "Maybe he is doing it because he thinks it is the right thing to do." Similarly, Governor Jack Markell (2016) discussed this theme with regard to his own legacy as governor of Delaware. He noted that he did not "sit around thinking about his legacy." During our conversation, Markell made it clear that he thought supporting transgender rights was the right choice and that it would make the lives of his citizens better. We believe that President Obama thought that backing transgender rights was the right thing to do. He did not have to fight this policy battle. He chose to do it. While we unsuccessfully tried to interview President Obama, we did receive a letter via e-mail from the White House noting the president's personal attention to this issue.[9] This letter listed the many actions that his administration had taken in support of transgender rights. It also discussed the arc of civil rights in the United States, the challenges faced by the transgender community, and the push for equality for all citizens. At the end of the letter, the president stated, "Please know I will keep pushing to advance the safety and dignity of every American as long as I hold this Office and beyond. Sincerely, Barack Obama." After he left office in 2017, we again attempted to interview President Obama. However, his press office declined the invitation but noted that the issue of transgender rights "was a topic dear to him."[10]

Executive Powers

In addition to the personal powers that presidents and governors can bring to bear on transgender rights policies, executive leaders from every level of government also have considerable formal authority to shape public policies. Here, we review the formal powers that have been used to shape transgender rights policies.

Veto

Presidents, governors, and even some mayors can block legislation that they disagree with, usually subject to legislative override provisions. One instance of a governor using his veto powers to block antitransgender legislation occurred in South Dakota in 2016. Governor Dennis Daugaard, a Republican, vetoed a bill that would have required transgender children enrolled in public schools to use bathrooms and locker rooms that matched their sex at birth (Smith 2016). Prior to Daugaard's veto, he met with a group of transgender people, including one individual whom he knew from his work at the Children's Home Society (Ferguson 2016). That meeting "helped put a human face" on the issues (Daugaard as quoted in Ferguson 2016). Similarly, Georgia governor Nathan Deal, a Republican, vetoed a bill that would have allowed discrimination against gay and transgender people under the guise of religious liberty (Somashekhar 2016). At the time of their vetoes, both Daugaard and Deal were in their second terms and were term limited.

Of course, not all gubernatorial vetoes have benefited the transgender community. In California in 2005, Governor Arnold Schwarzenegger (Republican) vetoed a bill allowing same-sex marriage (Gledhill 2005). We note this veto because same-sex marriage, despite commonly being thought of as a gay rights issue, clearly benefits transgender individuals as well. With same-sex marriage, they too can marry the partner of their choice without fear of having their sex or their partner's legal sex questioned and marriages nullified or blocked in cases like *In re Estate of Gardiner* (2002) or *In re Application for Marriage License for Nash* (2003). Additionally, in 2005, Hawaii governor Linda Lingle, another Republican, vetoed a gender-identity-inclusive bill that would have offered employment nondiscrimination protections to transgender people (Human Rights Campaign 2005). At times, just the threat of a veto is enough to force legislatures to modify legislation (e.g., Cameron 2000). For example, in a statement of administration policy, President George W. Bush threatened to veto a gay- and transgender-inclusive hate crimes bill (White House 2007). Likely as a result, that bill, H.R. 1592, was not taken up by the Senate despite passage by the House.

Appointment Powers

Presidents and governors have wide powers to nominate and appoint officials to various capacities. For the president, this includes, subject to the advice and consent of the Senate, federal district and appellate judges, justices to the Supreme Court, and the principal officers of government. In total, the president can appoint (directly, indirectly, or with approval of the Senate) approximately 8,000 individuals (Committee on Oversight and Government Reform 2012). Appointments are important because "personnel is policy" (Moynihan and Roberts 2010, 574); they have the power to shape, in accordance with administration policy priorities, the implementation of laws and the promulgation of regulations. In turn, political appointees can broadly affect the staffing of the bureaucracy because they can fill certain positions within their agencies with "Schedule C" appointees and noncareer Senior Executive Service personnel who are approved by the Office of Presidential Personnel.

We interviewed (2016) one such Schedule C appointee, Maya Rupert, who served as senior policy advisor to the secretary at the U.S. Department of Housing and Urban Development. As part of her responsibilities, Rupert provided Secretary Julián Castro with important policy information about gay and transgender rights given her previous work as policy director for the National Center for Lesbian Rights. She noted that the Victory Fund (an LGBT rights group that helps elect LGBT candidates to office) was very effective in getting LGBT-identified individuals placed into positions of authority during the Obama administration. These individuals "affected the culture of the organizations." Further, the Office of Personnel Management had a "bully pulpit on how people are talking and thinking" about transgender equality.

Importantly, President Obama's choice of Loretta Lynch to serve as attorney general made an impact on the development of transgender rights. On May 9, 2016, in response to North Carolina's passage of a law (HB2) that restricted restroom access for many transgender people, Lynch powerfully defended the rights and the dignity of transgender people in the announcement of civil rights enforcement action (Phillips 2016). The text of her speech, contained in appendix D, combined with the enforcement action (a federal civil rights lawsuit) taken against North Carolina, is likely the single most powerful affirmation of transgender rights by a ranking appointed or elected national official to date.

Other Obama administration cabinet secretaries also made important policy decisions that advanced the movement. For instance, in 2010, Secretary of State Hillary Clinton loosened State Department rules that governed gender markers on passports (Kruse 2016). This policy change was substantively important because it allowed transgender people to more easily access gender-conforming identification papers. Indeed, one transgender person felt so thankful for the policy change that she sent Secretary Clinton a thank you letter that discussed the importance of this for her life and business (Wikileaks 2016). The policy change also held symbolic significance, as National Center for Transgender Equality director Mara Keisling noted, "We had never, and I mean never, had the federal government do a pro-trans policy before" (Kruse 2016). Other appointees, such as Julián Castro, secretary of the Department of Housing and Urban Development (HUD), made policy changes as well. Under Castro, HUD advanced a rule that ensured that homeless shelters accept all individuals regardless of their gender identity. In the announcement of this rule, Castro said,

> Today, we take another important step to ensure full acceptance of transgender and gender non-conforming individuals in the programs HUD supports. . . . This new rule will ensure equal access to the very programs that help to prevent homelessness for persons who are routinely forced to choose between being placed in facilities against their gender identity or living on our streets. (HUD 2016)

In addition, some executive appointments can carry important symbolic weight to the transgender movement. In late 2009, President Obama made the first presidential appointments of openly transgender persons, Dylan Orr and Amanda Simpson, to positions in the Department of Labor and Department of Commerce (New York Times 2015). Similarly, in 2015, the Obama administration hired the first openly transgender person, Raffi Freedman-Gurspan, to serve in a White House staff position (Shear 2015). Sarah McBride was the first openly transgender individual to intern at the White House (Skiles 2016).

Although we are still in the early days of the Trump administration, he has not nominated open proponents of transgender issues (NBC News 2017a). However, three high-ranking public officials that he selected are known opponents of transgender rights. Attorney General Jeff Sessions, Mark Green as secretary of the army (his nomination was withdrawn), and Roger Severino to lead the Office of Civil Rights at the Department of Health and Human Services came under criticism for statements made against the morality of transgender individuals (NBC News 2017a). In fact, Green eventually removed himself from consideration because of harsh media attention that he received for statements that he made about people of color, as well as about gay and transgender individuals (BBC News 2017). Trump administration agency heads have begun to remove some of the policies from the Obama administration. For instance, even before the end of President Trump's first 100 days in office, the Department of Justice and the Department of Education rescinded the Obama administration's Title IX guidance letter on transgender students (NBC News 2017a). Further, Attorney General Sessions has been at the forefront of efforts to rollback protections with his guidance that

Title VII is not transgender inclusive (Savage 2017b) and via a memorandum expansively interpreting religious freedom in a way that may be harmful to the LGBT community (Zapotosky and Bailey 2017).

Executive leaders also often have the authority to nominate judges. Given the importance of judicial decisions to the evolution of transgender rights, these nominations are of keen interest to the movement. As a counterma-joritarian institution, the federal courts have been especially important to protecting the rights of minority groups. As noted in the previous chapter, with lifetime appointments to the bench, presidents can influence the arc of a movement for decades (well after the nominating president leaves office). For instance, two of President Obama's nominees to the Fourth Circuit of Appeals, Senior Circuit Court Judge Andre Davis and Judge Henry Floyd, were in the majority of the three-judge panel in *G.G. v. Gloucester County School Board* (2016). The dissenting opinion in the decision was written by a nominee of George H. W. Bush, Paul Niemeyer. Judges thought to be hostile to transgender rights can also block administration initiatives, particularly when lawsuits are strategically brought up in districts with sympathetic judges (i.e., venue shopping). One such federal judge in Texas, Reed O'Connor, was nominated to the bench by George W. Bush in 2007 and subsequently blocked implementation of the Obama administration's Department of Education guidelines on transgender people and Title IX with a nationwide injunction pending trial (Korte 2016). Judge O'Connor also blocked implementation, via an injunction, of the Obama administration's regulations under the Affordable Care Act, which we discuss further in the chapter on health care policy, that provided nondiscrimination protections to gay and transgender patients (Gorman 2016). Given the views of President Trump's early judicial nominations, notably Neil Gorsuch to the Supreme Court (Dejean 2017) and Damien Schiff to the Court of Federal Claims (Marcus 2017), we anticipate that his effect on transgender rights in the federal judiciary will be long, and likely negative. This is especially true given the advanced ages of many Supreme Court Justices at the beginning of the Court's 2017 term, particularly Ruth Bader Ginsburg, Stephen Breyer, and Anthony Kennedy. Indeed, as of this writing, Justice Kennedy has retired and will likely be replaced by a conservative. This is important because Kennedy is the author of many of the important pro-LGBT rights decisions issued by the Court, such as *Lawrence*, *Romer*, *Windsor*, and *Obergefell*. If President Trump were to win reelection in 2020 and serve a second full term, it is easily conceivable that he might nominate the majority of Supreme Court justices.

Gubernatorial appointment powers are limited by the relatively more fractured nature of executive authority in the states. Most states separately elect multiple executive branch officials (e.g., attorney general or secretary of state) with narrower portfolios of responsibility than the governor. Of these independently elected cabinet officers, attorneys general have had an important impact on transgender rights given their ability to bring lawsuits challenging federal law on behalf of their states. Texas attorney general Ken Paxton, a Republican, led the fight against the Obama administration's Title IX guidance to schools, which expanded the rights of transgender people, and against the transgender-inclusive regulations promulgated under the Affordable Care Act (Korte 2016; Gorman 2016). An attorney general might also decline to defend a state law that he or she finds questionable under federal law or constitutional principles. While serving as North Carolina's attorney general, Roy Cooper, a Democrat, refrained from defending the state in multiple lawsuits challenging North Carolina's antigay and antitransgender HB2 (Blythe 2016). As governor, Cooper, along with his successor as attorney general, Joshua Stein (D), subsequently entered into a proposed consent agreement with plaintiffs in the ongoing litigation over HB2 and the still discriminatory legislation that repealed it, HB142. If the federal district court approves the consent agreement, HB142 would be interpreted to not bar transgender people from using gender-corresponding public facilities that are under control of the executive branch (Lambda Legal 2017a).

As the chief legal officer in the state, an attorney general may also issue official opinions that, while not legally binding, can shape state or even national policy. Stryker (2008, 44–45) notes how a 1950s era opinion by California attorney general Edmund "Pat" Brown shaped trans treatment access in the United States for decades because it said that genital modification of transsexual individuals might constitute criminal mayhem and left doctors open to criminal liability. Virginia attorney general Mark Herring, a Democrat, controversially issued an opinion asserting that, despite not being given explicit statutory authority, local school boards may create sexual-orientation and gender-identity-inclusive nondiscrimination policies (Lavers 2015). Conversely, his predecessor, Virginia attorney general Ken Cuccinelli, a Republican, offered an opinion that sexual orientation and gender identity protections at state colleges and universities were not authorized under state law (Helderman 2010a).

Other elected state offices can also affect transgender rights. For instance, in 2011, Michigan secretary of state Ruth Johnson, a Republican, made it more difficult for transgender people to obtain sex marker changes on their driver's licenses. Her department's policy required an amended birth certificate before a license with a gender-conforming sex marker could be issued (Erickson 2015). The policy was challenged in court by the ACLU, and Johnson subsequently altered the policy to allow a passport, in addition to an amended birth certificate or a court order, in changing the sex of an individual (Baldas 2016). Independently elected officials might also set office nondiscrimination policies that are more inclusive or restrictive (within their discretion under state or federal law) than the rest of the state government. While running for attorney general in Virginia, Mark Herring specifically noted that, if elected, his office policy would be sexual orientation and gender identity inclusive (Lavers 2013).

Executive Orders and Memoranda

In their roles as chief executives of their bureaucracies, the president, governors, mayors, and city managers often have the authority to set policies by issuing executive orders or, in the case of the president, by signing presidential memoranda that restrict or enhance the rights of transgender people. For instance, in 2011 President Obama signed a presidential memorandum "directing all agencies engaged abroad to ensure that U.S. diplomacy and foreign assistance promote and protect the human rights of LGBT persons" (White House 2011). As previously noted in this chapter, in 2009 President Obama also directed the agencies to investigate and address the inequalities faced by same-sex couples. Conversely, President Trump issued a presidential memorandum directing the secretary of defense and secretary of homeland security to reinstate a prior ban on military service by transgender individuals until such time that removal of the ban would not "hinder military effectiveness and lethality, disrupt unit cohesion, or tax military resources" (White House 2017c). Over time, governors have also turned to executive orders as a means to protect transgender individuals within their states. Additionally, mayors in several major cities have issued executive orders to extend protections to local government employees (Sellers 2014a). Although ordinances are far more common among local governments (see chapter 9), executive actions have added protections as well.

One of the most common ways in which executive orders have affected the gay and transgender communities is through the treatment of current and prospective public employees. As of this writing, there are no explicit legal protections for gay and transgender people under national laws governing employment discrimination. Similarly, the majority of states lack these protections. However, it is not uncommon for executives within such jurisdictions to offer such protections to employees within the governmental bureaucracy via the use of executive orders. For instance, given the state legislature's inability to pass an employment discrimination law that included gender identity in 2009, Delaware governor Jack Markell, a Democrat, signed Executive Order 8 to include gender identity in discrimination protections for state employees (Delaware Governor's Office 2009; Markell 2016). Virginia governor Terry McAuliffe, also a Democrat, chose to issue a similar sexual-orientation and gender-identity-inclusive order, Executive Order Number One, upon taking office in 2014 (Virginia Governor's Office 2014). McAuliffe's actions were in stark contrast to that of his predecessor, Governor Bob McDonnell, a Republican, who removed earlier sexual-orientation-inclusive language from his executive order regarding discrimination in state government employment (Helderman 2010b).

As with all executive orders, transgender inclusive or exclusive orders can easily be undermined or overturned by a successor. Ohio governor John Kasich, a Republican, let lapse a sexual-orientation and gender-identity-inclusive nondiscrimination order from his predecessor, Governor Ted Strickland, a Democrat. Governor Kasich subsequently issued an executive order that included the sexual-orientation protections, but eliminated those for gender identity (Columbus Dispatch 2011). Additionally, the legality of executive orders might be challenged in court. In a case highlighting the importance of independently elected executives at the state level, Louisiana's attorney general, Jeff Landry (Republican), successfully challenged the state-level constitutionality of Governor John Bel Edwards's (Democrat) executive order that banned discrimination against gay and transgender state employees (Reuters 2016).

Executive leadership at the local level is determined in a number of different structural arrangements (e.g., council-manager systems, strong mayor-council systems); and local governments, under the advice or direction of a city manager or strong mayor, might choose to offer such protections to their employees. This might occur despite a lack of state-level action if it is not preempted by state law. In their report on municipal policies, HRC (2015) found that 177 of 406 cities included in the study provided these internal protections for public employees.

Nondiscrimination protections might also be extended beyond the confines of the particular state or federal bureaucracy through restrictions on contracts with outside vendors. For instance, in 2014, President Obama signed Executive Order 13672, which in addition to prohibiting gender-identity-based discrimination in the federal bureaucracy, also prohibited federal contractors and subcontractors from discriminating because of sexual orientation or gender identity (White House 2014). However, some of its effects were short-lived. Despite early assurances that enforcement of the ban would continue (White House 2017a), President Trump weakened compliance guidelines for federal contractors in March 2017 (White House 2017b; O'Hara 2017). States and cities have also regulated the personnel policies of their contractors. For instance, Virginia governor Terry McAuliffe signed an executive order banning state contracts with vendors that engage in discrimination against LGBT individuals (Vozzella 2017). Through 2015, at least ninety-three localities had adopted policies that required gender-identity-inclusive protections for government contractors (Human Rights Campaign 2015).

Gubernatorial Action

The president's executive leadership on transgender rights has received the majority of attention in this chapter, but state governors also play important leadership roles in shaping public policy on these issues. Drawing on a range of personal and formal powers that give them immense influence over public policy (Beyle and Ferguson 2008), governors are said to have the "best job in politics" (Rosenthal 2013). In fact, governors, compared to presidents, are significantly more likely to achieve their policy goals (Kousser and Phillips 2012), and thus can present viable advocacy opportunities for the transgender rights movement.

Delaware governor Jack Markell (2016) discussed this with us when he talked of using his political resources to help pass a 2013 transgender-inclusive nondiscrimination law in Delaware. Governor Markell spoke publicly about transgender rights and conferred with legislators about the bill. He "felt an obligation to explain" why he supported transgender inclusion in state nondiscrimination laws. Governor Markell's support for this issue is personal. One of his friends and supporters is a transgender person. He said that while he was philosophically inclined to support transgender inclusion, knowing Sarah McBride (a transgender person and family friend since she was in the seventh grade) helped with his understanding of the issues and with the authenticity of his support.

Indeed, state governments have been quite active in creating LGBT policies over the past four decades. Governors turned to executive orders to create protections for sexual orientation in the 1970s through the 1990s. This strategy was common when the LGBT movement struggled for the public's attention and support, leaving state legislatures with little incentive to pass statutory protections. Pennsylvania governor Milton Shapp (D) began this process when he issued an executive order in 1975 to protect public employees from discrimination based on sexual orientation. In the following two decades, governors from across the country followed this trend of extending protections to employees via executive orders. As Sellers (2016) finds, this was common for sexual-orientation-inclusive nondiscrimination policies— nearly thirty governors issued executive orders to protect sexual orientation or gender identity, or both. This happened when general *employment* protections for sexual orientation were broadly accepted in the country, but much of the country was staunchly against same-sex marriage and allowing gay adoption (Brewer 2008). Transgender identities were not even discussed in polling during much of this era.

These executive orders served as an early step forward in changing the culture within states. Many states with sexual-orientation protections established through executive orders eventually went on to adopt legislation that prohibited discrimination in several policy areas. Yet gender-identity-inclusive policies followed a different pattern of adoption than did sexual-orientation protections. One notable difference is that states did not adopt transgender protections until decades after Governor Shapp's original sexual-orientation-inclusive order. Minnesota passed the first state statute to protect transgender individuals in 1993, and Iowa governor Tom Vilsack (D) issued the first executive order to protect transgender public employees in 1999. Table 6.1 shows that these protections were rare prior to the 2000s. Unlike for sexual-orientation-inclusive nondiscrimination policies, gender-identity-inclusive legislation (rather than executive orders) continues to be the most common form of statewide protections for transgender workers. However, governors in states whose legislatures are controlled by the Republican Party, or by social conservatives, have turned to executive orders in the past two decades to protect transgender state employees from discrimination. As Mayer (1999) and Deering and Maltzman (1999) note, executive orders are an alternative for governors that confront an oppositional legislature.

Figure 6.1 shows that much of the executive attention to transgender rights occurred in the Midwest and Northeast. Pennsylvania governor Edward Rendell (D) ran his gubernatorial campaign on a platform of lower taxes and education reform, but early during his first year in office he issued an executive order to extend protections to include gender identity. Some Midwestern states soon followed suit. Indiana governor Joe Kernan (D) issued an executive order in 2004 and there was a flurry of activity in 2007 when governors in Kansas, Maryland, Michigan, and Ohio issued executive orders in the span of six months.[11]

This type of executive action was not new to the Midwestern states. Ohio had governor-issued sexual-orientation-inclusive protections for over a decade (1983–99). Yet partisan politics explains the inconsistent coverage in the state. Governor Bob Taft (R) removed these protections during his administration, but his successor, Ted Strickland (D), reinstated the policy in 2007 and added "gender identity" and "gender expression" to the list of protected classes. As previously noted, John Kasich (R) then removed those transgender-inclusive protections when he entered office. Kansas also saw their transgender protections rescinded once a Republican governor, Sam Brownback, took office in 2011. For Michigan governor Jennifer Granholm (D), her executive order built on a previous order in 2003 that banned discrimination based on sexual orientation.

The spread of transgender protections continued along the East Coast. Following a sexual-orientation-inclusive executive order by Parris Glendening (D) in 1995 and a statewide sexual-orientation-inclusive nondiscrimination law in 2001, Maryland governor Martin O'Malley issued a gender-identity-inclusive executive order in 2007. Governors also issued executive orders in Delaware (2009), New York (2009), and Massachusetts (2011). The orders in Delaware and Massachusetts were quickly followed up by transgender-

TABLE 6.1. Transgender-Inclusive Protections

State	Executive Order	Governor
Delaware	2009	Jack Markell
Indiana	2004	Joe Kernan
Iowa	1999	Tom Vilsack
Kansas	2007	Kathleen Sebelius
Kentucky	2003	Paul Patton
Kentucky	2008	Steve Beshear
Louisiana	2016	John Bel Edwards
Maryland	2007	Martin O'Malley
Massachusetts	2011	Deval Patrick
Michigan	2007	Jennifer Granholm
Montana	2016	Steve Bullock
New Hampshire	2016	Margaret Wood Hassan
New York	2009	David Paterson
North Carolina	2016	Pat McCrory
Ohio	2007	Ted Strickland
Pennsylvania	2003	Ed Rendell
Virginia	2014	Terry McAuliffe

Notes: Iowa Supreme Court nullified in 2000; Kansas removed in 2015; Kentucky removed in 2006; Louisiana order in 2016 was ruled unconstitutional later in the same year; Ohio removed in 2011; New York promulgated regulations in 2015 that define "sex" in New York's human rights law to include gender identity; and North Carolina restricts public accommodations by not allowing transgender individuals to use bathrooms that match their gender identity.

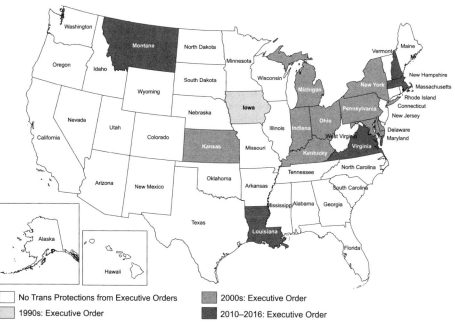

Figure 6.1. Protection Spread via Executive Orders 1999–2016. (Sellers 2016.)
Notes: States are coded based on when a governor first issued a transgender-inclusive executive order. Some states' executive orders are no longer in effect due to court rulings or subsequent governors revoking of protections. NC not included.

inclusive nondiscrimination statutes. Change was rapid in Massachusetts as Governor Deval Patrick (D) made transgender rights a major component of his reelection bid. He issued an executive order in February 2011 after winning reelection, and signed H.3810, "An Act Relative to Gender Identity," in November of the same year (State Library of Massachusetts 2017). Delaware governor Jack Markell (D) also signed transgender-inclusive legislation into law, just four years after his executive order. In 2014, Governor O'Malley signed a gender identity inclusive nondiscrimination law in Maryland, seven years after his executive order.

Governors continue to issue executive orders in the 2010s. Some governors in states unlikely to adopt transgender-inclusive legislation anytime soon issued executive orders upon entering office. Virginia governor Terry McAuliffe (D) did so in his early days in office in 2014. And in 2016 alone, governors in the ideologically conservative states of Louisiana, Montana, New Hampshire, and North Carolina issued executive orders adding protections. Within hours of taking office in January 2018, Virginia governor

Ralph Northam issued his first executive order and it prohibited gender identity and sexual orientation based discrimination in state employment and in the provision of public services. The order also directed a review of state procurement policies to ensure that they align with gay and transgender inclusive nondiscrimination guidelines (Commonwealth of Virginia Office of the Governor 2018).

The gay and transgender inclusive executive order issued by North Carolina governor Pat McCrory (R) requires special attention. It came in the wake of North Carolina's HB2 legislation, known as the "bathroom bill." In part, North Carolina Republicans, who dominated the state's legislature and controlled the governor's mansion, passed this legislation because they felt that it offered an electoral advantage in the upcoming 2016 elections (Hood 2016; Stam 2016). However, HB2 generated a public relations crisis that engulfed the state and the Republican politicians who championed the discriminatory legislation. Governor McCrory, in particular, was demonized and became the public face of HB2. There were many boycotts by businesses, entertainers, other governments, and advocacy organizations (Bort 2016). The state faced lawsuits and, as previously noted, the Obama administration challenged the law.

In the face of the intense blowback, Governor McCrory attempted to quell the furor by issuing an executive order to protect gay and transgender state workers (Shoichet 2016). Consequently, this executive order was less about adding protections than about diverting negative attention from the state and from Governor McCrory. The executive order held that the state could not discriminate against gay and transgender employees, but it also reinforced that transgender individuals must use the bathroom of their birth sex (Harrison 2016).[12] Even though the order was unpopular with many Republicans (Hood 2016), it remained in place during the remainder of the McCrory administration. Upon taking office after defeating McCrory in the 2016 election, Democratic governor Roy Cooper did not remove the protections for gay and transgender state workers. In fact, on October 18, 2017 he eliminated any discriminatory aspects of McCrory's earlier executive order via a new and more expansive executive order (Harrison 2017). Thus, part of HB2's legacy, even after its repeal in 2017, is a limited expansion of protections for LGBT individuals.

Executive Orders versus Legislation Adoption

While the 2000s and 2010s saw massive expansion in the number of statewide protections for transgender people, not all protections are created equally. Statutory nondiscrimination protection is preferable to unilateral executive action because it can offer protection beyond public employees. Executive orders also do not provide for permanent protections. In some states, the protections expire shortly after the administration ends, while in other states the executive order remains in effect until a subsequent governor removes them (Council of State Governments 2017). This occurred in Ohio and Kentucky.

Another concern is the authority of executives to act unilaterally. This varies depending on the executive powers in each state's constitution, but several governors had their executive orders blocked by their respective state supreme courts. For instance, the courts invalidated Iowa governor Tom Vilsack's 1999 executive order just a year after he issued it. Iowa governors had used executive orders to protect "sexual orientation" since 1975 (Sellers 2016), but Vilsack's order was the first to include "gender identity" as well. The courts determined that Iowa governors did not have authority to make such personnel changes in personnel rules unless approved by the legislature or public. As previously noted in this chapter, Louisiana governor John Bel Edwards (D) ran into similar problems in 2016 when the state attorney challenged the order and state courts deemed it to run afoul of the Louisiana Constitution.

Figure 6.2 shows that there is little overlap between states that add protections through legislation and executive orders. Only four of the states have both forms of protections. In all the cases, governors issued executive orders prior to the adoption of legislation. Massachusetts waited just months, while Maryland did not adopt comparable legislation until several years after O'Malley's executive order. Figure 6.2 also hints at a relationship of region to the type of policy adopted. Specifically, West Coast states predominantly adopted legislation. Montana's governor issued an executive order in 2016, but the remaining states passed statutes to create nondiscrimination policies. Even more conservative states, such as New Mexico and Utah, adopted legislation to protect transgender citizens from discrimination in a number of areas, such as housing and employment. The reverse pattern occurs along the Rust Belt. Governors in many of these states added protections through executive orders. More broadly, looking at the Midwestern and Northeastern states, these states have just one form of protection. Southern states typically do not have any protections, but some governors have issued executive orders.

The multiple policy vehicles for protections create an interesting schism across the states. States that adopt legislation tend to be the most liberal across the country (Sharp 2005). The states without legislation are split between those with no protections and limited protections through executive orders. Whether a state has protections or not is not simply a political

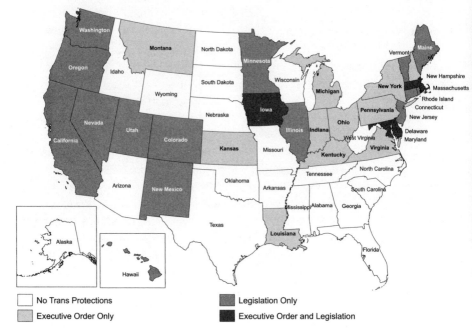

Figure 6.2. Protection Spread via Executive Orders or Legislation. (Information on legislation adoption is provided by Human Rights Campaign (2017), while executive order use is derived from Sellers (2016).

Notes: States are coded based on whether executive orders or legislation was ever on the books. No legislature rescinded protections, but some states' executive orders are no longer in effect.

control question. Liberal legislatures adopt transgender protections (Taylor et al. 2012), but sometimes governors step up to fill the void in moderate to conservative states. This is consistent with the strategic model proposed by executive branch scholars. The strategic model suggests that governors issue executive orders during divided government or when the legislature is more conservative (Deering and Maltzman 1999). The issuance of executive orders, when entering office, serves as part of an overall effort to shape their administration in accordance with their vision. Thus, governors act out of a perceived stalemate in the legislature.

Why Do Governors Issue Executive Orders?

In this section, we explore the factors that lead governors to issue executive orders protecting transgender individuals from discrimination in state government with an event history analysis covering the years 1993–2016.[13] While the first trans-inclusive executive order was issued in 1999, we start our analysis with the adoption of the first statewide transgender-inclusive nondiscrimination law in 1993. The model considers both political and social factors, as well as features specific to the governor to understand why they extend protections through executive orders. The dependent variable in our model is a dichotomous indicator for issuance of a gender-identity-inclusive executive order.

The political factors include the partisan makeup of the legislature as well as the party of the governor, collected from the *Book of States* for each year. Democratic Governor is simply a dichotomous indicator of whether the state had a Democratic governor. Lower Chamber (percent Democrats) and Upper Chamber (percent Democrats) control for the composition of the legislature. We expect governors to pursue legislation, rather than issue an executive order, when there are more Democrats in either of the chambers. More specifically, we expect governors to issue executive orders when legislation appears unlikely to pass (Deering and Maltzman 1999; Fine and Warber 2012). Therefore, we also control for Divided Government. It is coded as 0 if a political party has the governor's office and holds a majority within both chambers of the legislature (unified government). We also control for whether the state already has existing inclusive nondiscrimination law

Social factors also sway politicians' behavior. The Evangelical Population (percent within state) is drawn from the Association of Religion Data Archives.[14] We expect that states with higher percentages of Evangelicals to be more socially conservative, and thus governors will be less likely to issue executive orders. Conversely, governors should issue executive orders in state with more liberal citizens. As such, Liberal Citizen Ideology accounts for the ideology of citizens, as gauged by Berry et al. (1998). Interest group activity also influences policy adoption. We use LGBT Assets per capita to capture the ability of LGBT interest groups to lobby and pressure politicians (see appendix A).

The model also accounts for individual characteristics of the governors, including gender, tenure in office, and institutional power. Executives tend to utilize unilateral action at the start of their administration to advance their political agendas (Mayer 1999). This suggests that the variable Years Served in Office should have a negative relationship to executive action. To account for the differing institutional powers of governors, we use a time variant measure of Appointment Powers to capture institutional differences (Beyle 1968).[15] A governor's ability to select members of their administration increases as Appointment Powers increase.

Last, we control for temporal changes with a year variable and a media attention variable. Media attention to transgender issues is measured as an annual count of the number of *New York Times* stories that include transgender or transgender related terms.[16]

Analysis

The model is estimated using multilevel analysis to account for differences in traditions and political conditions from state to state. Event history analysis allows the states to drop from the analysis when a governor issues an executive order, but they otherwise remain in the dataset if other forms of protections are adopted in the legislature or determined by precedents via the courts.

Table 6.2 presents the results, showing that partisan control of government is important to explaining why governors issue these executive orders. Democratic governors are more likely to issue transgender-inclusive executive orders. This is likely because Democrats and Republicans had noticeably different stances on LGBT issues before any governor issued an executive order to protect gender identity and expression. The earliest protections ap-

TABLE 6.2. Event History Analysis of Gubernatorial Executive Orders, 1993–2016

	b_i	SE_b
Lower Chamber (% Democrats)	8.127	(5.780)
Upper Chamber (% Democrats)	−10.383⁺	(5.868)
Divided Government	1.249*	(0.658)
Democratic Governor	3.886**	(1.045)
Gender Identity Law	−0.654	(1.083)
Evangelical Population (% in State)	−0.062	(0.085)
Liberal Citizen Ideology	0.006	(0.037)
LGBT Assets	0.047	(0.109)
Female Governor	−2.124*	(1.100)
Years Served in Office	−0.360**	(0.142)
Appointment Power	1.521⁺	(0.830)
New York Times Coverage	−0.001	(0.002)
Year	0.756**	(0.146)
Constant	−1530.789	(292.724)
Total Observations	1,176	
χ^2	39.6**	

Notes: Results are from an event history analysis estimated with a logistic regression model. The dependent variable indicates whether a governor issued an executive order protecting transgender individuals from discrimination in state government. + $p < 0.10$, * $p < 0.05$, ** $p < 0.01$.

peared at the turn of the century (1999 and 2003). By the 1990s, public opinion had become more supportive of gay rights and the Democratic Party forged new alliances to win support from the lavender vote (Brewer 2008). Sellers (2016) notes that Democratic and Republican governors issued the earliest sexual orientation protections, but by the 1990s Democratic governors became the primary governors to issue executive orders to safeguard against discrimination based on sexual orientation and gender identity. Governors extended protections for sexual orientation to include gender identity, while others created comprehensive new policies to set the tone during the early days of their administrations (Sellers 2016).

Additionally, consistent with presidential literature, governors are more likely to issue executive orders when facing unfavorable conditions in the legislature (Deering and Maltzman 1999). Governors are more likely to issue executive orders both when confronted with divided government and when there are fewer Democrats in the upper chamber of the legislature. In fact, governors confronting divided government were more likely to issue executive orders by a factor of 3.49 when compared to governors with a unified government. Although the lower chamber variable is not statistically significant, the upper chamber and divided government together indicate that governors turn to executive orders to bypass a recalcitrant legislature.

Beyond the partisan effects, factors specific to the governor also shape decisions to use executive orders to pursue gender identity protections. Interestingly, female governors were less likely to issue an executive order. This is may be the result of female governors often serving in states that already have legislation on the books. We also find that governors are most likely to issue executive orders when they first enter office. In fact, many governors issued executive orders within the first month of their administration. The odds of a governor issuing an executive order declines by a factor of 1.43 for each year in office, and by a factor of 2.94 after three years. The Appointment Power of governors is positive and statistically significant, which indicates that governors who have more discretion over their administration are more likely to extend protections to transgender individuals. Surprisingly, state social factors, the presence of gender-identity nondiscrimination laws in the state, and media attention do not have statistically significant effects. There is also an increased likelihood of these executive orders over time.

Conclusion

It is clear that the executive branches of government at all levels have been crucial in shaping transgender rights in the United States over the past few decades. With formidable formal and informal policymaking and leadership tools at their disposal, executive leaders can have a dramatic impact on transgender rights policies. Further, policymaking in the executive branch avoids the majoritarian tendencies of the legislative branch, providing an important opportunity for the transgender rights movement despite its small size and relatively low levels of public support on many issues. Yet executive policymaking can be a double-edged sword. Executive orders can easily be overturned, and policymaking is highly dependent on personnel. As seen in the change from the Obama administration to the Trump administration, policy successes can swiftly be turned back with a change in the political winds.

Nonetheless, the Obama administration generated substantial gains for transgender rights. With the exception of inclusion of transgender protections in a hate crimes law and in the reauthorization of the Violence Against Women Act, most of the advancement came through executive branch action. From policy changes, to executive orders, to personnel actions, to regulation, the Obama administration made significant advances that helped the lives of transgender people. LGBT activists, led by organizations like the Human Rights Campaign, strongly advocated for these actions from the beginning of Obama's first term. However, much of the movement on this front came after 2011. For transgender rights, many of the gains occurred after Obama's reelection. While rewarding supporters is a motivation for elected officials, we also believe that the president was motivated to secure his legacy on LGBT rights in a challenging political environment. In addition, advocates like Dan Gurley (2016) note other, more altruistic motivations. This highlights how policymaking in the executive branch can often hinge on personal characteristics and motivations in ways that have provided opportunities for transgender rights advocates.

Governors, such as Jack Markell or Deval Patrick, have also sometimes been allies to the LGBT movement in many states. They have extended protections based on sexual orientation and gender identity over the past four decades. This tradition is likely to continue for the near future as several states added protections for transgender individuals in 2016. Policy diffusion has a regional component. Western and Northeastern states have more protections through legislation, while the Midwestern and Southern states primarily use executive orders if any protections are present. Political factors and factors specific to the governor drive gubernatorial use of executive orders. Governors issued trans-inclusive executive orders during divided government and when the legislature was composed of fewer Democrats. Additionally, Democratic governors were considerably more likely to extend protections through executive orders. Other factors specific to governors, such as time served in office, partisanship, and appointment powers, play a role in explaining executive order use. Governors entering office are more likely to issue trans-inclusive executive orders, as are governors who have greater authority to select members of their administration.

At the same time, our exploration reveals the limits of executive policymaking. The Obama administration took many steps forward on transgender rights, but the Trump administration can just as easily undo some of these policies. That there is an effort to do so is clear given Trump's own attempt to reinstate the ban on transgender military service and in the actions taken by the Departments of Justice and Education to rescind previous guidance on Title IX. The limits of executive policymaking are also evident at the state level, given that some executive orders have been struck down by the courts or overturned by later administrations. Thus, executive policymaking offers a potentially fruitful advocacy venue for the transgender community, but one that is limited.

CHAPTER 7

Direct Democracy and Transgender Rights

While the transgender rights movement has achieved some success in state legislatures and in state and national executive branches, many of these victories have received little public attention. This was particularly true in the 2000s when transgender issues were less salient. However, in recent years transgender rights policies have garnered more of the spotlight, especially when these policies have been placed on the ballot. In one of the most prominent battles over transgender rights, in November 2015 voters in Houston were given the opportunity to approve or reject the Houston Equal Rights Ordinance (HERO). This municipal policy extended broad nondiscrimination protections in city employment, city services, city contracting practices, housing, public accommodations, and private employment to include sexual orientation and gender identity. After a highly publicized and heated campaign that centered on transgender people and their bathroom usage, voters rejected HERO, 61 percent to 39 percent (Somashekhar 2015; Fernandez and Blinder 2015).

This prominent setback for the transgender community not only highlighted the challenges in expanding rights beyond the most liberal cities and states, but it also raised concerns about the ability of the movement to win when these issues are put to a popular vote. As the gay rights movement had shown, particularly on the issue of same-sex marriage, initiatives and referenda tended to result in policies that restricted, rather than expanded, the rights of sexual minorities (Haider-Markel, Querze, and Lindaman 2007; Haider-Markel and Meier 2003; Lewis 2011b). Indeed, there is a large body of literature warning of the dangers that direct democracy can pose to minority rights (Frey and Goette 1998; Gamble 1997; Haider-Markel et al. 2007; Lewis 2013). Should these warnings be heeded by transgender rights advocates? How have direct democracy institutions, including initiatives and referendums, affected the pursuit of transgender rights in the United States?

In this chapter, we examine the role of direct democracy institutions in shaping state and local policies regarding transgender rights.[1] After reviewing the theoretical challenges posed by putting minority civil rights to a popular vote, we empirically explore the relationship between direct democracy and nondiscrimination policy in the states. We then turn our attention to three local-level cases, where the inclusion of gender identity as a protected class was added to municipal nondiscrimination policies but was subsequently challenged through the popular referendum process.

Direct Democracy and Policy Responsiveness

Direct democracy institutions, including ballot initiatives and popular referendums, were adopted in many states during the early twentieth century as a reform designed to increase the responsiveness of state government to the people (Cronin 1989). Populists and Progressives criticized the representative branches of government for being corrupt and beholden to moneyed interests. To address these ills and make public policy more reflective of the public will, they advocated for a range of direct democracy reforms to allow citizens to circumvent elected officials and directly create policy on their own (Sullivan 1893; Haskell 2001).

Today, twenty-four states have some form of citizen legislative process, or direct democracy, including the direct initiative, indirect initiative, and popular referendum. Direct initiatives are policy proposals drafted by the people, which qualify for the ballot through a petitioning process, and are included on a statewide ballot. Indirect initiatives work similarly, but instead of being placed directly on the ballot, the legislature is given an opportunity to act on the proposal. If the legislature does not act, the proposal goes to the ballot. Popular referendums, commonly called "popular vetoes," allow the people to petition to have a policy proposal that was passed by the legislature placed on the ballot for a public vote. This process essentially gives the people veto power over the legislature.

In theory, these direct democracy institutions should lead to more responsive public policies in two ways. First, by allowing citizens to directly create public policy, the resulting policies are likely better reflections of public preferences than policies passed solely through representative democratic institutions, like the state legislature. This primary effect of direct democracy can be seen in the outcomes of ballot initiatives, where citizens can enact policies that have been ignored by the legislature. For example, legislative term limits have long been a popular reform that state legislatures, unsurprisingly, are not willing to pass. Yet many states have adopted them through ballot initiatives. Indeed, all but one state that passed legislative term limits did so through direct democracy institutions (Kousser 2005).

While this primary effect may be obvious, direct democracy can also affect policy responsiveness in a more indirect manner. By giving the people agenda setting power through the ability to place policy proposals on the ballot, direct democracy may also alter the behavior of elected officials and incentivize them to adopt policies closer to the preferences of the people (Romer and Rosenthal 1979; Gerber 1996; Matsusaka and McCarty 2001). This indirect effect can function in several ways. Ballot initiatives can serve as a signal to elected officials, indicating which policies have public support and allowing the legislature to enact them themselves in order to claim credit for popular policies. We see some evidence of this with the 2017 decision by Texas lieutenant governor Dan Patrick and state Senator Lois Kolkhorst to introduce a bill restricting transgender bathroom access in that state's public buildings. During their press conference about the proposal, they specifically referenced the referendum against Houston's HERO ordinance as support for their decision to pursue a statewide policy (Ura, Blanchard, and Wiseman 2017).[2] Ballot initiatives can also serve as credible threats. If the public is pursuing a relatively extreme policy through the direct democracy process, elected officials may act to preempt that policy by enacting a more moderate version. In this way, elected officials respond to public preferences in cases where they otherwise would have been satisfied with the status quo. Either way, the presence of direct democracy institutions changes the behavior of elected officials to make them more likely to respond to public preferences.

Empirical studies tend to find support for direct democracy's effect on policy responsiveness. Although this increased responsiveness has been clearly demonstrated when examining salient social issues, such as abortion (Matsusaka 1995, 2010; Gerber 1996, 1999; Arceneaux 2002), scholars have questioned whether this extends to all policy areas and political contexts (Lascher, Hagen, and Rochlin 1996; Lax and Phillips 2009, 2012). Burden (2005) posits that direct democracy is likely to enhance responsiveness to attitudes on specific and salient issues, but this does not extend to general ideological orientation and less salient issues. Nonetheless, recent work on state policy priorities shows that public mood has a significantly larger impact in direct democracy states (Lewis, Schneider, and Jacoby 2015). Leemann and Wasserfallen (2016), meanwhile, argue that direct democracy is most likely to enhance responsiveness in cases of "bad representation," where elite preferences diverge significantly from mass preferences, and less likely to have an impact in cases of "good representation."

Tyranny of the Majority

Though direct democracy likely increases policy responsiveness to public preferences, as Populist and Progressive reformers suggested, this responsiveness might come at a cost to minority groups. In the Federalist Papers, James Madison makes this point clear as he warns that "if a majority be united by a common interest, the rights of the minority will be insecure" (Madison [1787] 1999b, 291). Further, he argues that "pure democracy . . . can admit no cure for the mischief of factions" (Madison [1787] 1999a, 49). In other words, in a democratic system where the majority is empowered to set policy, minority groups, by definition, will be at a disadvantage. Thus, the rights of numerical minority groups are at risk because the majority always has the authority to revoke and restrict those rights. So, instead of "pure democracy," Madison advocates for a representative democratic system that is designed to filter the preferences of the public through elite representatives and place a check on the power of the majority through separated powers. In this way, representative government in the United States is designed to check and slow the power of the majority in order to protect the rights of minority groups. Direct democracy reforms, by contrast, are designed to speed up the process and empower the majority in order to increase policy responsiveness.

This poses an important question of whether the rights of minority groups are at higher risk in states with direct democracy institutions. Research on this question generally finds that these institutions do have the potential to harm minority rights (Gamble 1997; Haider-Markel et al. 2007; Lewis 2013). When public opinion is tilted against the rights of minority groups, states with direct democracy institutions are more likely to pass restrictive policies (Lewis 2011a, 2013). This is evident in the diffusion of affirmative action bans, English language laws, and a host of anti-gay-rights policies, such as same-sex marriage bans, across the states (Gamble 1997; Schildkraut 2001; Haider-Markel et al. 2007; Lewis 2011b, 2013).

However, direct democracy is not always associated with antiminority policies. In cases where the majority favors protections or the expansion of minority rights, the increased responsiveness driven by direct democracy institution can be favorable for minorities. For example, Lewis (2013) finds that racial profiling bans and hate crimes laws are more likely to pass in direct democracy states. Another study shows a more conditional result—

consistent with studies of responsiveness, citizen ideology has a larger impact on the adoption of sexual-orientation-inclusive nondiscrimination policies in direct democracy states (Taylor et al. 2012). In more liberal states, direct democracy increases the likelihood of passing these protections, but the likelihood of adoption is reduced in more conservative states. Similarly, Lewis and Jacobsmeier (2017) find that direct democracy enhances the effect of public opinion about same-sex marriage on state adoption of both same-sex marriage bans and a host of same-sex relationship recognition policies.

Since public opinion nationally is not very supportive of transgender people (Lewis et al. 2017), direct democracy may endanger transgender rights. Indeed, as seen in chapter 2, the nation tends to have relatively negative feelings toward transgender people. Yet public opinion on some issues, such as nondiscrimination protections, is more positive. In our 2016 survey, over 85 percent of respondents agreed that "[t]ransgender people deserve the same rights and legal protections as other Americans," and 71 percent support passing laws to protect transgender people from job discrimination (see figure 2.7). At the state level, public support for nondiscrimination policies is also high, recently estimated to range from 66 to 90 percent in 2011 (Flores, Herman, and Mallory 2015).

In all, the public seems to hold contradictory attitudes—they have negative feelings toward transgender people, but are supportive of transgender-inclusive nondiscrimination protections. Thus, it is not immediately apparent how direct democracy may shape policies in this area. On the one hand, negative public feelings may result in policies that restrict the rights of transgender people. On the other hand, high levels of support for nondiscrimination policies may provide an opportunity to secure rights through the direct democracy process. We explore this question empirically in the following sections, examining both direct and indirect effects at the state and local levels.

State Direct Democracy and Transgender Rights

At the state level, the question of the direct effect of direct democracy on transgender rights policies is straightforward. Through 2016, no policy proposal directly regarding transgender rights has appeared on a state ballot.[3] In recent years, a few policies have been proposed, but none of them has been able to make it past the petitioning stage to qualify for the ballot. For example, one proposal in California in 2014 aimed to veto a bill passed by the legislature and signed by the governor (AB 1266) that required public schools to allow students to participate in sex-segregated programs, including athletics, and use facilities consistent with their gender identity. In 2016, proposals to restrict access to public facilities based on biological sex failed to qualify for the ballot in California and Washington. That same year, proposals in Michigan and Arkansas sought to expand discrimination protections to include gender identity, but neither qualified for the ballot. More recently, the Montana Family Foundation is attempting to place an initiative on the 2018 ballot that would restrict restroom/locker room access to one's sex at birth. The proposal further defines sex as something fixed at birth and allows aggrieved citizens to sue governmental entities for damages, including for emotional distress, if they encounter a person of the "opposite sex" in one of these protected facilities (Billings Gazette 2017).[4] This initiative grew out of the failure of a similar bill in the Montana legislature during the 2017 legislative session (Michels 2017). In one 2018 referendum that has already qualified for the ballot, Massachusetts voters will review that state's 2016 gender-identity-inclusive public accommodations law (Johnson 2016a). Thus, through this writing, direct democracy has not had a direct effect on transgender rights policies at the state level. Whether it will in the future is still an open question.

Testing for Indirect Effects

There is not yet any evidence of direct effects of ballot measures on state transgender policies, but direct democracy may nonetheless be affecting the behavior of state lawmakers and, subsequently, the policies they enact. To test for the indirect effects, we examine a range of eight state-level policies designed to protect the rights of the transgender community. These policies were identified by the Human Rights Campaign (as of 2016) and include:

- Gender-identity-discrimination protections for public accommodations.
- Gender-identity-discrimination protections for housing.
- Gender-identity-discrimination protections for employment.
- Policies designed to facilitate gender marker changes on drivers' licenses and birth certificates.
- Bans on insurance exclusions for transgender health care.
- Hate crimes laws that cover gender identity.
- Bullying laws that cover gender identity.
- Gender-identity-discrimination protections for public schools.

As seen in table 7.1, just four states have enacted all eight policies (California, Oregon, Vermont, and Washington) three of which are high-use direct democracy states. Another six states have enacted seven of these protections. On the other end of the spectrum, twenty-two states have not enacted any of these policies and eight more adopted just one of the protections. The average number of protections per state is three. Discrimination protections and bullying policies are the most widespread; nineteen states have enacted nondiscrimination protections and twenty states have passed antibullying statutes. Bans on insurance exclusions for transgender health care are the least common, enacted in just nine states.[5]

To test the for the indirect effect of direct democracy on these policies, we estimate an Ordinary Least Squares (OLS) regression model where the dependent variable is an additive index of the number of transgender protections enacted, ranging from zero to eight. Since the indirect effect of direct democracy should function by enhancing responsiveness to public opinion, the primary independent variables measure support for gender-identity-inclusive nondiscrimination policy, the relative impact of direct democracy institutions in each state, and the interaction between these two measures. If direct democracy does increase responsiveness to public opinion, then the interaction should be positive. Public support for gender-identity-inclusive nondiscrimination policy is measured using a state-level Multilevel Regression and Poststratification (MRP) estimates derived from a 2012 national Gallup poll (Flores, Herman, and Mallory 2015).[6] The effect of direct democracy institutions, which vary significantly across the states in their usage and policy impact (e.g., Bowler and Donovan 2004), is gauged with a measure derived from a principal components analysis of Bowler and Donovan's Legislative Insulation and Qualification Difficulty Indices (2004) and the logged frequency of ballot measure use in the past ten years (e.g., Lewis 2013). The resultant Direct Democracy Impact variable ranges from zero for states without ballot initiatives or popular referendums to nearly five for California, which considers ballot initiatives very frequently and does not have many restrictions on its use.

In addition, the analyses account for several other factors that may affect transgender policies. This includes a Ranney Index of partisan control over the past ten years, where lower values indicate complete Republican control and higher values represent complete Democratic control (Ranney 1976; Klarner 2014). The strength of the state LGBT advocacy coalition is measured as the average combined asset value of LGBT rights organizations per capita from 1995 to 2015 (see appendix A). The potential strength of conservative Christian groups, which often advocate against transgender

TABLE 7.1. State Transgender Rights Protections, 2016

	Discrimination Protections				Gender Marker Changes	Healthcare Exclusion Bans	Hate Crimes	Bullying	Total Protections
State	Public Accommodations	Housing	Employment	Schools					
CA	✓	✓	✓	✓	✓	✓	✓	✓	8
OR	✓	✓	✓	✓	✓	✓	✓	✓	8
VT	✓	✓	✓	✓	✓	✓	✓	✓	8
WA	✓	✓	✓	✓	✓	✓	✓	✓	8
CO	✓	✓	✓	✓		✓	✓	✓	7
CT	✓	✓	✓	✓		✓	✓	✓	7
IL	✓	✓	✓	✓		✓	✓	✓	7
MA	✓	✓	✓	✓		✓	✓	✓	7
MN	✓	✓	✓	✓	✓	✓	✓		7
NY	✓	✓	✓	✓	✓	✓	✓		7
DE	✓	✓	✓	✓			✓	✓	6
MD	✓	✓	✓		✓	✓	✓		6
NV	✓	✓	✓	✓			✓	✓	6
NJ	✓	✓	✓	✓			✓	✓	6
HI	✓	✓	✓		✓			✓	5
IA	✓	✓	✓	✓				✓	5
ME	✓	✓	✓	✓				✓	5
NM	✓	✓	✓				✓		4
RI	✓	✓	✓					✓	4
UT					✓		✓		2
AK					✓				1
AZ					✓				1
AR								✓	1
KS					✓				1
MO							✓		1
NH								✓	1
NC								✓	1
WI					✓				1

Source: Human Rights Campaign (2016b).
Note: States not listed here have not enacted any of these policies.

rights, is measured as the percentage of the state population that belongs to an evangelical Christian or Mormon congregation (Association of Religious Data Archives 2010). Last, because higher education levels are associated with increased tolerance for outgroups (e.g., McCloskey and Brill 1983), the analysis includes the U.S. Census Bureau's percentage of the state population over the age of twenty-five with a college degree from the 2010 American Community Survey.

The results from the OLS regression analysis are presented in table 7.2. Overall, the model fits quite well, explaining nearly 70 percent of the cross-state variation in transgender protection policies. Unsurprisingly, public support for transgender nondiscrimination policies significantly affects the number of transgender policy protections adopted in the states. On average, in states without direct democracy institutions, a standard deviation increase in public support—about 6.5 percentage points—is associated with the adoption of an additional transgender protection. A larger increase of 10 points is associated with two more protections.

The coefficient for the interaction between Public Support and Direct Democracy Impact is also positive, indicating a small increase in responsiveness. For average-to-high impact direct democracy states (Direct Democracy Impact scores between 3 and 5), the effect of public opinion on the number of transgender protections is estimated to range from 0.293 to 0.348. In these states, a standard deviation increase in support is associated with the adoption of roughly two additional transgender protections. While this suggests a substantively significant effect of direct democracy institutions, the differ-

TABLE 7.2. Regression Analysis of State Transgender Protections Policies

	b_i	SE_b
Public Support	0.211[**]	(0.076)
Public Support X Direct Democracy Impact	0.028	(0.024)
Direct Democracy Impact	−1.853	(1.928)
Party Control (Ranney Index)	6.044[**]	(2.354)
LGBT Assets per capita	0.046	(0.064)
Evangelical Population Percentage	0.023	(0.026)
Percentage w/College Degree	0.183[**]	(0.075)
Constant	−22.718[**]	(5.192)
N	49	
Adjusted R^2	0.684	

Notes: Results are from an OLS regression model. The dependent variable is the number of transgender protections enacted in each state as of 2016. Nebraska is omitted due to its nonpartisan legislature.
[**] $p < 0.01$; one-tailed tests where appropriate

ences in effects between non-direct-democracy states and direct democracy states does not reach traditional levels of statistical significance (p = 0.133).

Two other factors also seem to affect the number of transgender protections a state adopts: party control and education levels. The coefficient for the Ranney Party Control Index shows that a shift from complete Republican control to complete Democratic control of government would be associated with the adoption of six of the eight protections. While that kind of partisan shift is unlikely, the result does reflect the large distinctions between the parties seen in differences in Republican dominated states, such as Idaho, and Democratic controlled states, such as Massachusetts. Education levels also have a significant effect. A standard deviation increase in the percentage of the population over twenty-five with a college degree—about 5 percentage points—is associated with the adoption of one additional transgender protection.

In all, the results suggest that there may be a modest indirect effect of direct democracy on the adoption of these transgender protections that functions by increasing state responsiveness to public opinion. Yet the difference in the effects of public opinion between direct democracy states and non-direct-democracy states is not clear from this analysis. Theoretically, the indirect effects of these institutions should stem from agenda-setting power that they give to the public. Since no state-level proposal in this policy area has appeared on the ballot as of this writing, and absent a more definitive statistical result, it is not clear, despite anecdotal evidence mentioned earlier, whether there have been enough prominent signals and threats to alter the behavior of policymakers. What is abundantly evident from the analysis, however, is that public opinion *in all states* significantly shapes policy process outcomes for transgender rights.

Local Direct Democracy and Transgender Rights

At the state level, direct democracy has, at most, only modestly affected transgender rights policies. At the local level, however, direct democracy has been utilized more frequently and prominently to address these issues. The HERO popular referendum in Houston is one clear example, but other municipal governments have also used direct democracy to consider transgender protection policies, specifically nondiscrimination policies. Since 2009, voters in at least twelve cities considered ballot measures on gender-identity-inclusive nondiscrimination policies (see table 7.3). Yet only one was a ballot initiative proposed by citizens. The rest were either legislative referendums or popular referendums challenging a law passed by the local legislature. Seven of the ballot measures have been presented to voters since 2014. The ballot measures have produced split outcomes for transgender rights. Six of the ballot measure resulted in repeals or rejections of nondiscrimination policies, while six served to ratify nondiscrimination protections enacted by the municipal governments.

Although there have been several local referenda that have directly af-

TABLE 7.3. Local Transgender Rights Ballot Measures

Place	Year	Type	Measure Title	Outcome
Gainesville, FL	2009	PR	Transgender Anti-discrimination Ordinance Referendum	Ordinance upheld, 58% to 42%
Kalamazoo, MI	2009	PR	Kalamazoo Discrimination Protection for Gays Referendum	Ordinance upheld, 62% to 27%
Traverse City, MI	2011	PR	Traverse City Non-Discrimination Ordinance Question	Ordinance upheld, 63% to 37%
Salina, KS	2012	LR	LGBT Anti-Discrimination Ordinance Question	Ordinance repealed, 54% to 46%
Anchorage, AK	2012	I	Anchorage Equal Rights Initiative	Proposal rejected, 57% to 43%
Fayetteville, AR	2014	PR	"Civil Rights Administration" Ordinance Veto Referendum	Ordinance repealed, 52% to 48%
Pocatello, ID	2014	PR	Sexual Orientation & Gender Expression Discrimination Referendum	Ordinance upheld, 50.4% to 49.6%
Chattanooga, TN	2014	PR	Health Benefits for Domestic Partners Referendum*	Ordinance repealed, 63% to 37%
Eureka Springs, AR	2015	PR	Anti-Discrimination Ordinance Referendum	Ordinance upheld, 71% to 29%
Fayetteville, AR	2015	LR	Uniform Civil Rights Protection Ordinance	Ordinance upheld, 53% to 47%
Springfield, MO	2015	PR	Sexual Orientation & Transgender Anti-Discrimination Ordinance Veto	Ordinance repealed, 51% to 49%
Houston, TX	2015	PR	Houston Equal Rights Ordinance Referendum	Ordinance repealed, 61% to 39%

Notes: Ballot measure types: I = Initiative; LR = Legislative Referendum; PR = Popular Referendum. *Chattanooga's "Health Benefits for Domestic Partners" ordinance included a various provisions to protect transgender people from discrimination in the workplace. Data updated through 2016.

fected transgender rights policies, citizens at the local level seem less likely use the initiative process to advance transgender policies. In most cases, citizens seem to be responding to local legislation rather than pursuing these issues themselves. Thus, there is evidence that direct democracy, especially through the referendum process, can directly shape local nondiscrimination policy. Yet it is not clear whether these referendums have had an indirect effect on policy as well.

Indirect Effects

To explore the indirect effects of direct democracy at the local level, we analyze a set of seven municipal transgender protection policies identified in the Human Rights Campaign's *2015 Municipal Equality Index*:

- Gender-identity-discrimination protections for public accommodations.
- Gender-identity-discrimination protections for housing.
- Gender-identity-discrimination protections for employment.
- Gender-identity-discrimination protections for municipal employment.
- Trans-inclusive health benefits for municipal employees.
- Municipal contractor nondiscrimination policy.
- Bullying laws that cover gender identity.

The *2015 Municipal Equality Index* surveys municipal policies related to LGBT rights in 408 cities, including the 50 state capitals, the 200 largest cities in the country, the cities of each state's 2 largest research universities, and 25 small, midsize, and large cities with the highest proportion of same-sex couples. On average, the cities in this sample had enacted two of the seven protections as of 2015. However, as seen in figure 7.1, the modal number of protections is zero, with another 25 percent of cities adopting just one protection. Only 5.5 percent of the cities in the sample had enacted all seven protections. The most common protection is a nondiscrimination policy for municipal employees, which is in effect in 177 cities. Antibullying policies are also quite common, covering most schools in 171 cities.[7] The least common protections are policies that ensure insurance coverage of transgender-related health services for municipal employees.

As with the state-level analysis, we model these local transgender protection policies as a function of public opinion, direct democracy institu-

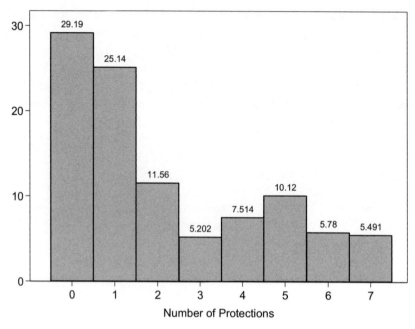

Figure 7.1. Municipal Transgender Rights Protections, 2015. (Human Rights Campaign, 2015 Municipal Equality Index.)

tions, and the interaction between the two primary independent variables. However, measuring these variables at the local level requires different approaches. Unfortunately, estimates of public opinion toward transgender rights policies are not available at the local level due to the relative sparseness of survey items that address these issues. Therefore, we utilize a more common indicator of political opinions: the ideological identification of citizens, estimated using MRP (Tausanovitch and Warsaw 2014).[8] Since we do not have access to data on ballot measure use and qualification rules at the local level, direct democracy is gauged with a simple dichotomous indicator of whether initiatives are available for citizens (Garret and Matsusaka 2008). At the local level, these institutions are much more common: over 80 percent of the cities in the sample have access to ballot initiatives. The model is also specified with several control variables, including local institutional factors such as the form of government, partisan elections, and at-large council elections. In addition, we account for socioeconomic factors such as median income, population (natural log), and, to assess the potential capacity of the local LGBT community, the per capita (k) number of same-sex partner households.[9]

The model is estimated using linear regression with state fixed effects.[10] The results are presented in table 7.4. Overall, the model accounts for nearly 60 percent of the variation in local transgender policies. This explanatory power is driven in large part by the state fixed effects, but also by citizen ideology. Indeed, the standardized coefficient for citizen ideology is by far the largest in the model at -0.507. The results show that cities that are more conservative tend to have fewer transgender protections. A standard deviation increase in citizen ideology (more conservative) is associated with roughly one less protection. This suggests that public opinion is a powerful factor shaping local transgender rights policies. However, the presence of initiatives does not seem to condition this effect. This null effect may result from the relatively simplistic measure of initiatives that cannot differentiate between various institutional arrangements that can make direct democracy easier to employ and the frequency of use at the municipal level. In addition, with over 80 percent of the sample having access to initiatives and the model showing a large impact of public opinion, the interaction term may be underestimating any conditioning effect.

The model also reveals two other significant factors: the size of the city and the number of same-sex-partner households. Larger cities tend to have significantly more transgender protections than smaller cities. This may indicate a relative increase in demand for these protections as populations increase. Similarly, cities with higher numbers of same-sex-partner house-

TABLE 7.4. Regression Analysis of Municipal Transgender Protection Policies

	b_i	SE_b
Citizen Ideology (Lib. → Cons.)	−3.823**	(1.000)
Citizen Ideology X Initiatives	0.021	(1.030)
Initiatives	−0.138	(0.524)
Mayor-Council System	−0.060	(0.248)
Partisan Elections	0.078	(0.363)
At-Large Council Elections	0.133	(0.220)
Median Income (k)	−0.002	(0.010)
Population (logged)	0.570**	(0.132)
Same-Sex Partner Households per capita (k)	0.024*	(0.013)
Constant	−1.263	(1.295)
N	345	
R^2	0.595	

Notes: Results are from an OLS regression model. The dependent variable is the number of transgender protections enacted in each city. State fixed effects states are included in the model, but not presented here. * $p < 0.05$; ** $p < 0.01$; one-tailed test where appropriate

holds per capita tend to have slightly more transgender protections. For a standard deviation increase in these households (about eight), the number of protections increases by about 0.2 protections. This may indicate that a more organized LGBT community might be more effective in lobbying for policy change.

In all, the local-level analysis finds little indirect impact of direct democracy on the enactment of transgender protections. Yet municipal governments do seems to be quite responsive to citizen ideology, regardless of whether the city has ballot initiatives (which most do). While this may be a result of the local-level direct democracy measure or the widespread use of ballot initiatives in municipalities, it may also indicate relatively low levels of public salience on these issues. Indeed, the direct effects of direct democracy have been felt entirely through referendums, suggesting that the public is not initiating policy proposals, but rather that they are reacting to policy proposals from elected officials. For some types of these policies, such as antibullying measures or gender-identity-inclusive nondiscrimination protections that cover public employees, there might be support by broad swaths of the public (see chapter 2). For other types of municipal policies, such as gender-identity-inclusive public accommodations or private employment protections, there might be a higher likelihood of backlash in some cities.

Case Studies

To further explore how direct democracy has been used to react to local-level policy proposals from elected officials, we examine three recent cases in more depth: Fayetteville, Arkansas; Eureka Springs, Arkansas; and Houston, Texas. These cases offer recent examples of both pro- and antitransgender rights outcomes across a range of city sizes and political contexts. We also restrict our cases to southern cities in this analysis to avoid the confounding effects that different regions of the country might have on this question. Additionally, nearly all states in the Northeast and on the West Coast have transgender-inclusive state laws that alleviate the need for local-level policies.

Fayetteville Referendums

Fayetteville is the third largest city in Arkansas, with a population of 78,960, and it is home to the state's flagship public university, the University of Arkansas. Its cultural identity centers on the university, but it also serves as the primary economic hub for northwest Arkansas and the Ozark region, which includes the corporate headquarters of Walmart in Bentonville. Ideologically, the city is relatively moderate by Arkansas standards, but is fairly conservative compared to other cities across the nation (Tausanovitch and Warshaw 2014).

During the summer of 2014, the Fayetteville City Council introduced a wide-ranging ordinance to bar discrimination based on race, ethnicity, national origin, age, gender, gender identity, gender expression, familial status, marital status, socioeconomic background, religion, sexual orientation, disability, and veteran status. The ordinance would provide protections in employment, housing, and public accommodations, and create a civil rights administrator position to enforce the law. Prior to the city council vote, opponents organized against the proposal, including fielding a robocall by Michelle Duggar, a celebrity from the reality TV show *19 Kids and Counting* and resident of the neighboring city of Springdale. The robocall raised concerns about how the gender identity protections would affect the safety of women and children in public bathrooms (Gill 2014a).

Despite this vocal opposition, the ordinance passed on August 19, six votes to two, after an amendment was included to exempt places of worship and tax-exempt properties (Gill 2014c). During the public debate preceding the council vote, opponents of the ordinance voiced concerns about religious freedom and bathrooms (Brantley 2014). The discussion also addressed the potential of a petition to force a popular referendum on the ordinance since a previous municipal nondiscrimination policy was rejected by voters in 1998. However, an amendment to place the ordinance directly on the ballot as a legislative referendum was rejected by the council (Gill 2014c).

As opponents of the ordinance warned, a petition drive to call for a popular referendum did proceed. Led by the group Repeal 119—which refers to the newly created Chapter 119 of the city code—over 5,000 signatures were submitted in September and the city clerk certified that there were enough to trigger a popular referendum, ultimately held on December 9 (Gill 2014b). The ensuing referendum campaign included a wide range of issues. Following the Duggar robocall, many opponents echoed public safety concerns related to bathrooms and locker rooms (Gill 2014d). Religious freedom, particularly around the issue of whether or not churches would be forced to host same-sex marriages under the public accommodations provision, continued to surface in messaging and debates. In addition, the Fayetteville Chamber of Commerce announced its opposition to the ordinance, arguing that the vague language of "perception" and "socioeconomic background" might place an undue burden on businesses. They also expressed skepticism about the civil rights administrator position and the process by which policy would be enforced, calling this part of the ordinance "incomplete." Opponents also expressed skepticism over the ordinance because it used similar language to model legislation posted by the Human Rights Campaign, viewed as an outsider group from Washington, DC. Supporters of the ordinance, including Mayor Lioneld Jordan and University of Arkansas chancellor David Gearhart, focused on pushing back against opponents' arguments and on advocating for civil rights. They noted that most large businesses already have their own trans-inclusive nondiscrimination policies, including Walmart (Gill 2014d). Despite the contentious campaign, just 29 percent of eligible voters cast ballots on December 9, 2014, and they voted to repeal the ordinance, 52 percent to 48 percent.

Although citizens were able to use the popular referendum to overturn the policy passed by the city council, the issue remained on the public agenda. Other cities in Arkansas introduced their own antidiscrimination policies in early 2015, including the capital city, Little Rock, and nearby Eureka Springs (see the full description below). The Fayetteville City Council introduced a revised version of the antidiscrimination ordinance, the Uniform Civil Rights Protection Ordinance. This proposal was very similar to the previous measure and provided protections against discrimination in employment, housing, and public accommodations to the same set of groups, but it also included a few key revisions. Instead of enforcing the ordinance through a civil rights administrator position, investigations under the revised proposal would be conducted by a seven-member Civil Rights Commission. The investigation and enforcement processes were also clearly outlined. In addition, exact definitions for discriminatory actions, key protected classes, and affected organizations, such as employers and religious groups, were provided (Gill 2015; Koon 2015). The revised ordinance passed on June 16, again by a 6–2 vote, but it was immediately referred to the public for approval through a legislative referendum set for September 8, 2015.

The second referendum campaign, like the revised ordinance itself, also differed slightly from the first campaign. Perhaps most importantly for supporters, the revisions to the proposal were enough to garner the support of the Fayetteville Chamber of Commerce, which had prominently opposed the original ordinance. The endorsement of the business community proved to be important enough that opponents of the ordinance, now led by Protect Fayetteville, continued to try to use the Chamber's former support in their messaging against the new ordinance (Gill 2015). However, besides this change in endorsement, the content of the public debate remained on concerns from opponents over religious freedom and transgender people in bathrooms. Proponents of the ordinance continued to highlight the importance of protecting civil rights, but they no longer had to contend with concerns about vague language and the procedural concerns of the business community. Another change in the campaign was less attention to celebrity endorsements or national advocacy groups. Indeed, the Human Rights Campaign, which had provided more than $166,000 in nonmonetary contributions in the 2014 fight, sat out the 2015 campaign due to concerns about the lack of inclusiveness of the revised ordinance's language (Sitek 2015).

On September 9, once again just 29 percent of voters cast ballots to determine the fate of Fayetteville's antidiscrimination ordinance. However, this time the ordinance was approved by voters, 53 percent to 47. In this case, the legislative referendum process was used to ratify the city council's actions. In all, the ability of citizens to petition to refer bills to the ballot allowed voters to not only have a direct impact on policy—by repealing the first ordinance—but also had an indirect effect, forcing revisions to the new ordinance and ensuring that voters would have another chance to vote on the ordinance through a legislative referendum.

Eureka Springs Referendum

Eureka Springs, Arkansas is a small resort city of 2,073 in the Ozark Mountains of northwest Arkansas. It has a liberal reputation in a conservative state and it has been dubbed by some as "the gay capital of the Ozarks" (Fausset 2015). This reputation has been supported in public policies, with the city creating one of the Arkansas' first domestic partnership registries in 2007 and issuing the state's first same-sex marriage licenses in 2014 (Bowden 2015).

In response to the Arkansas Senate's passage of a bill on February 9, 2015 to prohibit the creation or enforcement of antidiscrimination laws that exceed state policies (SB202), the Eureka Springs city council unanimously passed Ordinance 2203 that same night to bar discrimination based on "real or perceived race, ethnicity, national origin, age (if 18 years or older), gender, gender identity, gender expression, familial status, marital status, socioeconomic background, religion, sexual orientation, disability or veteran status" (Bowden 2015). The measure was passed quickly in order to be enacted prior to the state ban on local antidiscrimination policies, but this approach was criticized as circumventing due process. As a result, a petition drive to refer the policy to the ballot was initiated with the support of the Arkansas Family Council and the leader of Fayetteville's Repeal 119 organization (Cook 2015). In response to this criticism and the pending petition, the city council voted to refer the ordinance to the public for a vote themselves. The voters of Eureka Springs would determine the fate of the antidiscrimination ordinance on May 12, 2015 (Brantley 2015).

The campaign and public debate that ensued over Ordinance 2223 in Eureka Springs focused primarily around issues of tourism and religious freedom. In addition to the city's reputation as a gay-friendly tourist destination, the area is also home to a seven-story-tall statue called *Christ of the Ozarks* and *The Great Passion Play*, which retells the story of Jesus Christ and is one of the most visited outdoor theater productions in the country. Thus, much of the debate centered on how the new ordinance would affect tourism driven by this religious attraction. This concern was further highlighted at the state level, as the Arkansas legislature passed a series of religious freedom bills that garnered national attention (Davey, Robertson, and Pérez-Peña 2015). Countering these concerns, members of the city council cited the importance of providing protection against discrimination to all visitors, regardless of their sexual orientation or gender identity, emphasizing how protecting civil rights would burnish the city's tolerant and welcoming reputation. Indeed, Ordinance 2223 was featured in a gay tourist website, Out in Eureka (Fausset 2015).

Most of the messaging and public debate centered on LGBT rights, broadly conceived, rather than on transgender rights in particular. This likely derives from the content of the ordinance itself, as an entirely new antidiscrimination policy that added protections to a host of groups. Further, in the context of Eureka Springs' reputation as a gay-friendly tourist destination, it is not surprising that much of the messaging on both sides of the issue tended to focus on sexual orientation or use the umbrella language, such as LGBT. While a few opponents of the ordinance raised concerns about gender and bathrooms, this issue was not a prominent part of the public debate. Unlike Houston, the content of messaging was much broader and centered on issues of tourism, religious freedom, and civil rights.

On May 12, 2015, 810 voters cast ballots on the antidiscrimination ordinance, passing the referendum overwhelmingly—71 percent to 29 percent—and supporting the city policy. In this case, direct democracy was used to challenge the actions of the city council, but instead served to ratify the council's policy. Given the content of the debate surrounding the ordinance, which focused on broad civil rights language, combined with the relatively progressive political climate of the city, the outcome of the election is not very surprising. From this situation, it is not clear whether direct democracy had much of an impact on the policy outcome, either directly or indirectly. Indeed, this may be an example of Leemann and Wasserfallen's

(2016) "good representation," where the preferences of the city council already adequately reflected the preferences of the people of Eureka Springs. Regardless, for the LGBT communities in Eureka Springs and Fayetteville, the referendum victories would be short-lived. In 2015, Arkansas passed a law that preempted localities from enacting nondiscrimination ordinances that are more expansive than state law (which does not include sexual orientation or gender identity). The Arkansas Supreme Court later invalidated the existing LGBT-inclusive measures due to their nonconformance with state law (Hersher 2017).

Houston Referendum

The final case under examination here, the popular referendum on the Houston Equal Rights Ordinance (HERO), drew the most national attention. With well over two million residents, Houston is the fourth largest city in the United States and the largest city in Texas. As a major metropolitan area, it has a relatively diverse population. For a conservative state like Texas, it is relatively liberal, but its citizen ideology ranks as more moderate compared to other large cities across the country. Indeed, the city is divided politically between the two major parties, but it has leaned toward Democrats in recent years. When Annise Parker won the mayoral election in 2009, Houston became the nation's largest city to elect an openly gay or lesbian mayor. Parker went on to serve three terms and led the city during the HERO referendum.

The Houston City Council passed the Houston Equal Rights Ordinance on May 28, 2014. The ordinance would ban discrimination based on sex, race, color, ethnicity, national origin, age, familial status, marital status, religion, disability, genetic information, pregnancy, sexual orientation, and gender identity in housing, public accommodations, and employment. The ban would apply to businesses that serve the public, private employers, housing, city employment and city contractors, but it included religious exemptions. Violations could draw fines up to $5,000. After a nine-hour public debate, the city council passed the ordinance by an 11 to 6 vote (Morris 2014).

A petition drive to force the ordinance onto the ballot began soon after the council vote, and signatures were submitted on July 3, 2014. However, the mayor's office determined that there were not enough valid signatures after thousands of signatures were thrown out during the review process because the signatures were on invalid petition pages. The petitioners promptly sued the city and the case wound its way through the state court system over the following year, with the Texas Supreme Court ultimately siding with petitioners on July 24, 2015 (Elliot and Morris 2015). HERO was subsequently placed on the general election ballot for November 2, 2015.

Unlike the two Arkansas referendum campaigns, throughout the petitioning and referendum campaign the opponents of Houston's antidiscrimination ordinance focused their criticism primarily on the bathroom issue, dubbing it the "Sexual Predator Protection Act." Reverend Max Miller of the Baptist Ministers Association argued that "[w]e're standing up to protect our women and children" (Morris 2014). The referendum soon drew national attention, with a range of advocacy groups and celebrities becoming involved in the campaign (Foxhall 2015; Moyer 2015). Opponents' advertising utilized the tagline "No men in women's bathrooms," and included prominent endorsements from former Houston Astro Lance Berkman, Houston Texans owner Bob McNair, and Governor Gregg Abbott. Supporters of HERO focused on a broader civil rights-oriented message and were able to draw endorsements from national groups, such as the ACLU and Human Rights Campaign; corporations, like Apple and Hewlett Packard; and celebrities, including actresses Eva Longoria and Sally Field. Despite proponents' use of civil rights language, most of the debate continued to center on bathroom issues, framing the referendum as a public safety issue (Moyer 2015; Ross 2015).

The election results allowed opponents of the ordinance to declare victory with 61 percent of voters casting ballots to repeal HERO. Through the popular referendum process, citizens were able to directly affect and change the policies enacted by their elected representatives. However, the HERO referendum also reveals an important indirect effect. One of the important facets of the theory of the indirect effects of direct democracy is that it allows the public to set the political agenda. In this case, the referendum campaign shaped the agenda by focusing the content of the debate on bathroom access and concerns about public safety. Thus, the vote likely reflected public preferences on those issues, rather than the broader issues of employment or housing discrimination, religious freedom, or even economic concerns. Further, the HERO referendum demonstrated the power of the bathroom messaging strategy for opponents of transgender rights. Although the Houston campaign was not the first where this strategy was utilized, it is the highest-profile locality where its effectiveness has been shown.

Subsequent legislative efforts across the country to restrict bathroom access, including North Carolina's infamous HB2, reflect the success of that strategy. This point is especially relevant because the ordinance had covered a broad range of group classifications, including sex, race, color, ethnicity, national origin, age, religion, disability, pregnancy, genetic information, family, marital, and military status, but opponents were able to focus all of the attention on trans bathroom access. As we noted earlier, the "bathroom strategy" was also used by Texas lieutenant governor Dan Patrick to call for a statewide ban on restroom use that does not match one's biological sex. Positioning himself to the right of Governor Greg Abbott, a fellow Republican, Patrick was rumored to be considering a run for governor in 2018 (Weissert 2016). Position taking on the bathroom issue, and credit claiming if the statewide ban had passed, was a way to signal to conservative voters that he was the better choice to lead Texas.

Conclusion

The question of how direct democracy has affected transgender rights policies is an important one for understanding not only the present state of the transgender rights movement but also its future. Given the high-profile defeat of HERO and the theoretical concern over "tyranny of the majority," direct democracy certainly has the potential to be a significant obstacle to transgender rights. Yet direct democracy could also be used to advance and protect transgender rights in certain political contexts, when the public is supportive of protective policies and at the local level when state policy also offers localities home rule powers.

Despite this potential, the state and local level analyses presented here show only a small systematic impact of direct democracy on transgender rights so far. This small effect is likely driven by the relative sparseness of ballot measures that address transgender rights. Very few transgender rights protections or restrictions have been pursued via direct democracy institutions. Indeed, only reactive referendums have been employed at both the state and local levels in attempts to veto or ratify the decisions of elected officials; this pattern is similar to what has historically been observed for gay and lesbian rights policies (Haider-Markel, Querze, and Lindaman 2007; Haider-Markel and Meier 2003). The reluctance to use the initiative process to advance rights might reflect a fear of expanding the scope of conflict given the experiences of gay and lesbian advocates with direct democracy (Haider-Markel and Meier 1996). The small effects also may result from the relatively high level of responsiveness to public opinion that state and local governments have shown on these issues. In each of our analyses, public preferences were significant factors in shaping the adoption of transgender rights policies. This high level of policy representation may mitigate any large effect of direct democracy institutions (Leemann and Wasserfallen 2016). It also suggests that public opinion, regardless of whether citizens have access to direct democracy institutions, is critical in determining policy outcomes related to transgender rights.

Indeed, while there is not much evidence of a systematic effect of direct democracy, either in advancing or restricting transgender rights, our analyses certainly reveal the potential of an effect as the movement evolves. This potential effect is evident in the evolution of same-sex-marriage attitudes in recent decades. A spate of proposals to ban same-sex marriage appeared on ballots from 2004 to 2008, and public support for same-sex marriage declined in the short term. However, these direct democracy campaigns likely moderated the public's initial opposition to same-sex relationships, including civil unions and domestic partnerships, and in the long term support for same-sex marriage increased to majority levels after 2008 (Lewis and Jacobsmeier 2017; Pew Research Center 2016). Similarly, the referendums in Arkansas and Texas showed the power of campaigns to shape public understanding of issues related to gender identity. When framed as a civil rights protection, and with adequate buy-in from businesses, the public tends to be supportive of broad antidiscrimination policies. This is evident not only in relatively liberal-to-moderate cities of Eureka Springs and Fayetteville but also nationally, where most people support discrimination bans based on sexual orientation and gender identity (Flores, Herman, and Mallory 2015; Lewis et al. 2017). Yet, when framed more exclusively in terms of bathrooms (and public safety) or religious freedom, the public is far less supportive. In these contexts, direct democracy institutions have the potential to restrict transgender rights. However, even when opponents of transgender rights are successful in using direct democracy to thwart transgender rights, they provide an opportunity for transgender people and their allies to educate the public and increase contact with a marginalized group. In the end, that might prove beneficial to the advancement of transgender rights.

Transgender Policy

CHAPTER 8

Identity Documentation and the Regulation of Gender

In this chapter, we focus on the particular problems and solutions that identity documents pose for transgender people. Identity documents are issued at the state and federal levels. They include familiar items like birth certificates, passports, and driver's licenses. For some, there are also student identification cards or identifications derived from state and local government employment. At the federal level, identity documents include passports, Social Security cards, military/government identification cards, and immigration documents. These documents are important because they provide status and evidence that identifies a person to government authorities and those in the private sector. Proving identity might allow an individual to gain access to important government services like public schools or Social Security. Identity documents might be required when dealing with the police, when trying to board an airplane, or when getting a library card. Businesses in the private sector require individuals to provide identification documents when securing a car loan, setting up a bank account, applying for a credit card, obtaining a mortgage, being hired, or even picking up a concert ticket. Further, some identification documents are required to get other identification documents. For instance, for Americans born in the United States, one must provide a birth certificate to get a passport (United States Department of State, 2017a). In many states, identification is required to both register to vote and to vote. In short, these documents are essential for membership in the polity.

For transgender people, identification documents provide many challenges. A transgender person might have an identity that does not align with the name or gender identity, or both, listed on the birth certificate or on other identification documents. The individual might have some documents where the name and gender marker aligns with their gender identity while there is misalignment on other documents. Indeed, a recent study found that only 11 percent of transgender respondents had been able to update the name and gender on all of their identity documents (James et al. 2016). Further, 68 percent of transgender respondents had no identification documents where name and gender markers were aligned with their gender presentation. When there is misalignment between the identification document and gender presentation, a transgender person can have a difficult time proving who they are and what gender they are when dealing with governmental authorities or entities in the private sector. This can create enumerable hassles, embarrassments, and barriers. These nonaligning documents leave transgender individuals vulnerable to outing by the state. As such, a transgender person might be subjected to discriminatory treatment, harassment, or violence. James et al. (2016) report that 32 percent of transgender respondents who have shown an identification document that does not align with their gender presentation have been verbally harassed, denied services or benefits, or assaulted. Individuals who are racial/ethnic minorities or undocumented immigrants are even more likely to experience these negative interactions.

Nonaligning identity documents typically derive from two sources: names and gender markers. Name changes are often an important part of a transgender individual's transition. In the United States, these are commonly executed by a court order in the local jurisdiction where the person lives. Rules for doing so vary accordingly. In a recent survey (James et al. 2016), 36 percent of transgender individuals had attempted to legally change their name, but only 83 percent of those individuals successfully completed the change. The survey notes that nonbinary transgender people are far less likely than binary trans people to change their legal name or gender. In addition, those that cross-dress commonly did not change their name or gender. The study also finds that 30 percent of respondents have their preferred name on all identification documents, while 22 percent had their preferred name on some identification documents. Respondents with lower incomes or noncitizens were more likely to have no documents with their preferred name. This is likely a function of the costs to legally change one's name, including a variety of court-related fees and legal assistance costs. Respondents reported costs ranging from $0 to more than $2,000, with a modal cost between $100 and $249 (James et al. 2016). When changing a name, 22 percent of respondents felt that court officials did not treat them with respect.

Further, 23 percent of respondents noted that court officials misgendered them in pronoun or title usage.

Changing the gender marker on an identification document is also important because there are many instances where a person's legal sex might be relevant in policy. For instance, North Carolina's HB2 attempted to regulate restroom access in public buildings by requiring individuals to use facilities that correspond to the sex listed on the person's birth certificate. In addition, men are required to register for the Selective Service System, but women are not. Prisons and jails remain gender segregated. Many public and private schools have gendered dress codes. There are some single sex schools and colleges. Athletics, from youth and scholastic levels to adult recreation and professional competitions, are commonly divided by gender. Prior to the series of court cases that established marriage equality across the country, a person's legal sex also mattered in terms of his or her marriage rights (Greenberg and Herald 2005).[1] In addition, many essential services for society's most vulnerable, who are also disproportionately people of color, are sex segregated (Spade 2006). These include services and institutions such as drug treatment facilities, homeless shelters, and foster care facilities.

James and his coauthors (2016) find that only 12 percent of transgender people have their preferred gender on all of their identification documents, while an additional 21 percent of respondents had it on some of their documents. Meanwhile, they note that 67 percent of respondents had no identity documents with their preferred gender. As a result, most transgender people face considerable challenges accessing gender-segregated services and facilities based on gender markers on their identity documents. This challenge is likely even more daunting for more vulnerable populations, despite their need for an array of social services and institutional support.

When a transgender person's legal sex is relevant as a matter of policy, questions abound. What sex is the person? Can a person change their legal sex? If so, what is required to do so? Are specific medical treatments necessary? Who can make that determination? Are they always treated as the new legal sex as a matter of policy? What level of privacy is the transgender individual afforded in this process of changing sex? What can be done about life's paper trail that has all of the old information? What are the social implications of allowing people to change their sex on their birth certificate (Meyerowitz 2002)? Sadly, for transgender people, the policy framework for answering these questions often provides inconsistent and incoherent guidance (Taylor 2007).

Despite the abundance of legal requirements related to sex, Davis (2017) questions whether the use of sex in public policy is always related to legitimate government interests. For instance, he argues that the use of sex markers on identity documents does not bear a rational relationship to the goal of fraud prevention because roughly half of the population shares the classifications of male or female. Use of biometric information would be more rationally related to the goal of fraud prevention because it is universally held, invariable, and unique. Of course, some trans people also eschew the notion of binary sex categories. Many transgender activists, such as Davis (2017), are actively trying to "'disestablish' gender from the state by ending the state's authority to police the relation between one's legal sex assigned at birth, one's gender identity, and one's gender expression" (Currah 2006, 24). They envision a world where a person's sex is not a governmental or policy concern.[2]

While many policies are built upon sex segregation, there are relatively few statutes that legally define sex.[3] Historically, it was assumed that these categories were self-evident and immutable (Meyerowitz 2002). Sex is determined via genital inspection by the birth attendant and it is noted on the birth certificate. That document establishes legal sex as male or female (Greenberg 1999).[4] However, binary sex categories are problematic given the variety of intersexual conditions that undermine tradition notions of male and female (Greenberg 1999). Indeed, there are varieties of ways to assess an individual's sex. Greenberg (1999) lists the following:

- Genetic or chromosomal sex.
- Gonadal sex.
- Internal morphologic sex.
- External morphologic sex (genitalia).
- Hormonal sex.
- Phenotypic sex (secondary sexual features).
- Assigned sex and gender of rearing.
- Sexual identity.

Without statutory definitions of sex, in early court cases about medically changing sex during the 1960s physicians serving as expert witnesses relied on discussion of the above signifiers of sex to rebut arguments that sex is strictly genetic (Meyerowitz 2002). When successful, these arguments helped courts issue new birth certificates to trans people during an era when there was little statutory guidance or legal precedent. Since then, governments at all levels have developed a myriad of policies to address name and gender marker changes on identity documents.

Federal Policies

Passport

Since 2010, the Department of State has allowed transgender individuals to get a standard ten-year passport with an amended gender marker if a licensed physician certifies that the individual has had clinically appropriate treatment. Clinically appropriate treatment is defined by the physician. This policy was an Obama administration change that was ushered in by Secretary of State Hillary Clinton in June 2010 and amended in 2011 (Kruse 2016). It removed an older policy requiring documentation about the completion of specific surgeries to change the sex designation on a passport. If a name change to a current passport is also needed, proof of a legal name change is required via a court order or similar document. Individuals in the process of clinical treatment may get a limited two-year passport with proper documentation. Minor children are also eligible for amended gender markers on passports with the same rules (U.S. Department of State 2017b). Yet to date, the State Department does not allow for nonbinary gender markers, such as an X as opposed to an F or M.[5] In 2016, a federal judge ruled in favor of an intersex individual who had challenged the State Department's binary gender classification rules (*Zzyym v. Kerry* 2016). However, implementation of that ruling or a decision to appeal will be made by the Trump administration (LeGaL Foundation 2016). Indeed, through June 2017, the State Department has refused to comply with the ruling and litigation has been reopened by Lambda Legal (2017c).

Social Security

To change gender in Social Security records, transgender individuals need documents proving identity, such as a driver's license. In addition, a valid ten-year passport showing the new gender, an amended birth certificate showing the new gender, a court order recognizing a new gender, or a medical certification of appropriate treatment from a licensed physician must be provided (U.S. Social Security Administration 2016). The previous policy required documentation of particular surgeries, but the policy was expanded in 2013 by the Obama administration to allow for more flexibility (Goad 2013). In 2011, the Obama administration also ended the practice of informing employers when the gender of a worker did not match a person's Social Security records (Eilperin 2015). Name changes in Social Security records have no cost. A person can change his or her name with a court order, divorce decree, marriage record, or certificate of naturalization showing the new name (U.S. Social Security Administration 2017). Most transgender people are likely to use the court order (James et al. 2016). Despite the recent easing of gender marker change requirements by the Social Security Administration, James et al. (2016) report that only 23 percent of transgender respondents who wanted to change the gender marker in their Social Security records had done so. Name changes have been more common, and 43 percent of respondents had changed the name in their Social Security records.

Selective Service

According to the Selective Service System (2017b), individuals born male but who transition to female must still register with the Selective Service System. If transition occurs before the twenty-sixth birthday and the individual had previously registered, then she must also change her name with Selective Service. This requires a court order documenting the legal name change (Selective Service System 2017a). Female-born individuals are not required to register for Selective Service. However, they may face complications when applying for financial aid as a male. To remedy this issue, the Selective Service System will provide transgender men with a status letter noting an exemption after receipt of an application and birth certificate showing female birth (Selective Service System 2017b). If the individual has already changed his birth certificate, the transgender male can also provide other documentation noting a female to male transition (National Center for Transgender Equality 2005).

Immigration Documents

Transgender individuals may change name and sex markers on their immigration documents. Documents that can be amended include employment authorization documents, refugee travel documents, permanent resident cards, and certificates of citizenship or naturalization. To change the gender marker, the United States Citizenship and Immigration Services (USCIS) requires either a court order, a government-issued document reflecting the appropriate gender, or a letter from a licensed health-care professional stating that the requested gender designation is consistent with a person's gender identity. USCIS explicitly restricts gender options to male or female.

Individuals requesting name changes also need to provide appropriate documentation that is consistent with laws in the jurisdiction where the name change was performed (USCIS 2017b). In its last full day in power, the Obama administration issued a policy memo (PM-602–0141) that updated rules for a change of gender on immigration documents (USCIS 2017a). This followed on the heels of a 2012 policy memo (PM-602–0061) that loosened many of the requirements for amending these documents (USCIS 2012). Earlier USCIS policies required a federal court order to change the sex in a person's immigration file and did not recognize marriages involving transgender individuals to members of the same birth sex in spousal immigration petitions (USCIS 2004). However, the Board of Immigration Appeals case *In re Jose Mauricio Lovo-Lara* (2005) forced USCIS to treat such marriages according to the laws where the marriage occurred. In this instance, since North Carolina allowed transgender individuals to amend their birth certificates under state law and recognized the marriage of the transgender individual in question, USCIS was forced to recognize the marriage despite the federal Defense of Marriage Act's prohibitions on federal same-sex marriage recognition.[6] The Bush administration slow-walked the broader incorporation of *Lovo-Lara* and did not issue a policy memo until January 2009 (USCIS 2009).

State Policies

Driver's License/State-Issued Identification Card

The National Center for Transgender Equality (2016a) rated the requirements to change the gender marker on state driver's licenses, assessing the ease of the forms, who can attest to what is appropriate treatment, any requirements for particular surgical interventions, and any requirements for court orders or birth certificates. States that score higher have easier forms, a broader array of licensed professionals who can determine what appropriate treatment is, and no required legal documents. Table 8.1 provides the rankings by state. Most of the sixteen states where it is difficult to change the gender marker on a driver's license are in the South. Many of the states that modernized their policies did so between 2006 and 2015. For most people, changing the name on a driver's license will require a court order. James et al. (2016) report that 44 percent of respondents who wanted to change the name on their driver's license or state identification card had done it, but only 56 percent of respondents who had transitioned have done so. They also report that only 29 percent of respondents who wanted to change the gender marker on their driver's license or state identification card had completed it. However, among those who have transitioned, this figure rises to 42 percent. In addition to the policies regarding gender marker changes, states have also considered allowing nonbinary gender markers on driver's licenses. On June 26, 2017, the District of Columbia became the first jurisdiction to provide a nonbinary gender marker, X, with Oregon following in July (Segal 2017a), and California adopting the policy in October (Moon 2017).

Birth Certificate

Birth certificates are issued by states, territories, the District of Columbia, and New York City, which has its own vital records laws. Like many other forms of identification, these register a gender marker. As noted in earlier sections, the ability to amend a gender marker on a birth certificate is important because an amended birth certificate is often a requirement for gender

TABLE 8.1. State Driver's License/Identity Card Gender Marker Change Policies, 2016

Policy	Ease Rating	States
Easy-to-understand form, certification from a range of licensed professionals	A⁺	AK, CT, DE, DC, HI, ME, MA, MO, NH, NJ, NM, OR, PA, RI, VA, WA *(15 + DC)*
Easy-to-understand form, certification from a *limited* range of licensed professionals	A	CA, OH *(2)*
Easy-to-understand form, certification by a physician only	A-	CO, IN, NE, NV, WV *(5)*
No form, but no requirement of proof of surgery or court order; certification from medical/mental health professional	B⁺	AZ, FL, ID, IL, KS, MN, NY, VT, WI *(9)*
No form, and burdensome process requirements, but does not require proof of surgery, court order, or amended birth certificate	B	MD, MI, UT *(3)*
Unclear, unknown or unwritten policy	D	AR, MS, ND, SD *(4)*
Proof of surgery, court order, or amended birth certificate required	F	AL, GA, IA, KY, LA, MT, NC, OK, SC, TN, TX, WY *(12)*

Source: National Center for Transgender Equality (2016a).

marker changes on other identity documents. Meyerowitz (2002) notes that, by the mid-1960s, some states were amending the birth certificates of trans individuals. As noted earlier, this often occurred because of court cases that relied on the testimony of physicians who were called as expert witnesses to rebut arguments that sex is determined solely by chromosomes.[7] Today, approximately half the states have specific statutes that allow for birth certificate amendment by transgender people (see table 8.2). Many of these states adopted these policies in the 1970s and 1980s. Passage of these statutes was influenced by model legislation put forth by the Centers for Disease Control and Prevention in 1977 and 1992 (Taylor, Tadlock, and Poggione 2014).

However, birth certificates remain one of the most difficult documents to change. James et al. (2016) report that only 18 percent of transgender respondents have changed the name on their birth certificate. Of those who had transitioned, this figure rose to 24 percent of respondents. They also note that just 9 percent of transgender respondents have changed the gender marker on their birth certificate. Among respondents who had transitioned, 13 percent of respondents had changed the gender marker on their birth certificate. Most of those were people who adhere to a binary gender identity rather than those with a nonbinary identity.

Rules to change a birth certificate vary tremendously by state. Advocacy organizations such as Lambda Legal (2015) and the National Center for Transgender Equality (2017a) compile detailed descriptions of these policies.[8] In states such as Virginia, the bar to change the gender marker on the birth certificate is high. A court order noting that an individual's sex has been changed by surgical procedure is required (Va. Code Ann. §32.1–269). When a court order is required, an added barrier exists if the transgender person is no longer a resident of the birth state. Other states, such as North Carolina, might not require a court order but they still require a licensed physician to attest that sex reassignment surgery has been performed (N.C. Gen. Stat. §§ 130A-118). Some states, such as Missouri, will change the birth certificate after receipt of a court order regarding the performed surgical procedures but mark the birth certificate as amended (Mo. Ann. Stat. § 193.215). This makes it more likely that the document, even though changed, will out the transgender person and possibly subject them to discriminatory treatment (Boone 2017).

More recently, states like California (Cal. Health & Safety Code § 103426) and Iowa (Iowa Code Ann. § 144.23), along with New York City (Croffie 2017) and the District of Columbia (Riley 2013), have created policies that more easily allow transgender people to amend birth certificates. Many of these jurisdictions have relaxed the surgical standard to appropriate medical treatment as determined by a licensed health-care provider and have not required a court order (Lambda Legal 2015). In 2016, Nevada went a step further when it adopted a policy that did not require an affidavit from a health care provider (NAC 440.130). The new policy requires an affidavit from the petitioner along with a second affidavit from another person, or other documentation, that can confirm the assertions by the person in question. Because of its nonmedicalized nature, the National Center for Transgender Equality (2016c) hails this as the "most progressive" birth certificate policy in the nation. To increase privacy in these matters, Oregon, California, and the District of Columbia have also made it possible for transgender individuals to seal court cases involving gender identity changes or shield name and birth certificate changes from public notice, or do both (Hansen 2017; Riley 2013). In another notable development, some courts have allowed individuals to change their gender to nonbinary, hermaphrodite, or intersex (O'Hara 2016; Segal 2016). In December 2016, New York City issued the nation's first known birth certificate with intersex listed as the gender marker (Segal 2017b).

TABLE 8.2. State Birth Certificate Gender Marker Change Requirements, 2017

Requirement	States
Petitioner affidavit and a supplemental affidavit from anyone with personal knowledge of the petitioner's gender identity	NV *(1)*
No court order, health care provider certification of gender transition/identity	CA, CT, DE, DC, HI, IA, ME*, MD, MA*, MN, NY, NYC, OR, PA, RI*, WA *(14 + DC, NYC)*
Court order with health care provider certification of gender transition	IN, MS*, NH, TX, UT*, VT, VA, WV* *(8)*
No court order, health care provider certification of surgical sex change	AK*, AZ, FL, IL, KY*, MI, NE, NJ, NM, NC, ND* *(11)*
Court order with evidence of surgical sex change	AL*, AR, CO, GA, LA, MO*, MT*, OK, SC*, SD, WI*, WY* *(12)*
No gender marker changes allowed	ID, KS, OH, TN *(4)*

Sources: National Center for Transgender Equality (2017), Lambda Legal (2015).
*Birth certificate marked as amended

However, some states will not amend the gender marker on a birth certificate. States that fall into this category include Tennessee, Ohio, Idaho, and Kansas. Tennessee statutes expressly forbid it (Tenn. Code Ann. § 68-3-203(d)). Ohio's decision not to amend birth certificates is based on case law from *In re Ladrach* (1987). In that case, a transgender woman was denied the ability to enter into a marriage with a male because of a lack of statutory guidance specifically allowing for recognition of a gender change. The court in this instance viewed a birth certificate as a historical record of fact. Similarly, authorities in Kansas have interpreted *In re Estate of Gardiner* (2002) as not allowing birth certificate amendments. As such, in 2016 they overturned earlier regulations that allowed for amendment in the event of sex reassignment (Lowry 2016). Idaho officials cite a lack of statutory authority to amend birth certificates in the event of sex reassignment (Lambda Legal 2015). Their policy is currently being challenged in federal court by a Hawaii resident born in Idaho (Boone 2017).

Conclusion

This chapter examined some of the problems faced by transgender people when trying to update their identification documents. It also examined policies to amend the name and gender marker for some major types of identity documents. In general, name changes are easier to obtain than changes to the gender marker on identification documents. For most transgender people in the United States, the birth certificate is the most difficult document to change. In many states, there are difficult procedural hurdles, such as a court order or requirements for particular sex reassignment surgeries, or both. As of June 2018, four states will not amend these documents for issues related to transgender identity. Individuals who have transitioned are more likely to amend their documents than those in transition or those who have not transitioned. In addition, individuals with a binary gender identity are more likely to amend their identity documents than those who have nonbinary identities. Individuals who do not have identity documents that align with their gender presentation are more likely to experience negative interactions with authorities or other service providers. This problem more often afflicts some of the most vulnerable people in society.

CHAPTER 9

Discrimination and Civil Rights

Although there are important criticisms about the limitations of rights-based approaches to gay and transgender advocacy (Vaid 1995; Spade 2015), laws combating discrimination remain a useful tool for activists in the pursuit of equality. These types of civil rights laws are common for a number of protected classes such as race, sex, national origin, religion, and in some places sexual orientation. In this regard, advocacy for laws protecting transgender people follows a rich tradition. Yet, regardless of which protected class a law covers, it is difficult to win employment discrimination cases given the burden of proof on the plaintiff, information asymmetry between the parties, and court biases (Selmi 2001). Despite their limited effectiveness, these policies send a clear signal to the public that discrimination against a target group is not acceptable and might lead to sanctions and negative publicity. They also provide a tool to combat the extremely high levels of discrimination and poverty experienced by many in the transgender community (Grant, Mottet, and Tanis 2011; James et al. 2016).

In our federal system, nondiscrimination laws may operate at the national, state, or local level. Private companies often also have internal policies that prohibit discrimination. Indeed, more than 80 percent of Fortune 500 businesses have internal nondiscrimination policies that offer gender-identity-based protections (Human Rights Campaign 2017a). These policies can be beneficial to transgender people regardless of the jurisdiction where a company is located. However, in this chapter, we turn our attention to the common components of laws combating discrimination and provide an overview of policies and issues in this area.

Laws against Discrimination

Laws combating discrimination commonly describe who is protected (known as protected classes) and what actions are prohibited. For instance, the Civil Rights Act of 1964 offers protections on the basis of race, color, sex, religion, and national origin in the areas of employment and public accommodations. Separate laws address discrimination in other areas. For instance, housing discrimination on the basis of color, national origin, race and religion is addressed under the Civil Rights Act of 1968. Legislation to block sex-based discrimination in education is found in the Education Amendments of 1972 (commonly called Title IX). Some states ban discrimination in credit, insurance, or health care provision. Discrimination against the disabled is combatted by the Americans with Disabilities Act of 1990. However, transgender people are not granted any protections under the latter law because it has specific exclusions for transvestism, transsexualism, and gender identity disorders (see 42 USC 12211). These exclusions were challenged under an equal protection claim via the due process clause in the Fifth Amendment in the case *Blatt v. Cabela's Retail Inc.* (Trotta 2016). However, in May 2017, a federal district court declined to address those claims and instead took a narrow view of what the ADA exclusions entailed (Ramirez 2017). The decision in *Blatt* (2017) noted that despite the excluded identities, such individuals can have disabling conditions, such as gender dysphoria, that are covered under the ADA. Thus, Cabela's attempt to have the case dismissed was rejected.[1]

In statutory construction, it is advisable that legislation include enumerated categories and inclusive language. Without enumerated categories addressing trans identities, judicial or executive branch interpretation of laws might lead to unsatisfactory outcomes. For instance, unless a statutory reference to sexual orientation is explicitly transgender inclusive, courts have generally found that transgender individuals are not covered under sexual-orientation-inclusive policies (*Maffei v. Kolaeton Industry Inc., et al.* 1995; *Underwood v. Archer Management Services Inc.* 1994). The most common term used to signify transgender inclusion in statutes is "gender identity." Another relevant term is "gender expression." Sometimes, definitions include the words "actual or perceived" before gender identity or expression. For example, Vermont provides the following definition of gender identity (1 V.S.A. § 144):

The term "gender identity" means an individual's actual or perceived gender identity, or gender-related characteristics intrinsically related to an individual's gender or gender-identity, regardless of the individual's assigned sex at birth.

Although the federal government does not currently define gender identity in relation to employment nondiscrimination laws, it did define gender identity when the Matthew Shepard Hate Crimes Act was passed in 2009. Thus, in 18 USC 249, gender identity is defined as "actual or perceived gender-related characteristics." However, in some statutes transgender people might also be included in the definition of sexual orientation or in the definition of sex or gender. For example, in Minnesota statutes, sexual orientation is defined as follows (363A.03 Subd. 44):

> Sexual orientation: "Sexual orientation" means having or being perceived as having an emotional, physical, or sexual attachment to another person without regard to the sex of that person or having or being perceived as having an orientation for such attachment, or having or being perceived as having a self-image or identity not traditionally associated with one's biological maleness or femaleness. "Sexual orientation" does not include a physical or sexual attachment to children by an adult.

Colorado defines sexual orientation as follows (CRS 2-4-401):

> "Sexual orientation" means a person's orientation toward heterosexuality, homosexuality, bisexuality, or transgender status or another person's perception thereof.

California's penal code denotes sex and gender as follows (422.56):

> "Gender" means sex, and includes a person's gender identity and gender expression. "Gender expression" means a person's gender-related appearance and behavior whether or not stereotypically associated with the person's assigned sex at birth.

As shown above, there are multiple ways to explicitly include transgender people when writing legislation. From the perspective of transgender rights activists, there is not an ideal approach if the legislation explicitly covers them. The goal is to remove any ambiguity that could cause a court or executive agency to interpret the statute in a noninclusive manner.

Federal Law and Discrimination against Transgender People

As of November 2017, there are no federal laws that explicitly provide protections from discrimination based on gender identity. However, transgender individuals do have protections from discrimination in federal civilian government employment via Executive Order 13672, issued by President Barack Obama in 2014.[2] This order, which largely put gender identity on a par with sexual orientation in terms of civil service protections, also extended protections to employees of contractors working for the federal government. However, transgender individuals, like gays and lesbians, are not explicitly shielded from discrimination in private employment or public accommodations under the Civil Rights Act of 1964. Neither gender identity nor sexual orientation are protected classes in housing discrimination under the Civil Rights Act of 1968. Despite this, during the Obama administration the Department of Housing and Urban Development enacted some regulations, such as its Equal Access Rule (2012), that prohibited sexual-orientation and gender-identity-based discrimination in its programs and services.[3] And as we will discuss in the chapter on education policy, transgender people (along with gays and lesbians) are not explicitly protected from discrimination under Title IX.

As they have for gays and lesbians, repeated attempts to provide explicit statutory protections for transgender people in private employment via the Employment Nondiscrimination Act (ENDA) or comprehensive protections via the Equality Act have failed in Congress. In large part, this can be attributed to the supermajoritarian rules of the Senate and trends in partisan control of the chambers. Republicans tend to oppose this type of legislation (Taylor et al. 2012). They have controlled, with the exception of the 111th Congress (2009–10), at least one chamber of Congress since 1995.

Although there are not explicit statutory protections for sexual orientation and gender identity at the federal level, some legal precedents point to protection for transgender people.[4] Nevertheless, initial cases testing whether or not the sex discrimination prohibitions contained in Title VII of the Civil Rights Act of 1964 would protect transgender people were not especially encouraging. For example, in *Holloway v. Arthur Andersen* (1977), the Ninth Circuit Court of Appeals turned aside the plaintiff's contention that discrimination against transsexuals was not permissible because gender based discrimination was prohibited under Title VII. The court took a narrow view of what unlawful sex discrimination entailed and noted that transsexuals were not a protected class. Similarly, in *Sommers v. Budget Mar-*

keting Incorporated (1982), the Eighth Circuit held that transsexuals were not included under Title VII because of the plain meaning of the word sex and a lack of congressional intent. In *Ulane v. Eastern Airlines* (1984), the Seventh U.S. Circuit Court of Appeals held that discrimination was permissible under Title VII if it happened because of an individual's transsexual identity.

More recent decisions and interpretations of the sex discrimination prohibitions in Title VII by courts and the United States Civil Rights Commission mostly suggest that these protections are more inclusive of the transgender community. These cases largely hinge on a precedent in a landmark case that does not involve a transgender person or gender identity. The Supreme Court in *Price Waterhouse v. Hopkins* (1989) expanded Title VII sex discrimination protections to cover sex stereotyping. This has provided transgender rights advocates with a useful legal strategy—that discrimination against transgender people is prohibited gender stereotyping. This has frequently undermined precedents from earlier employment law cases, such as *Ulane*. Indeed, the Ninth Circuit Court of Appeals in *Schwenk v. Hartford* (2000), a case testing whether a transsexual person could be protected by the Gender Motivated Violence Act, noted that *Price Waterhouse* overturned Title VII precedents from those earlier cases. This line of Title VII reasoning has been utilized in several cases involving transgender plaintiffs. One of the key early decisions was *Smith v. City of Salem, Ohio* (2004) by the Sixth Circuit.[5] In this case, the plaintiff stated that he was a male with a gender identity disorder and as such was a member of a protected class (sex).[6] He was being discriminated against because his feminine behavior and appearance were not in conformance with how his supervisors felt a man should look or act. The appellate court agreed with this theory, and it overturned the district court that had erroneously followed the precedents that predated *Price Waterhouse*.

In another Title VII case, *Schroer v. Billington* (2008), the United States District Court for the District of Columbia found that the defendant unlawfully discriminated against a well-qualified transgender individual who was going to undergo sex reassignment. That decision was grounded both in the gender stereotyping approach discussed above and through the plain meaning of sex in the statutory language of Title VII. This latter approach was in sharp contrast to earlier cases like *Holloway*. The judge in the case drew a compelling analogy between sex discrimination and transsexual discrimination when he argued that laws against religious discrimination would protect converts between religions and not just members of a particular religion. Additionally, the decision noted that Title VII could be expansively interpreted beyond the principal concern of the legislators at the time of passage due to the precedent set in *Oncale v. Sundowner Offshore Services* (1998).

In *Oncale*, the justices unanimously held that Title VII's sexual harassment protections also covered unwanted and improper activity between members of the same sex, even though that was not the principal evil that concerned Congress.[7] This logic was also employed in a case involving the Georgia state legislature, *Glenn v. Brumby* (2011). In addition to following the sex stereotyping approach from *Price Waterhouse* and addressing *Oncale*, the Eleventh Circuit decision invoked the equal protection clause's prohibitions against unwarranted differential treatment for unpopular groups.

In a move that might influence other litigation in this area, the United States Equal Employment Opportunity Commission ruled, in *Macy v. Department of Alcohol, Tobacco, Firearms and Explosives* (2012), that discrimination based on gender identity, a change of sex, and transgender status is prohibited under Title VII protections. However, not all courts post–*Price Waterhouse* have taken this approach. In *Oiler v. Winn-Dixie* (2002), a federal district court in Louisiana dismissed a Title VII claim by a man who was fired for crossdressing while off duty. In *Etsitty v. Utah Transit Authority* (2007), the Tenth Circuit Court of Appeals echoed earlier rulings from the pre–*Price Waterhouse* era and held that Title VII does not protect transsexuals. It also found that the defendant's concerns about the plaintiff using the women's restroom while biologically male was a legitimate reason for termination and not prohibited sex stereotyping.

To date, the Supreme Court has not ruled directly on transgender inclusion under Title VII. However, as noted in our earlier chapters on the courts and the executive branch, the appellate courts have played a role in how federal agencies have interpreted the definition of sex in statutes and regulations. Rulings such as *Smith* and *Macy* provided substantial legal cover for attempts to interpret statutes in a transgender-inclusive manner during the Obama administration. The Trump administration has departed from this practice following guidance from Attorney General Jeff Sessions that holds that transgender people are not protected under Title VII (Savage 2017b). This change highlights the importance of enumerated categories in statutes. Although executive branch interpretations of laws against sex discrimination have provided important transgender rights gains, particularly during Barack Obama's presidency, these advances are far more fragile than laws on the books.

State Nondiscrimination Law

Compared to the national government, states have been more active in developing transgender rights policies. As we discussed in chapter 6, many states have gender identity protections in state government employment that were created by executive order. Additionally, the courts in some states, such as New Jersey, New York, and Connecticut, have chosen to use the logic of the *Price Waterhouse* decision in their rulings on transgender employment discrimination cases (Broadus 2006). Further, Levi and Klein (2006) note that some trans individuals have been able find shelter from discrimination under disability laws in a few states.

However, more clearly defined statutory protections are common and are preferred. As of 2017, twenty states and the District of Columbia provide nondiscrimination protections in employment and housing to transgender people. Nineteen states provide comprehensive protections that also encompass public accommodations. These states are displayed on figure 9.1. Many of the states that have these protections are clustered in the Northeast and in the West. In comparison, twenty-one states and Washington, DC provide comprehensive protections for gays and lesbians. Most states that adopted gay-inclusive laws prior to 2003 have had to "come back" for transgender inclusion. All of the states, except Delaware, that adopted sexual-orientation-inclusive protections after 2003 also expanded gender identity protections concurrently (Taylor and Lewis 2014). For the states that had to "come back," the process has been slow in most instances and the delay is attributed to the position of transgender people within the LGBT advocacy coalition (especially prior to 2003), the rise of same-sex marriage as a salient policy issue prior to *Obergefell*, and a general lack of awareness or concern by legislators (Taylor and Lewis 2014).

The average wait is about fifteen years for the states that have "come back" to pass trans inclusive nondiscrimination protections. Transgender people in Massachusetts had a lag of twenty-two years between the adoption of sexual orientation and gender identity protections, but Delaware's transgender community only waited four years. The two sexual-orientation-inclusive states that have yet to extend protections to transgender people via statute are New York (2001) and Wisconsin (1982).[8] Additionally, some states, such as California, Hawaii, and Massachusetts, have taken a piecemeal approach to extending rights. They have covered different components of discrimination policy at separate times. For instance, Massachusetts chose to extend employment, credit, and housing protections in 2011 and public accommodations protection in 2016.[9] Utah extended employment and housing protections in 2015, but not public accommodations. In general, states that adopt transgender-inclusive protections are more likely to do it under unified Democratic control of the state legislature and executive branch (Taylor

States that have adopted Gender Identity Inclusive State Anti-Discrimination Laws

Figure 9.1. Gender-Identity-Inclusive State Antidiscrimination Laws, June 2017. (National Gay and Lesbian Task Force, Human Rights Campaign.)

Notes: Gray shaded states have banned gender identity/expression discrimination in at least one area, including employment, public accommodations, and housing (twenty states and the District of Columbia) Dates of gender identity inclusion: Minnesota (1993); Rhode Island (2001); New Mexico (2003); California (2003 for employment and housing, 2005 for public accommodations); District of Columbia (2005); Illinois (2005); Maine (2005); Hawaii (2005 for housing, 2006 for public accommodations, 2011 for employment); New Jersey (2006); Washington (2006); Iowa (2007); Oregon (2007); Vermont (2007); Colorado (2007); Connecticut (2011); Nevada (2011); Massachusetts (2011 for housing and employment, 2016 for public accommodations); Delaware (2013); Maryland (2014); Utah (2015) for housing and employment New Hampshire (2018).

et al. 2012). Lax and Phillips (2009) note that on some LGBT issues, such as nondiscrimination in the areas of housing and employment, there is a bias toward conservative policymaking even when overwhelming majorities favor pro-LGBT policies (see also Flores et al. 2015). This does not bode well for the transgender movement in the short term since Republicans control (as of 2018) all of the state legislatures, except New York (where they control the Senate, but not the Assembly), in the 30 states that do not yet have comprehensive gender-identity-inclusive policies (National Conference of State Legislatures 2017a).

Local Nondiscrimination Policy

Given the conservative bias in state policymaking on LGBT rights laws, local governments have sometimes engaged in compensatory policymaking on these issues (Sharp 2005). Localities might create internal policies that ban gender identity discrimination in municipal employment. They might pass ordinances to ban discrimination in private employment, public accommodations, or housing, or all of them. As shown in figure 9.2, more than 200 localities have passed these gender-identity-inclusive ordinances to date (Human Rights Campaign 2016a). With some notable exceptions, such as Houston, many large cities have these policies.

In part, compensatory policymaking explains the large number of localities that have transgender-inclusive ordinances in Michigan, Ohio, and Pennsylvania. The lack of local action in some more liberal states is often due to the presence of transgender-inclusive state laws that remove the need for local policies. Local governments that pass transgender-inclusive nondiscrimination laws tend to have higher education levels, greater diversity, and more people engaged in management, business, science, and arts occupations. Researchers often refer to this as the "urbanism/social diversity model" (Wald, Button, and Rienzo 1996; Taylor et al. 2014). Institutional factors are also important to the passage of transgender-inclusive nondiscrimination policies at the local level. Cities that use strong mayor systems as opposed to council manager systems appear to be more receptive to transgender rights policies (Taylor et al. 2014). Adoption of transgender-inclusive policy is also contingent on the level of home rule authority that a locality has been granted by its state (Gossett 1999). Even where home rule powers exist, a state may choose to preempt local policies. Examples of states having done this include Tennessee and North Carolina. Further, local laws might also be struck down by the courts if they are in conflict with state laws. This occurred in Arkansas in 2017. As we found in our analysis of direct democracy, efforts to repeal local transgender rights laws with popular referendums, such as the 2015 Houston referendum, sometimes occur.

Public Accommodations and Bathrooms

The fight over Houston's Equal Rights Ordinance (HERO) in 2015 contained much messaging about transgender bathroom access. Privacy and safety are two common arguments in this messaging (Davis 2017). Often with the safety discourse, laws granting transgender people access to restrooms that

○ Cities that Prohibit Discrimination Based on Gender Identity in Public and Private Employment

Figure 9.2. Examples of American Cities That Prohibit Employment Discrimination Based on Gender Identity, June 2017

Notes: Compiled by the authors from news sources and the Human Rights Campaign; does not include all cities with these policies.

match their gender identity are portrayed as also allowing men to identify as women for nefarious purposes. This is the safety frame identified by Tadlock (2014). Westbrook and Schilt (2014) note that sex-segregated spaces, such as restrooms, tend to use biologically based criteria rather than identity based criteria for determining access. Due to perceived female vulnerability, they also note a marked difference in how women's spaces are policed relative to male designated spaces. In an inflammatory example of the security frame used by opponents of transgender rights, North Carolina state senator Chad Barefoot, a Republican, e-mailed figure 9.3 to his constituents to defend passage of HB2, a law that preempted a Charlotte LGBT-inclusive nondis-crimination ordinance.[10] HB2 also required that transgender people use the restroom that corresponds to the sex on their birth certificate.[11]

To date, the security frame used to deny transgender people restroom access that conforms to their gender identity or block their inclusion in public accommodations laws has been effective. Our surveys confirm that concerns over safety are quite common among Americans. In our 2016 poll, 52 percent of respondents agreed that allowing transgender people to use the restroom of their choice posed a security risk for women and children, with

Figure 9.3. Security Frame Image on HB2. (E-mail from North Carolina state Senator Chad Barefoot.)

GENDER-NEUTRAL RESTROOM

just one-third disagreeing with this security frame. Indeed, there is a long history of LGBT rights opponents using this tactic and it was employed in campaigns in Anchorage (AK), Gainesville (FL), Montgomery County (MD), and several other localities. Further back in time, Phyllis Schlafly and her allies deployed arguments about privacy between the sexes to assist in thwarting the Equal Rights Amendment during the 1970s and early 1980s (Levi and Redman 2010). Of course, restrooms, and who can go in them, have long been contested terrain. From women who attempted to gain access to public life but found no women's restrooms, to African Americans plagued by race-segregated facilities, to transgender people today, the bathroom has been a battlefield in many fights for civil rights (Davis 2017).

Concerns about the "bathroom issue" have led to delays, even in some inclusive states, in efforts to adopt public accommodations protections for transgender people. Perhaps most notably, this occurred in Massachusetts, a state often portrayed as very liberal on social issues, when it passed employment and housing protections in 2011. However, policymakers demurred on public accommodations to build legislative support for the other provisions given privacy and safety concerns about giving access to sex-segregated facilities based on aspects other than biology (MassLive 2011). The bill passed in 2011 (H.3810) reflected these concerns when it defined gender identity as follows:

"Gender identity" shall mean a person's gender-related identity, appearance or behavior, whether or not that gender-related identity, appearance or behavior is different from that traditionally associated with the person's physiology or assigned sex at birth. Gender-related identity may be shown by providing evidence including, but not limited to, medical history, care or treatment of the gender-related identity, consistent and uniform assertion of the gender-related identity or any other evidence that the gender-related identity is sincerely held as part of a person's core identity; provided, however, that gender-related identity shall not be asserted for any improper purpose.

The added focus on consistency, sincerely held, and improper purpose marks a sharp contrast from a bill (H. 502) earlier in the session that stated:

The term "gender identity or expression" shall mean a gender-related identity, appearance, expression, or behavior of an individual, regardless of the individual's physiology or assigned sex at birth.

Massachusetts did not pass public accommodations protections for transgender people until 2016, when the issue of transgender bathrooms burst into prominence during the national debate over North Carolina's HB2.

Courts have also addressed the transgender bathroom issue, with conflicting rulings. In *Cruzan v. Special School District # 1* (2002), the United States Court of Appeals for the Eighth Circuit held that women's restroom usage by a male-to-female transgender employee does not create a hostile work environment for other employees under Title VII. However, in *Etsitty v. Utah Transit Authority* (2007) the Tenth Circuit held that the firing of a transgender woman over concerns about her using the women's restroom was not prohibited under Title VII. North Carolina's HB2 was challenged on Title VII grounds in federal court as well. However, neither *Carcaño, et al. v. McCrory, et al.* nor a separate lawsuit by the Justice Department were decided before the law was repealed by the legislature.[12] State courts have weighed in on these matters, too. In *Goins v. West Group* (2001), Minnesota's Human Rights Act was determined to neither require nor prohibit employers from designating restroom access for either biological gender or gender self-image. As an ongoing policy debate at all levels of government, courts will be instrumental in determining whether transgender people will be able to secure unfettered access to public accommodations.

Religious Exemptions

A threat to LGBT-inclusive nondiscrimination laws is found in the Religious Freedom Restoration Act of 1993 (RFRA) (Haider-Markel and Taylor 2016). In *Burwell v. Hobby Lobby* (2014), the Supreme Court found that RFRA allowed owners of a privately held for-profit company to refuse to provide insurance coverage for contraception for employees as mandated by the Patient Protection and Affordable Care Act. Hobby Lobby argued that such coverage would be a violation of the owner's religious beliefs. Given the ruling and its justification, it is plausible that owners of closely held companies could use the same legal reasoning and attempt to discriminate against transgender or gay individuals, or same-sex couples, in hiring or in the course of their business operations. This concern is based on a passage in *Burwell* (2014, 46):

> The principal dissent raises the possibility that discrimination in hiring, for example on the basis of race, might be cloaked as religious practice to escape legal sanction. . . . Our decision today provides no such shield. The Government has a compelling interest in providing an equal opportunity to participate in the workforce without regard to race, and prohibitions on racial discrimination are precisely tailored to achieve that critical goal.

The majority opinion was silent about discrimination against LGBT people. However, as we have already discussed, gender identity and sexual orientation are not enumerated classes in the nation's major civil rights laws or in the laws of most states. It is possible that the expansive view of the RFRA in *Hobby Lobby* could override existing federal regulations or executive orders that provide limited protections in health care, housing, or employment. Indeed, there are increasing fears of this given the recent decision by Attorney General Sessions to expansively interpret religious freedom laws during the Trump administration (Zapotosky and Bailey 2017).

Although the Court ruled in *City of Boerne v. Flores* (1997) that federal RFRA does not apply to the states, many states have introduced their own RFRA legislation. Indeed, twenty-one states, concentrated in the South and Midwest, have passed RFRAs (National Conference of State Legislatures 2016, 2017b). However, only a few of these states have LGBT-inclusive antidiscrimination laws that would be threatened as of 2017. Still, state RFRAs could certainly undermine local-level nondiscrimination policies or hamper any LGBT-inclusive state laws.

Other possible threats to inclusive local or state laws exist in First Amendment's free speech and religious free expression protections. A case before the Supreme Court during the 2017–18 term, *Masterpiece Cake Shop, LTD v. Colorado Civil Rights Commission* examined these issues (Epps 2017). In this case, a bakery in Colorado refused to supply a wedding cake for a same-sex couple who was getting married. The baker's lawyers argue that a Colorado law barring discrimination in public accommodations, on the basis of sexual orientation (and gender identity), infringes on the owner's constitutionally protected freedoms. Lower courts have held this to be in violation of state policy. However in a 7–2 decision, the Supreme Court found that the Civil Rights Commission showed bias against the baker in applying the civil rights law. This narrow decision, largely based on facts unique to the case, avoided answering questions about the potential conflict between First Amendment protections and civil rights laws (Liptak 2018).

Transgender and Military Service

Historically, transgender people were blocked from serving in the armed forces. Unlike gay, lesbian, and bisexual service members, they were not provided any relief from the end of the Don't Ask Don't Tell (DADT) policy that that was lifted by Congress in 2011. However, transgender people had also never been the object of congressional policymaking in this area. Whereas DADT had been law, transgender people were only denied through several regulations that restricted their ability to join or remain in the armed services. For instance, Department of Defense Instruction 6130.03 set forth medical standards and disqualifying conditions for recruits. This blocked individuals who had a change of sex from joining the military and barred those with a history of "psychosexual conditions" such as transsexualism or transvestism.

Although these regulations were pernicious for transgender soldiers, they also provided an opportunity for change. Because regulations could be changed through executive branch action, and the Obama administration had been amenable to transgender rights, a policy window was open (Kingdon 1984). As such, activists such as Aaron Belkin at the Palm Center and organizations such as SPARTA and their allies waged a campaign to end this ban. They provided research about the positive impact of transgender soldiers and engaged in a spirited public relations campaign (Belkin 2016). For instance, Fiona Dawson's documentary *Transgender, at War and in Love* depicted the lives of two patriotic transgender soldiers, and this humanized the issues for the public.[13] Former surgeon general Jocelyn Elders and Rear

Admiral Alan Steinman, MD (2014) authored a report that found there was no medical rationale for banning transgender soldiers, and a study by the RAND Corporation (2016) found that transgender soldiers would have a minimal impact on force readiness. In our interview with Belkin (2016), he noted that the repeal was helped by the end of DADT. That policy change had generated momentum and created space for gay soldiers and sailors to advocate for transgender inclusion. One such ally was the first openly gay secretary of the army, Eric Fanning. Also important were well-placed officials, such as Under Secretary of Defense for Personnel and Readiness Brad Carson, who had shepherded through other important changes, such as opening combat positions to women. In addition, many in the military felt that "we had had this conversation [about LGBT inclusion]," and the opposition's "unit cohesion" argument had failed to be borne out in the years since the end of DADT (Belkin 2016). In June 2016, Secretary of Defense Ashton Carter announced an end to the ban on transgender service members (Rosenberg 2016).

However, even with the end of the ban there was still not a formal policy in place for transgender people entering the armed forces, only guidance from Secretary of Defense Carter. This provided an opening for his successor from the Trump administration, Defense Secretary Jim Mattis, to delay the policy (Lamothe 2017a). The Obama era directive also held that transgender service members could not be removed from service and that they must undergo an eighteen-month process before they can be certified by a doctor as stable in their gender preference. Transgender recruits, including officers, must also undergo the eighteen-month process, but this was to occur before they formally entered the military (Brook 2017). In effect, this policy barred recent graduates of military academies from receiving a military commission upon earning their degree.

However, as noted earlier, President Trump "tweeted" that he was going to reinstate the ban on transgender soldiers and he directed the Secretary of Defense to do so (White House 2017c). In discussing a review of the issue by a panel of experts, Secretary Mattis hinted that the study's findings would adhere to the president's directive when he noted that new political appointees "will play an important role in this effort" (Lamothe 2017b).

The Trump administration's proposed ban on transgender troops is facing an increasing number of lawsuits. In one lawsuit filed by the National Center for Lesbian Rights and GLBTQ Legal Advocates & Defenders on behalf of eight transgender service members, the Massachusetts state attorney general filed an amicus brief along with fourteen other state attorneys general to block the "irrational decision to reverse recent progress and reinstitute formal discrimination against transgender individuals" (LeBlanc 2017). While federal courts in California, DC, Maryland and Washington have issued preliminary injunctions on the ban pending decisions in these lawsuits, it is unclear what will happen to the careers of the transgender troops currently serving their nation (Wheeler 2017; Savage 2017a; Lavers 2017). However, thanks the myriad of court rulings blocking, at least temporarily, the Trump administration's intended direction on these matters, the military began accepting transgender recruits on January 1, 2018 (Ring 2018). Current estimates place the number of transgender troops at 6,600 (Brook 2017).

Conclusion

In this chapter, we briefly reviewed gains that transgender people have achieved through nondiscrimination law in court decisions, executive orders, and statutes at the national, state, and local levels. The gains have been significant, especially at the subnational level. We also identified challenges that transgender activists and their allies face. These challenges include the lack of explicit protection in the nation's major civil rights laws. Additionally, the arguments of transgender rights opponents around privacy and safety, especially on public accommodations and transgender people's access to restrooms based on gender identity, have been very effective at curtailing the recent success in passage of local and state discrimination protections. In addition, Republican control of most legislatures in states lacking trans inclusive protections has led to the blockage of many inclusive bills. Republican controlled legislatures, particularly in the South have sometimes preempted local trans inclusive laws. RFRAs and the *Hobby Lobby* decision offer another threat at the national level and in many states, and states are increasingly considering new laws to expand notions of religious freedom. However, transgender rights advocates still have opportunities to advance rights. The courts, particularly in terms of employment discrimination, have been an important vehicle for advancing transgender equality. Additionally, executive actions can sometimes offer relief even when advocates are faced with recalcitrant legislatures. Localities have also often provided a path forward when not preempted or otherwise blocked by state policy.

CHAPTER 10

Health Care Policy

with Ryan Combs

This chapter addresses health care policy and how it affects transgender individuals. Joining us in this chapter is Ryan Combs, a noted expert on health care policy in transgender populations. Like anyone, transgender people need access to affirming and competent health care to achieve good mental and physical health. Along with the significant positive changes in public opinion discussed in earlier chapters, recent years have seen major shifts in policies and practices related to transgender health care. Professional associations such as the American Medical Association, the American Psychiatric Association, the American Psychological Association, and the American Public Health Association have released statements in support of improved access to health care for this population (Lambda Legal 2016). Their statements find that numerous barriers to high-quality care exist for transgender individuals, such as discrimination and health insurance exclusions of transition-related treatment.

Transgender health, once a marginalized specialty in medicine, is moving toward the mainstream. In recent years, there has been a shift from a pathologizing health care model that treats transgender identities as illnesses, to an affirming health care model that focuses on the well-being of the transgender individual (Singer 2006). We see this shift in the American Association of Medical Colleges' (2014) comprehensive guidance to integrate transgender health into medical school curricula. It is also found in the movement toward less stigmatizing language about transgender people in the most recent edition of the American Psychiatric Association's *Diagnostic and Statistical Manual of Mental Disorders* (DSM-5) (Zucker et al. 2013), and in the statements of support from a variety of professional medical organizations (Lambda Legal 2016).

The increased attention to competent transgender care has likely facilitated transgender advocates' effective use of medical necessity-based political and legal arguments that give deference to increasingly supportive medical professionals (e.g., Nash 2011). Doctors, therapists, and medical service providers have long affected the lives of transgender people in both positive and negative ways (e.g., Stryker and Whittle 2006). Some physicians helped facilitate medical treatments for transgender people, but others served as gatekeepers, effectively barring treatments. In addition to the direct provision or withholding of services, they are authorities who wield cultural, social, and political power (Meyerowitz 2002; Stryker and Whittle 2006; Raymond 1979). They can shape public policy through recommendations, serve as expert witnesses or file amicus briefs in court proceedings, and shape public discourse.

In part, Jamison Green (2016), the former president of the World Professional Association for Transgender Health and the first transgender-identified head of the organization, explained that some of this positive shift was due to the hard-fought inclusion of transgender people within professional medical organizations. Whereas physicians and researchers drove early transgender medical treatments, patient perspectives have been incorporated into recent health care models. For instance, transgender people gained a voice within the World Professional Association for Transgender Health in the late 1990s and early 2000s.[1] Further, transgender people have shaped the provision of transgender health through grassroots activism and an increasing unwillingness to be controlled by researchers or health care providers (e.g., Denny 1992). They have criticized services or diagnoses that they have found lacking. Importantly, they have critiqued the diagnosis of Gender Identity Disorder for stigmatizing transgender identities (Zucker 2013 et al.). They have become knowledgeable participants in research and not just subjects in research about transgender health (Wilkinson 2006).

This chapter introduces key issues in transgender health and health care services in the United States. Then, it presents concerns related to health insurance coverage for transgender people. Examining selected policies and legal decisions concerning transgender health, it examines the strategies used to advance or constrain affirming policies and considers the strategies' relative successes or failures in light of the rapidly changing political landscape. It concludes with a discussion about future directions for transgender health policy.

Transgender Health Care

Transgender people have been seeking medical assistance to facilitate gender transition since at least the 1920s (Meyerowitz 2002).[2] Gender dysphoria, a phrase used in the DSM-5, describes a discordance between one's gender identity and the sex assigned to them at birth (American Psychiatric Association 2013). Psychiatrists once considered gender nonconformity to be a mental illness, but the growing scientific consensus is that transgender people's internal sense of their gender (i.e., their gender identity) cannot be altered to match their assigned sex (Cohen-Kettenis and Gooren 1999). Accordingly, the profession has taken steps to change the framing of transgender identities away from a pathological classification, to considering it a rare but normal variation of the human experience. This push was codified by a diagnostic change in the DSM-5 from gender identity disorder to gender dysphoria, recognizing that it is clinically significant distress caused by gender incongruence, and not the identity itself, that is diagnosable (American Psychiatric Association 2013; Zucker et al. 2013).

A medically facilitated gender transition is the accepted treatment for transgender people who experience gender dysphoria. The purpose of gender-affirming treatment is to produce changes to the primary and secondary sex characteristics to align the body with one's gender identity. Based on clinical experience and peer-reviewed evidence (e.g., Cohen-Kettenis and Gooren 1999), the World Professional Association for Transgender Health, the leading professional organization of clinicians and academics in the field, contends that gender-affirming treatments are medically necessary. They state that such treatments and surgical procedures have been demonstrated to be "beneficial and effective" and play an "undisputed role in contributing toward favorable outcomes" (World Professional Association for Transgender Health 2016).

Transgender health care is interdisciplinary. Doctors treating transgender people are in primary care, endocrinology, urology, plastic surgery, and other specialties. Medical treatment may include mental health counseling, hormone therapy, electrolysis or laser hair removal, and surgery. Surgeries for transgender men may include bilateral mastectomy (chest surgery), hysterectomy (removal of the uterus and potentially also the ovaries, fallopian tubes, and cervix), vaginectomy (removal of the vagina), salpingo-oophorectomy (removal of the fallopian tubes and ovaries), phalloplasty or metoidioplasty (construction of the penis), and body contouring (liposuction to masculinize body shape). For transgender women, surgeries may include facial feminization, breast augmentation, thyroid chondroplasty (reduction of the

Adam's apple), orchiectomy (removal of the testicles), penectomy (removal of the penis), vaginoplasty (construction of the vagina), and clitoroplasty (construction of the clitoris). Of course, this list is not exhaustive. Some transgender people, especially transgender women, also take part in speech and language therapy to become more comfortable with their voice and to learn how to use it safely. The decisions about which treatments a transgender person pursues are individual. Some transgender people need significant medical intervention to affirm their gender identity, while others do not need transition-related medical treatment at all.

Barriers to health care are also a key issue for this group. Transgender people are less likely to have health insurance coverage than other Americans, including those who identify as lesbian, gay, or bisexual (Baker, Durso, and Cray 2014; James et al. 2016). They are also less likely than cisgender people to have a health provider and to have seen a dentist in the past year (Meyer et al. 2017). Even when they do have access to a health provider, transgender people may face additional obstacles to obtaining appropriate health services. Many report having to educate their doctor about their health, being asked intrusive questions about their gender identity when presenting about an unrelated illness, and being refused care related to their gender transition, among other issues (James et al. 2016). Indeed, 33 percent of respondents in a recent survey had experienced a negative interaction with health care providers in the previous year due to their transgender status (James et al. 2016). One author on this project, Jami Taylor, provides some anecdotal evidence of this type of poor treatment. On one visit to her former doctor, the physician asked if the entire medical team could examine her genitalia because several of the nurse practitioners, nurses, and medical aides in the office had never worked with a transgender patient. After thirty minutes of sitting with her feet in stirrups while a parade of strangers reviewed and commented on her internal and external anatomy, she felt more like a medical exhibit or zoo animal than a patient. She had also been denied care at another office after being told that the doctor "does not treat your kind."

Further, treatments can be prohibitively expensive if the costs fall on the individual patient. While the extent of the problem is unknown, according to a 2015 survey of transgender adults about 25 percent of transgender people report having problems with health insurance in the past year related to being transgender, including denial of coverage for routine care (James et al. 2016). In addition, more than 55 percent of transgender respondents reported being denied insurance coverage for transition-related surgery and 25 percent were denied coverage for hormones in the past year (James et al. 2016). The cost of coverage for care related to gender transition is miniscule for insurance carriers, given the small size of the transgender population but out-of-pocket costs can be prohibitively high for transgender individuals, meaning that many are unable to access medically necessary services such as transition-related surgeries.[3] At the health system level, evidence suggests that coverage of medically necessary services for transgender people is cost effective because it leads to improved mental and physical health while having a negligible impact on overall premium costs (Padula, Heru, and Campbell 2016). Providing no care at all is unethical because it can have a great cost to the individual's health and well-being in both the short and long term (Stroumsa 2014).

Health Disparities and the Social Determinants of Health

Much of the discussion about transgender health focuses on transition-related treatments; however, transgender people are subject to the same diseases as the general population, such as heart disease, cancer, respiratory diseases, stroke, and diabetes. They also experience health disparities, which are avoidable differences in health status affecting certain groups. Being transgender carries a great deal of social stigma, therefore it is unsurprising that they report a disproportionately higher prevalence of poor mental and physical health when compared to cisgender people (Meyer et al. 2017). Transgender people are more likely to suffer from mental health problems such as anxiety, suicide, and substance misuse, and report more days per month of poor physical and mental health (Hendricks and Testa 2012; James et al. 2016; Meyer et al. 2017). HIV is a significant concern among transgender people, especially women of color (Baral et al. 2013). Violence is another important health issue; transgender people are at increased risk for multiple types of violence throughout their lifespan and are at an especially high risk of experiencing child abuse, sexual violence, and elder abuse (Stotzer 2009; Cook-Daniels and Munson 2010; Roberts et al. 2012). Older transgender people may also face difficulties, particularly if they become vulnerable due to physical frailty or if they have cognitive impairments. Many aging transgender people face a lack of social support due to family and social relationships that might have been changed due to a person's transition. There is a dearth of data about transgender health in many other areas of medicine, but the quantity and quality of research on this population appears to be increasing exponentially (e.g., Witten and Eyler 2012).

The social determinants of health—the conditions in which people live—drive health disparities at the population level (Marmot 2005). Economics, politics, and policy shape these conditions. Important factors for good health include the availability of resources such as education and jobs, fair treatment, social support, and safety. However, the reality for many transgender people is stark in this regard. The 2015 U.S. Transgender Survey, the largest to date (*n* = 27,715), found that transgender people experience disparities that include pervasive discrimination, harassment, and violence, economic hardship, and poor mental and physical health as compared to the overall U.S. population (James et al. 2016). Social marginalization and stigma, family breakdown, and homelessness are all contributing factors.

In ways that are not yet fully understood, the intersectional effect of multiple sources of oppression may compound the disparities for transgender people belonging to other socially marginalized groups, such as racial and ethnic minorities, people living in poverty, and people with disabilities (Lopez and Gadsden 2016). The negative impact of social inequity reduces the resources available to the individual and increases barriers to care. This, in turn, exacerbates health disparities. Data show that transgender people of color and those with disabilities face far worse health outcomes than the group as a whole (James et al. 2016).

Health Insurance

Having health insurance coverage is essential to accessing affordable health care in the United States due to the extremely high costs of medical treatment. Yet transgender people face several barriers to getting and using health insurance coverage. First, companies have historically refused insurance to many transgender people, particularly before the Affordable Care Act (ACA) began to protect people with preexisting conditions from denials of coverage. Second, many insurance companies have blanket transgender exclusions in place, meaning that their plans will not cover any services or procedures related to being transgender. A quarter of respondents to the U.S. Transgender Survey reported difficulty with insurance in the past year that was related in some way to their gender identity (James et al. 2016). Denials of coverage range from psychological support and assessment, to hormones, to surgical and other treatments described earlier in the chapter.

Third, insurance companies often deny coverage when the gender listed on a person's insurance plan does not match the gender associated with a particular treatment. An example of this would be when a transgender man is designated male on his insurance records but then requires a pelvic exam (Shaffer 2005). A transgender person may also need a mix of "gendered" treatments and screenings, for example a transgender woman who needs both a mammogram and a prostate exam or a transgender man who needs both testosterone and a Pap test. Binary sex designations in health systems do not consider the needs of transgender people. This affects care both related to, and unrelated to, their gender transition. It is unclear whether these denials are a function of intentional discrimination, a lack of foresight or consideration for gender diversity in health records systems, or both. When insurance companies deny coverage, the burden falls on the transgender patient to pay or appeal the bill.

Public and private payers rationalize blanket transgender exclusions by drawing upon outdated information, misinformation, or bias. Insurers have described gender reassignment as cosmetic, experimental, and unproven— none of which are in keeping with the current medical consensus (Green 1998a). As Stroumsa (2014) suggests, payers should make decisions about pursuing gender reassignment in the same way as any other treatment—by weighing the potential risks of the treatment versus the potential benefits and the risks involved in failing to treat. In many cases, insurers deny transgender people coverage for treatments that they approve for cisgender people.

However, the health insurance situation for transgender people is improving. Recently, there has been increasing public and private coverage of transition-related care. Baker (2017) identifies three principal reasons for this shift: the growing medical consensus around the necessity of such treatments, legal guidance and court decisions in favor of transgender health insurance nondiscrimination protections, and evidence that these treatments are cost effective.

Approaches to Advancing Transgender-Affirming Policies

Individual and Employer-Based Approaches

In the United States, transgender people have often self-funded their gender transition treatments due to the lack of insurance coverage. As such, access to treatment is often a function of socioeconomic class. Those with greater incomes are more likely to be able to access needed treatment while access is more precarious for those without financial resources (James et al. 2016). However, in recent decades, many transgender people, their doctors, and interest groups have argued that insurance companies should cover gender reassignment treatments due to medical necessity. This includes publicly funded payers such as Medicare, Medicaid, and TRICARE, a health program for members of the military and their families. Individuals, at times assisted by organizations such as the American Civil Liberties Union and the Transgender Legal Defense and Education Fund, have submitted appeals, filed complaints with state insurance regulators, and challenged the insurance denials in court. The legal arguments commonly used to challenge government denials by public programs have often been based on constitutional protections (e.g., Eighth Amendment for transgender prisoners) or federal Medicaid rules regarding medical necessity (e.g., *Pinneke v. Preisser* 1980). There are also Title VII arguments against discriminatory treatment in employer sponsored health care plans (e.g., *Baker v. Aetna* 2017).

Employers can elect to negotiate with insurance companies to remove transgender exclusions and add affirming policies to their health plans. In 2001, the City and County of San Francisco became the first major employer to announce insurance coverage of transition-related treatments when the San Francisco Board of Supervisors voted to remove transgender exclusions (Human Rights Campaign 2010b). Many public employers have followed suit, including states such as California, Massachusetts, New York, and Washington, and cities such as New York, Chicago, Boston, Phoenix, and Cincinnati. In addition, the number of private employers that provide insurance coverage for gender transitions has risen dramatically. The Human Rights Campaign's Corporate Equality Index shows the number of major employers providing inclusive coverage increased from forty-nine in 2009 to 647 in 2017 (Human Rights Campaign 2017a). Affirming policies and initiatives designed to increase LGBT inclusivity are part of wider efforts by many companies to increase their competitiveness in, and attractiveness to, a diverse workforce.

State Approaches

The rules concerning health insurance plans sold through state exchanges vary by state. Some states have enacted civil rights protections based on gender in public accommodations that apply to the health care context. Where implicit, administrators are increasingly interpreting existing gender-based protections as applying to transgender people. Discrimination because of gender identity in private insurance plans is prohibited in eighteen states and the District of Columbia. In addition, twelve states and the District of Columbia have changed their Medicaid rules to make gender transition coverage explicitly included (Baker 2017). For example, the California Department of Managed Health Care and the Department of Insurance issued nondiscrimination directives requiring health insurers to provide coverage for medically necessary treatment for transgender people when the same treatments are covered for cisgender people (California Department of Insurance 2013; Barnhart 2013). The majority of states, however, have no nondiscrimination protections or transgender affirmative coverage requirements. Further, some states have exclusions for sex reassignment procedures and restrictions on cosmetic and experimental treatments under their Medicaid policies (True 2012).

Prisoners

Consequential court cases have also involved transgender prisoners seeking new or continued treatment while in custody. In *Fields v. Smith* (2011), a federal court found that a Wisconsin law prohibiting funding for gender reassignment treatments had violated prisoners' constitutional right to equal protection and guarantee not to be subjected to cruel and unusual punishment. In *Kosilek v. Spencer* (2014), a prisoner who sought gender reassignment surgery presented an argument for medical necessity. A district court in Massachusetts found, and a three-judge panel of the First Circuit Court of Appeals affirmed 2–1, in favor of the plaintiff. However, the state sought additional review, and a panel of judges overturned the original decision 3–2 in 2014 (*Kosilek v. Spencer* 2014). The majority opinion stated that the nonsurgical treatment provided was satisfactory and that the ruling judge did not adequately consider the Department of Corrections' postsurgery security concerns. The Supreme Court declined to review the *Kosilek* case; therefore, the issue of gender transition care for prisoners remains unresolved.

Federal Approaches

Affordable Care Act Section 1557

The Obama administration led a strong top-down push for improving transgender health care access. This culminated in explicit nondiscrimination protections in Section 1557 of the Affordable Care Act (Patient Protection and Affordable Care Act 2010). Section 1557 gave civil rights protections on the basis of sex (among other characteristics) in health programs or activities that are administered by, or receive funds from, the federal government—that is, virtually all major health care providers. Prohibition of discrimination on the basis of sex has direct relevance because federal courts have increasingly interpreted sex discrimination laws as covering transgender people. Indeed, in 2012 the Department of Health and Human Services (HHS) clarified its interpretation of the Section 1557 sex discrimination prohibition as encompassing discrimination based on gender identity (Johnson 2012).

In May 2016, HHS issued a final rule on implementing Section 1557 (U.S. HHS Office of the Secretary 2016) and elucidating federal transgender nondiscrimination protections in health care. The final rule included protections from discrimination on the basis of both gender identity and sex stereotyping. The department's definition of gender identity acknowledged that gender could be nonbinary. However, on December 31, 2016, the day before it was due to go into effect, federal enforcement of the rule was enjoined nationwide by Judge Reed O'Connor of the United States District Court for the Northern District of Texas (*Franciscan Alliance, Inc. et al. v. Burwell* 2016).[4] In ruling for the plaintiffs, O'Connor found that the regulation could require coverage for gender transition treatments and reproductive-related services like abortions that would violate the Religious Freedom Restoration Act. The Trump administration is unlikely to defend the regulation on appeal, particularly after Attorney General Sessions noted that transgender identity is not covered under the Title VII definition of sex (Savage 2017b), leaving the future of the regulation's protections uncertain. Further, shortly into his administration, President Donald Trump and the Republican Congress began taking steps to dismantle the Affordable Care Act altogether. While these attempts have repeatedly failed (Roubein 2017), the future of the ACA is unclear. In addition, the Trump Administration's 2017 Executive Order on religious liberty and its January 2018 creation of a new Conscience and Religious Freedom Division in the HHS Office for Civil Rights may make it easier for health care workers to refuse treatment to transgender people on the basis of religious beliefs (Eilperin and Cha 2018).

Dismantling the ACA could have a substantial negative impact on transgender people. First, explicit transgender nondiscrimination protections could no longer be in place, meaning that many transgender people would have little recourse if they experienced mistreatment or inequities in health care.[5] Second, rolling back preexisting condition protections could mean that insurance companies might not insure transgender people with a history of gender transition. Third, gains in health insurance access due to Medicaid expansion and federal subsidies could reverse, resulting in many people becoming uninsured. These events would be a crushing blow for transgender health.

Medicare

Medicare is a publicly funded federal health insurance program that covers people over the age of sixty-five and younger people with certain disabilities or health conditions. Medicare specifically excluded "transsexual surgery" from 1989 until 2014 because these surgeries were considered experimental (Department of Health and Human Services Appeals Board 2014). Around the same time, a lawsuit from Denee Mallon, a transgender woman who had been denied coverage for sex reassignment surgery, spurred HHS to review the policy (Cha 2014).[6] After considering the advances in science and medicine, the HHS Appeals Board rescinded the exclusion (HHS Departmental Appeals Board 2014; Centers for Medicare and Medicaid Services 2014). Medicare already covered hormone therapy for transgender beneficiaries and the new policy indicates that Medicare will make decisions about the medical necessity of transition-related surgeries on a case-by-case basis (Centers for Medicare and Medicaid Services 2017). As a result, Mallon was able to undergo sex reassignment surgery in 2015 at age seventy-four.

The case-by-case determination approach based on medical necessity is consistent with other types of doctor and hospital services covered under Medicare. In addition, the National Center for Transgender Equality (2017b) notes that although different Medicare programs have slightly different rules about treatment access, both original Medicare and private Medicare programs, like Medicare Advantage or Medicare Part D, have appeals processes if case-by-case determinations are unsatisfactory. The potential impact of the ruling in Denee Mallon's case is highly significant given that Medicare is the largest health care program in the nation (Centers for Medicare and Medicaid Services 2013).

Military

TRICARE is the health plan provided to active duty military, retired military, members of the National Guard and Reserve, and their dependents. As of October 3, 2016, TRICARE provides mental health services and hormone therapy to transgender enrollees, but it still prohibits surgical care for non-active-duty beneficiaries (TRICARE 2016). Active duty service members can request a waiver based on medical necessity. The Department of Defense made the TRICARE health policy changes in preparation for July 1, 2017, when, for the first time, openly transgender people will be eligible to join the military (Department of Defense 2016). The costs associated with this decision, although they are comparatively low, are one of the flashpoints in the ongoing political controversy about transgender military service (Hamblin 2017). As noted in our earlier chapters on public opinion, public funding of medical treatments for gender dysphoria related care is unpopular. However, barring treatment access and forcing transgender individuals who wish to remain in the military back into an unhealthy silence will likely increase the negative health consequences that come with a lack of treatment. That will surely increase health care consumption and related costs in other ways.

With respect to transgender veterans, the Department of Veterans Affairs has published comprehensive directives on the care of transgender veterans (Veterans Health Administration 2013). These directives clarify what treatments are provided related to gender transition. While a Department of Veterans Affairs regulation explicitly excludes surgery from the medical benefits package, it will provide all other medically necessary care such as mental health services, hormone therapy, and pre- and postoperative evaluation and care. The directives outline medical and administrative processes that should take place when a veteran transitions and gives guidance on topics such as pronouns, room assignments, and bathrooms (Veterans Health Administration 2013). The document reports that field staff training was developed and implemented in FY 2012.

Bottom-Up Federal Approaches

Not all federal approaches have been top-down. As we discussed in earlier chapters and with the Denee Mallon case, litigation has been used to advance transgender rights in the health care field. Drawing from a separate case mentioned earlier in the volume, Internal Revenue Service arguments that hormone therapy and sex reassignment surgeries did not treat a medically recognized disease, and that such procedures were cosmetic, were successfully challenged in court (*O'Donnabhain v. Commissioner of Internal Revenue* 2010). In *O'Donnabhain*, the plaintiff's legal team demonstrated that gender identity disorder was a serious condition that was widely addressed in the medical literature, and they provided evidence that the petitioner had undergone appropriate medical treatment for this serious condition. As such, the plaintiff was able to deduct expenses related to her transition on her taxes, consistent with the limitations imposed on other medical conditions. Importantly for other transgender taxpayers, the Internal Revenue Service subsequently amended its policy to conform to the ruling (Internal Revenue Service 2011).

In the earlier chapter on nondiscrimination, we also noted the ongoing legal challenge to the blanket transgender exclusion in the Americans with Disabilities Act (*Blatt v. Cabela's Retail Inc.* 2017). A federal district court recently allowed a transgender plaintiff to proceed with an ADA case against her employer. If the case is successful, this could remove one of the last remaining federal policies that allow for de jure discrimination against transgender people.

Conclusion

Access to gender-affirming treatments specifically, and quality health care generally, requires consideration of both types of care in policy and practice. Advancement on transgender health requires policymakers to consider not only the questions of how and when to cover care related to gender transitions but also how to mitigate the social determinants of health that cause transgender people to have poor health in general.

Incremental, bottom-up approaches to increasing access to transition related health care include strategies such as appealing insurance denials, seeking court or regulatory remedies, advocating for inclusive employer-based coverage, and lobbying for gender-identity nondiscrimination protections at the state and local levels. These types of approaches have been taking place for several years. These efforts have brought about mixed results for individuals, but have had a positive effect overall.

Top-down federal approaches by the Obama administration would have addressed the issues with transgender health access in the majority of cases. However, many of these reforms are jeopardized by the starkly different policy priorities of the Trump administration and a Congress that is under unified Republican control. The Trump administration's priorities may also affect the future of litigation in this area. To date, the Trump administration and Congress have not indicated an interest in addressing transgender health. To the contrary, the Republican Party Platform includes a call for a return to the "original, authentic meaning" of nondiscrimination protections on the basis of sex that would not include protections for gender identity, sex stereotyping, or sexual orientation (Republican Party 2016, 35). To continue making advancements in the current political environment, an incremental, bottom-up approach may be the only viable option for transgender people and their advocates in the short to medium term.

Removing gender transition insurance exclusions and enacting transgender-inclusive nondiscrimination protections nationwide would go a long way toward improving care, but it alone cannot solve the problem of transgender health disparities. Policies relating to collecting and publishing data on transgender patient outcomes, in particular incorporating gender identity questions into large national surveys and electronic health records, are essential to better understanding the transgender population and improving their care (Stroumsa 2014).[7] The continued education and training of health providers is necessary to reduce prejudice and build cultural competency and transgender health expertise. Finally, reducing stigma and discrimination in society and addressing other social determinants of health are important to improving transgender health.

There is much cause for optimism despite the immediate concerns. Advancements in supportive public attitudes, public policy, and medical and legal practices since the turn of the twenty-first century suggest that attitudes toward, and policies concerning, transgender people in the United States will continue to improve. Researchers are producing a great deal of new evidence about the efficacy and cost effectiveness of gender dysphoria treatment. Professional organizations and health care providers are making great strides in improving transgender care. Transgender advocates and their allies are moving forward with demands that the health, dignity, and rights of transgender individuals be considered and respected at all levels of public policy.

CHAPTER 11

Education Policy

Education policy presents a virtual microcosm of many of the previously discussed policy areas in relation to transgender rights. Transgender students face a challenging environment throughout their educational career. They must navigate complex social interactions, administrative rules, and governmental policies that can all have a drastic impact on their academic and personal development. From an early age, transgender children and their families must address challenges to their own identities, including peer bullying, administrative recordkeeping policies, and sex-segregated facilities and activities (Beam 2007). According to a 2015 survey conducted by the Gay, Lesbian & Straight Education Network (GLSEN), transgender students face a daunting educational experience (Beam 2007; Kosciw et al. 2015). Three-quarters of transgender students surveyed reported feeling unsafe at school and 65 percent had experienced verbal harassment based on their gender expression. Nearly one-quarter of these students had experienced physical harassment as well. These challenges extend to school policies and the enforcement of those policies. About half of LGBTQ students that had been victimized found that reporting the incidents to the school was ineffective in stopping the harmful behavior.[1] Possibly, this signals either willful disregard by school officials, administrative bias, or an inability to address the situation in an effective manner. At least 60 percent of transgender students report that they are not allowed to use bathrooms or locker rooms corresponding with their gender identity. More than half of transgender students were prevented from using their preferred name or pronoun. Thus, the rights of students, like adults, are shaped by nondiscrimination laws, gender marker and identification policies, access to appropriate services, and the bureaucratic discretion of those enforcing the policies.

Yet education policy also poses some unique challenges for transgender rights. First, education policy in the United States is a highly decentralized policy area. Although national policies certainly have important impacts on education, state governments and local school districts have a large degree of autonomy. Many policies may be set on an even more local level, at each of the roughly 130,000 schools across the country. Next, schools, from kindergarten through college, tend to have a high degree of sex segregation, including gender-specific schools, classrooms, bathrooms, locker rooms, dormitories, dress codes, sports, and extracurricular activities. In the 2015 GLSEN survey, over 70 percent of LGBTQ students report that their school has some form of gender segregation, including gendered dress codes, awards, graduation attire, and even yearbook photos (Kosciw et al. 2015). Finally, education policies primarily apply to children, a vulnerable population whose welfare can elicit strong emotions and concern among policymakers and citizens alike. As noted in chapter 2, this can result in very muddled attitudes toward the treatment of transgender children. On one hand, most people support antibullying laws and allowing children to express their transgender identity. On the other hand, 60 percent of the public oppose using hormone blockers to delay puberty.

Given these unique challenges, we explore education policy relating to transgender rights across all levels of government, from the federal guidelines stemming from Title IX, to state nondiscrimination laws, to sex segregation policies in schools. The chapter not only examines public policies proffered by governments, but also examines the policies of nonprofit organizations that run many private schools and colleges, as well as athletic associations.

Title IX

Though education policy is highly decentralized, with a significant degree of authority at the state and local levels, federal policy has an important impact in this area as well. In particular, Title IX of the Education Amendments of 1972 bars schools that receive federal financial assistance from sex-based discrimination in education programs and activities (20 U.S.C. §§ 1681–1688). This policy is most commonly recognized as the regulation requiring equal opportunities and resources for sex-segregated athletic programs, but it has also shaped the educational landscape by requiring schools to promptly and effectively respond to incidents of sexual harassment and violence.

Title IX regulations on harassment have led to the development of some legal protections for gender identity or gender expression that stem from the logic of Title VII case law that barred employment discrimination based on gender stereotypes (Kimmel 2015). As noted in the chapter on nondiscrimination policy, court rulings in *Price Waterhouse v. Hopkins* (1989) and *Oncale v. Sundowner Offshore Services* (1998) set a precedent that sex discrimination protections encompass gender stereotyping. However, because this legal argument hinges on whether transgender discrimination is a form of gender stereotyping, it has not consistently been applied to transgender discrimination (Weiss 2013). This legal rationale requires that the plaintiff demonstrate that the harassment was motivated by gender stereotypes and their own gender nonconformity. From the court's perspective, a transgender identity is not a protected class and, in itself, is not enough to support a sex discrimination claim (Lee 2012; Rao 2013). In other words, this legal rationale may provide protection for gender nonconforming *expression*, but not necessarily for *identity*.

Still, Title VII court rulings that define the concept of sex discrimination to encompass gender stereotypes, combined with the Supreme Court's decision in *Davis v. Monroe County Board of Education* (1999) that schools districts could be held liable under Title IX for peer-to-peer sexual harassment, allows for a legal rationale to protect LGBT students against sex discrimination in schools (Rao 2013; Kimmel 2015). Indeed, courts have since found in favor of students experiencing peer-to-peer harassment based on sexual orientation due to sex stereotypes and gender nonconformity in several cases, including *Ray v. Antioch Unified School District* (2000), *Montgomery v. Independent School District No. 709* (2000), *Henkle v. Gregory* (2001), and *Theno v. Tonganoxie* (2005). These cases tend to focus on homophobia-based harassment; however, they all use sex stereotyping and gender nonconformity as the basis for their claims. As such, these precedents should provide a degree of protection for transgender students against harassment and violence in schools.

Importantly, legal scholars have argued that Title IX protections, if broadly applied to transgender students, in theory should go beyond harassment to include rights such as the recognition of preferred names and pronouns, access to facilities that correspond with a student's gender identity, gender-inclusive dress codes, and privacy (e.g., Weiss 2013). Yet court rulings on these broader applications of Title IX have produced mixed results, and many cases are still pending. For example, the Ninth Circuit Court of Appeals ruled in *Kastl v. Maricopa County Community College District* (2009) that though the Title VII and Title IX protections against sex discrimination cover gender-stereotyping-based discrimination, the Maricopa Community College did not bar a transgender woman from using the women's restroom for discriminatory reasons. It found that they did so out of safety concerns

(Buzuvis 2013). Some recent cases have resulted in favorable outcomes for transgender students through settlements or via consent agreements. Following a complaint brought to the Department of Education's Office of Civil Rights (OCR) in 2014, the Downey Unified School District (CA) agreed to allow a transgender girl to use the girl's facilities and to treat her as a female in all respects (OCR Case No. 09-12-1095). Another OCR complaint produced a voluntary resolution agreement in 2015 when the Central Piedmont Community College (NC) agreed to take steps to end discrimination against transgender students, allow them to use facilities that correspond with their gender identity, and allow for student records to be changed in order to reflect a student's gender identity (OCR Case No. 11-14-2265).

Title IX has been successfully used to provide protections for transgender students in specific schools, but a broader, precedent-setting ruling based on Title IX or any other law has yet to emerge. In the absence of this kind of precedent, the Department of Education issued a nationwide guidance in the form of a Dear Colleague Letter on May 13, 2016. The letter provided "significant guidance" to schools on how Title IX applied to transgender students and included examples of policies and practices to support transgender students. The DOE guidance stated that a student's gender identity will be treated as their sex for Title IX purposes and that schools may not treat transgender students differently from students of the same gender identity. It clarified that no medical diagnosis or treatment requirement was needed for a student to assert his or her gender identity. It required that transgender students have equal access to education programs and activities. Meeting the requirements entailed ensuring that identification documents and pronouns be consistent with a student's gender identity, that they have access to sex-segregated facilities (e.g., restrooms and locker rooms) and activities (e.g., athletics, single-sex classes, and housing) consistent with their gender identity, and that their privacy through education records is protected (United States Department of Education 2016b).

Absent clear court rulings on a broader application of Title IX to protect transgender students, the DOE guidance in 2016 served as an administrative directive to schools that receive federal funding to clarify how the DOE would assess compliance with Title IX. However, the guidance was not statutorily binding, and it could be overturned by courts and future administrations. Indeed, with the inauguration of President Trump, the DOE and the Department of Justice (DOJ) promptly rescinded the guidance on February 22, 2017. The new Dear Colleague Letter cited ambiguity in how courts have interpreted "sex" with regard to sex-segregated facilities, stemming from two recent cases. The first case was *G.G. v. Gloucester*

County School Board.[2] In 2014 Gavin Grimm, a transgender male student at Gloucester County High School (VA), filed a complaint with the DOJ under Title IX, after the school board passed a policy requiring students to use restrooms that correspond with their "biological gender." His request for a preliminary injunction against the policy while the complaint was reviewed was denied by the federal district court. This ruling held that Title IX regulations allow for sex-segregated facilities and that "sex" in these cases includes biological or birth sex. On appeal, the Fourth U.S. Circuit Court of Appeals sided with Grimm in August 2016 because it gave deference to the agency's interpretation of its own regulations on Title IX. The school board appealed. The Supreme Court was set to consider the case in March 2017. However, given that the relevant Title IX guidance had been rescinded by the Trump administration, the Court vacated the judgment and remanded the case back to the lower courts.[3] A similar case, but one that garnered less media attention, was *Evancho v. Pine-Richland School District* (PA). On behalf of three transgender students, Lambda Legal filed suit against a school district policy that denied restroom access based on gender identity. The federal district court ruled in favor of the transgender students and issued a preliminary injunction on February 27, 2017. It noted that the new school district policy may violate the equal protection clause of the U.S. Constitution, but also hinted that the Title IX claim would likely not be supported in light of the DOE's and DOJ's 2017 rescinding their earlier guidance. Subsequently, the parties reached a settlement that forced the school district to revise its restroom access policies, add gender identity to the school district's nondiscrimination policy, and make other transgender-inclusive policy changes (Lambda Legal 2017b).

The second major case addressing the 2016 Obama administration's DOE and DOJ letter is *State of Texas et al. v. United States of America et al.* (2016). This lawsuit was brought by Texas and twelve other states seeking a nationwide preliminary injunction against the 2016 DOE and DOJ guidance on Title IX and transgender students. The federal district court in Northern Texas granted the nationwide injunction in August 2016, ruling that the guidance likely went beyond the plain meaning of the Title IX regulations on sex discrimination and, therefore, improperly created new regulations without due administrative procedure.

As the law currently stands, Title IX protections against sex discrimination in schools provide only limited relief for transgender students. For instance, in *Miles v. New York University* (1997), a federal district court allowed a transgender woman's lawsuit over sexual harassment to proceed. In denying summary judgment to New York University, which argued that the plaintiff was not covered by Title IX because of her transsexual status, the court found that the conduct by the faculty member in question was related to sex and not to the plaintiff's transsexual status. However, at the time of the harassment, the faculty member did not know of the student's transsexual status. Thus, Title IX can be used to address peer-to-peer harassment and violence, following the sex stereotyping legal theory, but it does not necessarily apply to broader discrimination protections that would allow for equal treatment by gender identity. Since Title IX regulations allow for sex-segregated facilities, programs, and activities, and the courts have so far not equated "sex" in this context to gender identity, broad national-level protections through this policy may not be likely. Indeed, legal scholars, presaging the *Evancho v. Pine-Richland School District* (2017) opinion, contend that broad discrimination protections in schools are more likely to be won using equal protection constitutional arguments (Lee 2012; Buzuvis 2013). Alternatively, protections against discrimination based on gender identity could be more concretely secured with statutory nondiscrimination policies (Rao 2013).

State Policies

Given the legal complexity in applying national regulations to schools at the state and local levels through Title IX, state policies may provide more concrete and robust protections for transgender students. While there are no statutory protections for transgender people (and students) at the national level, fourteen states and the District of Columbia have enacted nondiscrimination protections explicitly for students and schools (see figure 11.1). For example, California amended the discrimination section of its Education Code in 2011 to read (CA EDC 220):

> No person shall be subjected to discrimination on the basis of disability, gender, gender identity, gender expression, nationality, race or ethnicity, religion, sexual orientation, or any other characteristic that is contained in the definition of hate crimes set forth in Section 422.55 of the Penal Code in any program or activity conducted by an educational institution that receives, or benefits from, state financial assistance or enrolls pupils who receive state student financial aid.

States with these types of education nondiscrimination policies overlap with the eighteen states that have broad nondiscrimination policies (see figure

States that have adopted Gender Identity Inclusive Education Anti-Discrimination Laws

Figure 11.1. Gender-Identity-Inclusive Education Antidiscrimination Laws, 2017
Notes: Gray shaded states have banned gender identity/expression discrimination in education.
Compiled by the authors from Human Rights Campaign 2017.

9.1 in chapter 9), with seven exceptions: New Hampshire, New Mexico, Hawaii, Maryland, Delaware, Rhode Island, and Utah all have broad non-discrimination laws, but do not yet have explicit education policies for students.[4] These states present opportunities for transgender rights advocates to expand protections to education policy. However, beyond these seven states, the prospects for new nondiscrimination policies in the near term remain low due to Republican control of all of the legislatures in all of the remaining thirty-two states (Kralik 2017).

Antibullying Policies

Another type of policy that has gained traction at the state level is antibullying laws. These laws are needed given pervasive discrimination and harassment faced by LGBTQ students (Kosciw et al. 2015). As such, advocacy groups like GLSEN provide model policies that states can modify to their

States with laws that address harrassment and/or bullying of students based on sexual orientation and gender identity (20 states & D.C.)

States with regulations that address harassment and/or bullying of students based on sexual orientation and gender identity (2 states)

States with laws that prevent school districts from specifically protecting LGBT students (2 states)

Figure 11.2. State Antibullying Policies, 2017. (Human Rights Campaign 2017.)

circumstances.[5] Broadly speaking, these policies prohibit a wide range of bullying and harassing behavior. They also require schools to develop policies to prevent, report, investigate, and punish bullying based on a range of student characteristics. Indeed, all states have some form of an antibullying law or policy. However, only twenty states and the District of Columbia list gender identity or expression as a protected characteristic in their policies (see figure 11.2). Two more states, Hawaii and West Virginia, cover gender identity in their school regulation codes that address discrimination, harassment, and bullying. An additional twenty-five states have antibullying laws that do not list any protected characteristics or categories. Even though most states do not explicitly address bullying of transgender students in their current policies, the public is highly supportive of these types of protections. Our June 2016 survey found that 86 percent of Americans agreed that laws should protect transgender children from bullying. This represents an opportunity for transgender rights advocates to further expand the number of states with gender-identity-inclusive antibullying policies.

Given such levels of support, these policies can be adopted in unexpected places. Indeed, figure 11.2 finds a southern state, North Carolina, with an antibullying policy. This was historic because it was the first statewide sexual orientation and gender-identity-inclusive law adopted in the South. This policy, the School Violence and Prevention Act, was passed by a legislature that was under Democratic control and signed into law by Governor Beverly Perdue (D) in 2009. This is consistent with research presented in chapter 4 about the political factors that allow for the adoption of most gay and transgender-inclusive law. The broad coalition of advocates pushing for the policy, including Equality North Carolina, trumpeted the public support that the proposal had in its messaging (e.g., Prevent School Violence NC 2009). A survey research firm, Public Policy Polling, found that 69 percent of North Carolina voters supported the measure (Public Policy Polling 2009). These levels of public support likely buoyed the advocacy coalition's efforts with Democrats in that highly partisan state. Indeed, Ian Palmquist (2017), the executive director of Equality North Carolina at the time, noted that "positive polling was probably helpful in persuading Democratic leadership to ask their members to take the vote."

Despite the high public support for these LGBT-inclusive antibullying policies, two states prevent schools from explicitly protecting LGBT students: Missouri and South Dakota. In addition to not listing protected categories of students in their antibullying policies, both states actively bar the enumeration of these categories. Missouri's policy states (Missouri Revised Statutes 160.775.3):

> Each district's antibullying policy shall be founded on the assumption that all students need a safe learning environment. Policies shall treat all students equally and shall not contain specific lists of protected classes of students who are to receive special treatment.

Similarly, South Dakota's antibullying law includes the exception that "no school district policy prohibiting bullying, whether it is existing or adopted pursuant to §§ 13-32-14 to 13-32-19, inclusive, may contain any protected classes of students" (SL 2012, ch. 96, § 1). Proponents of these bans on enumerated categories contend that it allows the policy to protect all students from bullying, regardless of the motivation. However, LGBT rights advocates point to research that suggests enumerating protected categories increases the efficacy of antibullying policies because it more clearly communicates to students, faculty, and administrators what types of behavior are covered under the policy. In addition, enumeration helps to create an environment conducive to creating supportive strategies for LGBT students (Human Rights Watch 2016; Hatzenbuehler and Keyes 2013; Russell et al. 2016).

Sex-Segregated Facilities and Activities

Whereas antibullying policies are one of the few near-valence education policies related to transgender rights, sex-segregated facilities are perhaps the most controversial. As seen in the previous discussions of Title IX and North Carolina's HB2, the debate over access to bathrooms, locker rooms, housing, and numerous activities that are segregated by gender has drawn national attention and considerable consternation on both sides of the issue. This controversy permeates education policy because sex segregation is quite common in the U.S. education system. Not only are facilities like bathrooms and locker rooms segregated, but classes, sports, extracurricular activities, and even entire schools are organized by gender.

States with gender-identity-inclusive nondiscrimination policies for education and public accommodations should, in theory, allow transgender students to use facilities that correspond with their gender identity. However, most of these states also have laws that allow for separate facilities based on sex as long as the facilities are comparable. As such, some state courts have sided with school districts that force transgender students to use gender neutral restrooms (often faculty restrooms) and have narrowly interpreted regulations that allow sex segregation to mean biological sex rather than gender identity (Hart 2014). Yet most of these cases have ultimately been decided in favor of the student, with decisions noting that the legislative intent of nondiscrimination laws takes precedent over narrow definitions of sex in state regulations (e.g., *Mathis v. Fountain-Fort Carson School District 8* [2013]; *Doe v. Regional School District Unit 26* [2014]). Importantly, and as illustrated in the *G.G. v. Gloucester County School Board* case, transgender students in states without gender-identity-inclusive protections for education and public accommodations have not secured favorable decisions. For example, in *Johnston v. University of Pittsburgh of the Commonwealth System of Higher Education et al.* (2015) a federal district court judge ruled that barring a transgender male student from men's bathrooms and locker rooms did not constitute sex discrimination under the federal Constitution, Title IX, or state nondiscrimination and education law. Yet a recent federal appeals court ruling granted a transgender student in Wisconsin injunctive relief to use the bathroom corresponding with his gender identity (*Whitaker v. Kenosha Unified School District* [2017]). In upholding the injunction, the court became the first to support a transgender student's claims under both Title IX and the equal protection clause of the Fourteenth Amendment, potentially providing constitutional protection for access to sex-segregated facilities.

Still, with mixed and evolving outcomes from the courts, states have recently tried to clarify policy on sex-segregated facilities. In 2013, California passed the School Success and Opportunity Act (AB 1266), which amended the existing gender-identity-inclusive education nondiscrimination policy to address sex-segregated facilities and activities (Cal. Educ. Code § 221.5):

> A pupil shall be permitted to participate in sex-segregated school programs and activities, including athletic teams and competitions, and use facilities consistent with his or her gender identity, irrespective of the gender listed on the pupil's record.

The addition of this single sentence to the state's nondiscrimination policy explicitly clarifies the extent to which the policy protects against discrimination in sex-segregated spaces (Harvard Law Review 2014). Similarly, Massachusetts, Washington, and Connecticut have drafted guidelines clarifying that transgender students should have access to facilities that correspond with their gender identity (National Education Association 2016). For example, in 2012 the Massachusetts Board of Elementary and Secondary Education adopted revised regulations and policy guidance in the wake of the state's 2011 inclusion of gender identity in their nondiscrimination laws. This guidance not only addressed sex-segregated facilities, including bathrooms and locker rooms, but also extended to all school activities (Massachusetts Department of Elementary and Secondary Education 2013):

> Whenever students are separated by gender in school activities or are subject to an otherwise lawful gender-specific rule, policy, or practice, students must be permitted to participate in such activities or conform to such rule, policy, or practice consistent with their gender identity.

A few states have moved to clarify the application of nondiscrimination protections in sex-segregated school facilities and activities by explicitly ensuring access based on gender identity. However, other states have sought to restrict this access. From 2013 to 2017, twenty-four states introduced bills to broadly restrict access to sex-segregated facilities based on biological or birth sex and fourteen states considered bills to explicitly limit the rights of transgender students at schools (Kralik 2017). The first to pass was North Carolina's controversial HB2 in 2016, which, among other restrictions, restricted access to single-sex multiple occupancy bathrooms and changing facilities based on biological sex (as stated on a birth certificate). However, after a considerable backlash, in which many businesses, entertainers, and athletic associations boycotted the state—with an estimated cost to the state of $3.7 billion over a decade (Dalesio and Drew 2017) —the state legislature repealed the portion of the law that restricted access to sex-segregated facilities in 2017. Yet the repeal of HB2 also included a provision barring all state agencies, including the state university system, from regulating multiple occupancy facilities (North Carolina House Bill 142/S.L. 2017–4). South Dakota's legislature also passed a restrictive "bathroom bill" in 2016, but Republican governor Dennis Daugaard vetoed the bill, preferring to allow local schools districts to address the issue (Pearce 2016). In 2017, the Texas Senate passed a broadly restrictive bathroom bill similar to North Carolina's HB2, but the measure failed to pass the Republican-controlled House of Representatives due to concerns about an economic backlash like the one that occurred in North Carolina (Ura 2017).

School Districts

States have considerable authority to shape education policies relating to transgender students, yet most states have not yet been able to come to an agreement on how to deal with these issues. This leaves the local school districts relative autonomy to address the rights of transgender students. Unfortunately, as noted in the introduction, most transgender students have had very negative experiences with school policies. Again, 60 percent of transgender students were forced to use sex-segregated facilities that did not match their gender identity, and half of transgender students were unable to use their preferred name or pronoun (Kosciw et al. 2015). This may be the result of a lack of school policies. Just 6 percent of LGBTQ students reported that their school had policies or guidelines regarding transgender or gender nonconforming students while 57 percent reported no school policies and another 37 percent were not sure (Kosciw et al. 2015).

Despite the ability to set policies regarding transgender students, many schools and school districts do not have clear policies or do not effectively communicate them to students, staff, and parents. To address this, LGBT advocacy groups, along with education groups, have begun to develop model policies and guidelines. One prominent example, "Schools in Transition: A Guide for Supporting Transgender Students," developed jointly by the ACLU, Gender Spectrum, the Human Rights Campaign, the National

Center for Lesbian Rights, and the National Education Association, provides an overview of the range of policies that are recommended to support and promote the well-being of transgender students (Orr et al. 2017):

- *Student Records and Information Systems*: To comply with state and national reporting requirements, schools should allow local student information systems to reflect a transgender student's preferred name and gender identity (e.g., class rosters, yearbooks, and student IDs) while maintaining other identity records such as birth certificates in order to satisfy external reporting requirements.
- *Names and Pronouns*: Create policies and guidelines allowing students to identify preferred names and pronouns and ensure that faculty, administrators, and peers respect these preferences.
- *Dress Codes*: Allow students to follow the gender specific dress code that corresponds with their gender identity.
- *Sex-Segregated Facilities and Activities*: Allow access to sex-segregated facilities and activities consistent with students' gender identities. This can include bathrooms, locker rooms, overnight field trips, health and physical education classes, athletics, proms and dances, and even graduation. Schools may even consider eliminating the gendered aspects of some of these activities. Be prepared to address concerns and misconceptions of cisgender students, parents, and staff regarding privacy and safety.
- *Bullying and Harassment*: Schools should have clear antidiscrimination and antibullying policies and procedures that enumerate gender identity as a protected class. Further, schools should actively foster a climate of inclusion and diversity, and encourage intervention as needed to protect transgender students.
- *Supportive Services*: Provide supportive services to help transgender students navigate school policies and their own transition process. This includes administrative support, counseling, and individualized education plans (IEPs).

Private Schools

Our focus on governmental policy and public education in this section fails to address an important provider of education services in the United States, private schools. In 2013, more than 33,000 private schools served more than four million students. Sixty-nine percent of these institutions had a religious affiliation (United States Department of Education 2016a). Private schools, including charter schools, have significant leeway to set their own policies. Despite this, government policies, such as Title IX or state nondiscrimination laws, may affect them in some instances. Notably, this may occur when private schools receive public funding. However, Betsy DeVos, secretary of education for the Trump administration, has been noncommittal on whether federal policies, such as Title IX, offer protections to LGBT students in private schools (ABC News 2017). In some instances, these institutions might also be shielded by religious freedom protections, such as the federal Religious Freedom Restoration Act and similar state laws. Large private providers of education services, such as parochial schools run by the Catholic Church or some Protestant denominations, have often been resistant to LGBT-inclusive policies. In addition, they might even deny admission to transgender students (e.g., Abeni 2016; Bowie 2017). Private schools are also not bound by the First Amendment's free speech guarantees. As such, they can stifle student expression in ways that public schools cannot. In general, LGBT students will have more legal protections in public school settings, but supportive private options might be available in some communities.

Colleges and Universities

Most of the attention to education policy regarding transgender students has been at the elementary and secondary levels of school (K-12), but similar issues confront colleges and universities. To a large degree, these postsecondary institutions have been more proactive in pursuing policies to support transgender students. According to Campus Pride, at least 1,036 colleges and universities have nondiscrimination policies that explicitly provide protections based on gender identity or gender expression, or both (Beemyn 2017). However, as discussed above, the presence of nondiscrimination policies does not ensure equal treatment and access to facilities, resources, and activities on campus. Indeed, one of the key court decisions against Title IX inclusion of gender identity protections, *Johnston v. University of Pittsburgh of the Commonwealth System of Higher Education et al.* (2015), comes from a university with a nondiscrimination policy that includes gender identity and expression.

In addition, other supportive policies are not nearly as widespread. For example, just 213 schools offer gender-inclusive housing, 163 schools enable students to use preferred names for campus records and documents, and only 76 schools cover transition-related medical expenses under student health insurance (Beemyn 2017). Access to sex-segregated facilities is typically unclear on most campuses, especially following the rescindment of the DOE's Letter of Guidance on Title IX in 2017.

In addition to the absence of clear policies regulating access to sex-segregated facilities and activities, two areas of college life are exempted from the sex discrimination provisions in Title IX: single-sex schools and social fraternities and sororities. Of the thirty-seven women's colleges in the United States, just seven have addressed gender identity, in varying ways, in their admissions policies (Beemyn 2017). Some of these colleges only admit students who identify as women, excluding genderqueer or gender nonbinary students and transgender men. Others accept applications from students who identify as women or were assigned female at birth (typically with caveats about gender identity). Single-sex colleges, particularly those that serve women, have also grappled with the status of current students who transition from one gender to another while in college. Mount Holyoke offers the most inclusive policy, considering all students except cisgender men (Davis 2017).

Social fraternities and sororities are also exempt from Title IX sex discrimination policies. With over 9,000 chapters and 700,000 current undergraduate members, social fraternities and sororities constitute a significant portion of the college student population (National Panhellenic Conference 2017; North-American Interfraternity Conference 2017). These social organizations usually have single-sex membership policies, but these policies are not governed by the government or even the national fraternal associations. Instead, each organization can determine its own membership rules (Tran 2012). Yet few organizations have created formal gender-identity-inclusive membership policies, with most occurring at the campus level. For example, the Panhellenic Council at Brown University voted to require its sororities to allow any individual identifying as a woman to participate in recruitment (Everett 2016). Though most national fraternities keep their membership policies private, to date only three national fraternities and three national sororities have adopted gender-identity-inclusive policies (Tran 2012; Ruiz 2016). In 2016, Harvard College adopted a policy to encourage these types of private social organizations to be more inclusive by limiting members' involvement in officially sanctioned college organizations and withholding endorsement letters for student fellowships if they were not inclusive (Harvard College 2016).

Athletics

One of the common issues confronting most of the education policies regarding transgender students are sex-segregated facilities and activities. This issue is also obviously central to athletics, where most sports have traditionally been segregated by gender. However, in addition to the challenges presented by sex-segregated facilities, such as bathrooms, locker rooms, and housing, discussed throughout this chapter, sex segregation in athletics also incorporates debates over competitive fairness driven by average physiological differences between men and women (Davis 2017; Carroll 2014; Jones et al. 2017). On average, men tend to have taller, leaner, and more muscular bodies. They typically have higher anaerobic capacities and muscular power (Buzuvis 2011). These physiological differences underlie the critical assumption that men have an athletic advantage over women and thus athletics should be segregated by gender.

As a result, athletic policies have long sought to ensure competitive fairness by enforcing sex segregation through sex testing and verification (Ha et al. 2014). Yet the development of these policies has produced considerable controversy as athletic governing bodies grapple with the complexities of determining nonbinary gender, even from a biological or physiological perspective. For example, the International Olympic Committee has used sex verification policies using chromosomal and hormonal tests, designed to ensure that all competitors in women's sports were female. However, this approach has not identified any male "impostors" seeking an athletic advantage, but has only disqualified women with disorders of sex development and intersex women such as Caster Semenya (Ha et al. 2014; Cooky and Dworkin 2013).

In addition to the complexity of biological gender, the assumption of a gender-based athletic advantage is limited because the assumed physiological differences between male and female athletes are based on averages. There is a significant overlap between the distributions of male and female athletes in height, strength, muscle tone, and anaerobic capacity (Gooren and Bunck 2004). This point is particularly relevant for youth athletics, where physiological differences may not be as significant, especially for prepubescent athletes (Buzuvis 2011). In addition, the concern that transgender women may have an unfair advantage in athletic competition ignores the physiological effects of estrogen administration and testosterone suppression on plasma testosterone levels, muscle mass, hemoglobin, and insulin-like growth factor-1 (Gooren and Bunck 2004). With time, this treatment in transgender females increases the already substantial physiological overlap that exists between natal men and women. However, some physiological differences between males and females that occur after puberty, such as height, are not affected by medical treatment (Reeser 2005). In addition, any advantages bestowed because of male socialization in sports might also be residual (e.g., Landers and Fine 1996). Yet it is unlikely that there is a fairness-based justification for a blanket exclusion of transgender students from athletics (Jones et al. 2017).

Indeed, opposite of their intended effect, policies that require students to compete in athletics in the gender of their birth may actually lead to unfair advantages for some transgender athletes. This is evident in the case of Mack Beggs, a transgender male, who was forced to compete in the girls wrestling division in 2017. Beggs began transitioning in 2015 and had been undergoing hormone treatments, including testosterone injections, for a year. Yet the University Interscholastic League, which governs school athletics in Texas, requires students to compete with the gender reported on their birth certificate. Despite challenges from opponents who argued that Beggs had an unfair advantage due to his hormone treatments, the University Interscholastic League kept him in the girls division, where he ultimately won the Texas state girls wrestling championship (Babb 2017).

Carroll (2014) points out other issues related to the participation of transgender individuals in athletics. One concern is whether transgender females take opportunities from natal females. However, this assumes that transgender females are not real females and thus are undeserving of opportunities to participate. It also ignores that gender identity is a core aspect of a person's identity. Further, there are arguments that segregating women from men in athletics is a form of sexism that leaves females in an inferior status (Davis 2017; McDonagh and Pappano 2008). Additionally, attention to possible unfair advantages held by transgender women ignores the plight of transgender men in sport. Blanket bans on transgender participation because of fears about transgender women penalize transgender men, such as Mack Beggs, when there is no evidence that they have any physiological advantages, when competing against men, stemming from transition or testosterone treatment (Gooren and Bunck 2004). However, testosterone is often a banned substance. Therefore, transgender men can be vulnerable to charges of doping in athletic competition (Reeser 2005). To remedy some of these inequities, Davis (2017) calls for the use of physiological features such as height, weight, age, and androgen levels as sorting measures in sports competition instead of sex categories.

As noted earlier, Title IX protects student athletes against sex discrimination, but it is not yet clear how it applies to sex-segregated athletic policies.

The New York Supreme Court struck down the U.S. Tennis Association's chromosome testing policy that led to the exclusion of Renee Richards, a transgender woman, from the U.S. Open in 1976, declaring the policy an example of improper sex discrimination under state law (*Richards v. U.S. Tennis Association* 1977). However, a case has yet to be decided that challenges policies governing student athletics, which often require birth certificates to prove gender conformity (Buzuvis 2016). As such, states and nonprofit athletic associations continue to set the policies governing transgender students' participation in athletics.

State Interscholastic Athletic Associations

Although California's groundbreaking School Success and Opportunity Act explicitly includes athletics, sex segregation in athletics and allowing students to compete with the sex that is consistent with their gender identity are not topics addressed in most state education policies. Instead, these policies are set by nonprofit organizations that oversee student athletic competition in the state. The National Federation of State High School Associations recommends the National Center for Lesbian Rights' model policy, which states (LGBT Sports Foundation 2016):

> All students should have the opportunity to participate in [state athletic association] athletics/activities in a manner that is consistent with their gender identity, irrespective of the gender listed on a student's records and without prior medical or mental health care.

This inclusive policy recognizes a student's right to participate in athletics in a gender-consonant manner, and it provides model procedures to notify the school and the state athletic association, as well as outlining an appeals process.

To date, state athletic associations have adopted a wide range of gender eligibility policies, only some of which are inclusive (see table 11.1). Texas, North Carolina, and Alabama determine eligibility strictly by birth certificates. Three other states (Indiana, Louisiana, Nebraska) will allow transgender athletes to participate in their preferred gender division only with medical proof of gender reassignment treatments. Idaho's policy mirrors the National College Athletic Association policy (described below), with different hormone treatment requirements for transgender women and transgender men. The most common approach (nineteen states) has been a policy based on gender identity, but with limitations or exceptions. For example, Delaware requires an official record (birth certificate, driver's license, or passport) or a physician's certification of medical treatments to determine a student's gender identity. Georgia allows each school to make its own determination on a case-by-case basis. An increasing number of states (sixteen states and Washington, DC), have adopted inclusive, gender consonant policies without limitations. Another eight state athletic association policies do not address transgender athletes or sex segregation explicitly.

National Collegiate Athletic Association

At the collegiate level, athletics is governed by the National Collegiate Athletic Association (NCAA), which adopted a new gender eligibility policy in 2011. In the report outlining the new policies, the NCAA highlighted the importance of inclusiveness while also addressing concerns about competitive equity. In particular, Griffin and Carroll (2011) contest the assumption that transgender women would have a competitive advantage over cisgender women, noting that prepubescent transitions avoid many potential physiological advantages and that physiological gender differences tend to be overgeneralized. The report also emphasizes that hormone treatments, such as estrogen and testosterone suppression, typically bring hormone levels into gender-normal ranges within one year (see also Gooren and Bunck 2004; Ljungvist and Genel 2005). The focus on hormone treatments also extends to concerns about doping by using testosterone (defined as a banned substance) to gain a competitive advantage, regardless of gender identity. As such, the NCAA policy is not broadly inclusive, but rather sets eligibility based on gender identity and hormone treatments (National Collegiate Athletic Association 2011, 13):

- 1. A trans male (FTM) student-athlete who has received a medical exception for treatment with testosterone for diagnosed Gender Identity Disorder or gender dysphoria and/or Transsexualism, for purposes of NCAA competition may compete on a men's team, but is no longer eligible to compete on a women's team without changing that team status to a mixed team.
- 2. A trans female (MTF) student-athlete being treated with testosterone suppression medication for Gender Identity Disorder or gender dysphoria and/or Transsexualism, for the purposes of

TABLE 11.1. State Athletic Association Gender Eligibility Policies, 2017

Policy Type	Example	States
Gender-Consonant	All students should have the opportunity to participate in CIF activities in a manner that is consistent with their gender identity, irrespective of the gender listed on a student's records. (California Interscholastic Federation)	CA, CO, CT, DC, FL, MD, MA, MN, NV, NH, RI, SD, UT, VT, VA, WA, WY
Gender-Consonant with Conditions	A transgender student . . . shall be eligible to participate in interscholastic athletics in a manner that is consistent with the student's gender identity, under any of the following conditions: a. The student provides an official record, such as a revised birth certificate, a driver's license or a passport, demonstrating legal recognition of the student's reassigned sex, or b. A physician certifies that the student has had appropriate clinical treatment for transition to the reassigned sex, or c. A physician certifies that the student is in the process of transition to the reassigned sex. (New Jersey State Interscholastic Athletic Association)	DE, IL, IA, NJ, NM, NY
Case-by-Case or School Determination	The GHSA will honor a gender determination made by a member school. (Georgia High School Association)	AK, AZ, GA, KS, KY, ME, MI, PA, WI
Hormone Treatments by Gender	A trans male (female to male) student-athlete who has undergone treatment with testosterone for gender transition may compete on a boys team but is no longer eligible to compete on a girls team without changing the team status to a mixed team. A trans female (male to female) student-athlete being treated with testosterone suppression medication for gender transition may continue to compete on a boys team but may not compete on a girls team without changing it to a mixed team status until completing one calendar year of documented testosterone-suppression treatment. (Missouri State High School Activities Association)	ID, MO, OH, OK, OR
Birth Certificate	A student's gender is denoted by what is listed on the birth certificate. (North Carolina High School Athletic Association)	AL, NC, TX
Medical Treatments	Proof of a student's changed gender is shown by the following: providing reliable medical evidence that the student-athlete has undergone sex change . . . (Indiana High School Athletic Association)	IN, LA, NE
No Policy		AR, HI, MS, MT, ND, SC, TN, WV

Source: TRANSATHLETE.com.

NCAA competition may continue to compete on a men's team but may not compete on a women's team without changing it to a mixed team status until completing one calendar year of testosterone suppression treatment.

- Any transgender student-athlete who is not taking hormone treatment related to gender transition may participate in sex-separated sports activities in accordance with his or her assigned birth gender.
- A trans male (FTM) student-athlete who is not taking testosterone related to gender transition may participate on a men's or women's team.
- A trans female (MTF) transgender student-athlete who is not taking hormone treatments related to gender transition may not compete on a women's team.

As noted earlier, this policy has served as model for several state athletic associations even though it is less inclusive than the policy recommendation of the National Federation of State High School Associations. However, the NCAA also establishes several best practice guidelines that encourage inclusion, including inclusive access to facilities and housing, preferred pronouns and names, inclusive dress codes, community education on transgender issues, and the protection of privacy (Griffin and Carroll 2011). Notably, the NCAA was also a formidable participant in the boycott of North Carolina during the battle over HB2 (Boren 2017).

Conclusion

In all, this chapter highlights the complexity of transgender rights in education policy. Many of the policies mirror other transgender rights policies, such as nondiscrimination policy, but education policy tends to be more decentralized and more focused on sex-segregation policies. Further, since education policies affect children, it tends to be a highly emotional policy area.

Although much of the recent political debate has centered on national-level guidance on Title IX and related court cases, state and local policies, including nongovernmental policies, are key forces shaping this policy area. With an absence of clear national nondiscrimination policies regarding education and schools, state policies addressing bullying, nondiscrimination, and sex-segregated facilities have become the key battlegrounds for transgender rights advocates. Many states have recently adopted protective policies for transgender students, but other states have begun to push back, barring the enumeration of transgender rights and feeding into unfounded security and safety fears. Meanwhile, local school districts and colleges in most states have a large degree of autonomy to create and enforce policies that affirm transgender students' rights. Private K-12 schools and colleges do as well. We not only see this in terms of enforcement of antibullying policies but also in providing access to sex-segregated facilities and activities, including athletics and social events. Thus, the experiences of transgender students rely heavily on local institutional policies and inclusiveness. Given this ad hoc framework, many transgender students find inadequate protection.

CHAPTER 12

Criminal Justice and Trans Identities

Like many minority populations in the United States, the relationship that transgender people have with the criminal justice system is complex, and many transgender people rarely perceive equal treatment or protection from the system (James et al. 2016, 185). In this chapter, we examine how the criminal justice system interacts with the transgender community, with trans people as victims, perpetrators, and prisoners. We begin with a discussion of transgender-inclusive hate crime laws. We also address the criminalization of trans people, transgender issues in jails and prisons, and relevant case law. The chapter discusses incarceration policies such as confinement with prisoners of the opposite gender or the placement of transgender inmates in administrative segregation. Our discussion highlights policies and court decisions regarding treatment for a transgender prisoner's gender-identity-related medical issues. Along the way, the chapter gives attention to police-transgender community relations.

Criminal Policies Protecting Transgender People

Since the 1970s, activists for minority populations have increasingly pushed for new laws that increase criminal penalties for crimes motivated by bias toward a particular group (Haider-Markel 2006; Jenness 1995; Jenness and Broad 1997). Often called hate crime laws, the proposed policies have tended to focus on protecting minority groups, such as the disabled and African Americans. These laws often increase penalties for crimes ranging from vandalism, to assault, to murder, when it is believed that the perpetrator(s) committed the crime based on bias toward the protected group. The argument in support of these laws has been that these crimes are committed not just to harm the victim but also to send a broader message that the targeted group is devalued in society.

Early hate crime laws tended to focus on race, ethnicity, and gender. However, as more states and localities began to consider these laws in the 1980s and 1990s, there was a greater push to include categories such as sexual orientation, disability, veteran status, and gender identity (Haider-Markel 1998, 2006). Many versions of these laws required statistics collection or police training for hate crimes, or both, but did not allow for increased penalties. For example, the federal Hate Crimes Statistics Act of 1990 defined hate crimes and required the Federal Bureau of Investigation to collect statistics on crimes motivated by bias against religion, race, ethnicity, gender, disability, and sexual orientation. The act did not create a federal category of crime labeled hate crime, nor did it enhance penalties for bias motivated crime. In 1994, Congress enhanced the 1990 Hate Crimes Statistics Act by passing the Violent Crime Control and Law Enforcement Act, which included a section called the Hate Crimes Sentencing Enhancement Act that tasked the U.S. Sentencing Commission to provide guidelines on longer sentences for bias crimes (Haider-Markel 2006, 820). Although the act did not create penalty enhancement for hate crimes, it did allow prosecutors and judges to call for, and impose, longer sentences for crimes motivated by bias. It also included the categories of gender and sexual orientation. The same year, Congress also passed the Violence Against Women Act of 1994, which created new criminal penalties and civil remedies for victims of violent crimes that were motivated by gender bias, though it did not explicitly include gender identity (Haider-Markel 2006).[1] In 2001, Congress passed the National Local Law Enforcement Enhancement Act, which authorized, but did not require, the attorney general to investigate and prosecute anti-LGBT crimes as violations of federal civil rights law.

Because the federal government was sluggish in response to hate crime violence, more states adopted some version of hate crime laws in the 1980s. Increasingly these laws included penalty enhancements as well as data collection and training requirements (Allen, Pettus, and Haider-Markel 2004; Haider-Markel 2006; Jenness and Broad 1997). State hate crime laws have also tended to cover a greater number of groups, such as gays and lesbians. Some of these laws even provided additional funding for training police and prosecutors about hate crimes (Haider-Markel 2006).

Local governments have considered hate crime policies as well, often after well-publicized acts of violence. One example occurred in Toledo, Ohio, when three men viciously attacked a transgender woman in broad daylight. This 2014 attack left her grievously wounded and garnered much media attention, in part because the victim was a well-known transgender activist. In response, with Council Member Jack Ford sponsoring the measure, the Toledo City Council unanimously passed a transgender-inclusive hate crime ordinance (Messina 2014).

However, at times these policies have encountered resistance from courts based on First Amendment concerns or via referendums due to opposition from the public. For example, a 1980s St. Paul, Minnesota ordinance seeking to criminalize vandalism such as cross-burning was struck down because the Supreme Court considered it an infringement on free speech (*R.A.V. v. City of St. Paul* 1992), and because the perpetrators could be prosecuted under arson and vandalism laws. Likewise, a 1993 arson attack on a gay actor's home in Springfield, Missouri led to quick action on the part of the city council to adopt a hate crime ordinance that included sexual orientation. However, the ordinance was repealed via a public referendum vote early the following year (Haider-Markel and O'Brien 1999).

Currently, forty-five states and the District of Columbia have some version of laws that enhance penalties for bias motivated crimes. Yet, as shown in figure 12.1, only seventeen of these laws cover gender identity (another eleven states cover gender [not shown] and an additional fourteen cover sexual orientation). Minnesota was the first state to include gender identity in its hate crime statute in 1993, which was an update to its 1989 law that covered sexual orientation.[2] This pattern is similar to other states that tended to adopt hate crime laws protecting sexual orientation in the late 1990s or early 2000s, only to come back and include gender identity in the statute more recently (e.g., Rhode Island, which included sexual orientation in 2001 and returned to include gender identity in 2012).

Under the Obama administration, and following considerable state and local activity, the national government returned to the issue of hate crimes (discussed in greater detail in chapter 4). The Matthew Shepard and James Byrd Jr. Hate Crimes Prevention Act was passed by Congress in 2009 and signed by President Obama. The act explicitly includes protections based on actual or perceived gender as well as gender identity, making this the first transgender affirmative federal law passed by Congress that mentions gender identity. The act created penalties for hate crimes, enhanced the power of federal authorities in hate crime cases, provided funding for investigations, and required the FBI to track statistics on hate crimes involving gender and gender identity. The first conviction for a hate crime based on gender identity, under this law, occurred in May 2017 when Joshua Vallum was sentenced to forty-nine years in prison for killing his former girlfriend, seventeen-year-old Mercedes Williamson, a transgender woman (Stack 2017).[3]

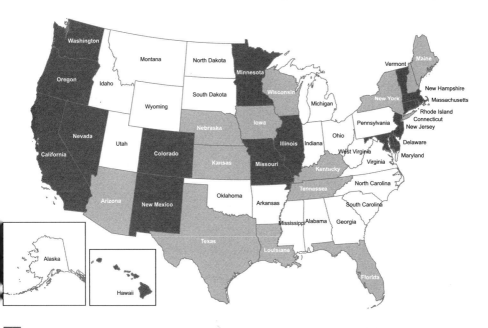

Address hate or bias crimes based on sexual orientation and gender identity (17 states & D.C.)

Address hate or bias crimes based on sexual orientation only (13 states)

Figure 12.1. State Hate Crime Laws Including Gender Identity and Sexual Orientation, 2017

Notes: Compiled by the authors based on data from the Human Rights Campaign and state legislation searches described in chapter 4.

Finally, when the Violence Against Women Act was up for renewal in 2012–13, LGBT advocates fought to include sexual orientation and gender identity. Additional protections were also sought for Native Americans and immigrants. The Senate was the first to pass the inclusive, but limited bill, and the House passed the Senate version in February 2013. President Obama signed the reauthorization measure on March 7, 2013.

Crimes, Violence, and the Transgender Community

By creating enhanced penalties for crimes motivated by bias, hate crime laws are designed to deter crimes against particular groups, including transgender people. However, hate crime laws may be more symbolic than substantive in their impact (Haider-Markel 2002). Nonetheless, as more states and the national government have enacted hate crime laws, the number of hate crimes reported to the FBI had declined prior to 2016.[4] In 2015, there were 6,837 single-bias hate crime offences involving over 7,000 victims. Only 1.7 percent of these involved gender identity bias and nearly 18 percent involved sexual orientation bias; the vast majority (nearly 60 percent) of incidents involved a race or ethnicity bias.[5] The total number of reported single-bias hate crime offences has declined from 9,160 in 2008 (see table 12.1), which is a further decline from the peak of 11,451 offences in 2001. The decline in hate crimes through 2015 was consistent with overall declines in all types of crime since the 1990s, even though Americans perceive that all types of crime have been increasing in recent years (Gramlich 2017). However, the hate crimes statistics released by the FBI for 2016 showed a troubling uptick in the number of bias-related crimes (Berman 2017). This included increases in attacks against LGBT-identified people. Of these, there were 130 bias incidents related to gender identity (111 antitransgender and 19 gender nonconforming). That represented 2 percent of single bias incidents in the FBI dataset (Federal Bureau of Investigation 2017).

However, like all crime, the hate crimes reported to the FBI are voluntarily reported by local police departments and are widely understood to be underreported (Haider-Markel 2006).[6] Indeed, the DOJ Office of Justice Programs, Bureau of Justice Statistics issues its own report on hate crimes, based on its victimization survey, which is an annual survey of American adults to assess crime victimization and interactions with police. The victimization survey consistently finds that less than half of all crimes are reported to police and that police do not pursue cases in many of the reports.

Hate crime victims are even less likely to report crimes to police (Haider-Markel 2006). For example, the 2012 victimization survey reveals that an estimated 292,790 Americans were victimized by hate crimes and almost 60 percent of these incidents were not reported to police (Wilson 2014). Almost 90 percent of these incidents were violent; 26 percent involved a gender bias and another 13 percent involved a sexual orientation bias. By comparison, about 53 percent of violent crime is reported to police (Gramlich 2017). Likewise, the National Coalition of Anti-Violence Programs (NCAVP) says that 1,036 incidents of LGBTQ violence or harassment were reported to its twelve member programs in 2016, with 31 percent of these victims identifying as transgender or gender nonconforming (NCAVP 2016). Of the total victims, only 41 percent interacted with police because of the incident (NCAVP 2016, 15).

Although transgender people represent a small portion of hate crime victims, there is evidence to suggest that they are at greater risk for violent hate crimes, and are more likely to suffer significant bodily harm and death because of these crimes (Grant, Mottet, and Tanis 2011; James et al. 2016).[7] In one study, nearly one in ten transgender respondents reported that "they were physically attacked in the past year because of being transgender" and 46 percent were verbally harassed (James et al. 2016, 198). Of the twenty-eight NCAVP-recorded LGBTQ homicides in 2016, 68 percent were of transgender or gender nonconforming people; all of these victims, except one, were also people of color (NCAVP 2016, 28).[8] Likewise, Matt Foreman (2016) indicated that when he was with the NYC Gay & Lesbian Anti-Violence Project, 100 percent of the victims of violent crime that he dealt with were gender nonconforming.

Criminalizing Transgender People and the Criminal Justice System

As an ostracized group, transgender people are more likely to participate in the underground economy, which can include engaging in illegal activity. James et al. (2016, 14) found that 20 percent of transgender respondents in a national survey had turned to the underground economy, including sex work for hire. Participants in these illicit markets are more likely to face violence and become victims; 41 percent of transgender people in the underground economy had been physically attacked in the past year (James et al. 2016, 202). Additionally, police sometimes have made the situation worse by victimizing transgender people further: "Of those who interacted with the police while doing or thought to be doing sex work, 86 percent reported some form of police harassment, abuse, or mistreatment, including

TABLE 12.1. Hate Crime Offenses Reported to the FBI, 2008–2015

Year	Total Offenses	Sexual Orientation	Gender Identity	Sexual Orientation %	Gender Identity %
2008	9,160	1,617	0	17.7	0
2009	7,775	1,436	0	18.5	0
2010	7,690	1,470	0	19.1	0
2011	7,240	1,508	0	20.8	0
2012	6,705	1,318	0	19.7	0
2013	6,921	1,402	33	20.8	0.5
2014	6,835	1,178	109	18.4	1.7
2015	6,837	1,219	118	17.8	1.7

Notes: Compiled by the authors based on data found in Federal Bureau of Investigation (various years).

being verbally harassed, physically attacked, or sexually assaulted by police" (James et al. 2016, 158). Likewise, the National Coalition of Anti-Violence Programs (2016, 34) finds that a significant proportion of victims of hate incidents that interacted with police as a result of the incident reported police indifference or misconduct. Even though transgender people are at higher risk for interactions with the criminal justice system because they are more likely to be victims of crime, and they are somewhat more likely to participate in the illicit economy because of well-documented employment discrimination, we also know that trans people are often criminalized simply for who they are. Historically, there were many laws criminalizing non-gender-conforming behavior. One of the earliest examples of this was an "appearance" law passed by Columbus, Ohio in 1848. This ordinance forbade adults from "appearing in public in a dress not belonging to his or her sex" (News Desk 2015). Similar laws were adopted in cities around the country in the mid-nineteenth century. In the twentieth century, some of these laws were revised to only target men who dressed as women. Included in this group of laws are ordinances passed in Denver, Colorado in 1954 and Miami, Florida in 1965 (News Desk 2015). In the 1970s, many of these laws began to be overturned in court, including the 1973 striking down of an 1851 Chicago, Illinois ordinance.[9] However, police persisted in enforcing some of these laws. For example, fifty-three people were arrested in Houston, Texas in 1977 for violating an 1861 crossdressing ordinance; that law was thrown out by a court in 1980 (News Desk 2015).

Some of the laws banning cross-gender appearance in public stayed on the books until the twenty-first century, but, once explicitly challenged, the laws have been overturned. However, the use of the police and criminal law to enforce gender norms continues to structure interactions between transgender people and the criminal justice system (Amnesty International 2006; Cahill 2017; Grant, Mottet, and Tanis 2011; James et al. 2016; Mallory, Hasenbush, and Sears 2015).

In one example of the policing of gender norms, Daum (2015) argues that police engage in trans-profiling and selectively enforce solicitation laws to regulate the ability of trans people to move freely in public space. Police often treat transgender people as prostitutes (James et al. 2016; Mallory, Hasenbush, and Sears 2015), and this is even more likely for trans people of color (Daum 2015). Daum (2015) and others have simply referred to this as "walking while trans."

Transgender people also report harassment and violence on the part of the police. In a large-scale survey of transgender adults in the United

States, 22 percent of respondents reported being harassed by the police and 6 percent indicated they had been assaulted by police (Grant, Mottet, and Tanis 2011). In one of the most dramatic examples of police violence, surveillance video in Memphis, Tennessee captured a police officer holding down a transgender woman, Duanna Johnson, while another officer beat her and sprayed her with pepper spray. The incident occurred in the booking area of the Shelby County Jail after Johnson had been arrested for solicitation. Months later Johnson was found murdered with a gunshot wound to the head (Brown 2008). In a San Antonio case, a police officer lost his job and was convicted of "official repression" after sexually assaulting a trans woman on his patrol in 2010 (Kapitan 2011).

Inmate Rights

The cases and statistics above make it clear that transgender people face an inordinate amount of scrutiny from the criminal justice system. Moreover, once brought into the system for charges, transgender people may face abuse and assault. This pattern continues through the imprisonment of convicted trans people. For transgender inmates, housing and facility access are a primary concern because decisions on these matters can directly influence the safety and health of any inmate. If, for example, a female transgender inmate is housed in a general population male prison rather than a female prison, she is much more likely to suffer from violence and sexual assault. Indeed, because most transgender people have not undergone gender confirmation surgeries, most transgender inmates are housed in facilities based on their sex assigned at birth, not their gender identity. The levels of violence are astounding. One study (the National Transgender Discrimination Survey) found that 13 percent of all transgender inmates reported sexual assault by another inmate and 6 percent reported assault by a prison guard or staff. Black and Latino inmates reported even higher rates of assault, and male-to-female transgender inmates reported sexual assault rates that were over eight times higher than those of female-to-male transgender inmates (Cahill 2017, 136).

Importantly, in 1976 the Supreme Court first ruled that inmates have the right to be safe and receive medical care under the cruel and unusual punishment clause of the Eighth Amendment (*Estelle v. Gamble* 1976). This ruling established a legal foundation for addressing the incarceration issues of transgender people. Additionally, the Prison Rape Elimination Act (PREA) of 2003, and the related implementation directives developed by the Obama administration in 2012, has helped to improve the safety of LGBT inmates, but these were narrow first steps (Cahill 2017).

The PREA was intended to study and reduce the incidence of sexual assault in virtually all government detention facilities, including federal prisons, local jails, and immigration detention centers, by establishing the National Prison Rape Reduction Commission to research the topic. It also focuses on the establishment of national standards, and provides funds to survey inmates. Additional funds to research the topic are provided through grants (Mair, Frattaroli, and Teret 2003). The Obama administration's standards, which were adopted in 2012 by the Department of Justice, included input from LGBT organizations that focused on increased protection for "vulnerable detainees." The standards advise administrators to collect data on "whether the inmate is or is perceived to be gay, lesbian, bisexual, transgender, intersex, or gender nonconforming" (Cahill 2017, 141). Additionally, Cahill (2017, 141–42, 146) notes that the PREA standards require[10]

- Training of correctional staff on LGBT and intersex issues
- LGBT and intersex inmates be flagged as more vulnerable
- Confidential screening of new inmates within seventy-two hours for vulnerable status
- Investigation of sexual abuse must consider whether the incident was motivated by LGBT or intersex status
- Ending "protective custody" for LGBT prisoners (which was often a default to solitary confinement)
- Ending dedicated wings or units for LGBT inmates, unless ordered by a legal settlement
- Segregated housing should be temporary and only used as a last resort
- Transgender women should be housed in women's facilities and transgender men should have housing determined on a case-by-case basis that "respect[s] the gender identity of individuals"
- Ending most cross-gender searches
- Transgender and intersex inmates be allowed to shower separately from other inmates.

In May 2018, the Trump administration issued a directive to roll back changes made by the Obama administration on the housing of transgender prisoners. The new guidelines house prisoners according to biological sex. However, in rare circumstances, transgender inmates can be sent to facilities consistent with their gender identity. Factors that will be taken into consideration include institutional safety, other potential ways to mitigate risk to the detainee, inmate history, and progress toward medical transition (Benner 2018; Department of Justice 2018).

Beyond the PREA implementation standards, a number of important court cases have followed the ruling in *Estelle v. Gamble* (1976). For example, in *Farmer v. Brennan* (1994) the U.S. Supreme Court ruled that a "prison official may be held liable under the Eighth Amendment for acting with 'deliberate indifference' to inmate health or safety if he knows that inmates face substantial risk of serious harm and disregards that risk by failing to take reasonable measures to abate it." The Court also indicated that excessive risks include situations where an inmate belongs to "an identifiable group of people who are frequently singled out for violent attacks by other inmates" (*Farmer v. Brennan* 1994, as quoted in Cahill 2017, 141). In this instance, a transgender woman (Dee Farmer) had been housed in a male prison and had often been raped and beaten by other inmates. Since the *Farmer* ruling, a number of other court decisions have established that LGBT and gender nonconforming inmates constitute an "at risk" group, requiring prison officials to take steps to protect their health and safety (Cahill 2017, 141).

Health Care

Health care is also a significant issue for transgender inmates and the issue has generated a significant amount of litigation. These cases have helped to establish some health care rights for transgender inmates. As noted, *Estelle v. Gamble* (1976) and *Farmer v. Brennan* (1994) established some general rights for LGBT and intersex health care that have led to additional court cases. For example, a Wisconsin state law that prohibited government funding of gender reassignment treatments was ruled to be an unconstitutional violation of the equal protection clause and of the cruel and unusual punishment clause. The ruling by a federal district court was upheld by the Seventh Circuit (*Fields v. Smith* 2011).[11] Lambda Legal and the ACLU were directly involved in the case.

Like lesbian, gay, or bisexual inmates, transgender inmates also have high needs for prevention and testing for HIV, other sexually transmitted diseases, and for hepatitis C. Yet much of the focus on the health care rights of transgender inmates has been on access to hormone therapies and sex reassignment surgery. The litigation in these areas has been mixed, and none of the cases have established a national precedent. In addition, many corrections administrators have balked at these treatments, sometimes under the direction of elected officials. In federal courts, transgender inmates have received some support for hormone therapies, but much less support for surgeries.

As noted in chapter 5, in *Kosilek v. Spencer* a prisoner receiving hormone therapy sought gender reassignment surgery as a medical necessity. A federal district court in Massachusetts found, and a three-judge panel of the First Circuit court affirmed 2–1, in favor of the plaintiff. However, the state sought additional review and a panel of judges overturned the original decision 3–2 in 2014 (*Kosilek v. Spencer* 2014). The majority opinion stated that the nonsurgical treatment provided was satisfactory and that the ruling judge did not adequately consider the Department of Corrections' postsurgery security concerns. The Supreme Court declined to review the *Kosilek* case, allowing the lower court ruling to stand.

Additional cases have found some success, but they have not set national precedents. Transgender inmate Ophelia De'lonta pursued transition medical treatment in Virginia in 1999. Her case led to hormone treatments in 2004, but she had to sue for transition surgery in 2011. After an initial loss, a federal panel supported her legal argument about deliberate indifference to an inmate's health. However, De'lonta was granted parole in 2014 before the state's appeal was heard (Spies 2015).[12]

In California, the progress and outcomes of several court cases have helped to ensure that many transgender inmates are able to have access to hormone therapy (Allen 2016; St. John 2015a, 2015b) and state policy on gender transition surgery has been revised to potentially cover these procedures (Pérez-Peña 2015). In particular, the historic settlement between Shiloh Quine and the state of California ensures that transgender inmates will have access to all "medically necessary treatment for gender dysphoria, including surgery" (Transgender Law Center 2015). This was the first of its kind policy in any state, but it is limited to California.

Conclusion

Transgender people have often been criminalized in the United States as well as being disproportionately the victims of crime and violence. Those entering the criminal justice system are often subjected to harassment and abuse by police and corrections officials. Nevertheless, significant progress has been achieved in the past few decades.

Laws that criminalize transgender people, including laws against appearing in public as a gender other than one's birth sex, have been repealed or found to be unenforceable. Meanwhile, localities and states have increasingly included gender identity in hate crime laws that enhance penalties for crimes motivated by bias toward a group. National laws have also been revised to support transgender people, including the adoption of a federal hate crime policy in 2009 that includes gender identity.

Within the criminal justice system, progress has been somewhat slower. Transgender people are still more likely to receive harassing treatment from police, and sometimes to be subjected to violence by police. For incarcerated transgender people, the situation improved somewhat under the Obama administration. Their national policy and implementation guidelines helped corrections officials identify at risk inmates, such as gay and transgender people. These guidelines increased the likelihood that a transgender inmate's rights, safety, and health would be protected. However, the Trump administration has worked to reverse these changes. Litigation has largely ensured that transgender people have access to hormone therapies, but only California provides public funding for transition-related surgery. As litigation over these issues continues, it is likely that more of the health needs of transgender inmates will be addressed over time.

Conclusion

On Memorial Day, 2016, I (Jami Taylor) was in Washington, DC, preparing to interview a few sources for this book. With some time to kill, I went over the National Portrait Gallery. After winding my way through paintings of presidents and other famous Americans, I stumbled upon the section of the museum that highlights pioneers in the battle for civil rights in America. There were artworks memorializing the achievements of civil rights icons like Rosa Parks, César Chávez, and Dr. Martin Luther King. As I walked past the bust of Dr. King, I looked at the wall and there was a picture of LGBT rights pioneer and transgender activist Sylvia Rivera. I was absolutely gobsmacked. Stunned. Here I was in the National Portrait Gallery, *The National Portrait Gallery*, and there was a picture of Sylvia Rivera, a key early activist in trans and gay rights. She was a Latina trans woman who was involved in the Stonewall Riots and she later cofounded, with Marsha P. Johnson, an early trans rights advocacy organization, Street Transvestite Action Revolutionaries. Prior to her death in 2002, Rivera also fought to highlight how the concerns of gender variant people and the socially marginalized were being sidelined by the assimilationist parts of the gay rights movement. Yet today, it is clear that the transgender movement is not sidelined. Indeed, transgender rights have reached the point where a trans woman can be honored in the National Portrait Gallery for her service to transgender and LGBT rights, as well as civil rights generally. Transgender activist Riki Wilchins (2002) once called her "the Rosa Parks of the modern transgender movement." I was really choked up because it was another high-profile indicator of how far transgender rights have advanced. I left in awe.

As this story shows, the transgender movement has come a long way. As of 2018, the transgender rights movement in the United States has been able to secure a remarkable string of policy achievements in the few decades that the term transgender has existed (Stryker 2008). Since the beginning of the modern transgender movement in the 1980s and 1990s, transgender rights advancements have been achieved across all levels of government and in a range of policy areas. At the national level, gender identity and sexual orientation were added to the federal hate crimes law with the passage of the Matthew Shepard and James Byrd Jr. Hate Crimes Prevention Act in 2009. Recent federal district and appellate court rulings have determined that the sex discrimination protections under Title VII of the Civil Rights Act of 1964 encompass sex stereotyping and thus may provide protection for transgender employees. The Obama administration issued a series of executive actions to advance transgender rights. These ranged from easing gender marker changes for federal documents such as passports and Social Security records, to securing discrimination protections in a variety of government programs, to allowing transgender people to serve in the military. Although the Trump administration is rolling back some of these protections, it is unlikely that it will remove all of them. At the subnational level, twenty states specifically include gender identity in their antibullying policies. Nineteen states comprehensively bar gender identity discrimination in employment, housing, and public accommodations. Seventeen states include gender identity in their hate crimes law, and fourteen have passed more narrowly tailored protections against discrimination in schools. Many local governments, from municipalities to schools districts, have adopted their own policies that provide protections for transgender rights. Finally, the majority of large businesses also provide protections in their internal policies.

As we noted at the outset of the book, policy changes are one of the common ways that we assess the work of social movements. Indeed, the achievements of the transgender rights movement are astonishing for such a small and historically marginalized political group. In a majoritarian democracy like the United States, policy successes typically require a significant amount of resources—political access, money, and votes (e.g., Olson 1965; Schlozman 1984; Gilens 2012). Yet, with an estimated national population of just 1.4 million people, or 0.6 percent of the population (Flores et al. 2016) that has faced widespread discrimination, poverty, and violence (Grant, Mottet, and Tanis 2011; James et al. 2016), the transgender community has nonetheless been able to find ways to secure political and policy victories against the odds. These surprising successes, themselves, constitute an intriguing puzzle. Put simply, how are they doing that?

Of course, this rather simple question does not lend itself to an equally simple answer. Throughout the book, we explored a range of social, political, and institutional factors that have contributed to the policy successes of the transgender rights movement and, in many cases, to the limits of the successes and the challenges that the movement faces in the coming years. While there is no quick and easy answer to our research question, the analyses covered in these pages have revealed a range of important insights into the remarkable rise of transgender rights and the future challenges and opportunities for the movement.

Summary of Findings

Building a Transgender Rights Social Movement

Our analyses of the development of the transgender rights movement identified several critical factors that contribute to recent policy successes. Importantly, the transgender rights movement developed independent organizations and became accepted, somewhat begrudgingly, as part of the broader LGBT advocacy coalition. By participating in a larger coalitional movement, transgender rights advocates leveraged more financial, organizational, and political resources than they could generate by themselves. They also could take advantage of the gay and lesbian advocacy community's ties to the Democratic Party. In addition, they gained access to the policymaking process more effectively than they would have otherwise been able to do on their own. Further, gay and lesbian advocates have proven to be important ambassadors to the public and policymakers alike, increasingly normalizing transgender inclusion in LGBT advocacy. In legislatures, gay or lesbian legislators have been important champions for transgender rights, providing crucial representation given the paucity of transgender elected officials. Gay and lesbian activists are also sometimes excellent surrogate lobbyists for transgender rights because of legislator discomfort with trans people.

However, the inclusion of the transgender community in this advocacy coalition was not always a foregone conclusion. The development of queer politics and core values built upon a shared experience of oppression due to the violation of gender norms has been critical in allowing for transgender inclusion in the more robustly organized gay rights movement. This conceptual development was also aided by more practical developments, such as the response to the HIV/AIDS epidemic. Likewise, the growth of queer theory in academia and its dispersion among a new generation of activists helped to inform advocacy organization practices over time and make them more transgender inclusive. The professionalization of transgender advocacy, with its necessary attention to identity politics, helped to facilitate transgender inclusion by making sure that transgender people "had a seat at the table." That many trans people had long-standing connections in the gay or lesbian communities assisted in this process, as did shared political opponents. And increased media attention to transgender people and transgender issues has increased public familiarity with the concerns of the trans community, thus making their incorporation in LGBT advocacy easier as well.

Inclusion in the umbrella LGBT movement has certainly been important to the advancement of transgender rights, but it has not been without its own challenges. Assimilationist strategies by gay people often marginalized or completely excluded transgender rights. Indeed, until recently, transgender rights have not been at the top of the advocacy coalition's policy priorities. The movement has often had to "come back" to secure rights based on gender identity that had previously been won for rights based on sexual orientation (Taylor and Lewis 2014). The achievement of marriage equality, a key policy objective for many gay rights groups over the past several years, has been a boon to transgender advocacy. It lessened competition for the limited resources held by LGBT groups, and it no longer competes in the policy space for attention. Indeed, the battle for marriage equality eclipsed nearly all other LGBT policy goals for the better part of two presidencies. With that fight over, LGBT groups that specialize in litigation have rapidly increased their attention to transgender issues in their legal advocacy. Further, gaining marriage equality provided another policy win for transgender people because it negated the importance of sex and gender in a major civil institution.

Public Opinion

Another important factor shaping both the policy successes and challenges of the transgender rights movement is public opinion. Drawing on several national surveys, we found public attitudes toward transgender people to be complex and, currently, quite mutable. Americans hold negative feelings toward transgender people as a group. They report relatively low levels of personal comfort with transgender people, and large portions of the public express moral or personal opposition to the very concept of transgender. However, at the same time majorities tend to favor discrimination protections for transgender people and believe that transgender people deserve the same rights as all Americans. The seemingly contradictory nature of public attitudes toward transgender people, on the one hand, and transgender rights, on the other, helps explain policy successes in areas that highlight human and civil rights, such as employment nondiscrimination and hate crime policies, and the limits in other areas that emphasize personal feelings of discomfort, such as bathroom accessibility.

Yet the complex nature of public opinion toward transgender people and their rights seems to be highly fluid. When given the opportunity to select an option of "neither agree nor disagree," a substantial portion of the public chooses this option, likely indicating attitude ambivalence or nonattitudes on the topic. In other words, we find that many people are still not familiar with transgender concepts. Nor are they familiar with policy implications related to the issues raised by the transgender rights movement. This fluidity may provide the transgender rights movement with both challenges and opportunities since many people are still learning about the issues and are open to framing and persuasion efforts (Broockman and Kalla 2016). Further, the relatively low level of familiarity with transgender rights policies suggest that public opinion is likely to be positively affected by the increasing exposure to transgender people in the media and through interpersonal contact (Flores et al. 2017a; Tadlock et al. 2017).

Indeed, we found that several factors shape individuals' attitudes toward transgender people and transgender rights. Attitudes toward transgender people are primarily shaped by personality traits, values, and experience. Moral traditionalists and respondents with high levels of disgust sensitivity tend to have attitudes that are more negative toward transgender people. Conversely, those with egalitarian values tend to have views that are more positive. In addition, interpersonal contact with both transgender people and gays and lesbians increased positive attitudes toward transgender people. The latter is very important given the significantly larger size of the gay and lesbian communities relative to the trans community. While these factors remain significant in forming political and policy attitudes, other factors also emerge. Interestingly, partisanship and ideology only seem to have significant effects on attitudes relating to public policies. Authoritarianism is also a significant factor for these political attitudes.

Political Institutions and Opportunity Structure

The American transgender rights movement developed within a federal and democratic institutional structure with a separation of powers between branches. This provided a range of policy advocacy opportunities in different institutional venues and at different levels of government. Transgender advocates, like the advocates for other groups, have many access points and venues in which to find policy gains. They can strategically shop for, and often find, favorable policymaking venues. In legislatures, from city councils to the U.S. Congress, trans and LGBT groups have made significant strides in gaining increased policy recognition and protections. For some policies, such as antidiscrimination protections and hate crimes, the trans movement has been able to build on the earlier successes of the gay movement and pursue incremental policy changes that are less controversial. Particularly in the 2000s, the trans movement sometimes benefited by obtaining these protections concurrently with gays and lesbians, occasionally as a little noticed afterthought. Activists could share information about these successes in their advocacy. Early victories provided relevant policy information that could be shared in other jurisdictions. These examples were useful in lobbying and they facilitated the diffusion of these policies.

In other policy areas, such as those relaxing rules about gender identification on official documents, there is no parallel set of gay rights laws. Thus, the transgender movement sometimes has been forced to go it alone. However, as witnessed during the Obama administration, there is increasing attention from LGBT advocates to these transgender specific measures. Even here, where policies are not incremental changes, the backlash has often been weak. Further, conservative jurisdictions that have not supported sexual-orientation-inclusive policies have sometimes provided significant policy changes, such as birth certificate amendment laws or allowing sex markers on driver's licenses to be changed. Frequently, this is done without much fanfare.

Like other minority civil rights movements before it, the transgender rights movement has also successfully turned to the courts as a "judicial safety net" to provide civil rights protections. These venues, often more isolated from electoral and partisan pressures (especially at the national level), allow transgender rights advocates to pursue policies from a legal framework that highlights civil rights and equal protection under the law, even in the context of negative public opinion and partisan opposition in many areas of the country. While most areas of litigation on transgender rights are still ongoing, there have been some notable policy achievements. Because the U.S. Supreme Court's ruling in *Price Waterhouse v. Hopkins* (1989) found that Title VII's sex discrimination clause provides protection against discrimination based on sex stereotyping, several federal district and appellate courts have extended these protections to cover transgender people. A similar legal argument has also held sway in some recent Title IX cases at the federal district and appellate levels, such as *G.G. v. Gloucester County School Board* (2016). Several cases regarding the rights of transgender prisoners have also been successfully litigated, with the Eighth Amendment's prohibition against cruel and unusual punishment providing a legal rationale to provide gender-identity-related health care to transgender prisoners and to challenge sex-segregated facilities based on sex assigned at birth.

The executive branches of government have also proven to be fruitful venues for transgender rights advocacy. Bureaucratic policymaking can avoid majoritarian pressures while shaping the implementation of critical policies that affect the everyday lives of transgender people. For example, a rule passed by the State Department in 2010 eased the standards for changing gender markers on passports. Similar changes happened at the Social Security Administration, which ended the practice of sending gender no match letters to the employers of transgender people. In addition, executive leaders like presidents and governors can shape policy through unilateral action, personnel, and symbolic leadership. Our analysis revealed the ways in which significant gains were made at the national level during the Obama administration. Obama issued an executive order prohibiting gender-identity-based discrimination in federal employment in 2014, and he filled his cabinet with officials that pursued transgender rights in their departments. The administration's ability to take these actions was enabled by court cases that provided a legal rationale for the actions, such as *Smith v. City of Salem* (2004) and the EEOC decision in *Macy v. Holder* (2012). Though gay and transgender rights were not always a top priority for his administration, by Obama's second term it was clear that they had become a key component of his legacy building. This was a function of the pressure placed by LGBT advocates on the president, the evolution of public attitudes on LGBT issues, the lack of opportunities elsewhere, and his beliefs about equality. Beyond his policy actions, Obama ultimately pushed the Democratic Party to be more inclusive through his rhetoric and symbolic leadership. In doing so, the transgender rights movement is now a recognized partner in the Democratic coalition, with its policy goals embedded in the party platform. Going forward, many aspiring Democratic candidates will find it difficult to ignore transgender issues even though they are still unlikely to make them front-and-center campaign issues in many parts of the country. Any reluctance to embrace transgender rights in Democratic circles is certainly lessened given the actions of President Trump and his administration on transgender rights. Given Trump's low approval ratings, Democrats are incentivized to be in opposition to these discriminatory actions. Similarly, we documented how North Carolina Democrats rallied around the transgender rights cause after passage of HB2 by a deeply unpopular Republican governor and Republican-led legislature in North Carolina.

Of course, state executives have also played crucial roles in advancing transgender rights. Governors have often been at the forefront of providing discrimination protections using executive orders before the legislature is willing, or where it is unwilling, to adopt statutory protections. We also found that governors have wielded their veto pens to block bills that would restrict the rights of transgender people, as when Governor Daugaard (R-SD) vetoed a bill to require students to use bathrooms that corresponded with the sex assigned at birth rather than their gender identity. Anecdotally, Republican governors might be more willing to veto such changes when they are term limited and cannot run for reelection. Our analysis revealed that transgender-inclusive executive orders are common early in gubernatorial terms, during divided governments, and by Democratic governors. Further, some governors, such as Jack Markell in Delaware, used their political capital to advocate for transgender-inclusive policies in their state. Another influential state official is the attorney general. In some instances, attorney generals can play a role in advancing transgender rights by declining to defend discriminatory laws, as was done by Roy Cooper in North Carolina, or by issuing favorable advisory opinions.

At the state and local level, we also found that direct democracy institutions, such as ballot initiatives and referenda, have the potential to shape policy outcomes related to transgender rights. To date, these institutions primarily have been used to challenge legislative actions to expand nondiscrimination policies to cover gender identity. However, in many cases these popular referendums have served to ratify these protections rather than to veto them. Analysis of the referendum campaigns also reveals the power of framing these issues, as we found a correlation between civil rights messaging and support for transgender rights. Opposition to these policies coincided with messages emphasizing personal discomfort and security concerns related to bathroom access.

This potential to shape public opinion toward LGBT rights through direct democracy campaigns is not only evident in these early transgender related referendums but was also apparent in the battle over same-sex marriage in the past few decades. In both cases, direct democracy served to not only enhance the impact of public opinion on policy outcomes (both directly and indirectly), but it also seems to have shaped the content of public preferences as well. These campaigns familiarize the public with the LGBT community and the issues at stake. In particular, the unwanted campaigns against the measures forced gay couples and families to reveal a public face that many Americans had not seen before; those seeking marriage were not single people looking for one-night stands. Instead, they were committed long-term couples and families nurturing children; the opposing campaigns to referenda were able to share these images and educate the public. Moreover, even though LGBT rights activists lost many of those referenda by wide margins, the campaigns and successful bans on same-sex marriage generated policy feedback that helped reframe the debate and educate the public, which allowed for dramatic opinion shifts and future agenda setting. We largely expect the same thing to occur if opponents to transgender rights engage in a similar tactic.

The Future of Transgender Rights: Challenges and Opportunities

Although the transgender rights movement has had remarkable success in the past few decades, significant challenges remain. One of the most prominent challenges derives from the movement's patterns of success. First, geographically, we have seen policy successes in the most liberal states, typically in the Northeast and Western regions of the United States. The maps displayed in this book tend to show the same set of 14–20 states that have adopted pro-transgender policies. As seen in table 7.1, twenty states had passed four or more of the eight policies evaluated by HRC (each including some form of gender-identity-inclusive nondiscrimination policy), but ten more had just one or two policies, and the rest had not adopted any policies. This geographic pattern certainly corresponds to partisan and ideological patterns in the country. It raises the question of whether transgender rights policies at the state level may be close to reaching their limit. For many conservative states in the South and Midwest, transgender rights have made virtually no progress via legislative action, other than on birth certificate policies. And even those latter policies are often deemed inadequate and unnecessarily discriminatory by most trans activists.

This geographic pattern is also related to partisan and ideological patterns in policy success and support seen throughout the book. One factor enabling the passage of pro-transgender policies has been the integration of a gay and transgender rights agenda into the Democratic Party platform. Yet this integration may be a double-edged sword. Although it fosters policy progress in Democratic-controlled states, cities, and in Democratic administrations at all levels of government, it may hinder progress on these issues in areas where the Republican Party holds more sway, and where voters oppose anything Democrats represent. This is particularly problematic given the historic low ebb of Democratic control in state legislatures, at the gubernatorial level, and with unified Republican control in Washington (as of 2017).

In an era of polarized partisan politics, the transgender rights movement's affiliation with the Democratic Party may erect barriers toward broader bipartisan support. At the same time, the libertarian portion of the Republican base might provide some opportunities for cooperation on issues that avoid the intrusive force of government intervention.

The benefits and limitations of partisan integration in recent years are abundantly clear in the dynamics of executive policymaking at the national level. Whereas the Obama administration sought to bolster its legacy through a range of pro-transgender policies, from employment discrimination to Title IX protections to easing gender marker changes, the Trump administration is on track to reverse many of these policy advances in just its first year in office. The DOE and DOJ have already rescinded gender-identity-inclusive guidance on Title IX. The administration is not pursuing a case (*Franciscan Alliance v. Burwell* 2016) to enforce a nondiscrimination clause in the Affordable Care Act as it applies to gender identity, and it is taking steps to roll back HHS regulations related to this policy (National Center for Transgender Equality 2017c). A series of legal cases and court injunctions aside, a ban on transgender people in the military is under policy development based on direction from President Trump. These reversals not only highlight the limits of partisan integration but also reveal the limits of executive policymaking. Unlike legislative policymaking, these rules and guidances can be overturned, somewhat easily, by a subsequent administration. However, public opinion shifts toward civil rights protections for transgender people may make that politically difficult if current patterns continue. Of course, many of the Trump administration's policy gambits may be altered by his successor as well. Yet one thing that will not be easily altered is the reshaping of the judiciary by President Trump. His judicial nominations have already begun to move the federal courts in a direction that will likely be hostile to LGBT rights.

The challenge of partisanship may also extend to public support for transgender rights. Analysis of our national surveys shows that partisanship is a significant determinant of support for transgender policies. In a previous analysis, we found that the effect of partisanship was greater for evaluations of transgender people compared to evaluations of gay men and lesbians (Lewis et al. 2017). In addition, Republican identifiers are less likely than Democratic identifiers to vote for a transgender candidate who shares their views on political issues (Haider-Markel et al. 2017). Because of the multidimensionality in people's attitudes about transgender rights and the feelings of disgust that transgender people activate in some individuals, it is also possible for Republicans to create partisan wedges in electoral politics around the bathroom issue, access to medical treatment, and sports participation. Use of these potential wedge issues is also advanced by the fact that relatively few people have personal contact with transgender individuals, which we know increases comfort and positive feelings, even if that does not directly translate into policy support (Flores et al. 2017a; Tadlock et al. 2017).

Yet despite these limits and challenges, the transgender rights movement also has several opportunities for advancement in the coming years. In particular, public support for transgender rights may be ripe for large shifts similar to the changes in support for gay rights issues such as same-sex marriage. A 2017 Gallup poll found that 64 percent of Americans believed that same-sex marriage should be legal, an increase of 20 to 25 points over levels of support in 2004 and 2005 (Gallup 2017b). This represents a near complete reversal of opinion from 1996, when just 27 percent supported same-sex marriage and 68 percent were opposed. As noted in the chapters on public opinion, a substantial portion of the public does not hold clear attitudes toward transgender people and related policies. This may allow for substantial shifts in opinion as the public becomes more familiar with these issues, and it makes the education role of advocacy organizations all the more paramount.

Although there is the potential for opinion to shift in a negative direction, perhaps as a result of backlash from government decisions, a positive change is more likely. First, as people become more familiar with transgender people through the media and through increased interpersonal contact, they are likely to hold more positive attitudes toward transgender people as a group (Allport 1954; Tadlock et al. 2017). Indeed, Flores et al. (2017a) found that mere exposure to an image of a transgender person increased evaluations of transgender people as a group. Next, while partisanship may present a barrier to broader support for transgender rights, it does not seem to consistently affect personal feelings toward transgender people, such as group affect and personal comfort. This point is important because group affect may influence transgender policy attitudes. In addition, religiosity—a significant limit on support for gay rights—is less influential in shaping attitudes toward transgender people (Lewis et al. 2017). Unlike biblical prohibitions on homosexuality, there are fewer direct prohibitions in the Bible. Indeed, the controversial and extremely conservative televangelist Pat Robertson has made public statements opining that gender reassignment is not sin (Brydum 2013). Some other faith traditions, notably Reform and Conservative Judaism and Shia Islam, have also long been accepting of sex reassignment. And as our legislative chapter reveals, the evangelical population overall, which has played a significant role in shaping gay rights policy, appears to have little influence on the adoption of transgender-inclusive rights policies.

We also expect that increased familiarity with specific policies, whether it is bathroom access, gender marker changes, or health care, is likely to reduce opposition to transgender rights in the longer term. As noted in the direct democracy chapter and above, as the public becomes more exposed to these issues through ballot initiative and referendum campaigns, the movement can use these as (perhaps unwanted) "teaching moments" to expose the broader public to the issues faced by trans people in their families. Moreover, we do know that exposure to transgender discrimination, combined with a process of self-evaluation of experiences of discrimination, can radically shift attitudes about trans equality (Broockman and Kalla 2016). A similar dynamic may result from the legislative and executive policymaking processes as well, as the exposure to bills and agenda items, even those that are limited in scope, "softens up" policymakers to policy ideas and solutions (Haider-Markel 2010).

Indeed, the battle over North Carolina's HB2 exhibits these traits. While a discriminatory law, it also was a yearlong transgender public education campaign, unexpectedly facilitated by Republicans in North Carolina's General Assembly and by Governor Pat McCrory. It provided a high-profile opportunity for LGBT activists to talk to the public about transgender rights. It provided an opening for transgender individuals to talk about their struggles and thus increase contact and parasocial contact. The heavy-handed action by government made life for transgender people more difficult, but it also made transgender people more sympathetic. They became victims of a mean-spirited government policy. President Obama and Attorney General Loretta Lynch weighed in. The business community opposed it as well. The state and national backlash to the law stiffened the resistance of Democrats, who were often leery of LGBT issues in the South. Even Democrats who voted for HB2 in the House were now open to learning about the issue. They were apologizing for the vote and quickly evolving (Ring 2016a). HB2 and transgender rights became a partisan issue. Democrats, such as those who chose to walk out in the Senate rather than cast a vote, took a position on record. They bludgeoned Republicans with the issue, particularly Governor McCrory. And McCrory lost his reelection campaign in large part because of his strong support for this ill-considered law. When a movement wants policy change, moving from a nonissue to a partisan issue is a sign that success. It is even better for your movement when that shifts helps defeat a high-profile opponent in the process. This episode almost certainly caused policymakers in other states, such as Texas, to be more cautious when considering discriminatory legislation.

In addition, the transgender rights movement's association with and continued inclusion in the broader LGBT advocacy coalition also presents opportunities. In terms of public opinion, association with the LGBT movement should have a positive effect on attitudes toward transgender rights. Ratings of gay men and lesbians tend to be higher than for transgender people, and may act to increase evaluations of transgender people over time. Further, Tadlock et al. (2017) find that interpersonal contact with gays and lesbians has a positive effect on attitudes toward transgender people and rights, suggesting a positive effect by association. Current trends show that the number of people reporting knowing someone who is gay or lesbian is growing (Brewer 2008), which should lead to increased support for transgender rights.

Inclusion in the LGBT advocacy coalition should also continue to pay dividends for transgender rights advocates. Transgender rights have become more central to the advocacy coalition in recent years and, as a result, have become a higher priority. As noted in chapter 1, the major LGBT groups are no longer excluding transgender rights, and they have embraced the more universal concept of gender nonconformity that unifies the whole coalition. Further, with same-sex marriage legalized across the country, LGBT groups have begun the process of "coming back" for gender identity inclusive language in nondiscrimination policies and other transgender rights priorities. With gays and lesbians serving as ambassadors for the trans community, as we note in earlier chapters, the education and contact effects for policymakers and the public become multiplied fivefold beyond what trans people might be able to do by themselves.

Although the transgender rights movement still faces significant challenges, our analyses of the remarkable rise of this historically marginalized group implies cautious optimism for the future. As a dynamic and emerging issue among the public, there is great potential for positive shifts in public support driven by increasing familiarity, interpersonal contact, and knowledge of transgender people and issues. This should build on existing successes in the legislative, judicial, and executive policymaking arenas. There are certain to be setbacks in the short term and notably during the Trump administration, but the transgender rights movement has developed into a robust and institutionalized social movement that can "outpunch its weight class" through its inclusion in the LGBT advocacy coalition and in the Democratic Party. It is also advantaged by the highly permeable nature of the American political system.

Appendix A

LGBT Organization Financial Data

These IRS Business Master Files (BMF) obtained from the National Center for Charitable Statistics contain information about all active nonprofit organizations that have registered for tax-exempt status with the IRS. Our data includes organizations covered by tax code sections 501(c)(3), 501(c) (4) and other 501(c) types (National Center for Charitable Statistics n.d.). When downloading the data, we obtained employment identification number, name, state, income, asset, revenue code subsection, and the National Taxonomy of Exempt Entities (NTEE) classification code. Because the National Center for Charitable Statistics (NCCS) holdings are inconsistent as to whether data was collected annually, quarterly, or monthly, we queried the last record available in each calendar year. Our search terms included the following NTEE codes:

- G81: AIDS
- H81: AIDS Research
- P88: LGBT Centers
- R26: Lesbian and Gay Rights

In our dataset, we elected to include AIDS coded organizations because of the historical connection, in the U.S. context, between gay rights advocacy and the fight against HIV/AIDS. Because organizations are only afforded one NTEE code that is based on its major organizational purpose (National Center for Charitable Statistics 2008), we chose to expand our search for LGBT groups by looking for keywords in the organization name field. This included a variety of common LGBT-rights-related terms like gay, lesbian, bisexual, and transgender. Names for organizations not addressed by common keywords were also identified by consulting various editions of the *Encyclopedia of Associations, Encyclopedia of Associations: Regional, State and Local Organizations*, members of the Equality Federation, members of Centerlink, and various other online sources. We did not include groups like the American Civil Liberties Union because they serve multiple constituencies. The specific search terms used in the NCCS search were the following:

gay, lesbian, bisex, transgend, equality, lgb, glb, tranvest, transsex, transex, transyouth, trans youth, transkid, trans kid, lavender, pride, queer, crossdress, cross dress, gender education, freedom to marry, right to marry legal fund, gender rights, basic rights, fairness west, fairness campaign, fairness education, fairness wv, audre lord, one iowa, the triangle foundation, outfront, cimarron alliance, matthew shepard, national black justice coalition, soulforce, sylvia rivera, trans student, truth wins out, bilitis, love makes a family, log cabin republican, second self, arcus foundation, guilford green, new harvest foundation, cream city foundation, delaware valley legacy fund, adam foundation inc, stonewall community foundation, philanthrofund foundation, san diego human dignity foundation, gill foundation, equity foundation, horizons foundation, atticus circle, fine by me, stonewall democrat, one colorado, fairness campaign, louisiana trans advocates, massequality, outfront minnesota, promo, empire state pride agenda, transohio, gender justice, fair wisconsin, marriage equality, equal rights washington, citizens for equal protection, coloradans for fairness, lexington fairness, arizona human rights, center advocacy project, your family friends, center advocates, action wisconsin, project 515, point foundation, trevor project, our space community center, one-n-ten, wingspan, the centers at car, bienestar human services, stonewall alliance, pacific center for human growth, inside out youth services, out boulder, triangle community center, sexual minority, compass community center, metropolitan charities inc, sunshine social services, family tree community center, center on halsted, community alliance and action, quad citians affirming, up center of champaign, indiana youth group, rainbow serenity, out center, ruth ellis center, kaleidoscope youth center, youth outright, time out youth, stonewall columbus, living room, delta foundation of pittsburgh, attic youth center, resource center of dallas, montrose counseling center, roanoke diversity center, rosmy, oasis youth center, rainbow center, village vida, centerlink, palette fund, keshet, dykes on bikes, dyke march, gender information, survivor project, gender public advocacy, female-to-male international, pflag, integrity, dignity, universal fellowship of metropolitan community, black and white men together, artemis singers, asians and friends, rainbow alliance, bay area physicians for human rights, stonewall community, binet usa, capitol forum, chevrei tikva, chiltern mountain, colage, community united against violence, out proud, outproud, outright, fortunate families, greater seattle business association, hetrick martin institute, identity inc, indiana youth group, key west business guild, manhattan mustangs, men of all colors together, metropolitan community church, milwaukee gamma inc, new ways ministry, outside in, pacific center for human growth, radical faeries, rainbow families, seventh day adventist kinship international, shaar zahav, stonewall columbus, stonewall youth, tampa bay business guild, the relatives inc, tom homann law association, dulles triangles, trikone, utah associated garden clubs, we are family, more light presbyterians, lutherans concerned, reconcilingworks, congregation kol ami, congregation or chadash, congregation shaar zahav, american foundation for equal rights, american veterans for equal rights, getequal action, out and equal, marry me movement, oklahomans for equality, business guild.

Because the keyword searches within the NCCS database were "like" searches, derivations of keywords were picked up. For instance, a search for organizations with gay in the name would pick up an organization with gaylord in the name as well. Thus, the initial dataset of approximately 1.7 million records needed significant cleaning to remove non-LGBT-related groups. Except for the four types of NTEE coded groups above, organization records were reviewed individually for inclusion as LGBT related or not. To make the determination, the review included searches of organization websites, available 990 tax forms, and Internet news searches for the organization. Non-LGBT-related groups were dropped from the dataset. We also removed a few groups that advocate against LGBT rights but have LGBT rights related terms in their organization name (e.g., Americans for Truth about Homosexuality). In total, our data covers 5,216 LGBT organizations that appeared in the BMF files. Because we look at annual data over time (1995–2015), these 5,216 organizations collectively produce a dataset with 53,402 observations over twenty-one years.

All organizations were then categorized into a classification scheme of activities that emerged from the data:

1. Advocacy (e.g., Human Rights Campaign), n = 743
2. Culture and sport (e.g., Portland Gay Men's Chorus), n = 215
3. AIDS related, n = 2,591
4. Religious congregations (e.g., Metropolitan Community Churches), n = 167
5. Social support (e.g., Parents Families Friends of Lesbians and Gays—PFLAG), n = 745
6. Pride and similar events (e.g., Charlotte Pride), n = 198
7. Unknown, n = 0 (this category was dropped as we investigated groups)
8. LGBT funding and scholarships (e.g., Gill Foundation), n = 40
9. Professional and student organizations (e.g., Tampa Bay Business Guild), n = 151
10. Religious-based LGBT advocacy (e.g., Soulforce), n = 132
11. LGBT community centers (e.g., Houston Gay and Lesbian Community Center), n = 170
12. Archives, studies, media (e.g., Ohio Lesbian Archives), n = 32
13. LGBT health (e.g., Transgender Health Empowerment), n = 32

When classifying the organizations, we relied on the organization name, website information, IRS 990 tax forms available via Guidestar, and Internet news searches to make a determination on the nature of their primary activity. Additionally, we maintained consistent classification over all yearly observations of an organization. Because of the sheer number of AIDS related groups, G81 and H81 coded NTEE groups were automatically assigned to the AIDS category unless there was an obviously miscoded organization (e.g., a group on beauty aids). Additionally, any organization with HIV or AIDS in the title was moved to the AIDS related category. A handful of organizations had name and or mission changes over their lifespan. When classifying these organizations, the team relied on the balance of the organization's history and information about its mission.

Data Collapse

The 53,402 observations and their income, asset, and organization type data—e.g., 501(c)(3)—were collapsed in Stata v.13 by state and year. This yielded a dataset with 1,071 observations (50 states + DC x 21years = 1,071). A separate collapse on the same variables but without the organization types culture and sport (2), AIDS related (3), and religious congregations (4) was performed. After dropping these types of organizations, this left 20,682 observations for 2,243 organizations. When collapsed by state and year, this yielded a separate 1,071 observation dataset. Each dataset was then merged with price index and population data from the following sources:

Data for the Price Index
• Bureau of Economic Analysis (National Income and Product Accounts, table 1.1.4)
• We used the Annual Price Index for Domestic Products
  • The exception was for 2015. We used the second quarter Price Index because we concluded data collection from NCCS at that time.

Data for Population
• 1990 Census
• 2000 Census
• 2010 Census (including corrections)
• 2014 American Community Survey (1 year)

To convert our collapsed nominal income and asset measures to real 2009 dollars, we used the following formula:

• income real = income/(price index/100)

To put our real collapsed income and asset figures in per capita terms, we divided income and assets by the state population as reported in census years and by the American Community Survey (ACS) for 2014. For other years, we interpolated the population in a straight line method between census years or the ACS. Population for 2015 was extrapolated by the annual change between 2010 and 2014. In this volume's various analyses, we use the dataset that drops the organizations that were coded as culture and sport, AIDS-related, or religious congregations. Primarily, we will use the assets per capita measure.

Appendix B

Interviews

To answer the question of how transgender rights became included with gay rights, we interviewed approximately fifty-five activists and policymakers and reviewed the literature in the field. These elite interviews were conducted with a mix of longtime transgender activists, LGBT rights professionals, policymakers, and academics. Respondents were selected based on literature review, snowball sampling, and longtime observation of the transgender and LGBT rights movement. Of course, access and a willingness to speak on the record were important factors as well. The interviews reflect a broad cross-section of transgender rights advocates and LGBT rights advocates from the 1990s through 2017. These interviews were also conducted at multiple points in time. These include during the dissertation work of Jami Taylor (2008) during 2005–7, in 2012 as part of the work published by Taylor and Lewis (2014), and during 2016–17 as part of this project. We also used multiple interview mediums. These include telephone, e-mail, and in-person interviews. Many of the in-person interviews were conducted in Washington, DC, with the help of the generous financial assistance from the American Political Science Association's Centennial Center for Political Science and Public Affairs and from the University of Toledo. While we cannot share the names of the activists from the previous work due to institutional review board rules on that research, we are able to share more than forty names, in table B.1, of those interviewed specifically for this project. With respect to the older interviews and as noted in Taylor and Lewis (2014), those drew from a wide variety of state and national advocacy groups. Beyond those organizations already mentioned in Table B.1, these include Equality Michigan, Equality Pennsylvania, Gay and Lesbian Advocates and Defenders, and the Transgender Law Center, among others. Given the restrictions on past interview work, we will rely more heavily on the interviews conducted in 2016 and 2017.

Because our respondents have worked in different organizational contexts, in different capacities, and sometimes in different eras, they have different insights on questions related to transgender advocacy. Some are even opponents of transgender rights. Therefore, we did not ask each respondent the same questions. After all, it makes no sense to ask people not engaged in litigation efforts about litigation efforts. Similarly, one cannot gain insights into events that occurred in the 1990s from people who are too young to remember them. Questions and themes of inquiry were selected based on likely respondent knowledge and organization position from an instrument approved by the University of Toledo's Institutional Review Board. Because we are interested in policymaking, organizational level decision-making, and movement information, this was not deemed human subjects research.

TABLE B.1. Elite Interviews, 2016–2017

Name	Affiliation	Past Affiliations
Anonymous	Funder for LGBT Issues	
Beemyn, Genny	Amherst College	
Belkin, Aaron	Palm Center	
Bowman, Lynne	Human Rights Campaign	Equality Ohio, Equality Federation
Boylan, Jennifer Finney	Barnard College, GLAAD	
Broadus, Kylar	Trans People of Color Coalition	National Gay and Lesbian Task Force, National Black Justice Coalition
Currah, Paisley	Brooklyn College	
Davis, Heath Fogg	Temple University	
Denny, Dallas		American Educational Gender Information Service, Southern Comfort
Dunn, Mason	Massachusetts Transgender Political Coalition	
Flynn, Roddy	Director, Congressional LGBT Caucus	
Foreman, Matt	Haas, Jr. Fund	National Gay and Lesbian Task Force, Empire State Pride Agenda, NYC Gay & Lesbian Anti-Violence Project
Furmansky, Dan		Equality Maryland
Gaber, Mark	Jenner & Block	
Graham, Jeff	Georgia Equality	
Green, Jamison		World Professional Association for Transgender Health, FTM International
Gurley, Dan		Equality North Carolina, chief of staff to Rep. Cass Ballenger, Republican National field director/deputy political director
Hood, John	John William Pope Foundation	John Locke Foundation
Howes, Hilary	Gender Rights Maryland	
Keisling, Mara	National Center for Transgender Equality	
Kleinschmidt, Mark		Mayor, Chapel Hill, NC
Maril, Robin	Human Rights Campaign	
Markell, Jack	Governor of Delaware	
McBride, Sarah	Human Rights Campaign	Center for American Progress
McGowan, Sharon	Department of Justice	American Civil Liberties Union
Minter, Shannon	National Center for Lesbian Rights	
Ore, Addison		Equality North Carolina, Triad Health Project
Palmquist, Ian	Equality Federation	Equality North Carolina

TABLE B.1.—*Continued*

Name	Affiliation	Past Affiliations
Peterson, Karen	Delaware state senator	
Poling, Parker Hamilton	Chief of staff, Rep. Patrick McHenry	
Rupert, Maya	U.S. Dept. of Housing and Urban Development	National Center for Lesbian Rights
Sanchez, Diego	PFLAG	Staffer for Rep. Barney Frank
Scott, Gunner	Pride Foundation	Massachusetts Transgender Political Coalition
Seaton, Liz		National Center for Lesbian Rights, Human Rights Campaign, Equality Maryland, Free State Justice
Spade, Dean	Seattle University	Sylvia Rivera Law Project
Stam, Paul	Majority Leader, North Carolina House of Representatives	
Suffredini, Kasey	Freedom for All Americans	Gill Action
Thompson, Ian	American Civil Liberties Union	
Tobin, Harper Jean	National Center for Transgender Equality	
Wilchins, Riki Anne	True Child	GenderPAC, Transexual Menace
Wisnecki, Hope	Human Rights Campaign	

Appendix C

Survey Items for Scatter Plots in Chapter 2

Survey Items for Personal Contact with Transgender People (figure 2.5)
- Do you personally know or work with anyone who is transgender? HRC/Greenberg Quinlan, July 19, 2002.
- Now thinking about the people that you know . . . Please tell me whether you have a close friend or family member who is . . . transgender. PRRI, August 14, 2011; June 7, 2015; February 19, 2017.
- Do you have a close friend or family member who is transgender? PRRI/Princeton, December 18, 2013; CVR, June 25, 2015; CNN/ORC, May 1, 2016.
- Do you personally know or work with someone who is transgender? University of Illinois-Springfield, July 24, 2015.
- Now thinking about the people that you know, do you know someone who is gay/lesbian or transgender who is . . . a family member, a close friend, an acquaintance such as a co-worker or someone you know from school or college (Select all that apply for each row.) GfK, October 11, 2015; CVR, June 29, 2016.
- Do you personally know someone who is transgender or gender fluid? PT/Marist, May 14, 2016.
- Now, not thinking about people you may have seen, read, or heard about, but only whom you know, do you personally know or work with someone who is transgender, that is, someone who does not identify with their birth gender like a person born as a man who now identifies and is living as a woman or a person born as a woman who now identifies and is living as a man? NBC/Wall Street Journal, May 19, 2016.

- Do you personally know someone who is transgender? AP/NORC, July 13, 2016; Pew, September 12, 2016.
- How familiar are you with transgender people . . . (know family or friends)? Williams Institute/IPSOS, August 5, 2016.
Survey Items for Attitudes toward Transgender Restroom Policies (figure 2.11)
- Overall, would you say you favor or oppose laws that require transgender individuals to use facilities that correspond to their gender at birth rather than their gender identity? Do you favor/oppose that strongly or somewhat? CNN/ORC, May 1, 2015.
- In terms of policies governing public restrooms, do you think these policies should—[ROTATED: require transgender individuals to use the restroom that corresponds with their birth gender (or should these policies) allow transgender individuals to use the restroom that corresponds with their gender identity]? Gallup, May 8, 2016.
- Do you think transgender or gender fluid people should be allowed to choose the public restroom with which they identify or should be required to follow the sex on their birth certificate in using a public restroom?; PT/Marist, May 14, 2016.
- Do you think people who are transgender—that is, someone who identifies themselves as the sex or gender different from the one they were born as—should be allowed to use the public bathrooms of the gender they identify with or should they have to use the public bathrooms of the gender they were born as? CBS/New York Times, May 17, 2016.
- Now, North Carolina recently passed a law that prevents transgender people from using public restrooms that match the gender with which they identify and instead requires them to use public restrooms based upon their gender at birth. Do you believe transgender people should be allowed to use the public restroom of the gender with which they identify or should they be legally prevented from doing so or do you not have an opinion one way or the other? NBC/ Wall Street Journal, May 19, 2016; AP/NORC, July 13, 2016.
- In terms of policies governing public restrooms, do you think these policies should require trans individuals to use the restroom that corresponds with their birth gender; or allow transgender individuals to use the restroom that corresponds with their gender identity? University of Kansas, June 29, 2016.
- Please tell me how strongly you FAVOR or OPPOSE each of the fol-

lowing: Laws that require people to use restrooms that match the sex listed on their birth certificate—do you strongly favor, favor, oppose, or strongly oppose this? University of Delaware, July 13, 2016.

- Agree/disagree: Transgender people should be allowed to use the restroom associated with their gender identity. Williams Institute/ IPSOS, August 6, 2016

- Agree/disagree: Laws that require transgender individuals to use bathrooms that correspond to their sex at birth rather than their current gender identity. PRRI, August 16, 2016; PRRI, February 19, 2017.

- And if you had to choose, which comes closest to your view? Transgender people should be . . . [Allowed to use the public restrooms of the gender with which they currently identify] or [Required to use the public restrooms of the gender they were born into]. Pew, September 12, 2016.

Appendix D

Remarks by Attorney General Loretta E. Lynch on HB2

On May 9, 2016, Attorney General Loretta Lynch provided a powerful rebuttal to North Carolina's discriminatory legislation known as HB2. The text of this speech is below (Department of Justice 2016):

> Attorney General Loretta E. Lynch Delivers Remarks at Press Conference Announcing Complaint Against the State of North Carolina to Stop Discrimination Against Transgender Individuals Washington, DC United States-Monday, May 9, 2016.

Remarks as prepared for delivery

Good afternoon and thank you all for being here. Today, I'm joined by [Vanita] Gupta, head of the Civil Rights Division at the Department of Justice. We are here to announce a significant law enforcement action regarding North Carolina's Public Facilities Privacy & Security Act, also known as House Bill 2.

The North Carolina General Assembly passed House Bill 2 in special session on March 23 of this year. The bill sought to strike down an anti-discrimination provision in a recently passed Charlotte, North Carolina, ordinance, as well as to require transgender people in public agencies to use the bathrooms consistent with their sex as noted at birth, rather than the bathrooms that fit their gender identity. The bill was signed into law that same day. In so doing, the legislature and the governor placed North Carolina in direct opposition to federal laws prohibiting discrimination on the basis of sex and gender identity. More to the point, they created state-sponsored discrimination against transgender individuals, who simply seek to engage in the most private of functions in a place of safety and security—a right taken for granted by most of us.

Last week, our Civil Rights Division notified state officials that House Bill 2 violates federal civil rights laws. We asked that they certify by the end of the day today that they would not comply with or implement House Bill 2's restriction on restroom access. An extension was requested by North Carolina and was under active consideration. But instead of replying to our offer or providing a certification, this morning, the state of North Carolina and its governor chose to respond by suing the Department of Justice. As a result of their decisions, we are now moving forward.

Today, we are filing a federal civil rights lawsuit against the state of North Carolina, Governor Pat McCrory, the North Carolina Department of Public Safety, and the University of North Carolina. We are seeking a court order declaring House Bill 2's restroom restriction impermissibly discriminatory, as well as a statewide bar on its enforcement. While the lawsuit currently seeks declaratory relief, I want to note that we retain the option of curtailing federal funding to the North Carolina Department of Public Safety and the University of North Carolina as this case proceeds.

This action is about a great deal more than just bathrooms. This is about the dignity and respect we accord our fellow citizens and the laws that we, as a people and as a country, have enacted to protect them—indeed, to protect all of us. And it's about the founding ideals that have led this country—haltingly but inexorably—in the direction of fairness, inclusion, and equality for all Americans.

This is not the first time that we have seen discriminatory responses to historic moments of progress for our nation. We saw it in the Jim Crow laws that followed the Emancipation Proclamation. We saw it in fierce and widespread resistance to *Brown v. Board of Education*. And we saw it in the proliferation of state bans on same-sex unions intended to stifle any hope that gay and lesbian Americans might one day be afforded the right to marry. That right, of course, is now recognized as a guarantee embedded in our Constitution, and in the wake of that historic triumph, we have seen bill after bill in state after state taking aim at the LGBT community. Some of these responses reflect a recognizably human fear of the unknown, and a discomfort with the uncertainty of change. But this is not a time to act out of fear. This is a time to summon our national virtues of inclusivity, diversity, compassion, and open-mindedness. What we must not do—what we must never do—is turn on our neighbors, our family members, our fellow Americans, for something they cannot control, and deny what makes them human. This is why none of us can stand by when a state enters the business of legislating identity and insists that a person pretend to be something they are not, or invents a problem that doesn't exist as a pretext for discrimination and harassment.

Let me speak now to the people of the great state, the beautiful state, my state of North Carolina. You've been told that this law protects vulnerable populations from harm—but that just is not the case. Instead, what this law does is inflict further indignity on a population that has already suffered far more than its fair share. This law provides no benefit to society—all it does is harm innocent Americans.

Instead of turning away from our neighbors, our friends, our colleagues, let us instead learn from our history and avoid repeating the mistakes of our past. Let us reflect on the obvious but often neglected lesson that state-sanctioned discrimination never looks good in hindsight. It was not so very long ago that states, including North Carolina, had signs above restrooms, water fountains, and on public accommodations keeping people out based upon a distinction without a difference. We have moved beyond those dark days, but not without pain and suffering and an ongoing fight to keep moving forward. Let us write a different story this time. Let us not act out of fear and misunderstanding, but out of the values of inclusion, diversity, and regard for all that make our country great.

Let me also speak directly to the transgender community itself. Some of you have lived freely for decades. Others of you are still wondering how you can possibly live the lives you were born to lead. But no matter how isolated or scared you may feel today, the Department of Justice and the entire Obama Administration wants you to know that we see you; we stand with you; and we will do everything we can to protect you going forward. Please know that history is on your side. This country was founded on a promise of equal rights for all, and we have always managed to move closer to that promise, little by little, one day at a time. It may not be easy—but we'll get there together.

I want to thank my colleagues in the Civil Rights Division who have devoted many hours to this case so far, and who will devote many more to seeing it through. At this time, I'd like to turn things over to Vanita Gupta, whose determined leadership on this and so many other issues has been essential to the Justice Department's work.

Appendix E

Methodology and Sample, June 2015 Clear Voice Research Survey

A nonprobability sample of 2,102 subjects was recruited by Clear Voice Research (CVR) to participate in an online survey measuring political attitudes. We developed our instrument by modifying questions from existing sources, such as the 2011 PRRI Survey, the General Social Survey, and American National Election Studies and developing some original questions. The survey was fielded from June 12 to June 25, 2015. Members of the panel complete an extensive member profile survey before they are invited to participate in a particular research project. CVR requires double opt-in to surveys, Internet Protocol (IP) verification, USPS address verification, and phone or SMS (Short Message Service) text-message verification. Participants are recruited from existing Clear Voice respondent pools via e-mail; of the 51,492 invites, 2,102 agreed to participate and completed most of the survey.

The demographic characteristics of this panel closely resemble that of the United States population on several important traits. The table below displays the demographics of this sample compared to MTurk (Amazon Mechanical Turk) samples (adapted from Berinsky et al. 2012) and the National Annenberg Election Study, or NAES (Johnston, Jamieson, and Mutz 2008). These particular comparisons are shown so as to compare the CVR sample to a nonprobability sample like MTurk and a probability sample like NAES. Further, these comparisons are made as opposed to a comparison with Census data since Census data does not include party identification, which is an important component of our models.

Given the wide variety of nonprobability sampling methods that are used, we believe that the transparent method by which the CVR sample is drawn provides sufficient justification for its use. Also, since we investigate our hypotheses through use of both the CVR nonprobability sample along with the GfK nationally representative sample, we are confident that the inferences we make from the CVR-based models are valid since they are mostly duplicated with the GfK-based models. For further discussion on the usage of nonprobability samples, see Baker et al. (2013).

In our survey, we sometimes use terminology that is not the preferred nomenclature of LGBT activists. For instance, the choice of the term "sex change" in some questions as opposed to "sex reassignment surgery" or "gender confirmation surgery" reflects a need to use unambiguous terminology that the average respondent will most likely understand. We also acknowledge that this reifies notions of a gender binary.

TABLE E.1. Survey Demographics

Demographics	Clear Voice June 2015	MTurk	NAES 2008
Female	49.2%	60.1%	56.62%
Age (mean years)	50.6	20.3	50.05
Education (% completing college*)	39.7%	-	37.1%
White	80.5%	83.5%	79.12%
Black	9.2%	4.4%	9.67%
Asian	3.2%	-	2.53%
Latino (a)	4.1%	-	6.3%
Multiracial	2.3%	-	2.37%
Party Identification			
• Democrat	44.3%	40.8%	36.67%
• Independent	23.4%	34.1%	20.82%
• Republican	32.3%	16.9%	30.61%
N	2,102	484–551	19,234

Appendix F

GfK Survey

Our data used in chapter 3 is derived from a nationally representative poll that was conducted via GfK's KnowledgePanel (*N* = 1,020) on October 9–11, 2015. GfK draws the panel by probability from a sampling frame derived from a U.S. Postal Service Computerized Delivery Sequence File. This address-based sample avoids some problems associated with missing cell-phone-only households. Respondents cannot opt-in to this panel. GfK supplies Internet service/equipment to lessen participation bias (GfK n.d.). We sampled adults age eighteen and older. To ensure national representativeness, the GfK data were weighted by their proprietary system that factors in several variables: age, sex, education, race, household income, Internet status, and region. We developed our instrument by modifying questions from existing sources, such as the 2011 PRRI Survey, the General Social Survey, and American National Election Studies, and by developing some original questions. The questions used in the chapter 3 analyses are presented in tables F.1–F.3. In our survey, we sometimes use terminology that is not the preferred nomenclature of LGBT activists. For instance, the choice of the term "sex change" in some questions as opposed to "sex reassignment surgery" or "gender confirmation surgery" reflects a need to use unambiguous terminology that the average respondent will most likely understand. We also acknowledge that this reifies notions of a gender binary.

TABLE F.1. Dependent Variables, Chapter 3

Variable	Question Wording and Response Categories
Group Affect: • Transgender people • Gay men and lesbians	We'd like to get your feelings toward some of our organizations and groups who are in the news these days. We'd like you to rate groups using something we call the feeling thermometer. Ratings between 50 degrees and 100 degrees mean that you feel favorable and warm toward the group. Ratings between 0 degrees and 50 degrees mean that you don't feel favorable toward the group and that you don't care too much for that group. You would rate the group at the 50 degree mark if you don't feel particularly warm or cold toward the group.
Personal Comfort Scale: • Transgender • Crossdresser • Transsexual	Are you, personally, comfortable or uncomfortable you are around someone who is . . . [transgender] 1) Comfortable 2) Somewhat comfortable 3) Somewhat uncomfortable 4) Uncomfortable
Candidates Scales: • City council race • State legislative race • Governor's race • U.S. House Race	If an openly transgender [gay or lesbian] candidate were to run for an office and they were the candidate that most shared your views on political issues, how likely would you be to vote for that candidate: 1) Definitely vote for the transgender [gay or lesbian] candidate 2) Probably vote for the transgender [gay or lesbian] candidate 3) Probably vote for someone else 4) Definitely vote for someone else
Policy Scales*: • Seven-item Body Policy Scale • Seven-item Civil Rights Scale • Five-item Gay Rights Scale	We provide a few statements about transgender people. Please tell us how much you agree or disagree with each one. 1) Strongly agree 2) Somewhat agree 3) Neither agree nor disagree 4) Somewhat disagree 5) Strongly disagree

*Items for each policy scale are shown in table F.2.

TABLE F.2. Policy Attitude Scale Items, Chapter 3

Policy Attitude Scale	Policy Items
Transgender Body	Legal protections that apply to gay and lesbian people should also apply to transgender people.
Policy	Congress should pass laws to protect transgender people from job discrimination.
	Congress should pass laws to protect transgender people from discrimination in public accommodations like restaurants and movie theaters.
	Laws should protect transgender children from bullying in schools.
	Transgender people deserve the same rights and protections as other Americans.
	Laws to prevent employment discrimination against transgender people.
	Allowing transgender people to serve openly in the military.
Transgender Civil Rights Policy	Insurance companies should **not** be required to pay for medical treatment related to transgender health issues.
	Allowing transgender people to use public restrooms that are consistent with the way that they express their gender.
	Allowing transgender people to adopt children.
	Allowing transgender people to change the sex listed on their driver's license or state ID card.
	Allowing Medicare to pay for a transgender person's sex change surgery.
	Allowing Medicare to pay for a transgender person's hormone therapy.
	Allowing students who have had a sex change to play college sports as a member of their current gender.
	Legal protections that apply to gay and lesbian people should also apply to transgender people.
Gay Civil Rights	Congress should pass laws to protect gay men and lesbians from job discrimination.
Policy	Congress should pass laws to protect gay men and lesbians from discrimination in public accommodations.
	Laws should protect gay or lesbian children from bullying in schools.
	Businesses should have the right to refuse services to gay men or lesbians based on religious beliefs.
	Allowing gays and lesbians to adopt children.

TABLE F.3. Question Wording of Independent Variable Scales, Chapter 3

Scale/Item	Wording
Moral Traditionalism	*Below is a series of statements about contemporary society. Please indicate the degree to which you agree or disagree with each statement.* (5 pt. response) • The world is always changing and we should adjust our view of moral behavior to those changes. • The newer lifestyles are contributing to the breakdown of our society. • We should be more tolerant of people who choose to live according to their own moral standards, even if they are very different from your own. • This country would have many fewer problems if there were more emphasis on traditional family ties.
Egalitarianism	*Below is a series of statements about contemporary society. Please indicate the degree to which you agree or disagree with each statement.* (5 pt. response) • Our society should do whatever is necessary to make sure that everyone has an equal opportunity to succeed. • We have gone too far in pushing equal rights in this country. • One of the big problems in this country is that we don't give everyone an equal chance. • This country would be better off if we worried less about how equal people are. • It is not really that big of a problem if some people have more of a chance in life than others. • If people were treated more equally in this country we would have many fewer problems.
Authoritarianism	*Which one is more important for a child to have?* • Independence or Respect for Elders • Curiosity or Good Manners • Obedience or Self-Reliance • Being Considerate or Well Behaved
Disgust Sensitivity	*Please tell us how the following statements describe you.* (4 pt. response; extremely like me (1) to not at all like me (4)) • I never let any part of my body touch the toilet seat in a public washroom. • I probably would not go to my favorite restaurant if I found out that the cook had a cold. • I use hand sanitizer on a daily basis. • I am perfectly fine with drinking water from the same cup as an acquaintance of mine.

Notes

Introduction

1. In this book, we use the terms trans and transgender interchangeably.

2. Prior to her surgery, Jami was given access to one little used multiperson women's restroom in a rarely used building. It served as her locker room so that she could go to the gym. She was very happy with this accommodation and applauded the university for helping her.

3. Although a few municipalities had offered legal protections to gender variant individuals in the 1970s and early 1980's (Taylor et al. 2014) and some states allowed transsexual individuals to change their birth certificates if they underwent sex reassignment (e.g., Taylor, Tadlock, and Poggione 2014), there were few legal protections for what we now call transgender people.

4. The DSM-5 goes on to indicate that the incongruence must be manifested by at least two or more of a multitude of conditions in adults and adolescents. For children, the diagnosis requires at least six conditions, one of which must be Criterion A1, "A strong desire to be of the other gender or an insistence that one is the other gender (or some alternative gender different from one's assigned gender)" (Kraus 2015, 1152).

5. For James's website, Transsexual and Transgender Road Map, see http://www.tsroadmap.com/index.html

Chapter 1

1. The individual protested was Sandy Stone, who would go on to write a seminal article in trans studies, "The Empire Strikes Back: A Posttranssexual Manifesto."

2. Utah's sexual orientation and gender-identity-inclusive nondiscrimination law passed in 2015 was not comprehensive. It does not address public accommodations.

3. Delaware would "come back" to the issue of transgender protections in 2013.

4. Transgender-only groups were identified in Stata by searching the organization name variable for the string "TRANS." These were then reviewed manually to drop organizations that included gay, lesbian, or bisexual identities in the name. We also

manually added known trans groups such as the Sylvia Rivera Law Project, FTM International, and the Society for the Second Self (Tri-Ess). Some groups, like Massachusetts Transgender Political Coalition, have a separate fiscal sponsor (MPTC 2016) and are thus not included in the dataset. This data was then collapsed in Stata to show the sum by year for the groups. For the Human Rights Campaign, we add income and asset data for two component parts, Human Rights Campaign Foundation (a 501(c)(3) organization) and the Human Rights Campaign Inc. (a 501(c)(4) organization). We did not include HRC PAC, a political action committee, because it is not a 501(c) organization. See appendix A for further information about the data.

5. Jami Taylor's meeting and interview with the North Carolina Family Policy Council was held October 3, 2006 at their Raleigh office. She met with John Rustin, the policy director. Rustin would later become the director of the organization and lead them during the HB2 fight. Rustin and his organization would strongly support HB2 (Rustin 2016; Tan 2016).

6. Another contributing factor was the gender essentialism that some members of the feminist movement promoted (Raymond 1979).

7. As of this writing, GLAAD's board is cochaired by Jennifer Finney Boylan.

8. The search included the terms transgend!, transsex!, gender identity, transvest!, genderqueer!, and crossdress! We used these roots and the ! wildcard so that derivations of the terms, like transgendered, would be captured in the query.

9. Unlike the *New York Times* search, the broadcast media search was beset by limitations in the data. LexisNexis broadcast media transcripts vary tremendously by network, over time, and in which programs are covered. We included NBC, ABC, CBS, NPR, CNN and Fox. LexisNexis does not have NBC holdings prior to 1995. Of course, Fox was a later network entry. Despite these limitations, in more recent periods we clearly see that networks are increasingly covering transgender stories.

Chapter 2

1. The 2002 survey was a proprietary poll fielded for the Human Rights Campaign by Lake, Snell Perry & Associates. We thank the Human Rights Campaign for providing us with the data.

2. For a comparison of how the Clear Voice Research sample is representative of the U.S. adult population, see appendix E.

3. CVR recruited survey participants by e-mailing 51,492 empaneled members. Prior to recruitment, CVR conducted an extensive member profile survey and used Internet protocol, postal address, and phone or text message verification to reduce duplication of respondents and to allow data collection to meet demographic targets.

4. GfK draws the panel by probability from a sampling frame derived from a U.S. Postal Service Computerized Delivery Sequence File. This address-based sample avoids some problems associated with missing cell-phone-only households. Respondents cannot opt-in to this panel. GfK supplies Internet service/equipment to lessen participation bias. We sampled adults age eighteen and older. To ensure national representativeness, the GfK data were weighted by their proprietary system that factors in several variables: age, sex, education, race, household income, Internet status, and region.

5. CVR followed the same recruitment pattern as in the 2015 survey based on contacts with just over 50,000 empaneled members.

6. Most of these questions come from the Genderism and Transphobia scale as develop by Hill and Willoughby (2005).

7. The unwillingness of the public to support medical treatments for youth with gender dysphoria is especially troubling given that it is youth where transgender people, if denied their gender identity, are more likely to adopt negative lifestyles.

8. For a more detailed exploration of public support for transgender candidates, see Haider-Markel et al. (2017).

9. The 2002 data point is not included in figure 2.5 because it is a temporal outlier and obscures the more recent trends.

10. Our original article also included estimated opinion in the District of Columbia. We excluded the District of Columbia in this chapter because it is not a state. Support for transgender military service in Washington, DC, was estimated to be 85 percent.

11. The results were 44 percent "strongly favor," 23 percent "somewhat favor," 13 percent "somewhat oppose," 19 percent "strongly oppose," and 1 percent "don't know."

12. It should be pointed out that nearly all polling questions about the bathroom issue, even our own, ignore the diversity of identities under the transgender umbrella. As such, they are limited. Polling questions that ask about requiring transgender people to use the restroom of their birth gender ignores that many transgender people have undergone medical procedures to change their sex and are often legally members of that sex under state law. Even North Carolina's HB2 policy acknowledged this because it did not target those that had changed their birth certificate under state law. That would have created a statutory conflict.

13. Question wordings are listed in appendix C.

14. This question asked respondents to select all response options that apply. This is why the percentages in the following sentence add up to greater than 100 percent.

15. Such polling might also be used by opponents to undermine claims. For example, during the 2007 fight over transgender inclusion in the Employment Nondiscrimination Act, the Human Rights Campaign commissioned a poll finding that 70 percent of LGBT Americans supported passing a non-transgender-inclusive version of the bill. This was used to bolster the position of HRC on transgender exclusion (Eleveld 2007c).

Chapter 3

1. Disgust can also be an emotional state. But sensitivity to disgust is a trait, not a discrete emotional state in reaction to a specific attitude object. Substantial social psychology research examines disgust sensitivity rather than the emotional reaction of disgust per se, allowing greater comparison with our analyses.

2. A Cronbach alpha test reveals a scale reliability coefficient of 0.96.

3. For further analysis of this data, see Haider-Markel et al. (2017).

4. Our survey asked multiple questions about some topics. With respect to the questions about employment laws, one specified that Congress should pass a nondiscrimination law while the other question examined general support for these laws.

5. We recoded negatively phrased questions so that all policy items are coded in the same direction. For further information on these measures, see Miller et al. (2017).

6. Our battery of four disgust sensitivity questions was adapted from Haidt, McCauley, and Rozin (1994). For the sake of brevity in our survey, we edited their question "You take a sip of soda, and then realize that you drank from the glass that an acquaintance of yours had been drinking from." We developed the question "I use hand sanitizer on a daily basis."

7. We did not ask questions about bisexual candidates.

Section III

1. Freedom to Marry ended operations in 2016 after marriage equality was achieved.

2. In order to determine the largest financial players in the LGBT movement, we reviewed our 2014 data obtained via IRS Business Master Files from the National Center for Charitable Statistics. Among the groups that primarily engage in LGBT advocacy (not including those that focus specifically on health), we identified 135 LGBT organizations that had more than $100,000 in revenue. Of these organizations, only three organizations had revenues exceeding ten million dollars. These are the two tax code entities under the banner of the Human Rights Campaign and Lambda Legal. This list does not include political action committees. It only includes 501(c) organizations.

3. This e-mail exchange between Jami Taylor and Shannon Minter occurred on July 8, 2008.

Chapter 4

1. The search was conducted by keyword through bill subject and synopsis for the years 1990 through 2016. The keyword search terms used were gender identity, sex change, sex designation, transgender, sex reassignment, and the combination of sex AND birth AND certificate.

2. Keyword search performed between July 26, 2016 and August 1, 2016.

3. The variations of the search terms resulted in the same number of database hits as did the original search terms. Cursory examination of the records revealed them to be the same hits.

4. Local political subculture was measured with same-sex partner households (percentage of all households), nonfamily households (percentage of all households), percentage of females in labor force, percentage of the civilian population age sixteen and up employed in management, business, science and arts occupations, percentage of the population that is a member of an evangelical or Latter-day Saints congregation, percentage of the population that is white, and whether the city is located in a southern state. Institutional factors were form of government (manager council or mayor-council), home rule authority from Wood (2011), and whether there was a statewide nondiscrimination law. Regional diffusion was measured as the percentage of cities

with more than 100,000 residents in the census subregion. We also control for population change between years, median income, and unemployment rate.

5. As we were finishing this book in November 2017, two transgender people, Andrea Jenkins and Phillipe Cunningham, were elected to city council seats in Minneapolis, Minnesota. However, that city already has some transgender inclusive policies, such as a nondiscrimination ordinance.

6. For purposes of disclosure, Rep. Stam was Jami Taylor's state legislator while she lived in Willow Spring, North Carolina. She lobbied him on transgender inclusion. While he disagreed, they maintained a cordial relationship. He was even a guest lecturer in her class at North Carolina State University.

7. Hawaii included sexual orientation in its state employment law in 1991. In 2011, the state would cover gender identity and expression in employment. Governor Linda Lingle, a Republican, vetoed a bill in 2005 that would have enacted transgender inclusive employment nondiscrimination protections.

8. In 1992, Massachusetts voters elected Althea Garrison (R-Suffolk), an African American woman, to the state's House of Representatives. However, she was not out at the time that she ran. A story in the *Boston Herald* later outed her. Garrison was ostracized and defeated during her reelection bid. Garrison became a perennial candidate. In 2012, New Hampshire voters elected openly transgender Stacie Laughton to its lower chamber. However, Laughton was unable to take office because of a prior felony conviction (Eltagouri 2017b).

9. In addition, Maine, Nevada, New York, and Washington either allow bureaucratic discretion to administrators in these cases or have administrative codes to address this process (Taylor et al. 2013, 253). Other states do often amend birth certificates, but lack specific statutory authority regarding the conditions under which a change can be made (247).

10. Data compiled by the authors from Human Rights Campaign (http://www.hrc. org/state-maps/hate-crimes) and the Movement Advancement Project (http://www. lgbtmap.org/equality-maps/hate_crime_laws).

11. We use the nominate version of the Berry et al. (2010) measures of ideology as reported from Klarner (2013). In initial models, we also included variables capturing partisan control of the legislature and governor's office, with the expectation that Democratic control would increase the likelihood of hate crime policy adoption. However, neither measure was statistically significant nor did either measuring substantively improve the model. Given high collinearity with other variables in the model, we do not display those estimates in table 4.1. Additionally, we used the measure of direct democracy employed in chapter 7 as an independent variable and as an interaction term with citizen ideology. Neither measure was statistically significant nor did their inclusion substantively change the results reported in table 4.1.

12. This is the average percentage that losing candidates got in this year's election (of the total vote) and in the elections whose values were in the three calendar years prior to that. The average is weighted by the number of seats up for election in each chamber-year. Party competition data for 2012 to 2017 are extrapolated for each state. The data are from Klarner (2013).

13. In this analysis, the measure drops groups coded as culture and sport, AIDS

related, and religious congregations. We also thank Benjamin Rogers of the University of Kansas for his help in creating this measure.

14. We use the evangelical rates from the 1980, 1990, and 2000 Religious Congregations and Membership surveys, available from Association of Religion Data Archives at www.thearda.com and collected by the Association of Statisticians of American Religious Bodies. The years 1993–95 have 1990 values; 1996–2005 have 2000 values; and 2006–16 use 2010 values. Following Erikson, Wright, and McIver (1993), we include membership in the Church of Jesus Christ of Latter-day Saints as part of this measure.

15. In the cases of Alaska and Hawaii, we treat each state as contiguous with California, Oregon, and Washington. Likewise, we treat California, Oregon, and Washington as contiguous with Alaska and Hawaii for each state year.

16. The sign for the evangelical population is positive in this model, but this is likely the result of collinearity. If the model is estimated without the direct democracy variable, the sign for evangelical population is in the expected negative direction. Most states in the South, where evangelicals are most prevalent, do not have voter-initiated ballot initiatives.

17. The amendment was sponsored by Senator Gordon Smith (R-OR).

18. However, the subtitle of the measure had continued to be the Matthew Shepard Act, and in an April 2009 floor speech Rep. Mike Honda (D-CA) raised the specter of Shepard's death. He suggested that the measure might prevent the deaths of transgender people, such as Angie Zapata, a trans woman who had been killed in Colorado (Congressional Record 2009, E1004).

19. The conviction of Joshua Vallum in the 2015 killing of Mercedes Williamson marked the first time that anyone had been convicted under the transgender-inclusive provisions of the Matthew Shepard and James Byrd Jr. Hate Crimes Prevention Act (NBC News 2017b).

20. H.R. 3685 did pass out of committee and was approved by the House in a 235 to 184 vote on November 7, 2007. Rep. Frank introduced a separate bill that included gender identity, but that bill went nowhere (Eleveld 2007b). Versions of ENDA including gender identity have now passed both chambers (House, 2007, and Senate, 2013) but never in the same session (Cox 2013).

Chapter 5

1. Meyerowitz (2002) discusses early birth certificate amendment cases dating back to the 1960s. There were also trans related marriage and discrimination cases in the 1970s and 1980s. However, the transgender political movement organized in the late 1980s and early 1990s.

2. After a year of boycotts, lawsuits, and the defeat of Governor Pat McCrory, HB2 was repealed on March 30, 2017. However, because local governments were preempted from regulating public accommodations and there was a moratorium on localities passing nondiscrimination ordinances, many LGBT activists were not satisfied with the repeal measure (Fausset 2017).

3. This strategy may indeed be effective; recent research shows that exposure to pictures of transgender people reduces discomfort and transphobia among subjects (Flores et al. 2017a).

4. A total of 193 cases were identified via our supplementary approach. After cleaning the dataset to remove duplicates and instances where trans-related search terms were only tangential to the legal question, or the cases that entailed crimes against transgender people, 167 cases remained. In our research, we noted the attorneys involved in the litigation, the parties, any filed amicus briefs, the legal venue, year, and the area of focus.

5. To classify whether the attorney was from an advocacy organization, we relied on LexisNexis Academic to list the lawyer's firm or we relied on advocacy organization press releases. Cooperating attorneys are not included. It is plausible that our method undercounts the work of advocacy groups.

6. A year variable correlates very highly with our salience measure for the *New York Times* (r = .8359) and with our financial resources variable (r = .9472). As such, we provide alternate model specifications that include or omit year with these variables.

7. We used LexisNexis to search the *New York Times*. Blog entries are not included for later years. The annual search terms were transgend! OR transsex! OR gender identity OR transvest! OR genderqueer! OR crossdress!

8. We use the term transsexual in this sentence because the decisions in those cases use this term.

9. This may change given the Equal Employment Opportunity Commission's decision in *Baldwin v. Department of Transportation* (2015) that found a claim of sexual-orientation-based discrimination is also discrimination based on sex.

10. We use the term "comprehensive" to denote protections in employment, housing, and public accommodations. As of June 2017, Utah also has protections in housing and employment.

11. In an October 2017 reversal of the Obama administration's policy, Attorney General Jeff Sessions ordered the Justice Department to take the position that Title VII does not provide protections to transgender people (Savage 2017b).

12. See H.R. 3185 in the 114th Congress.

13. Judge Tigar rejected the First Circuit's en banc decision in *Kosilek* as not binding in the Ninth Circuit.

14. The North Carolina law was enacted as part of a backlash to advances in LGBT rights. It was passed after the city of Charlotte added sexual orientation and gender identity to its antidiscrimination ordinance.

15. Opponents of transgender rights also successfully venue shopped a similar transgender rights case regarding the definition of sex under regulations pertaining to the Affordable Care Act to the same federal district court judge, Reed O'Connor, in *Franciscan Alliance v. Burwell*. On December 31, 2016, O'Connor issued an injunction blocking enforcement of a regulation issued by the Department of Health and Human Services that interpreted the prohibition of sex discrimination as being gender-identity inclusive (Kass 2017).

16. We discuss this further in the next chapter.

17. See *In re Application for Marriage License for Nash*, 2003-Ohio-7221; *In re Estate*

of Gardiner, 42P.3d 120 (Kan. 2002); Littleton *v. Prange*, 9 S.W.3d 233 (Tex. App 1999); *Kantaras v. Kantaras*, Case no. 2D03–1377 (Fla. App. 2004).

Chapter 6

1. We note that many of these same agencies are at the forefront of rolling back these policies during the Trump administration.

2. On December 31, 2016, an injunction barring enforcement of the gender-identity-inclusive aspects of the regulation was issued by a federal district court in Texas (Kass 2017). As of this writing, litigation on this matter is ongoing. The ACLU has attempted to intervene in the matter to defend the policy (American Civil Liberties Union 2017). The Department of Health and Human Services is also reviewing the rule, and it has successfully argued that the litigation should be stayed pending that review (Gurrieri 2017). Subsequently, Attorney General Jeff Sessions issued a determination that gender identity is not covered by the definition of sex under Title VII (Savage 2017b). This will almost certainly shape any HHS revision to the rule.

3. We of course acknowledge that city managers are not elected. They are appointees of the city council.

4. Concerning the Americans with Disabilities Act of 1990, Senator Jesse Helms (R-NC) offered an amendment, (SP. 716), to the legislation (S.933) that stated "the term 'disabled' or 'disability' shall not apply to an individual solely because that individual is a transvestite." This was agreed by voice vote on September 7, 1989, and was contained in Section 508 of the bill. Further, the definitions contained in Section 511 of the bill specifically denied disability coverage to a host of LGBT-related concepts by definition. These were:

Sec. 511. Definitions.

(a) Homosexuality and Bisexuality—For purposes of the definition of "disability" in section 3(2), homosexuality and bisexuality are not impairments and as such are not disabilities under this Act.

(b) Certain conditions—Under this Act, the term "disability" shall not include—

(1) transvestism, transsexualism, pedophilia, exhibitionism, voyeurism, gender identity disorders not resulting from physical impairments, or other sexual behavior disorders;

(2) compulsive gambling, kleptomania, or pyromania; or

(3) psychoactive substance use disorders resulting from current illegal use of drugs.

However, the legislative history makes clear that "homosexuality and bisexuality were never considered impairments under this Act and therefore were never covered as disabilities" (Committee on Education and Labor 1990, 415). Additionally, the legislative history states, "other conditions listed are physical or mental impairments and could have been covered under this Act absent this provision. However, under this provision, the conditions listed are now excluded as disabilities. The Committee wishes to note, however, that if a person with one of the listed conditions also has another disability, which is still covered under this Act, and the person is discriminated against on the basis of the covered disability, that discriminatory act is still prohibited" (Committee on Education and Labor 1990, 415).

5. In regard to President Bush's exchange with Ms. Akwai, the *New York Times* (Bumiller 2004) reported: "Last spring, during a class of 1968 Yale reunion that he held at the White House, Mr. Bush had a particularly striking encounter with Petra Leilani Akwai, who in 2002 had a sex-change operation. At Yale, Ms. Akwai was known as Peter Clarence Akwai. "I was in the receiving line, I was dressed in an evening dress, and I was being escorted by a male friend from the Yale class of 1986," Ms. Akwai said in a telephone interview this weekend from Germany, where she lives. "And I said, 'Hello, George.' And in order for him not to be confused, in case he hadn't been briefed, because our class was all male, I said, 'I guess the last time we spoke, I was still living as a man.' "And he said, Ms. Akwai recounted, 'But now you're you.' "Ms. Akwai said the president seemed completely comfortable. "He leaned forward and gave me a little sort of smile," she said. "I thought it was a sincere thing, and it was very charming.'"

6. President Obama's utterance of the word transgender in the 2015 State of the Union Address is in contrast to his second inaugural address where he failed to use the word, despite discussing the Stonewall Rebellion. He was publicly rebuked for not doing so by an eleven-year-old transgender girl (Graf 2013).

7. President Obama was criticized for his evolving attitudes on same-sex marriage during his public life (e.g., Schwarz 2015).

8. This letter required that under Title IX's sex discrimination protections, schools must treat transgender students the same as other students of the same gender identity. Transgender students were entitled to equal access to educational programs. Schools have a responsibility to give transgender students a safe and nondiscriminatory environment. Schools were required to use pronouns that correspond to the student's gender identity. Transgender students should be treated according to their gender identity in the areas of restroom and shower access, athletic participation, single-sex education, and housing. Schools also had to maintain the privacy of transgender students (United States Department of Education 2016b).

9. The e-mail communication from the White House was sent to Jami Taylor on July 25, 2016.

10. The e-mail communication from the former president's press office was sent to Jami Taylor on June 20, 2017.

11. Ohio (2007–10S; May 17, 2007); Kansas (2007–24; August 21, 2007), Maryland (2007–16; August 22, 2007), Michigan (2007–24; November 21, 2007). See Sellers (2016) for more discussion of the historical development of these orders.

12. Transgender persons with birth certificates corresponding to their gender identity were not individually affected by this provision.

13. North Carolina's executive order was not included in this analysis. That executive order did not apply to public accommodations (restrooms) for government workers, so protections are limited compared to other states. Additionally, the circumstances that led to Governor McCrory's executive order suggest that North Carolina is an outlier in terms of motivation to add protections and the extent that it protects employee's gender identity.

14. We use the evangelical rates from the 1980, 1990, and 2000 Religious Congregations and Membership surveys, available from Association of Religion Data Archives at www.thearda.com and collected by the Association of Statisticians of American Religious Bodies. The years 1993–95 have 1990 values; 1996–2005 have 2000 values; and 2006–16 use 2010 values. Following Erikson, Wright, and McIver (1993), we include membership in the Church of Jesus Christ of Latter-day Saints as part of this measure.

15. The Institutional Power variable originally created by Thad Beyle includes several elements of gubernatorial power—partisan control in the legislature, ability to set the budget, veto powers, tenure potential, selection method for major offices within the administration, and appointment powers. Unlike Beyle's original measure, the variable in our data set is time variant. The appointment powers variable deals most directly with how capable a governor is to influence staffing in their administration. As such, it is most directly related to personnel policy.

16. This data was obtained in LexisNexis on April 22, 2017. The search string included transgend! OR transsex! OR gender identity OR transvest! OR genderqueer! OR crossdress! for relevant terms appearing in stories found in the print edition of the *New York Times*.

Chapter 7

1. The research in this chapter was generously supported by Siena College's Diversity Action Committee and the Center for Undergraduate Research and Creative Activity. We thank Ryan Knipple for their assistance in data collection and content analysis.

2. Surprisingly, SB 3 later failed to secure passage in the regular session and in a special session (Montgomery and Fernandez 2017). The latter episode led to great discord within the Texas Republican Party as moderates in the lower chamber, led by House Speaker Joe Straus (R-San Antonio), refused to take up SB 3 after it has passed the state senate.

3. Maine's 1999 law about sexual-orientation nondiscrimination included "gender expression" in the definition of sexual orientation. It was repealed by referendum, Maine Question 6, in 2000 by 50.38 percent to 49.62 percent (Maine Legislature 2000; Ballotpedia 2017). Maine Question 1 in 2005 was also a voter-initiated veto referendum to overturn a state law that prohibited discrimination based on sexual orientation. However, the law in question defined gender identity or expression as part of sexual orientation. Q1 failed 44.9 percent to 55.1 percent (Maine Public Laws, 1st Regular Session of the 122nd) (Ballotpedia 2005). Because the Maine measures did not directly address transgender inclusion, we do not include them in our analysis.

4. The Montana Supreme Court reviewed a challenge to the proposed language by the ACLU. It unanimously found that the proposed initiative required revision to conform with state law and tasked the state's attorney general with this task (Billings Gazette 2017).

5. The HRC coding includes protections afforded by executive orders, court rulings, and various executive interpretations of existing law, so some states do not have statutory protections. For example, New York does not have statutes protecting transgender people from discrimination, but Governor Andrew Cuomo's administration

has issued regulations through the New York State Human Rights Law that offer protections to transgender people (New York State Governor Press Office 2015). Alternative coding that excludes these regulatory policies by New York does not substantively change the results of the subsequent analyses.

6. Alternative measures, such as citizen ideology (e.g., Enns and Koch 2013), produce remarkably similar results.

7. The Municipal Equality Index codes a city as having antibullying policies if 75 percent or more of the students in the city are covered by a policy.

8. Some cities included in the Municipal Equality Index do not have corresponding estimates of citizen ideology or indicators of direct democracy. Thus, the sample in the regression analysis includes 336 observations.

9. Income and population variables are U.S. Census data from Warshaw and Tausanovitch's replication dataset (2015). Estimates of per capita same-sex households are from the Williams Institute's Census 2010 Snapshot (2011). Alternative specifications also include indicators of home rule powers (Wood 2011) and form of government (Nelson and Svara 2010), but this reduced the analytical sample by over 100 cases due to missing data. Results from these specifications did not differ substantially from those presented in table 7.4.

10. Alternative estimation approaches, including various count and multilevel models, produce substantively similar results.

Chapter 8

1. As such, some marriages involving transgender people had been invalidated or blocked by the courts. See, for example, *In re Ladrach* 1987; *Littleton v. Prange* 1999; *In re Estate of Gardiner* 2002; and *In re Application for Marriage License for Nash* 2003. Various rulings such as *Obergefell* have made the marriage implications of these decisions moot. However, they still might affect public policy. Ohio and Kansas deny transgender people the ability to amend their birth certificates because of the *Ladrach* and *Gardiner* decisions.

2. As of this writing California, Oregon, and Washington, DC, have laws that allow individuals to identify sex as nonbinary on state-issued identification. In California individuals can choose an x to indicate nonbinary or third gender (Moon 2017).

3. As of this writing, conservative activists in Montana are attempting to create such a definition via a ballot initiative (Billings Gazette 2017).

4. Birth certificates establish legal sex most of the time. However, some courts have refused to acknowledge the amended birth certificates of transgender people. One such example of this occurred in the case *In re Application for Marriage License for Nash* (2003).

5. The United Nations agency responsible for setting international travel standards, the International Civil Aviation Organization, recognizes "X" as an unspecified gender marker. This marker is currently used in passports in Australia, Bangladesh, Canada, Germany, India, Malta, Nepal, New Zealand, and Pakistan.

6. Of course, this provision of the Defense of Marriage Act would be struck down in *U.S. v. Windsor* (2013).

7. The first case to set precedent in this area is *Anonymous v. Weiner* (1966). In this

instance, New York's Supreme Court denied the petition of a transgender woman to amend her birth certificate. She had first been denied by the New York City Department of Health. We do not spend significant time with this case because New York currently amends birth certificates of transgender people due to policy changes in the state.

8. We used these sources extensively in this section. Citations of relevant state code came from those sources.

Chapter 9

1. As of this writing in 2017, the case is proceeding.

2. As of this writing, this will remain policy during the Trump administration (White House 2017a).

3. See RIN 2501-AD49 and RIN 2506-AC40 for regulations passed by HUD addressing gender-identity-based discrimination.

4. Given the scope of this work, we do not focus on sexual orientation under the definition of sex in Title VII. See *Baldwin v. Dept. of Transportation* (2015) for a precedent that might provide for sexual-orientation-based protections.

5. See also the Sixth Circuit's similar ruling in *Barnes v. Cincinnati* (2005).

6. We follow the court's ruling in *Smith* and refer to the plaintiff as a male.

7. Writing for the Court in *Oncale* (1998), Justice Antonin Scalia noted: "We see no justification in the statutory language or our precedents for a categorical rule excluding same-sex harassment claims from the coverage of Title VII. As some courts have observed, male-on-male sexual harassment in the workplace was assuredly not the principal evil Congress was concerned with when it enacted Title VII. But statutory prohibitions often go beyond the principal evil to cover reasonably comparable evils, and it is ultimately the provisions of our laws rather than the principal concerns of our legislators by which we are governed. Title VII prohibits 'discriminat[ion] . . . because of . . . sex' in the 'terms' or 'conditions' of employment. Our holding that this includes sexual harassment must extend to sexual harassment of any kind that meets the statutory requirements."

8. New York governor Andrew Cuomo, via the New York State Division of Human Rights, issued regulations in 2015 that clarified that gender-identity-based discrimination is prohibited sex discrimination in New York law. Additionally, this regulation, 9 NYCRR 466.13, notes that discrimination based on gender dysphoria is prohibited under state disability law (New York State Division of Human Rights 2015).

9. The Massachusetts protections for public accommodations will be put to a public referendum in 2018.

10. North Carolina state senator Chad Barefoot (R-Franklin and Wake) sent an e-mail to his constituent mailing list with a subject line of "What the Media Won't Report About Yesterday" on March 24, 2016. The graphic for figure 9.3 was contained in that e-mail. With this graphic, a headline noted that "Senate Unanimously Votes to Stop Radical Ordinance Allowing Men into Public Bathrooms with Women and Young Girls." Jami Taylor received this communication from Senator Barefoot because she used to live in the 18th District.

11. Defenders of HB2 noted that transgender individuals who undergo medical sex reassignment procedures could amend the sex on their birth certificate under North Carolina law (G.S. § 130A-118). However, this provision only benefitted individuals born in North Carolina or in other states that will amend the birth certificate of a trans person. Notably, this omitted neighboring Tennessee.

12. The legislation that repealed HB2, HB142, was controversial in its own right because it preempted localities from regulating restroom access and it placed a moratorium on localities passing nondiscrimination ordinances until December 1, 2020. Plaintiffs from the *Carcaño* case and their attorneys explored legal challenges to HB142 (Craver 2017). With Governor Cooper, the parties moved to end litigation via a consent decree that would interpret HB142 in a nondiscriminatory manner toward transgender people (Lambda Legal 2017a).

13. Dawson's film was featured in the online version of the *New York Times* on June 4, 2015. See https://www.nytimes.com/2015/06/04/opinion/transgender-at-war-and-in-love.html

Chapter 10

1. At the time, the World Professional Association for Transgender Health was named the Harry Benjamin International Gender Dysphoria Association.

2. Historically, gender transition was called sex or gender reassignment. More recently, it has also been described as gender-affirming treatment.

3. Recent estimates suggest there are approximately 1.4 million transgender people in the United States, which is 0.6 percent of the population (Flores et al. 2016). Our polling data from the GfK survey (conducted in 2015) supported this estimate.

4. The rule relating to ACA Section 1557 can still be used to sue in federal courts.

5. The American Health Care Act of 2017 would not have repealed ACA Section 1557.

6. The National Center for Lesbian Rights, ACLU, GLAD and Mary Lou Boelcke, a civil rights attorney, initiated the legal challenge for Ms. Mallon (GLAD 2013).

7. The Trump administration has noted that it will not collect information about sexual orientation or gender identity in the 2020 Census. However, this is consistent with past Census Bureau practices (Green 2017).

Chapter 11

1. The GLSEN School Climate Survey asked LGBTQ students about the effectiveness of reporting incidents of harassment and assault, but did not break down the responses by sexuality and gender identity.

2. See the American Civil Liberties Union of Virginia for all case documents and details: https://acluva.org/17406/grimm-v-gloucester-county-public-school-board/

3. Subsequently, Grimm graduated from high school. In May 2018 a federal district court judge ruled in favor of Grimm and gave the school district and Grimm's lawyers thirty days to have a conference meeting to settle on a new policy for transgender students (Stevens 2018). However, the school district is currently appealing the ruling

(Balingit 2018). Also during May 2018, another appellate court, the 3rd Circuit in *Doe v. Boyertown Area School District*, turned aside a complaint from cisgender students who felt uncomfortable sharing facilities with transgender students (Stern 2018).

4. It is possible, and indeed likely, that some of these states might define public accommodation to include schools or other education facilities.

5. GLSEN provides a model state-level antibullying policy at https://www.glsen. org/sites/default/files/GLSEN%20state%20model%20legislation.pdf

Chapter 12

1. In *United States v. Morrison* (2000), the Supreme Court declared the civil portion of the Violence Against Women Act unconstitutional.

2. Minnesota also adopted a law banning employment discrimination in 1993 that included both sexual orientation and gender identity. Activists and openly gay state legislators tied the issues together (Haider-Markel 2010).

3. Although the Trump administration has appeared to have little interest in protecting LGBT people, the Justice Department did take the unusual move in October 2017 of sending a federal hate crimes lawyer to prosecute a man accused of murdering a transgender teenager in Iowa (Gurman 2017).

4. As of this writing, the FBI has not released 2017 statistics for hate crimes. Media accounts and the work of advocacy groups point toward an increase (Smith and Trotta 2017).

5. All hate crimes statistics data are from the FBI (see https://www.fbi.gov/investigate/civil-rights/hate-crimes).

6. Underreporting or not reporting at all is even common among federal law enforcement agencies; in fact, the FBI has not been consistently reporting its own hate crime investigations (Thompson and Schwencke 2017).

7. Those tracking violence against transgender people recorded twenty-two violent deaths in 2016 and twenty-eight violent deaths in 2017 (see http://www.hrc.org/resources/violence-against-the-transgender-community-in-2017).

8. The twenty-eight homicides cited do not include the forty-nine people killed at an LGBT nightclub, Pulse, in Orlando, Florida.

9. The Supreme Court of Illinois struck down the Chicago ordinance in 1978 (*City of Chicago v. Wallace Wilson*, 1978).

10. See also National Institute of Corrections (2012).

11. The Wisconsin law, the Inmate Sex Change Prevention Act, had also banned public funds from being used for hormone therapy.

12. The relevant cases were *De'Lonta v. Angelone* (2003) and *De'Lonta v. Johnson* (2013).

References

ABC News. 2012. "Transcript: Robin Roberts ABC News Interview with President Obama." ABC News. Accessed January 25, 2017. http://abcnews.go.com/Politics/transcript-rob-in-roberts-abc-news-interview-president-obama/story?id=16316043

ABC News. 2017. "DeVos Non-Committal on Private School LGBT Discrimination." ABC News. Accessed November 13, 2017. http://abcnews.go.com/amp/Politics/wire-Story/devos-hedges-banning-discrimination-lgbt-students-47864789

Abeni, Cleis. 2016. "Alumni Condemn Catholic School's Exclusion of Trans Students." *Advocate*, March 6. Accessed November 13, 2017. https://www.advocate.com/transgender/2016/3/06/alumni-condemn-catholic-schools-exclusion-trans-students

Adorno, Theodor E., Else Frenkel-Brunswik, Daniel J. Levinson, and R. Nevitt Sanford. 1950. *The Authoritarian Personality*. New York: Harper and Row.

Air Transport Association of America v. City and County of San Francisco, 992 F. Supp. 1149 (N.D. Cal. 1998).

Allen, Mahalley D., Carrie Pettus, and Donald P. Haider-Markel. 2004. "Making the National Local: Specifying the Conditions for National Government Influence on State Policymaking." *State Politics and Policy Quarterly* 4 (3): 318–44.

Allen, Samantha. 2016. "Transgender Prisoners Deserve Surgery." *Daily Beast*, February 25. Accessed June 21, 2017. http://www.thedailybeast.com/transgender-prisoners-deserve-surgery

Allport, Gordon W. 1954. *The Nature of Prejudice*. Cambridge, MA: Addison-Wesley.

Amenta, Edwin, Bruce Carruthers, and Yvonne Zylan. 1992. "A Hero for the Aged? The Townsend Movement, the Political Mediation Model, and U.S. Old-Age Policy, 1934–1950." *American Journal of Sociology* 98 (2): 308–39.

American Civil Liberties Union. 2012a. "Agreement Reached on Illinois Policy for Issuing New Birth Certificates for Transgender Individuals." ACLU of Illinois press release, July 30, http://www.aclu-il.org/agreement-reached-on-illinois-policy-for-issuing-new-birth-certificates-for-transgender-individuals/

American Civil Liberties Union. 2012b. "K.L. v. State of Alaska, Department of Administration, Division of Motor Vehicles." Accessed November 12, 2017. https://www.aclu.org/cases/kl-v-state-alaska-department-administration-division-motor-vehicles

American Civil Liberties Union. 2017. "Franciscan Alliance v. Burwell." Accessed October 7, 2017. https://www.aclu.org/cases/franciscan-alliance-v-burwell

American Psychiatric Association. 2013. *Diagnostic and Statistical Manual of Mental Disorders (DSM-5)*. Arlington, VA: American Psychiatric Publications.

Amnesty International. 2006. "Stonewalled—Still Demanding Respect: Police Abuses against Lesbian, Gay, Bisexual and Transgender People in the USA." London: Amnesty International Publications. https://www.amnesty.org/en/documents/AMR51/001/2006/en/

Andersen, Ellen. 2009. *Out of the Closets and into the Courts: Legal Opportunity Structure and Gay Rights Litigation*. Ann Arbor: University of Michigan Press.

Andrews, Kenneth, and Bob Edwards. 2004. "Advocacy Organizations in the U.S. Political Process." *Annual Review of Sociology* 30: 479–506.

Anonymous Source (board member, Funders for LGBT Issues), interviewed by Jami Taylor, telephone, November 4, 2016.

Anonymous v. Weiner, 270 N.Y.S. 2d319 (1966).

Arceneaux, Kevin. 2002. "Direct Democracy and the Link between Public Opinion and State Abortion Policy." *State Politics & Policy Quarterly* 2 (4): 372–87.

Associated Press, 2016. "Black Youth Project: Associated Press–NORC GenForward Survey." AP-NORC Center for Public Affairs Research, pollster. Cornell University, Ithaca, NY: Roper Center for Public Opinion Research, iPOLL, distributor, accessed March, 28, 2017.

Association of American Medical Colleges. 2014. "Implementing Curricular and Institutional Climate Changes to Improve Health Care for Individuals Who Are LGBT, Gender Nonconforming, or Born with DSD." Accessed June 4, 2017. https://www.aamc.org/download/414172/data/lgbt.pdf

Association of Religion Data Archives. 2010. "Sources of Religious Congregations & Membership Data." Accessed March 11, 2011. http://www.thearda.com/mapsReports/RCMS_Notes.asp

Auer v. Robbins, 519 U.S. 492 (1997).

Babb, Kent. 2017. "Transgender Wrestler Mack Beggs Identifies as a Male: He Just Won the Texas State Girls Title." *Washington Post*, February 25.

Bagdett, M. V., and Jody Herman. 2011. "Patterns of Relationship Recognition by Same Sex Couples in the United States." Williams Institute, November. Accessed February 27, 2017. http://williamsinstitute.law.ucla.edu/wp-content/uploads/Badgett-Herman-Marriage-Dissolution-Nov-2011.pdf

Bailey, Robert. 1999. *Gay Politics, Urban Politics: Identity and Economics in the Urban Setting*. New York: Columbia University Press.

Baker, Kellan. 2017. "The Future of Transgender Coverage." *New England Journal of Medicine* 376: 1801–4.

Baker, Kellan, Laura Durso, and Andrew Cray. 2014. "Moving the Needle: The Impact of the Affordable Care Act on LGBT Communities." Washington, DC: Center for American Progress.

Baker, Reg, J. Michael Brick, Nancy A. Bates, Mike Battaglia, Mick P. Cooper, Jill A. Dever, Krista J. Gile, and Roger Tourangeau. 2013. "Report of the AAPOR Task Force on Non-Probability Sampling." Oakbrook Terrace, IL: American Association for Public Opinion Research.

Baker v. Aetna Life Insurance et. al. __ F. Supp. 3d __, 2017 WL 131658 (N.D. Tex. Jan. 13, 2017).

Baldas, Tresa. 2016. "Transgender Win: Sex-change Rules Eased for Michigan Driver's Licenses." *Detroit Free Press*, August 24. Accessed January 18, 2017. http://www.freep. com/story/news/local/michigan/2016/08/24/michigan-eases-sex-change-rules-drivers-licenses-no-surgery-needed/89265354/

Baldwin v. Dep't of Transportation, EEOC Appeal No. 0120133080 (July 15, 2015).

Balingit, Moriah. 2018. "Va. School Board Appeals Decision in Landmark Transgender Student Case. *Washington Post*, June 1. Accessed June 5, 2018 from https://www.washingtonpost.com/local/education/va-school-board-appeals-decision-in-landmark-transgender-student-case/2018/06/01/4e9c8898-65ea-11e8-99d2-0d678ec08c2f_story. html?noredirect=on&utm_term=.1cffe778f9f8

Ballotpedia. 2005. "Maine Reject Extension of Civil Rights Protections Regardless of Sexual Orientation, Question 1 (2005).' Accessed January 6, 2017. https://ballotpedia.org/ Maine_Reject_Extension_of_Civil_Rights_Protections_Regardless_of_Sexual_Orientation,_Question_1_(2005)

Ballotpedia. 2017. "Maine Civil Rights and Prevent Discrimination Based on Sexual Orientation, Question 6 (2000)." Accessed January 5, 2017. https://ballotpedia.org/Maine_ Civil_Rights_and_Prevent_Discrimination_Based_on_Sexual_Orientation,_Question_6_(2000)

Baral, Stefan D., Tonia Poteat, Susanne Strömdahl, Andrea L. Wirtz, Thomas E. Guadamuz, and Chris Beyrer. 2013. "Worldwide Burden of Hiv in Transgender Women: A Systematic Review and Meta-Analysis." *Lancet Infectious Diseases* 13: 214–22.

Barbash, Fred. 2016. "Wis. Transgender Boy Who Won the Right to Run for Prom King Wins Right to Sue to Use the Boy's Bathroom—for Now." *Washington Post*, September 22, https://www.washingtonpost.com/news/morning-mix/wp/2016/09/22/wis-transgender-boy-who-won-right-to-run-for-prom-king-wins-right-to-use-boys-bathroom-for-the-time-being/

Barclay, Scott, Mary Bernstein, and Anna-Maria Marshall, eds. 2009. *Queer Mobilizations: LGBT Activists Confront the Law*. New York: New York University Press.

Barker, David C., and James D. Tinnick III. 2006. "Competing Visions of Parental Roles and Ideological Constraint." *American Political Science Review* 100 (2): 249–63.

Barnes v. Cincinnati, 401 F.3d 729, 735 (6th Cir. 2005).

Barnhart, Brent A. 2013. "Gender Nondiscrimination Requirements." Department of Managed Health Care, April. Accessed June 4, 2017. http://translaw.wpengine.com/ wp-content/uploads/2013/04/DMHC-Director-Letter-re-Gender-NonDiscrimination-Requirements.pdf

Barth, Jay, L. Marvin Overby, and Scott H. Huffmon. 2009. "Community Context, Personal Contact, and Support for an Anti-Gay Rights Referendum" *Political Research Quarterly* 62 (2): 355–65.

Barton, Gina. 2005. "Prisoner Sues State over Gender Rights." JSOnline.com, January 23, http://www.jsonline.com.news/wisconsin.181956101.html

Baumgartner, Frank, and Bryan Jones. 1993. *Agendas and Instability in American Politics.* Chicago. University of Chicago Press.

BBC News. 2017. "Trump's Army Secretary Nominee Mark Green Withdraws." *BBC News,* May 5. Accessed May 15, 2017. http://www.bbc.com/news/world-us-canada-39826909

Beam, Cris. 2007. *Transparent: Love, Family, and Living the T with Transgender Teenagers.* Orlando: Harcourt.

Becker, Amy B., and D. A. Scheufele. 2011. "New Voters, New Outlook? Predispositions, Social Networks, and the Changing Politics of Gay Civil Rights." *Social Science Quarterly* 92 (2): 324–45.

Beemyn, Brett. 2003. "Serving the Needs of Transgender College Students." *Journal of Gay & Lesbian Issues in Education* 1 (1): 33–50.

Beemyn, Genny (director, Stonewall Center, University of Massachusetts Amherst), interviewed by Jami Taylor, telephone, October 7, 2016.

Beemyn, Genny. 2017. "Trans Policy Clearinghouse. Campus Pride 2017" Accessed May 16, 2017.. https://www.campuspride.org/tpc/

Belkin, Aaron (founding director, Palm Center), interviewed by Jami Taylor, telephone, May 23, 2016.

Benford, Robert D. 1992. "Social Movements." In *The Encyclopedia of Sociology*, edited by Edgar F. Borgatta and Marie L. Borgatta, 1880–86. New York: Macmillan.

Benford, Robert D., Timothy B. Gongaware, and Danny L. Valadez. 2000. "Social Movements." In *Encyclopedia of Sociology 2nd edition*, edited by Edgar F. Borgatta and Rhonda J. V. Montgomery, 2717–27. New York: Macmillan Reference.

Benjamin, Harry. 1966. *The Transsexual Phenomenon.* New York: Julian Press.

Benner, Katie. 2018. "Federal Prisons Roll Back Rules Protecting Transgender People." *New York Times*, May 11. Accessed June 6, 2018 from https://www.nytimes.com/2018/05/11/us/politics/justice-department-transgender-inmates-crime-victims.html

Bentz, Eva, Lukas Hefler, Ulrike Kaufmann, Johannes Huber, Andrea Kolbus, and Clemens Tempfer. 2008. "A Polymorphism of the CYP17 Gene Related to Sex Steroid Metabolism Is Associated with Female-to-Male but Not Male-to-Female Transsexualism." *Fertility and Sterility* 90 (1): 56–59.

Berg, Justin Allen. 2009. "Core Networks and Whites' Attitudes toward Immigrants and Immigration Policy." *Public Opinion Quarterly* 73 (1): 7–31.

Berinsky, Adam J., Gregory A. Huber, and Gabriel S. Lenz. 2012. "Evaluating Online Labor Markets for Experimental Research: Amazon.com's Mechanical Turk." *Political Analysis* 20: 351–68.

Berman, Mark. 2017. "Hate Crimes in the United States Increased Last Year, the FBI Says." *Washington Post*, November 13 Accessed November 13, 2017. https://www.washingtonpost.com/news/post-nation/wp/2017/11/13/hate-crimes-in-the-united-states-increased-last-year-the-fbi-says/?utm_term=.21f053edf785

Berman, Mark, and Amber Phillips. 2017. "North Carolina Governor Signs Bill Repealing and Replacing Transgender Bathroom Law amid Criticism." *Washington Post*, March 30 Accessed June 28, 2017. https://www.washingtonpost.com/news/post-nation/wp/2017/03/30/north-carolina-lawmakers-say-theyve-agreed-on-a-deal-to-repeal-the-bathroom-bill/?utm_term=.e7b323ca0bbf

Berry, Frances Stokes, and William D. Berry. 2014. "Innovation and Diffusion Models in

Policy Research." In *Theories of the Policy Process,* edited by Paul A. Sabatier and Christopher M. Weible, 307–62. Boulder, CO: Westview.

Berry, William D., Richard C. Fording, Evan J. Ringquist, Russell L. Hanson, and Carl E Klarner. 2010. "Measuring Citizen and Government Ideology in the US States: A Reappraisal." *State Politics & Policy Quarterly* 10 (2): 117–35.

Berry, William D., Evan J. Ringquist, Richard C. Fording, and Russell L. Hanson. 1998. "Measuring Citizen and Government Ideology in the American States, 1960–93." *American Journal of Political Science* 42 (1): 327–348.

Beyle, Thad. 1968. "The Governor's Formal Powers: A View from the Governor's Chair." *Public Administration Review* 28 (6): 540–45.

Beyle, Thad, and Margaret Ferguson. 2008. "Governors and the Executive Branch." In *Politics in the American States, 9th edition,* edited by Virginia Gray and Russell Hanson, 192–228. Washington, DC: CQ Press.

Billings Gazette. 2017. "The Plain Meaning of Montana Bathroom Initiative." *Montana Standard.com,* September 24. Accessed October 7, 2017. http://mtstandard.com/opinion/editorial/the-plain-meaning-of-montana-bathroom-initiative/article_7917e806–435c-544f-83b3–6bd03dddc642.html

Bishin, Benjamin G., Thomas J. Hayes, Matthew B. Incantalupo, and Charles Anthony Smith. 2015. "Opinion Backlash and Public Attitudes: Are Political Advances in Gay Rights Counterproductive?" *American Journal of Political Science* 60 (3): 625–48. doi:10.1111/ajps.12181.

Bishop, Elena P., and Noel Myricks. 2004. "Sex Reassignment Surgery: When Is a He a She for the Purpose of Marriage in the United States?" *American Journal of Family Law* 18 (1): 30–35.

Blatt v. Cabela's Retail, Inc., 5:14-cv-04822-JLS (E.D. Pa. 2017).

Blumenstein, Rosalyne, Barbara Warren, and Lynn Walker. 1998. "Appendix: The Empowerment of a Community." In *Current Concepts in Transgender Identity,* edited by Dallas Denny, 427–30. New York: Garland Publishing.

Blythe, Anne. 2016. "NC Attorney General Refuses to Defend State from HB2 Legal Challenge." *News & Observer,* March 30. Accessed January 22, 2017. http://www.newsobserver.com/news/politics-government/state-politics/article68780657.html

Bobo, Lawrence, and Frederick Licari. 1989. "Education and Political Tolerance: Testing the Effects of Cognitive Sophistication and Target Group Affect." *Public Opinion Quarterly* 53 (3): 285–308.

Bobrow, Emily. 2016. "How Two Producers of 'Transparent' Made Their Own Trans Lives More Visible." *New York Times Magazine,* September 18 Accessed June 12, 2017. https://www.nytimes.com/2016/09/18/magazine/how-two-producers-of-transparent-are-making-trans-lives-more-visible-starting-with-their-own.html?_r=0

Bolin, Anne. 1988. *In Search of Eve: Transsexual Rites of Passage.* South Hadley, MA: Bergin and Garvey.

Bolin, Anne. 1998. "Transcending and Transgendering: Male-to-female Transsexuals, Dichotomy, and Diversity. In *Current Concepts in Transgender Identity,* edited by Dallas Denny, 63–96. New York: Garland Publishing.

Boone, Rebecca. 2017. "Transgender Woman Sues Idaho over Birth Certificate Policy." Associated Press, April 19 Accessed May 31, 2017. https://www.usnews.com/news/best-states/idaho/articles/2017–04–19/transgender-woman-sues-idaho-over-birth-certificate-policy

Boren, Cindy. 2017. "NCAA Ends Boycott of North Carolina after Repeal, Replacement of Bathroom Law. *Washington Post*, April 4. Accessed October 9, 2017 from https://www.washingtonpost.com/news/early-lead/wp/2017/04/04/ncaa-ends-boycott-of-north-carolina-after-repeal-replacement-of-bathroom-law/?utm_term=.45b1a4130f23

Bornstein, Kate. 1994. *Gender Outlaw: On Men, Women, and the Rest of Us*. New York: Routledge.

Bort, Ryan. 2016. "A Comprehensive Timeline of Public Figures Boycotting North Carolina over the HB2 'Bathroom Bill'." *Newsweek*, September 14. Accessed May 25, 2017. http://www.newsweek.com/north-carolina-hb2-bathroom-bill-timeline-498052

Boswell, Holly. 1991. "The Transgender Alternative." *Chrysalis Quarterly* 1 (2): 29–31.

Boushey, Graeme. 2010. *Policy Diffusion Dynamics in America*. New York: Cambridge University Press.

Bowden, Bill. 2015. "Eureka Springs Quickly Passes Anti-Prejudice Law." *Arkansas Democrat-Gazette*, February 10.

Bowers v. Hardwick, 478 U.S. 186 (1986).

Bowie, Liz. 2017. "Private School Loses State Voucher Money over Anti-LGBT Policy." *Baltimore Sun*, October 13. Accessed November 13, 2017. http://www.baltimoresun.com/news/maryland/education/bs-md-school-voucher-discrimination-20171012-story.html

Bowler, Shaun, and Todd Donovan. 2004. "Measuring the Effects of Direct Democracy on State Policy: Not All Initiatives Are Created Equal." *State Politics & Policy Quarterly* 4 (3): 345–63.

Boylan, Jennifer Finney (professor, Barnard College), interviewed by Jami Taylor, telephone, September 9, 2016.

Boylan, Jennifer Finney. 2003. *She's Not There: A Life in Two Genders*. New York: Broadway Books.

Bowman, Lynne (senior regional field director, Human Rights Campaign), interviewed by Jami Taylor, telephone, October 16, 2016.

Bramlett, Brittany H. 2012. "The Cross-Pressures of Religion and Contact with Gays and Lesbians, and Their Impact on Same-Sex Marriage Opinion." *Politics and Policy* 40 (1): 13–42.

Brantley, Max. 2014. "Fayetteville Council Votes 6–2 for Civil Rights Ordinance That Protects Gay, Transgender People." *Arkansas Times*, August 19.

Brantley, Max. 2015. "Holy War in Eureka Springs Over Civil Rights Ordinance." *Arkansas Times*, March 6.

Brewer, Paul R. 2003. "The Shifting Foundations of Public Opinion about Gay Rights." *Journal of Politics* 65 (4):1208–20.

Brewer, Paul R. 2007. *Value War: Public Opinion and the Politics of Gay Rights*. Lanham, MD: Rowman and Littlefield.

Broadus, Kylar (executive director, Trans People of Color Coalition), interviewed by Jami Taylor, telephone, June 2, 2016.

Broadus, Kylar. 2006. "The Evolution of Employment Discrimination Protections for Transgender People." In *Transgender Rights*, edited by Paisley Currah, Richard Juang, and Shannon Price Minter, 93–101. Minneapolis: University of Minnesota Press.

Broockman, David, and Joshua Kalla. 2016. "Durably Reducing Transphobia: A Field Experiment on Door-to-Door Canvassing." *Science* 352 (6282): 220–24.

Brook, Tom Vanden. 2017. "Transgender Cadets at Military Academies Can Graduate but Not Serve." *USA Today*, May 10. Accessed May 17, 2017. https://www.usatoday.com/ story/news/politics/2017/05/10/transgender-troop-ban-president-donald-trump-defense-secretary-jim-mattis/101527662/

Brown, Robbie. 2008. "Murder of Transgender Woman Revives Scrutiny." *New York Times*, November 17. http://www.nytimes.com/2008/11/18/us/18memphis.html

Brydum, Sunnivie. 2013. "Watch: Pat Robertson Says Being Transgender Is Not a Sin." *Advocate*, July 29. Accessed October 9, 2017. https://www.advocate.com/politics/transgender/2013/07/29/watch-pat-robertson-says-being-transgender-not-sin

Buechler, S. 1995. "New Social Movement Theories." *Sociological Quarterly* 36 (3): 441–64.

Bugg, Sean. 2004. "Trans Mission." *MetroWeekly*, August 18. Accessed April 24, 2017. http://www.metroweekly.com/2004/08/trans-mission/

Bull, Chris, and John Gallagher. 1996. *Perfect Enemies: The Battle between the Religious Right and the Gay Movement*. New York: Crown Publishers.

Bullough, Bonnie, and Vern Bullough. 1998. "Transsexualism: Historical Perspectives, 1952-Present." In *Current Concepts in Transgender Identity*, edited by Dallas Denny, 15–34. New York: Garland Publishing.

Bullough, Vern. 2000. "Transgenderism and the Concept of Gender." *International Journal of Transgenderism* 4 (3). Accessed July 17, 2005. http://www.symposion.com/ijt/gilbert/ bullough.htm

Bumiller, Elizabeth. 2004. "White House Letter; On Gay Marriage, Bush May Have Said All He's Going To." *New York Times*, March 1 Accessed January 27, 2017. http://www. nytimes.com/2004/03/01/us/white-house-letter-on-gay-marriage-bush-may-have-said-all-he-s-going-to.html

Burack, Cynthia. 2008. *Sin, Sex, and Democracy: Antigay Rhetoric and the Christian Right*. Albany: State University of New York Press.

Burden, Barry C. 2005. "Institutions and Policy Representation in the States." *State Politics & Policy Quarterly* 5 (4): 373–93.

Burwell v. Hobby Lobby, 573 U.S. ___ (2014).

Butler, Judith. 1990. *Gender Trouble: Feminism and the Subversion of Identity*. New York: Routledge.

Button, James W., Barbara A. Rienzo, and Kenneth D. Wald. 1997. *Private Lives, Public Conflicts: Battles over Gay Rights in American Communities*. Washington, DC: CQ Press.

Buzuvis, Erin. 2011. "Transgender Student-Athletes and Sex-Segregated Sport: Developing Policies of Inclusion for Intercollegiate and Interscholastic Athletics." *Seton Hall Journal of Sports and Entertainment Law* 21 (1): 1–59.

Buzuvis, Erin. 2013. "'On the Basis of Sex': Using Title IX to Protect Transgender Students from Discrimination in Education." *Wisconsin Journal of Law, Gender & Society* 28: 219–43.

Buzuvis, Erin. 2016. "'As Who They Really Are': Expanding Opportunities for Transgender Athletes to Participate in Youth and Scholastic Sports." *Law and Inequality: A Journal of Theory and Practice* 34: 341–84.

Cahill, Sean 2017. "From 'Don't Drop the Soap' to PREA Standards: Reducing the Sexual Victimization of LGBT People in Juvenile and Criminal Justice Systems." In *LGBTQ Politics: A Critical Reader*, edited by Marla Brettschneider, Susan Burgess, and Cricket Keating, 134–52. New York: New York University Press.

Califia, Patrick. 1997. *Sex Changes: The Politics of Transgenderism*. San Francisco: Cleis Press.

California Code, Health and Safety Code § 1365.5. 2009.

California Department of Insurance. 2013. "Gender Nondiscrimination in Health Insurance." Sec. 2561.2. p.676.32. Accessed June 4, 2017. http://translaw.wpengine.com/wp-content/uploads/2013/04/CDI-Gender-Nondiscrimination-Regulations.pdf

Callahan, David. 2015. "No One Left Behind: Tim Gill and the New Quest for Full LGBT Equality." *Inside Philanthropy*, August 25 Accessed June 20, 2017. https://www.insidephilanthropy.com/home/2015/8/25/no-one-left-behind-tim-gill-and-the-new-quest-for-full-lgbt.html

Cameron, Charles M. 2000. *Veto Bargaining: Presidents and the Politics of Negative Power*. Cambridge: Cambridge University Press.

Cameron, Lindsey, and Adam Rutland. 2006. "Extended Contact through Story Reading in School: Reducing Children's Prejudice toward the Disabled." *Journal of Social Issues* 62 (3): 469–88.

Cameron, Loren. 1996. *Body Alchemy: Transsexual Portraits*. Pittsburgh, PA: Cleis Press.

Campbell, Amy L. 2002. "Raising the Bar: Ruth Bader Ginsberg and the ACLU Women's Rights Project." *Texas Journal of Women and the Law* 11(2): 157–243.

Campbell, Andrea Louise. 2003. *How Policies Make Citizens: Senior Political Activism and the American Welfare State*. Princeton: Princeton University Press.

Capehart, Jonathan. 2012. "Obama Leads on Marriage Equality, the NAACP and Others Follow." *Washington Post*, May 20 Accessed January 30, 2017. https://www.washingtonpost.com/blogs/post-partisan/post/obama-leads-on-marriage-equality-the-naacp-and-others-follow/2012/05/20/gIQAScBkdU_blog.html?utm_term=.c25d89e5519f

Carcaño et al. v. McCrory et al., No. 1:16-cv-00236 (M.D. NC. August 26, 2016).

Carmines, Edward G., and James A. Stimson. 1981. "Issue Evolution, Population Replacement, and Normal Partisan Change." *American Political Science Review* 75 (1): 107–18.

Carroll, Helen. 2014. "Joining the Team: The Inclusion of Transgender Students in United States School Based Athletics." In *Routledge Handbook of Sport, Gender and Sexuality*, edited by Jennifer Hargreaves and Eric Anderson, 367–75. New York: Routledge.

Casey, Logan. 2016. "Emotional Agendas: Disgust and the Dynamics of LGBT Politics." PhD diss., University of Michigan.

Centers for Disease Control and Prevention. 1977. "1977 Revision of the Model State Vital Statistics Act and Model State Vital Statistics Regulations". Accessed January 17, 2017. http://www.cdc.gov/nchs/data/misc/mvsact77acc.pdf

Centers for Disease Control and Prevention. 2012. "HIV Planning Guidance." Accessed December 16, 2016. https://www.cdc.gov/hiv/pdf/policies_funding_ps12–1201_HIV_Planning_Guidance.pdf

Centers for Medicare and Medicaid Services. 2013. "CMS Press Toolkit." Accessed October 8, 2017. https://www.cms.gov/Newsroom/PressToolkit.html

Centers for Medicare and Medicaid Services. 2014. "Invalidation of National Coverage Determination 140.3—Transsexual Surgery." Department of Health and Human Services. Accessed June 4, 2017. https://www.cms.gov/Regulations-and-Guidance/Guidance/Transmittals/Downloads/R189BP.pdf

Centers for Medicare and Medicaid Services. 2017. "Gender Dysphoria and Gender Reassignment Surgery." Department of Health and Human Services. Accessed June 4, 2017. https://www.cms.gov/regulations-and-guidance/guidance/transmittals/2017downloads/r194NCD.pdf

Cha, Ariana Eunjung. 2014. "Ban Lifted on Medicare Coverage for Sex Change Surgery." *Washington Post*, May 30. Accessed June 6, 2017. https://www.washingtonpost.com/national/health-science/ban-lifted-on-medicare-coverage-for-sex-change-surgery/2014/05/30/28bcd122-e818–11e3-a86b-362fd5443d19_story.html?utm_term=.be08d6362f20

Chambers, Jennifer. 2016. "Secretary of State Makes Changing Gender on ID Easier." *Detroit News*, March 15, http://www.detroitnews.com/story/news/politics/2016/03/15/secretary-state-makes-changing-gender-easier/81839546/

Chauncey, George. 2005. *Why Marriage? The History Shaping Today's Debate over Gay Equality*. Cambridge, MA: Basic Books.

Chevron v. Natural Resources Defense Council, 467 U.S. 837 (1984).

Chong, Dennis. 1991. *Collective Action and the Civil Rights Movement*. Chicago: University of Chicago Press.

City of Boerne v. Flores, 521 U.S. 507 (1997).

City of Chicago v. Wilson, 75 Ill. 2d 525 (1978).

Clawson, Rosalee, and Zoe Oxley. 2013. *Public Opinion: Democratic Ideals, Democratic Practice, Second Edition*. Thousand Oaks, CA: CQ Press.

Clements-Nolle, Kristen, Rani Marx, Robert Guzman, and Mitchell Katz. 2001. "HIV Prevalence, Risk Behaviors, Health Care Use, and Mental Health Status of Transgender Persons: Implications for Public Health Intervention." *American Journal of Public Health* 91 (6): 915–21.

CNN. 2009. "Holder Pushed Hate Crimes Law; GOP Unpersuaded." *CNN*, June 25. http://politicalticker.blogs.cnn.com/2009/06/25/holder-pushes-hate-crimes-law-gop-unpersuaded/#more-57796

Cohen, Jeffrey. 1997. *Presidential Responsiveness and Public Policy-making: The Public and the Policies That Presidents Choose*. Ann Arbor: University of Michigan Press.

Cohen-Kettenis, Peggy T., and Louis Gooren. 1999. "Transsexualism: A Review of Etiology, Diagnosis and Treatment." *Journal of Psychosomatic Research* 46 (4): 315–33.

Columbus Dispatch. 2011. "Kasich Alters Order on Work Rights." *Columbus Dispatch*, January 22. Accessed January 22, 2017. http://www.dispatch.com/content/stories/local/2011/01/22/kasich-alters-order-on-work-rights.html

Colvin, Roddrick A. 2007. "The Rise of Transgender-Inclusive Laws: How Well Are Municipalities Implementing Supportive Nondiscrimination Public Employment Policies?" *Review of Public Personnel Administration* 27 (4): 336–60.

Combs, Ryan. 2014. "Key Issues in Transgender Healthcare Policy and Practice." In *Transgender Rights and Politics: Groups, Issue Framing, and Policy Adoption*, edited by Jami Taylor and Donald Haider-Markel, 231–25. Ann Arbor: University of Michigan Press.

Comer, Matt. 2011. "Equality NC Receives $10K for Amendment Fight." *Q Notes*. Accessed

June 20, 2017. https://goqnotes.com/10148/equality-nc-receives-ten-thousand-dollars-for-amendment-fight/

Committee on Education and Labor. 1990. *Legislative History of Public Law 101–336, The Americans With Disabilities Act: Prepared for the Committee on Education and Labor, U.S. House of Representatives, One Hundred First Congress, Second Session.* Washington, DC: U.S. Government Printing Office.

Committee on Oversight and Government Reform, U.S. House of Representatives, 112th Congress. 2012. "United States Government Policy and Supporting Positions." Accessed January 22, 2017. https://www.gpo.gov/fdsys/pkg/GPO-PLUMBOOK-2012/pdf/GPO-PLUMBOOK-2012.pdf

Commonwealth of Virginia Office of the Governor. 2018. "Executive Order Number One (2018)." Accessed January 21, 2018 http://governor.virginia.gov/media/9834/eo-1-equal-opportunity.pdf

Congress.gov. 2009. S.909—Matthew Shepard Hate Crimes Statistics Prevention Act. https://www.congress.gov/bill/111th-congress/senate-bill/00909/cosponsors

Congressional Record. 2009. "Extensions of Remarks, Various Dates." Washington, DC: U.S. Government Publishing Office. Accessed: https://www.gpo.gov/fdsys/pkg/CREC-2009–04–28/pdf/CREC-2009–04–28-pt1-PgE1003–3.pdf#page=2

Conover, Pamela J. 1988. "The Role of Social Groups in Political Thinking." *British Journal of Political Science* 18 (1): 51–76.

Converse, Philip E. 1964. "The Nature of Belief Systems in Mass Publics." In *Ideology and Discontent,* edited by D. E. Apter. New York: Free Press.

Cook, Alana. 2015. "Eureka Springs Chamber Expresses Concerns over Anti-Discrimination Law." *Carroll County News,* February 23.

Cook-Daniels, Loree, and Michael Munson. 2010. "Sexual Violence, Elder Abuse, and Sexuality of Transgender Adults, Age 50+: Results of Three Surveys." *Journal of GLBT Family Studies* 6: 142–77.

Cooky, Cheryl, and Shari L. Dworkin. 2013. "Policing the Boundaries of Sex: A Critical Examination of Gender Verification and the Caster Semenya Controversy." *Journal of Sex Research* 50 (2): 103–11.

Corbett v. Corbett, [1970] 2 All E.R. 33 (Divorce Ct.).

Council, John. 2016. "Why Conservative States Handpicked This Texas Judge for Transgender Bathroom Challenge." Law.com, August 24, http://www.law.com/sites/almstaff/2016/08/24/why-conservative-states-handpicked-this-texas-judge-for-transgender-bathroom-challenge/?slreturn=20160725120023

Council of State Governments. 2017. *The Book of States.* Accessed January 10, 2017. http://knowledgecenter.csg.org/kc/category/content-type/bos-2016

Cox, Ramsey. 2013. "Senate Passes Gay Rights Bill." *The Hill,* November 7. Accessed: http://thehill.com/blogs/floor-action/senate/189599-senate-approves-enda-in-historic-step-on-gay-rights

Craig, Stephen C., Michael D. Martinez, James G. Kane, and Jason Gainous. 2005. "Core Values, Value Conflict, and Citizens' Ambivalence about Gay Rights." *Political Research Quarterly* 58 (1): 5–17.

Craver, Richard. 2017. "LGBT Plaintiffs Plan to Target Bill That Did Away with HB2." *Winston-Salem Journal,* May 2. Accessed May 18, 2017. http://www.journalnow.

com/news/elections/state/lgbt-plaintiffs-plan-to-target-bill-that-did-away-with/article_00896f21–9922–5a2d-8af4–948fd3670ba7.html

Croffie, Kwegyirba. 2017. "Hundreds Have Changed Genders on NYC Birth Certificates." *CNN*, March 10. Accessed May 31, 2017. http://www.cnn.com/2017/03/10/health/new-york-birth-certificate-gender-marker-change/

Cronin, Thomas E. 1989. *Direct Democracy: The Politics of Initiative, Referendum, and Recall.* Cambridge: Harvard University Press.

Cruzan v. Special School District # 1. 294 F.3d 981 (8th Cir.2002).

Currah, Paisley (professor, Brooklyn College), interviewed by Jami Taylor, telephone, October 7, 2016.

Currah, Paisley. 2006. "Gender Pluralisms under the Transgender Umbrella." In *Transgender Rights*, edited by Paisley Currah, Richard Juang, and Shannon Minter, 3–31. Minneapolis: University of Minnesota Press.

Currah, Paisley, Richard Juang, and Shannon Price Minter, eds. 2006a. *Transgender Rights*. Minneapolis: University of Minnesota Press.

Currah, Paisley, Richard Juang, and Shannon Price Minter. 2006b. "Introduction." In *Transgender Rights*, edited by Paisley Currah, Richard Juang, and Shannon Minter, xiii–xxiv. Minneapolis: University of Minnesota Press.

Currah, Paisley, and Shannon Minter. 2000. *Transgender Equality: A Handbook for Activists and Policymakers*. Washington, DC: National Gay and Lesbian Task Force.

Curry, Tom. 2012. "The 'Evolution' of Obama's Stance on Gay Marriage." *NBC News*, May 9. Accessed January 25, 2017. http://nbcpolitics.nbcnews.com/_news/2012/05/09/11623172-the-evolution-of-obamas-stance-on-gay-marriage?lite

Dahl, Robert. 1957. "Decision-making in a Democracy: The Role of the Supreme Court as a National Policy Maker." *Journal of Public Law* 6: 279–95.

Dalesio, Emery P., and Jonathan Drew. 2017. "Price Tag of North Carolina's LGBT Law: $3.76B." Associated Press, March 27.

Daley, Andrea, Steven Solomon, Peter A. Newman, and Faye Mishna. 2007. "Traversing the Margins: Intersectionalities in the Bullying of Lesbian, Gay, Bisexual and Transgender Youth." *Journal of Gay and Lesbian Social Services* 19 (3–4): 9–29.

Dasti, Jerry. 2002. "Advocating a Broader Understanding of the Necessity of Sex-Reassignment Surgery under Medicaid." *New York University Law Review* 77 (6): 1738–1775.

Daum, Courtenay W. 2015, "The War on Solicitation and Intersectional Subjection: Quality-of-Life Policing as a Tool to Control Transgender Populations." *New Political Science* 37 (4): 562–81.

Davey, Monica, Campbell Robertson, and Richard Pérez-Peña. 2015. "Indiana and Arkansas Revise Rights Bills, Seeking to Remove Divisive Parts." *New York Times*, April 2.

Davis, Heath Fogg (associate professor, Temple University), interviewed by Jami Taylor, telephone, June 2, 2016.

Davis, Heath Fogg. 2014. "Sex-Classification Policies as Transgender Discrimination: An Intersectional Critique." *Perspectives on Politics* 12 (1): 45–60.

Davis, Heath Fogg. 2017. *Beyond Trans: Does Gender Matter?* New York: New York University Press.

Davis v. Monroe County Bd. of Ed. (97–843) 526 U.S. 629 (1999).

De Cuypere, G., M. Van Hemelrijck, A. Michel, B. Carael, G. Heylens, R. Rubens, and S. Monstrey. 2007. "Prevalence and Demography of Transsexualism in Belgium." *European Psychiatry* 22 (3): 137–41.

Deering, Christopher J., and Forrest Maltzman. 1999. "The Politics of Executive Orders: Legislative Constraints on Presidential Power." *Political Research Quarterly* 52 (4): 767–83.

Dejean, Ashley. 2017. "Gorsuch Hints That He's Deeply Critical of LGBT Rights." *Mother Jones*, June 26. Accessed October 7, 2017. http://www.motherjones.com/politics/2017/06/gorsuch-hints-that-hes-deeply-critical-of-lgbt-rights/

De Koster, Willem, and Jeroen Van der Waal. 2007. "Cultural Value Orientations and Christian Religiosity: On Moral Traditionalism, Authoritarianism, and Their Implications for Voting Behavior." *International Political Science Review* 28 (4): 451–67.

Delaware Governor's Office. 2009. "Executive Order Number Eight." Accessed January 22, 2017. http://governor.delaware.gov/wp-content/uploads/sites/24/2016/12/EO008.pdf

De'lonta v. Angelone 330 F.3d 630, 634 (4th Cir. 2003).

De'lonta v. Johnson 708 F.3d 520, 522–23 (4th Cir 2013).

De'lonta v. Johnson et al., 11–7482 (4th Cir. 2013).

D'Emilio, John. 2007. "Will the Courts Set Us Free? Reflections on the Campaign for Same-Sex Marriage." In *The Politics of Same-Sex Marriage*, edited by Craig G. Rimmerman and Clyde Wilcox, 39–64. Chicago: University of Chicago Press.

D'Emilio, John. 2002. *The World Turned: Essays on Gay History, Politics, and Culture.* Durham: Duke University Press.

Democratic Party. 1988. "1988 Democratic Party Platform." Gerhard Peters and John T. Woolley, *American Presidency Project.* Accessed June 8, 2017. http://www.presidency.ucsb.edu/ws/?pid=29609

Democratic Party. 1992. "1992 Democratic Party Platform." *American Presidency Project.* Accessed June 8, 2017. http://www.presidency.ucsb.edu/ws/?pid=29610

Denny, Dallas (former executive director, American Educational Gender Information Service), interviewed by Jami Taylor, telephone, May 24, 2016.

Denny, Dallas. 1992. "The Politics of Diagnosis and a Diagnosis of Politics: The University-Affiliated Gender Clinics, and How They Failed to Meet the Needs of Transsexual People." *Chrysalis Quarterly* 1 (3): 9–20.

Denny, Dallas. 2006. "Transgender Communities of the United States in the Late Twentieth Century." In *Transgender Rights*, edited by Paisley Currah, Richard Juang, and Shannon Price Minter, 171–91. Minneapolis: University of Minnesota Press.

Department of Defense. 2016. "Department of Defense Transgender Policy." Accessed June 4, 2017. https://www.defense.gov/News/Special-Reports/0616_transgender-policy/

Department of Health and Human Services Departmental Appeals Board. 2014. "Ncd 140.3, Transsexual Surgery, Docket No. A-13–87, Decision No. 2576." Accessed June 4, 2017. https://www.hhs.gov/sites/default/files/static/dab/decisions/board-decisions/2014/dab2576.pdf

Department of Health and Human Services. 2016. "Nondiscrimination in Health Programs and Activities 45 CFR Part 92 RIN 0945–AA02." *Federal Register* 81, (96) (May 18): 31375–473.

Department of Justice. 2016. "Attorney General Loretta E. Lynch Delivers Remarks at

Press Conference Announcing Complaint against the State of North Carolina to Stop Discrimination against Transgender Individuals, Washington, DC- Monday, May 9, 2016." Accessed June 26, 2017. https://www.justice.gov/opa/speech/attorney-general-loretta-e-lynch-delivers-remarks-press-conference-announcing-complaint

Department of Justice. 2018. *Transgender Offender Manual*. Accessed June 6, 2018 from https://www.documentcloud.org/documents/4459297-BOP-Change-Order-Trans-gender-Offender-Manual-5.html

Dettwyler, Katherine. 2011. *Cultural Anthropology and Human Experience: The Feast of Life*. Long Grove, IL: Waveland Press.

Devor, Aaron, and Nicholas Matte. 2004. "ONE Inc. and Reed Erickson: The Uneasy Collaboration of Gay and Trans Activism, 1964–2003." *GLQ: A Journal of Lesbian and Gay Studies* 10 (2): 179–209.

Dhejne, Cecilia, Katarina Oberg, Stefan Arver, and Mikael Landen. 2014. "An Analysis of All Applications for Sex Reassignment Surgery in Sweden, 2016–2010: Prevalence, Incidence, and Regrets." *Archives of Sexual Behavior* 43: 1535–45.

Docter, Richard. 2008. *Becoming a Woman: A Biography of Christine Jorgensen*. New York: Hayworth Press.

Doe v. Regional School District Unit 26. Case No. Pen-12–582 (ME S.Ct., Jan. 30, 2014)

Dolan, Kathleen. 2004. *Voting For Women: How the Public Evaluates Women Candidates*. Boulder, CO: Westview Press.

Doran, Will. 2017. "Here's How Every NC Legislator Voted on the HB2 Repeal Bill." *News & Observer*, March 31. Accessed October 8, 2017. http://www.newsobserver.com/news/politics-government/politics-columns-blogs/under-the-dome/article141701219.html

Dresden, Hilton. 2017. "Obama Makes Final Efforts to Protect Transgender Rights in Bathrooms." *Out Magazine*, January 9. Accessed May 25, 2017. http://www.out.com/news-opinion/2017/1/09/obama-makes-final-efforts-protect-transgender-rights-bathrooms

Dresser, Michael, and Erin Cox. 2014. "O'Malley Signs Transgender Rights Bill." *Baltimore Sun*, May 14. Accessed June 28, 2017. http://www.baltimoresun.com/news/maryland/politics/blog/bs-md-last-signing-20140514-story.html

Druckman, James N., Erik Peterson, and Rune Slothuus. 2013. "How Elite Partisan Polarization Affects Public Opinion Formation." *American Political Science Review* 107 (1): 57–79.

Dunn, Mason (executive director, Massachusetts Political Coalition). Interviewed by Jami Taylor, telephone, May 25, 2016.

Dvorak, Petula. 2017. "A Transgender Candidate Takes on Virginia's 'Minister of Private Parts'." *Washington Post*, July 31. Accessed October 4, 2017. https://www.washingtonpost.com/local/a-transgender-candidate-takes-on-virginias-minister-of-private-parts/2017/07/31/2faf54ae-75f6–11e7–9eac-d56bd5568db8_story.html?utm_term=.88e4d694eec8

Edgell, Penny, Douglas Hartmann, Evan Stewart, and Joseph Gerteis. 2016. "Atheists and Other Cultural Outsiders: Moral Boundaries and the Non-Religious in the United States." *Social Forces* 95 (2): 607–38.

Egan, Patrick, Nathaniel Persily, and Kevin Wallsten. 2008. "Gay Rights." In *Public Opinion and Constitutional Controversy*, edited by Nathaniel Persily, Jack Citrin, and Patrick Egan, 234–66. New York: Oxford University Press.

Eggen, Dan. 2012. "Obama's Gay Marriage Announcement Followed by Flood of Campaign Donations." *Washington Post*, May 10. Accessed January 25, 2017. https://www.washingtonpost.com/politics/obamas-gay-marriage-announcement-followed-by-flood-of-campaign-donations/2012/05/10/gIQA2ntCGU_story.html?utm_term=.87c88bcce290

Eidelson, Josh. 2017. "Gay-Rights Advocates Look to Cities as Firewall against Rollback." *Bloomberg Politics*, January 24. Accessed June 28, 2017. https://www.bloomberg.com/news/articles/2017–01–24/gay-rights-advocates-look-to-cities-as-firewall-against-rollback

Eilperin, Juliet. 2015. "Obama's Quiet Transgender Revolution." *Washington Post*, November 30. Accessed January 30, 2017. https://www.washingtonpost.com/politics/obamas-quiet-transgender-revolution/2015/11/30/6879527e-95e4–11e5-b5e4–279b4501e8a6_story.html?utm_term=.dc5b08cc71d9

Eilperin, Juliet, and Ariana Eunjung Cha. 2018. "New HHS Civil Rights Division to Shield Health Workers with Moral or Religious Objections. *Washington Post*, January 17. https://www.washingtonpost.com/national/health-science/trump-administration-creating-civil-rights-division-to-shield-health-workers-with-moral-or-religious-objections/2018/01/17/5663d1c0-fbe2–11e7–8f66–2df0b94bb98a_story.html?undefined=&utm_term=.0e63e7cf615d&wpisrc=nl_headlines&wpmm=1

Elazar, Daniel. 1984. *American Federalism: A View from the States*. 3rd ed. New York: Harper and Row.

Elders, Jocelyn, and Alan Steinman. 2014. "Report of the Transgender Military Service Commission." Palm Center. Accessed May 23, 2017 at http://archive.palmcenter.org/files/Transgender%20Military%20Service%20Report_0.pdf

Eleveld, Kerry. 2007a. "Donna Rose on Why She Resigned as the Only Transgender Member of HRC's Board." *Advocate*, October 4. Accessed February 10, 2017. http://www.advocate.com/news/2007/10/04/donna-rose-why-she-resigned-only-transgender-member-hrcs-board

Eleveld, Kerry. 2007b. "ENDA to Be Separated into Two Bills: Sexual Orientation and Gender Identity." *Advocate*, September 29. https://www.advocate.com/news/2007/09/29/enda-be-separated-two-bills-sexual-orientation-and-gender-identity

Eleveld, Kerry. 2007c. "Poll: 70% of LGBT Respondents Support Noninclusive ENDA." *Advocate*, November 7. Accessed October 4, 2017. https://www.advocate.com/news/2007/11/07/poll-70-lgbt-respondents-support-noninclusive-enda

Eleveld, Kerry. 2015. *Don't Tell Me to Wait: How the Fight for Gay Rights Changed America and Transformed Obama's Presidency*. New York: Basic Books.

Elliot, Rebecca, and Mike Morris. 2015. "Texas Supreme Court Says City Must Repeal HERO or Put It on Ballot." *Houston Chronicle*, July 24.

Eltagouri, Marwa. 2017a. "Meet Andrea Jenkins, the First Openly Transgender Black woman Elected to Public Office in the U.S." *Washington Post*, November 8. Accessed: https://www.washingtonpost.com/news/the-fix/wp/2017/11/08/meet-andrea-jenkins-the-openly-transgender-black-woman-elected-to-public-office-in-the-us/?undefined=&utm_term=.7be005cbe945&wpisrc=nl_politics&wpmm=1

Eltagouri, Marwa. 2017b. "Transgender People Have Been Elected Before, but They Can Finally Let the Voters Know." *Washington Post*, November 8. Accessed November 10,

2017. https://www.washingtonpost.com/news/retropolis/wp/2017/11/08/transgender-people-have-been-elected-before-but-they-can-finally-let-the-voters-know/?utm_term=.88389ffef85f

Engel, Stephen. 2007. "Organizational Identity as a Constraint on Strategic Action: A Comparative Analysis of Gay and Lesbian Interest Groups." *Studies in American Political Development* 21 (1): 66–91.

Enns, Peter K., and Julianna Koch. 2013. "Public Opinion in the U.S. States: 1956 to 2010." *State Politics & Policy Quarterly* 13 (3): 349–72.

Epps, Garrett. 2016. "Breyer Brings Back Courtesy—at a Cost." *Atlantic*, August. Accessed September 23, 2016. http://www.theatlantic.com/politics/archive/2016/08/breyer-brings-back-courtesybut-at-what-cost/494666/

Epps, Garrett. 2017. "When Beliefs and Identities Clash in Court." *Atlantic*, September. Accessed January 22, 2018 from https://www.theatlantic.com/politics/archive/2017/09/when-beliefs-and-identities-clash-in-court/540069/

Epstein, David, and Sharyn O'Halloran. 1999. *Delegating Powers: A Transaction Cost Politics Approach to Policy Making under Separate Powers.* Cambridge: Cambridge University Press.

Erickson, Erica. 2015. "ACLU Files Lawsuit against Michigan's SOS Office on Gender Policy." *Fox News Detroit.* May 21. Accessed January 18, 2017. http://www.fox2detroit.com/news/324380-story

Erikson, Robert S., Gerald C. Wright, and John P. McIver. 1993. *Statehouse Democracy: Public Opinion and Policy in the American States.* Cambridge: Cambridge University Press.

Estelle v. Gamble, 429 U.S. 97 (1976).

Etsitty v. Utah Transit Authority, 502 F.3d 1215 (10th Cir. 2007).

Evancho v. Pine-Richland School District, Civil No. 2: 16–01537 (W.D. Pa. Feb. 27, 2017).

Everett, Gwen. 2016. "Sororities to Allow All Female-Identifying Students to Rush." *Brown Daily Herald*, February 2.

Eyler, A. E., and K. Wright. 1997. "Gender Identification and Sexual Orientation among Genetic Females with Gender-Blended Self-Perception in Childhood and Adolescence." *International Journal of Transgenderism* 1 (1). Accessed July 18, 2016. http://web.archive.org/web/20070502000856/http://www.symposion.com/ijt/ijtc0102.htm

Faderman, Lillian. 1991. *Odd Girls and Twilight Lovers: A History of Lesbian Life in Twentieth-Century America.* New York: Columbia University Press.

Farmer v. Brennan, 511 U.S. 825 (1994).

Faulkner, Jason, Mark Schaller, Justin H. Park, and Lesley A. Duncan. 2004. "Evolved Disease-Avoidance Mechanisms and Contemporary Xenophobic Attitudes." *Group Processes & Intergroup Relations* 7 (4): 333–53.

Fausset, Richard. 2015. "In Arkansas, Gay Rights Ordinance Highlights Clash between Two Faces of Tourism." *New York Times*, April 19.

Fausset, Richard. 2017. "Bathroom Law Repeal Leaves Few Pleased in North Carolina." *New York Times*, March 30. Accessed June 5, 2017. https://www.nytimes.com/2017/03/30/us/north-carolina-senate-acts-to-repeal-restrictive-bathroom-law.html

Fausto-Sterling, Anne. 1993. "The Five Sexes: Why Male and Female Are Not Enough." *Sciences* (March/April): 20–24.

Fausto-Sterling, Anne. 2012. *Sex/Gender: Biology in a Social World.* New York: Routledge.

Federal Bureau of Investigation. Various Years. "Hate Crime Statistics." Washington, DC: Uniform Crime Reports. https://ucr.fbi.gov/ucr-publications#Hate

Federal Bureau of Investigation. 2017. *Uniform Crime Report: Hate Crimes Statistics, 2016.* Accessed November 13, 2017. https://ucr.fbi.gov/hate-crime/2016/topic-pages/incidentsandoffenses.pdf

Feeley, Malcolm M., and Edward L. Rubin. 1998. *Judicial Policy Making and the Modern State: How the Courts Reformed America's Prisons.* New York: Cambridge University Press.

Feinberg, Leslie. 1992. *Transgender Liberation: A Movement Whose Time Has Come.* New York: World View Forum.

Feinberg, Leslie. 1996. *Transgender Warriors: Making History from Joan of Arc to RuPaul.* Boston: Beacon Press.

Feinberg, Leslie. 1998. *Trans Liberation: Beyond Pink or Blue.* Boston: Beacon Press.

Feldman, Stanley. 1988. "Structure and Consistency in Public Opinion: The Role of Core Beliefs and Values." *American Journal of Political Science* 32 (2): 416–40.

Ferguson, Dana. 2016. "Gov: Transgender Meeting 'Helped Me See Things through Their Eyes'." *Argus Leader,* February 23. Accessed May 25, 2017. http://www.argusleader.com/story/news/politics/2016/02/23/governor-daugaard-meets-transgender-students/80792620/

Fernandez, Manny, and Alan Blinder. 2015. "Opponents of Houston Rights Measure Focused on Bathrooms, and Won." *New York Times,* November 4.

Ferraro, Thomas. 2009. "U.S. House Passes 'Hate Crime' Bill That Bush Opposed." Reuters, April 29. Accessed October 6, 2017. http://www.reuters.com/article/us-usa-congress-hate/u-s-house-passes-hate-crime-bill-that-bush-opposed-idUSTRE53S8IM20090429

Fetner, Tina. 2008. *How the Religious Right Shaped Lesbian and Gay Activism.* Minneapolis: University of Minnesota Press.

Fields v. Smith, 653 F.3d 550 (7th Cir. 2011).

Fine, Jeffrey A., and Adam Warber. 2012. "Circumventing Adversity: Executive Orders and Divided Government." *Presidential Studies Quarterly* 42 (2): 256–74.

Firestone, Andrew. 2012. "Sciortino, Patrick Celebrate Transgender Bill." *Somerville Times,* January 25. Accessed June 28, 2017. http://www.thesomervillenews.com/archives/22588

Fleming, Dana. 2012. "Massachusetts Passes Transgender Rights Bill." Massachusetts Bar Association, January. Accessed June 28, 2017. http://www.massbar.org/publications/lawyers-journal/2012/january/massachusetts-passes-transgender-rights-bill

Flores, Andrew R. 2015a. "Attitudes toward Transgender Rights: Perceived Knowledge and Secondary Interpersonal Contact." *Politics, Groups, and Identities* 3 (3): 398–416.

Flores, Andrew R. 2015b. "Examining Variation in Surveying Attitudes on Same-Sex Marriage: A Meta-Analysis." *Public Opinion Quarterly* 79 (2): 580–93.

Flores, Andrew R., and Scott Barclay. 2016. "Backlash, Consensus, Legitimacy, or Polarization: The Effect of Same-Sex Marriage Policy on Mass Attitudes." *Political Research Quarterly* 69 (1): 43–56.

Flores, Andrew R., Taylor N. T. Brown, and Andrew S. Park. 2016. "Public Support for Transgender Rights: A Twenty-three Country Survey." Los Angeles: Williams Institute, UCLA School of Law.

Flores, Andrew R., Donald P. Haider-Markel, Daniel C. Lewis, Patrick R. Miller, Barry L.

Tadlock, and Jami K. Taylor. 2017a. "Challenged Expectations: Mere Exposure Effects on Attitudes about Transgender People and Rights." *Political Psychology*. doi:10.1111/pops.12402.

Flores, Andrew R., Donald P. Haider-Markel, Daniel C. Lewis, Patrick R. Miller, Barry L. Tadlock, and Jami K. Taylor. 2017b. "In Every State, Majorities Oppose Trump's Proposed Ban on Transgender Military Service." *Washington Post Monkey Cage*, August 4. https://www.washingtonpost.com/news/monkey-cage/wp/2017/08/04/in-every-state-majorities-oppose-trumps-proposed-ban-on-transgender-military-service/?utm_term=.d8351bc26f0c

Flores, Andrew R., Jody L. Herman, Gary J. Gates, and Taylor N. T. Brown. 2016. "How Many Adults Identify as Transgender in the United States?" Williams Institute, June, http://williamsinstitute.law.ucla.edu/wp-content/uploads/How-Many-Adults-Identify-as-Transgender-in-the-United-States.pdf

Flores, Andrew R, Jody L. Herman, and Christy Mallory. 2015. "Transgender Inclusion in State Non-Discrimination Policies: The Democratic Deficit and Political Powerlessness." *Research & Politics* 2 (4): https://doi.org/10.1177/2053168015612246.

Flynn, Taylor. 2006. "The Ties That Don't Bind: Transgender Family Law and the Unmaking of Families." In *Transgender Rights*, edited by Paisley Currah, Richard Juang, and Shannon Minter, 32–50. Minneapolis: University of Minnesota Press.

Fominaya, Cristina. 2010. "Collective Identity in Social Movements: Central Concepts and Debates." *Sociology Compass* 4 (6): 393–404.

Ford, Zack. 2015. "Utah Bill Would Ban LGBT Discrimination, with Some Big Exceptions," *Think Progress*, March 6. Accessed: https://thinkprogress.org/utah-bill-would-ban-lgbt-discrimination-with-some-big-exceptions-767990f9a9fc

Fording, Richard C. 1997. "The Conditional Effect of Violence as a Political Tactic: Mass Insurgency, Welfare Generosity, and Electoral Context in the American States." *American Journal of Political Science* 41 (1): 1–29.

Foreman, Matt (former executive director, National Gay and Lesbian Task Force), interviewed by Jami Taylor, telephone, November 30, 2016.

Foxhall, Emily. 2015. "Actors, Politicians Speak Up for HERO as Vote Nears." *Houston Chronicle*, October 31.

France, David. 2000. "An Inconvenient Woman." *New York Times Magazine*, May 28. Accessed February 1, 2017. http://www.nytimes.com/2000/05/28/magazine/an-inconvenient-woman.html

Franciscan Alliance, Inc. et al. v. Burwell. 2016. U.S. District Court for the Northern District of Texas. 7:16-cv-00108-O.

Frey, Bruno S., and Lorenz Goette. 1998. "Does the Popular Vote Destroy Civil Rights?" *American Journal of Political Science* 42 (4): 1343–48.

Frye, Phyllis Randolph. 2000. "Facing Discrimination, Organizing for Freedom: The Transgender Community." In *Creating Change: Sexuality, Public Policy and Civil Rights*, edited by John D'Emilio, William B. Turner, and Urvashi Vaid, 451–68. New York: St. Martin's Press.

Furmansky, Dan (former executive director, Equality Maryland), interviewed by Jami Taylor, telephone, October 21, 2016.

Gaber, Mark (attorney, Jenner & Block), interviewed by Jami Taylor, telephone. October 19, 2016.

Galanter, Marc. 1974. "Why the 'Haves' Come Out Ahead: Speculations on the Limits of Legal Change." *Law & Society Review* 9 (1): 95–160.

Gallup. 2017a. "Gay and Lesbian Rights." Accessed April 3, 2017. http://www.gallup.com/poll/1651/gay-lesbian-rights.aspx

Gallup. 2017b. "US Support for Gay Marriage Edges to New High." Gallup, May 15 Accessed June 22, 2017. http://www.gallup.com/poll/210566/support-gay-marriage-edges-new-high.aspx

Gamble, Barbara S. 1997. "Putting Civil Rights to a Popular Vote." *American Journal of Political Science* 41 (1): 245–69.

Gamson, Joshua. 1995. "Must Identity Movements Self-Destruct? A Queer Dilemma." *Social Problems* 42 (3): 390–407.

Gamson, Joshua. 1998. *Freaks Talk Back: Tabloid Talk Shows and Sexual Nonconformity.* Chicago: University of Chicago Press.

Gamson, William. 1990. *The Strategy of Social Protest 2nd edition.* Belmont, CA: Wadsworth.

Garner, Andrew. 2013. "Ambivalence, the Intergroup Contact Hypothesis, and Attitudes about Gay Rights." *Politics & Policy* 41 (2): 241–66.

Garret, Elizabeth, and John G. Matsusaka. 2008. "Legal Landscape Database." Initiative and Referendum Institute and USC–Caltech Center for the Study of Politics. Accessed June 15, 2016. http://www.iandrinstitute.org/data.cfm

Garretson, Jeremiah J. 2014. "Changing with the Times: The Spillover Effects of Same-Sex Marriage Ballot Measures on Presidential Elections." *Political Research Quarterly* 67 (2): 280–92.

Garretson, Jeremiah J. 2015. "Exposure to the Lives of Lesbians and Gays and the Origin of Young People's Greater Support for Gay Rights." *International Journal of Public Opinion Research* 27 (2): 277–88.

Gash, Alison. 2015. *Below the Radar: How Silence Can Save Civil Rights.* New York: Oxford University Press.

Gates, Gary. 2011. "How Many People Are Lesbian, Gay, Bisexual, and Transgender?" Williams Institute. Accessed June 7, 2017. https://williamsinstitute.law.ucla.edu/wp-content/uploads/Gates-How-Many-People-LGBT-Apr-2011.pdf

Gates, Gary J. 2017. "In U.S., More Adults Identifying as LGBT." *Gallup.* January 11. Accessed May 30, 2018: http://news.gallup.com/poll/201731/lgbt-identification-rises.aspx

Geer, John. 1996. *From Tea Leaves To Opinion Polls: A Theory of Democratic Leadership.* New York: Columbia University Press.

Gerber, Elisabeth R. 1996. "Legislative Response to the Threat of Popular Initiatives." *American Journal of Political Science* 40 (1): 99–128.

Gerber, Elisabeth R. 1999. *The Populist Paradox: Interest Group Influence and the Promise of Direct Legislation.* Princeton: Princeton University Press.

Gerstein, Josh. 2017. "Sessions Vows Assault on Hate Crimes." *Politico*, June 29. Accessed October 6, 2017. http://www.politico.com/blogs/under-the-radar/2017/06/29/jeff-sessions-federal-hate-crime-laws-transgender-240087

GfK. 2015. "GFK KnowledgePanel." Accessed November 19, 2015. http://www.gfk.com/us/Solutions/consumer-panels/Pages/GfK-KnowledgePanel.aspx

G.G. v Gloucester County School Board, 132 F. Supp. 3d 736 (E.D. Va. Sept. 17, 2015).

G.G. v Gloucester County School Board, 822 F.3d 709 (4th Cir. 2016).

G.G. v. Gloucester County School Board, No. 4: 16–1733 (4th Cir. Apr. 7, 2017).

Gilens, Martin. 1999. *Why Americans Hate Welfare: Race, Media, and the Politics of Antipoverty Policy*. Chicago: University of Chicago Press.

Gilens, Martin. 2012. *Affluence and Influence: Economic Inequality and Political Power in America*. Princeton: Princeton University Press.

Gill, Todd. 2014a. "Duggar Family Spends $10,000 to Help Repeal 119 Candidates in Fayetteville City Council Election." *Fayetteville Flyer*, October 31. Accessed June 14, 2016. https://www.fayettevilleflyer.com/2014/10/31/duggar-family-spends-10000-to-help-repeal-119-candidates-in-city-council-election/

Gill, Todd. 2014b. "Fayetteville Clerk Certifies Enough Signatures for Civil Rights Vote." *Fayetteville Flyer*, September 29. Accessed June 14, 2016. https://www.fayettevilleflyer.com/2014/09/29/fayetteville-clerk-certifies-enough-signatures-for-civil-rights-vote/

Gill, Todd. 2014c. "Fayetteville Passes Civil Rights Ordinance." *Fayetteville Flyer*, August 20. Accessed June 14, 2016. https://www.fayettevilleflyer.com/2014/08/20/fayetteville-passes-anti-discrimination-ordinance/

Gill, Todd. 2014d. "Understanding the Dec. 9 Civil Rights Special Election." *Fayetteville Flyer*, December 1. Accessed June 14, 2016. https://www.fayettevilleflyer.com/2014/12/01/understanding-the-dec-9-civil-rights-special-election/

Gill, Todd. 2015. "Fayetteville Voters Approve Civil Rights Ordinance." *Fayetteville Flyer*, September 8. Accessed June 14, 2016. https://www.fayettevilleflyer.com/2015/09/08/fayetteville-voters-approve-civil-rights-ordinance/

Giugni, Marco G. 1998. "Was It Worth the Effort? The Outcomes and Consequences of Social Movements." *Annual Review of Sociology* 24: 371–93.

Gjorgievska, Aleksandra. 2014. "Laverne Cox Is the First Transgender Person Nominated for an Emmy—She Explains Why That Matters." *Time*, July 10. Accessed July 14, 2016. http://time.com/2973497/laverne-cox-emmy/

GLAAD. 2016. "GLAAD Works with Hollywood to Help Create Transgender Roles and with Casting Transgender Actors." Accessed June 12, 2017. https://www.glaad.org/blog/glaad-works-hollywood-help-create-transgender-roles-and-casting-transgender-actors

GLAD. 2013. "LGBT Groups Challenge Medicare Exclusion of Transgender Care." Accessed October 8, 2017. https://www.glad.org/post/lgbt-groups-challenge-medicare-exclusion-transgender-care/

Gledhill, Lynda. 2005. "Schwarzenegger Vetoes Gay Marriage Bill as Promised." *San Francisco Chronicle*, September 29. Accessed January 18, 2017. http://www.sfgate.com/news/article/Schwarzenegger-vetoes-gay-marriage-bill-as-2605909.php

Glenn v. Brumby, 663 F.3d 1312 (11th Cir. 2011).

Goad, Benjamin. 2013. "Feds Unveil New Policy for Transgender People to Update Gender in Records." *The Hill*, June 15. Accessed May 30, 2017. http://thehill.com/regulation/administration/305799-feds-unveil-new-policy-for-transgender-people-to-change-sex-in-social-security-records

Goins v. West Group 635 N.W.2d 717 (Minn. 2001).

Goodridge v. Department of Public Health, 798 N.E.2d 941 (Mass. 2003).

Gooren, Louis and Mathijs Bunck. 2004. "Transsexuals and Competitive Sports." *European Journal of Endocrinology* 151: 425–29.

Gorman, Steve. 2016. "U.S. Judge Blocks Transgender, Abortion-Related Obamacare Protections." Reuters, December 31. Accessed January 18, 2017. http://www.reuters.com/article/us-usa-obamacare-idUSKBN14L0OP

Gossett, Charles. 1999. "Dillon's Rule and Gay Rights: State Control over Local Efforts to Protect the Rights of Lesbians and Gay Men." In *Gays and Lesbians in the Democratic Process: Public Policy, Public Opinion, and Political Representation*, edited by Ellen Riggle and Barry Tadlock, 62–88. New York: Columbia University Press.

Graf, Amy. 2013. "Transgender Girl, 11, Writes Inspirational Response to Obama Inaugural Speech." *SFGate.com*, January 25. Accessed January 25, 2017. http://blog.sfgate.com/sfmoms/2013/01/25/transgender-girl-11-writes-inspirational-response-to-obama-inaugural-speech/

Graham, Jeff (executive director, Georgia Equality), interviewed by Jami Taylor, telephone, May 23, 2016.

Gramlich, John. 2017. "5 Facts about Crime in the U.S." Fact Tank: *News in the Numbers*, February 21. Pew Research Center. http://www.pewresearch.org/fact-tank/2017/02/21/5-facts-about-crime-in-the-u-s/

Grant, Jaime, Lisa Mottet, and Justin Tanis. 2011. *Injustice at Every Turn: A Report of the National Transgender Survey*. Washington, DC: National Gay and Lesbian Task Force. Accessed March 28, 2012. http://www.thetaskforce.org/downloads/reports/reports/ntds_full.pdf

Gray, Virginia, and David Lowery. 1996. *The Population Ecology of Interest Representation: Lobbying Communities in the American States*. Ann Arbor: University of Michigan Press.

Green, Emma. 2017. "Why the Trump Administration Won't Ask about LGBT Americans on the 2020 Census." *Atlantic*, March 29. Accessed October 8, 2017. https://www.theatlantic.com/politics/archive/2017/03/trump-census-lgbt/521229/

Green, Jamison (former president, World Professional Association for Transgender Health), interviewed by Jami Taylor, telephone, October 1, 2016.

Green, Jamison. 1998. "FTM: An Emerging Voice." In *Current Concepts in Transgender Identity*, edited by Dallas Denny, 145–62. New York: Garland Publishing.

Green, Jeff. 2016. "Gay Political Power Reaching Record as U.S. Attitudes Shift." *Bloomberg Politics*, July 11. Accessed January 4, 2017. https://www.bloomberg.com/politics/articles/2016-07-11/gay-political-power-reaching-record-as-u-s-attitudes-shift

Green, Richard. 1998a. "Conclusion to Transsexualism and Sex Reassignment: Reflections at 25 Years." In *Current Concepts in Transgender Identity*, edited by Dallas Denny, 419–23. New York: Garland Publishing.

Green, Richard. 1998b. "Mythological, Historical, and Cross-Cultural Aspects of Transsexualism." In *Current Concepts in Transgender Identity*, edited by Dallas Denny, 3–14. New York: Garland Publishing.

Green, Richard. 2000. "Family Co-occurrence of 'Gender Dysphoria': Ten Sibling or Parent-Child Pairs." *Archives of Sexual Behavior* 29 (5): 499–507.

Greenberg, Julie. 1999. "Defining Male and Female: Intersexuality and the Collision between Law and Biology." *Arizona Law Review* 41: 265–78.

Greenberg, Julie, and Marybeth Herald. 2005. "You Can't Take It with You: Constitutional Consequences of Interstate Gender-Identity Rulings." *Washington Law Review* 80 (4): 819–85.

Gregory, Alice. 2015. "Has the Fashion Industry Reached a Transgender Turning Point?" *Vogue*, April 25. Accessed July 14, 2016. http://www.vogue.com/13253741/andreja-pejic-transgender-model/

Griffin, Pat, and Helen Carroll. 2011. "NCAA Inclusion of Transgender Student-Athletes." NCAA Office of Inclusion. https://www.ncaa.org/sites/default/files/Transgender_Handbook_2011_Final.pdf

Grossman, Matt, and Brendon Swedlow. 2015. "Judicial Contributions to US National Policy Change since 1945." *Journal of Law and Courts* 3 (Spring): 1–35.

Gurley, Dan (former Republican National Committee field director, deputy political director 2004), interviewed by Jami Taylor, Raleigh, NC, May 9, 2016.

Gurman, Sadie. 2017. "Justice Dept. to Help in Iowa Case of Slain Transgender Teen." *ABC News*, October 15. http://abcnews.go.com/Politics/wireStory/justice-dept-iowa-case-slain-transgender-teen-50498650

Gurrieri, Vin. 2017. "HHS Wins Stay in Suit Challenging Transgender Bias Rule." *Law360*, July 10. Accessed October 7, 2017. https://www.law360.com/articles/942852/hhs-wins-stay-in-suit-challenging-transgender-bias-rule

Ha, Nathan Q., Shari L. Dworkin, Maria Jose Martinez-Patino, Alan D. Rogol, Vernon Rosario, Francisco J. Sanchez, Alison Wrynn, and Eric Vilain. 2014. "Hurdling over Sex? Sport, Science, and Equity." *Archives of Sexual Behavior* 43 (6): 1035–42.

Haider-Markel, Donald P. 1997. "Interest Group Survival: Shared Interests versus Competition for Resources." *Journal of Politics* 59 (3): 903–12.

Haider-Markel, Donald P. 1998. "The Politics of Social Regulatory Policy: State and Federal Hate Crime Policy and Implementation Effort." *Political Research Quarterly* 51 (1): 69–88.

Haider-Markel, Donald P. 2001. "Policy Diffusion as a Geographical Expansion of the Scope of Political Conflict: Same-Sex Marriage Bans in the 1990s." *State Politics & Policy Quarterly* 1 (1): 5–26.

Haider-Markel, Donald P. 2002. "Regulating Hate: State and Local Influences on Law Enforcement Actions Related to Hate Crime." *State Politics and Policy Quarterly* 2 (2):126–60.

Haider-Markel, Donald P. 2006. "Hate Crimes." In *Social Issues in America: An Encyclopedia*, edited by James Ciment, 815–25. Armonk, NY: M. E. Sharpe.

Haider-Markel, Donald P. 2007. "Representation and Backlash: The Positive and Negative Influence of Descriptive Representation." *Legislative Studies Quarterly* 32 (1): 107–34.

Haider-Markel, Donald P. 2010. *Out and Running: Gay and Lesbian Candidates, Elections, and Policy Representation*. Washington, DC: Georgetown University Press.

Haider-Markel, Donald P., and Mark R. Joslyn. 2005. "Attributions and the Regulation of Marriage: Considering the Parallels between Race and Homosexuality." *PS: Political Science and Politics* 38 (2): 233–40.

Haider-Markel, Donald P., and Mark R. Joslyn. 2008. "Understanding Beliefs about the Origins of Homosexuality and Subsequent Support for Gay Rights: An Empirical Test of Attribution Theory." *Public Opinion Quarterly* 72 (2): 291–310.

Haider-Markel, Donald P., and Mark R. Joslyn. 2013. "Politicizing Biology: Social Movements, Parties, and the Case of Homosexuality." *Social Science Journal* 50 (4): 603–15.

Haider-Markel, Donald P., Mark R. Joslyn, and Chad J. Kniss. 2000. "Minority Group

Interests and Political Representation: Gay Elected Officials in the Policy Process." *Journal of Politics* 62 (2): 568–77.

Haider-Markel, Donald P., and Kenneth J. Meier. 1996. "The Politics of Gay and Lesbian Rights: Expanding the Scope of the Conflict." *Journal of Politics* 58 (2): 332–49.

Haider-Markel, Donald P, and Kenneth J. Meier. 2003. "Legislative Victory, Electoral Uncertainty: Explaining Outcomes in the Battles over Lesbian and Gay Civil Rights." *Review of Policy Research* 20 (4): 671–90.

Haider-Markel, Donald P., Patrick Miller, Andrew Flores, Daniel C. Lewis, Barry Tadlock, and Jami K. Taylor. 2017. "Bringing 'T' to the Table: Understanding Individual Support of Transgender Candidates for Public Office." *Politics, Groups, and Identities* 5 (3): 399–417.

Haider-Markel, Donald P., and Sean P. O'Brien. 1997. "Creating a 'Well Regulated Militia': Policy Responses to Paramilitary Groups in the American States." *Political Research Quarterly* 50 (3): 551–65.

Haider-Markel, Donald P., and Sean P. O'Brien. 1999. "Values in Conflict: Local Government Response to Hate Crime." In *Culture Wars and Local Politics*, edited by Elaine B. Sharp, 137–57. Lawrence: University Press of Kansas.

Haider-Markel, Donald P., Alana Querze, and Kara Lindaman. 2007. "Lose, Win, or Draw? A Reexamination of Direct Democracy and Minority Rights." *Political Research Quarterly* 60 (2): 304–14.

Haider-Markel, Donald P., and Jami K. Taylor. 2016. "Two Steps Forward, One Step Back: The Slow Forward Dance of LGBT Rights in America," In *After Marriage Equality: The Future of LGBT Rights*, edited by Carlos A. Ball, 42–72. New York: New York University Press.

Haidt, Jonathan, Clark McCauley, and Paul Rozin. 1994. "Individual Differences in Sensitivity to Disgust: A Scale Sampling Seven Domains of Disgust Elicitors." *Personality and Individual Differences* 16 (5): 701–13.

Halberstam, Judith. 1998. "Transgender Butch: Butch/FTM Border Wars and the Masculine Continuum." *GLQ: A Journal of Gay & Lesbian Studies* 4 (2): 287–310.

Halley, Janet. 1994. "Sexual Orientation and the Politics of Biology: A Critique of the Argument from Immutability." *Stanford Law Review* 46 (3): 503–68.

Hamblin, James. 2017. "The Cost of Banning Transgender Service Members. *Atlantic*, July 26. Accessed October 8, 2017. https://www.theatlantic.com/health/archive/2017/07/things-that-cost-more-than-medical-care-for-transgender-soldiers/534945/

Hansen, Kristina. 2017. "Oregon Governor Signs Transgender Equity Bill into Law." Associated Press, May 31. Accessed May 31, 2017. https://www.usnews.com/news/best-states/oregon/articles/2017–05–31/oregon-governor-signs-transgender-equity-bill-into-law

Harrison, Brian, and Melissa Michelson. 2017. *Listen, We Need to Talk: How to Change Attitudes about LGBT Rights*. New York: Oxford University Press.

Harrison, Steve. 2016. "What Gov. McCrory's Executive HB2 Order Does and Doesn't Do." *Charlotte Observer*, April 13. Accessed May 25, 2017. http://www.charlotteobserver.com/news/politics-government/article71414247.html

Harrison, Steve. 2017. "Advocates Disagree about How Sweeping Cooper's Transgender Bathroom Order Would Be." *Charlotte Observer*, October 20. Accessed November 12,

2017. http://www.charlotteobserver.com/news/politics-government/article180056436.html

Hart, Lindsay. 2014. "With Inadequate Protection under the Law, Transgender Students Fight to Access Restrooms in Public Schools Based on Their Gender Identity." *Northern Kentucky Law Review* 41: 315–37.

Hartocollis, Anemona. 2017. "A Transgender Student Won Her Battle. Now It's War." *New York Times*, April 2. Accessed June 28, 2017. https://www.nytimes.com/2017/04/02/us/transgender-students-township-illinois.html

Harvard College. 2016. "Single-Gender Organizations." http://www.harvard.edu/media-relations/media-resources/popular-topics/single-gender-social-organizations

Harvard Law Review. 2014. "Transgender Youth and Access to Gendered Spaces." *Harvard Law Review* 127 (6): 1722–45.

Haskell, John. 2001. *Direct Democracy or Representative Government? Dispelling the Populist Myth.* Boulder, CO: Westview Press.

Hatzenbuehler, Mark L., and Katherine M. Keyes. 2013. "Inclusive Anti-bullying Policies and Reduced Risk of Suicide Attempts in Lesbian and Gay Youth." Supplement to *Journal of Adolescent Health* 53 (1): S21–S6.

Heaney, Michael. 2004. "Outside the Issue Niche: The Multidimensionality of Interest Group Identity." *American Politics Research* 32 (6): 611–51.

Helderman, Rosalind. 2010a. "Virginia Attorney General to Colleges: End Gay Protections." *Washington Post*, March 5. Accessed January 22, 2017. http://www.washingtonpost.com/wp-dyn/content/article/2010/03/05/AR2010030501582.html?sid=ST2010031204121

Helderman, Rosalind. 2010b. "Virginia Governor's Anti-Bias Order Removes Language Regarding Sexual Orientation." *Washington Post*, February 9. Accessed January 22, 2017. http://www.washingtonpost.com/wp-dyn/content/article/2010/02/09/AR2010020903739.html

Hendricks, Michael L., and Rylan J. Testa. 2012. "A Conceptual Framework for Clinical Work with Transgender and Gender Nonconforming Clients: An Adaptation of the Minority Stress Model." *Professional Psychology-Research and Practice* 43: 460.

Henkle v. Gregory, 150 F. Supp. 2d 1067 (D. Nev. 2001).

Henningsson, Susanne, Lars Westberg, Staffan Nilsson, Bengt Lundström, Lisa Ekselius, Owe Bodlund, Eva Lindström, Monika Hellstrand, Roland Rosmond, Elias Eriksson, and Mikael Landén. 2005. "Sex Steroid Related Genes and Male-to-Female Transsexualism." *Psychoneuroendocrinology* 30 (7): 657–64.

Herbst, Susan. 1993. *Numbered Voices: How Opinion Polling Has Shaped American Politics.* Chicago: University of Chicago Press.

Herek, Gregory M. 2000. "Sexual Prejudice and Gender: Do Heterosexuals' Attitudes toward Lesbians and Gay Men Differ?" *Journal of Social Issues* 56 (2): 251–66.

Herek, Gregory M. 2002. "Gender Gaps in Public Opinion about Lesbians and Gay Men." *Public Opinion Quarterly* 66 (1): 40–66.

Herek, Gregory M., and John P. Capitanio. 1996. "'Some of My Best Friends': Intergroup Contact, Concealable Stigma, and Heterosexuals' Attitudes toward Gay Men and Lesbians." *Personality and Social Psychology Bulletin* 22: 412–24.

Herek, Gregory M., and Eric K. Glunt. 1993. "Interpersonal Contact and Heterosexuals' Attitudes toward Gay Men: Results from a National Survey." *Journal of Sex Research* 30 (3): 239–44.

Hersher, Rebecca. 2017. "Arkansas Supreme Court Strikes Down Local Anti-Discrimination Law." *NPR.org*, February 23. Accessed October 7, 2017. http://www.npr.org/sections/thetwo-way/2017/02/23/516702975/arkansas-supreme-court-strikes-down-local-anti-discrimination-law

Hertzog, Mark. 1996. *The Lavender Vote: Lesbians, Gay Men, and Bisexuals in American Electoral Politics*. New York: New York University Press.

Hetherington, Marc J., and Jonathan D. Weiler. 2009. *Authoritarianism and Polarization in American Politics*. Cambridge: Cambridge University Press.

Highland Local School District v. U.S. Dept. of Education, No. 2:16-CV-524 (S.D. Oh. September 26, 2016).

Hill, Darryl B., and Brian L. B. Willoughby. 2005. "The Development and Validation of the Genderism and Transphobia Scale." *Sex Roles* 53 (7–8): 531–44.

Hillman, Betty Luther. 2011. "'The Most Profoundly Revolutionary Act a Homosexual Can Engage In': Drag and the Politics of Gender Presentation in the San Francisco Gay Liberation Movement, 1964–1972." *Journal of the History of Sexuality* 20 (1): 153–81.

Hillman, Betty Luther. 2015. *Dressing for the Culture Wars: Style and the Politics of Self-Presentation*. Lincoln: University of Nebraska Press.

Hiltzik, Michael. 2000. "Through the Gender Labyrinth." *Los Angeles Times*, November 19. Accessed July 20, 2016. http://articles.latimes.com/2000/nov/19/magazine/tm-54188

Hodson, Gordon, and Kimberly Costello. 2007. "Interpersonal Disgust, Ideological Orientations, and Dehumanization as Predictors of Intergroup Attitudes." *Psychological Science* 18 (8): 691–98.

Holbrook, Thomas M., and Emily Van Dunk. 1993. "Electoral Competition in the American States." *American Political Science Review* 87 (4): 955–62.

Holden, Dominic. 2016a. "Federal Appeals Court Considers Trans Student's Right to Use Boys Restroom." *BuzzFeed*, January 27.

Holden, Dominic. 2016b. "Transgender Student Settles Locker Room Case with University of Pittsburgh." *BuzzFeed*, March 29.

Holian, David B. 2004. "He's Stealing My Issues! Clinton's Crime Rhetoric and the Dynamics of Issue Ownership." *Political Behavior* 26 (2): 95–124.

Hollingsworth v. Perry 570 U.S. __(2013).

Holloway v. Arthur Andersen 566 F.2d 659 (9th Cir. 1977).

Hood, John (president, John William Pope Foundation), interviewed by Jami Taylor, telephone, September 15, 2016.

Horberg, E. J., Christopher Oveis, Dacher Keltner, and Adam B. Cohen. 2009. "Disgust and the Moralization of Purity." *Journal of Personality and Social Psychology* 97 (6): 963–76.

Howard, Robert M., and Amy Steigerwalt. 2012. *Judging Law and Policy: Courts and Policymaking in the American Political System*. New York: Routledge.

Howell, William G., and Kenneth R. Mayer. 2005. "The Last 100 Days." *Presidential Studies Quarterly* 35 (3): 533–53.

Human Rights Campaign. 2002. "Human Rights Campaign Survey." Lake Snell Perry and Associates, pollster.

Human Rights Campaign. 2005. "Equality from State to State 2005." Accessed January 21, 2017. http://www.hrc.org/files/assets/resources/2005statetostate.pdf

Human Rights Campaign. 2010a. "Matthew Shepard and James Byrd, Jr. Hate Crimes Prevention Act." Washington, DC: Human Rights Campaign. http://www.hrc.org/resources/matthew-shepard-and-james-byrd-jr.-hate-crimes-prevention-act

Human Rights Campaign. 2010b. "San Francisco Transgender Benefit." Accessed June 4, 2017. http://www.hrc.org/resources/san-francisco-transgender-benefit

Human Rights Campaign. 2011. "Human Rights Campaign Survey" Greenberg Quinlan Rosner Research, pollster. Cornell University, Ithaca, NY: Roper Center for Public Opinion Research, iPOLL, distributor. Accessed March 28, 2017.

Human Rights Campaign. 2014. "With Executive Order, Obama Takes His Place in History." Accessed January 29, 2017. http://www.hrc.org/blog/with-executive-order-obama-takes-his-place-in-history

Human Rights Campaign. 2015. "2015 Municipal Equality Index." Washington, DC: Human Rights Campaign.

Human Rights Campaign. 2016a. "Cities and Counties with Non-Discrimination Ordinances That Include Gender Identity." Accessed May 9, 2017. http://www.hrc.org/resources/cities-and-counties-with-non-discrimination-ordinances-that-include-gender

Human Rights Campaign. 2016b. "Maps of State Laws & Policies 2016." December 1. http://www.hrc.org/state_maps

Human Rights Campaign. 2016c. "Obama Administration Policy Advancements on Behalf of LGBT Americans." Accessed May 26, 2016. http://www.hrc.org/resources/obama-administration-policy-legislative-and-other-advancements-on-behalf-of

Human Rights Campaign. 2017a. "Corporate Equality Index: List of Businesses with Transgender-Inclusive Health Insurance Benefits." Accessed June 4, 2017. http://www.hrc.org/resources/corporate-equality-index-list-of-businesses-with-transgender-inclusive-heal

Human Rights Campaign. 2017b. "New HRC Poll: Improving Favorability toward Transgender People." Accessed October 4, 2017. https://www.hrc.org/blog/new-hrc-poll-improving-favorability-toward-transgender-people

Human Rights Campaign. 2017c. "School Anti-Bullying." Washington, DC: Human Rights Campaign.

Human Rights Campaign. 2017d. "State Maps of Laws & Policies." Accessed February 22, 2017. http://www.hrc.org/state-maps

Human Rights Watch. 2016. "'Like Walking through a Hailstorm': Discrimination Against LGBT Youth in US Schools." New York: Human Rights Watch.

Hyman v. City of Louisville, 132 F.Supp.2d 528 (2001).

In re Application for Marriage License for Nash, 2003-Ohio-7221.

In re Estate of Gardiner, 42P.3d 120 (Kan. 2002).

In re Jose Mauricio Lovo-Lara, 23 I&N Dec. 746 (BIA 2005).

In re Ladrach, 32 Ohio Misc.2d 6 (1987).

Internal Revenue Service. 2005. "Office of Chief Counsel Internal Revenue Service Memorandum Number: 200603025." Accessed January 28, 2017. https://www.irs.gov/pub/irs-wd/0603025.pdf

Internal Revenue Service. 2011. "IRB No. 2011–47." Accessed June 4, 2017. https://www.irs.gov/pub/irs-aod/aod201103.pdf

Internal Revenue Service. 2017. "Political and Lobbying Activities." Accessed October 4, 2017. https://www.irs.gov/charities-non-profits/charitable-organizations/political-and-lobbying-activities

Ishak, Mohd. Shuhaimi Bin Haji, and Sayed Sikandar Shah Haneef. 2014. "Sex Reassignment Technology: The Dilemma of Transsexuals in Islam and Christianity." *Journal of Religion and Health* 53 (2): 520–37.

IowaPolitics.com. 2009. "U.S. Rep. King: 'Thought Crimes' Bill Will Damage Religious Freedom in America." *IowaPolitics.com*, April 28. Accessed: https://web.archive.org/web/20090520131111/http://www.iowapolitics.com/index.iml?Article=156914

Jackman, Mary, and Marie Crane. 1986. "'Some of My Best Friends are Black . . .': Interracial Friendship and Whites' Racial Attitudes." *Public Opinion Quarterly* 50 (4): 459–86.

Jacobs, Ethan. 2008. "Scott to Head MTPC, HRC and Local Orgs Provide Support." *Bay Windows*, July 12. Accessed January 4, 2017. http://www.baywindows.com/scott-to-head-mtpc-hrc-and-local-orgs-provide-financial-support-54721

Jagose, Annamarie. 1996. *Queer Theory: An Introduction.* New York: New York University Press.

James, Sandy, Jody Herman, Sue Rankin, Mara Keisling, Lisa Mottet, and Ma'ayan Anafi. 2016. *The Report of the 2015 U.S. Transgender Survey.* Washington, DC: National Center for Transgender Equality. Accessed May 9, 2017. http://www.transequality.org/sites/default/files/docs/usts/USTS%20Full%20Report%20-%20FINAL%201.6.17.pdf

Jarvis, Craig, Colin Campbell, and Lynn Bonner. 2017. "NC Senate, House Approve HB2 Repeal Compromise." *News & Observer*, March 30. Accessed October 8, 2017. http://www.newsobserver.com/news/politics-government/state-politics/article141656549.html

Jasper, James. 2010. "Cultural Approaches in the Sociology of Movements." In *Handbook of Social Movements across Disciplines*, edited by Bert Klandermans and Conny Roggeband, 59–109. Boston, MA: Springer.

Jenness, Valerie. 1995. "Social Movement Growth, Domain Expansion, and Framing Processes: The Gay/Lesbian Movement and Violence against Gays and Lesbians as a Social Problem." *Social Problems* 42 (1):145–70.

Jenness, Valerie, and Kendal Broad. 1997. *Hate Crimes: New Social Movements and the Politics of Violence.* Hawthorne, NY: Transaction Publishers.

Jenness, Valerie, and Ryken Grattet. 2001. *Making Hate a Crime: From Social Movement to Law Enforcement.* New York: Russell Sage Foundation.

Johnson, Chris. 2012. "HHS Affirms Trans Protections in Health Care Reform." *Washington Blade*, August 7. Accessed June 4, 2017. http://www.washingtonblade.com/2012/08/07/hhs-affirms-trans-protections-in-health-care-reform/

Johnson, Chris. 2016a. "Mass. Ballot Measure Seeking to Undo Trans Law Certified for 2018." *Washington Blade*, October 12. Accessed January 5. http://www.washingtonblade.com/2016/10/12/ballot-measure-seeking-to-overturn-mass-trans-law-certified-for-2018/

Johnson, Chris. 2016b. "State Advocates Reflect on Rift over Bathroom Protections." *Washington Blade*, November 7. Accessed June 18, 2017. http://www.washingtonblade.com/2016/11/07/state-groups-reflect-rift-bathroom-protections/

Johnson, Chris. 2017. "10 Years Later, Firestorm over Gay-Only ENDA Vote Still Informs Movement." *Washington Blade*, November 6. Accessed November 10, 2017. http://www.washingtonblade.com/2017/11/06/10-years-later-firestorm-over-gay-only-enda-vote-still-remembered/

Johnston, Hank, Enrique Larana, and Joseph R. Gusfield. 1994. "Identities, Grievances, and New Social Movements." In *New Social Movements*, edited by Hank Johnston, Enrique Larana, and Joseph R. Gusfield, 3–35. Philadelphia: Temple University Press.

Johnston, Richard, Kathleen Hall-Jamieson, and Diana Carole Mutz. 2008. "National Annenberg Election Survey." Annenberg Public Policy Center. https://services.annenbergpublicpolicycenter.org/naes08/phone/index.html

Johnston v. University of Pittsburgh, 97 F. Supp. 3d 657 (W.D. Pa. 2015), appeal dismissed (March 30, 2016).

Jones, Bethany Alice, Jon Arcelus, Walter Bouman, and Emma Haycraft. 2017. "Sport and Transgender People: A Systematic Review of the Literature Relating to Sport Participation and Competitive Sport Policies." *Sports Medicine* 47 (4): 701–16.

Jones, Philip Edward, Paul R. Brewer, Dannagal G. Young, Jennifer L. Lambe, and Lindsay H. Hoffman. 2018. "Explaining Public Opinion toward Transgender People, Rights, and Candidates." *Public Opinion Quarterly*. Online early view.

Jouvenal, Justin. 2017. "Federal Judge in D.C. Blocks Part of Trump's Transgender Military Ban." *Washington Post*, October 30. Accessed November 2, 2017. https://www.washingtonpost.com/local/public-safety/federal-judge-in-dc-blocks-part-of-trumps-transgender-military-ban/2017/10/30/41d41526-bd94-11e7-59c-fe2b598d8c00_story.html?utm_term=.8eda4c66d5dc

K.L v. Alaska Dept. of Admin., No. 3AN–11–05431 C, 2012 WL 2685183 (Alaska Sup. Ct. Mar.12, 2012).

Kane, Melinda D. 2007. "Timing Matters: Shifts in the Causal Determinants of Sodomy Law Decriminalization, 1961–1998." *Social Problems* 54 (2): 211–39.

Kantaras v. Kantaras, Case no. 2D03–1377 (Fla. App. 2004).

Kapitan, Craig. 2011. "Official Oppression Earns Ex-Cop a Year behind Bars." *San Antonio Express News*, January 18. http://www.mysanantonio.com/news/local_news/article/Official-oppression-earnsex-cop-a-year-behind-bars-963942.php

Kass, Dani. 2017. "Texas Judge Blocks ACA Transgender Rule." *Law360*, January 3. Accessed October 7, 2017. https://www.law360.com/articles/876664/texas-judge-blocks-aca-transgender-rule

Kastl v. Maricopa Cnty. Cmty. Coll. Dist., 325 Fed. Appx. 492 (9th Cir. 2009).

Katz, Jonathan. 2016. "What Happened to North Carolina?" *New York Times Magazine*, October 7. Accessed October 8, 2017. https://www.nytimes.com/2016/10/07/magazine/what-happened-to-north-carolina.html

Keck, Thomas M. 2009. "Beyond Backlash: Assessing the Impact of Judicial Decisions on LGBT Rights." *Law and Society Review* 43 (1): 151–85.

Keisling, Mara (executive director, National Center for Transgender Equality), interviewed by Jami Taylor, telephone, April 29, 2017.

Kiley, Jocelyn, and Shiva Maniam. 2016. "Lesbian, Gay, and Bisexual Voters Remain a Solidly Democratic Bloc." Pew Research Center, October 25. Accessed June 21, 2017. http://www.pewresearch.org/fact-tank/2016/10/25/lesbian-gay-and-bisexual-voters-remain-a-solidly-democratic-bloc/

Kimmel, Adele P. 2015. "TItle IX: An Imperfect but Vital Tool to Stop Bullying of LGBT Students." *Yale Law Journal* 125 (7): 2006–36.

King, Dave. 1996. "Cross-dressing, Sex-changing and the Press." In *Blending Genders: Social Aspects of Cross-dressing and Sex-changing*, edited by Richard Ekins and Dave King, 133–50. London: Routledge.

King, Gary, James Honaker, Anne Joseph, and Kenneth Scheve. 2001. "Analyzing Incomplete Political Science Data: An Alternative Algorithm for Multiple Imputation." *American Political Science Review* 95 (1): 49–69.

King, Mark E., Sam Winter, and Beverley Webster. 2009. "Contact Reduces Transprejudice: A Study on Attitudes towards Transgenderism and Transgender Civil Rights in Hong Kong." *International Journal of Sexual Health* 21 (1): 17–34.

King v. Governor of N.J., 767 F.3d 216 (3d Cir. 2014).

Kingdon, John W. 1984. *Agendas, Alternatives, and Public Policies*. Boston: Little, Brown.

Kinnard, Meg. 2014. "Teen Sues DMV after Being Told to Remove Makeup." *Post and Courier*, September 1. Accessed January 28, 2017. http://www.postandcourier.com/politics/teen-sues-dmv-after-being-told-to-remove-makeup/article_b836b498–70ad-5da4–94f6–8c9e28a7afce.html

Kiritsy, Laura. 2005. "Rep Backs Law Protecting Gender Identity." *Bay Windows*, November 3. Accessed January 4, 2017. http://www.baywindows.com/rep-backs-law-protecting-gender-identity-66229

Kitschelt, Herbert. 1986. "Political Opportunity Structures and Political Protest: Antinuclear Movements in Four Democracies." *British Journal of Political Science* 16 (1): 57–85

Klarman, Michael J. 2013. *From The Closet to the Altar: Courts, Backlash, and the Struggle for Same-Sex Marriage*. New York: Oxford University Press.

Klarner, Carl E. 2014. Klarner Politics 2014 Accessed May 12, 2014. http://www.indstate.edu/polisci/klarnerpolitics.htm

Klarner, Carl. 2013. "Other Scholars' Competitiveness Measures." doi:hdl:1902.1/22519, Harvard Dataverse, V1, UNF:5:we2ixYigyI3GVaDGKsU58A==.

Kleinschmidt, Mark (former mayor of Chapel Hill, North Carolina), interviewed by Jami Taylor, telephone, June 15, 2017.

Klimas, Jacqueline, and Bryan Bender. 2018. "Trump Moves to Ban Most Transgender Troops." *Politico*, March 23. Accessed May 23, 2018 from https://www.politico.com/story/2018/03/23/trump-transgender-troops-ban-483434

Koon, David. 2015. "Fayetteville City Council Approves New LGBT Protection Ordinance, Referendum Set for Sept. 8." *Arkansas Times*, June 16.

Korematsu v. U.S. 323 U.S. 214 (1944).

Korte, Gregory. 2016. "Judge in Texas Blocks Obama Transgender Bathroom Rules." *USA Today*, August 22. Accessed January 18, 2017. http://www.usatoday.com/story/news/politics/2016/08/22/texas-judge-temporarily-blocks-obamas-transgender-directive/89094722/

Kosciw, Joseph G., Emily A. Greytak, Noreen M. Giga, Christian Villenas, and David J. Danischewski. 2015. "The 2015 National School Climate Survey: The Experience of Lesbian, Gay, Bisexual, Transgender, and Queer Youth in Our Nation's Schools." New York: GLSEN.

Kosilek v. O'Brien, 774 F.3d 63 (1st Cir. 2014).

Kosilek v. Spencer, 889 F. Supp. 2d 190 (D. Mass., 2012).

Kosilek v. Spencer. 2014. 1st Circuit. 12–2194.

Kousser, Thad. 2005. *Term Limits and the Dismantling of State Legislative Professionalism.* New York: Cambridge University Press.

Kousser, Thad, and Justin H. Phillips. 2012. *The Power of American Governors: Winning on Budgets and Losing on Policy.* New York: Cambridge University Press.

Koyama, Emi. 2006. "Whose Feminism Is It Anyway? The Unspoken Racism of the Transgender Inclusion Debate." In *The Transgender Studies Reader,* edited by Susan Stryker and Stephen Whittle, 698–705. New York: Routledge.

Kraft, Michael, and Scott Furlong. 2015. *Public Policy: Politics, Analysis and Alternatives, 5th Edition.* Thousand Oaks, CA: CQ Press.

Kralik, Joellen. 2017. "'Bathroom Bill' Legislative Tracking." Washington, DC: National Conference of State Legislatures. http://www.ncsl.org/research/education/-bathroom-bill-legislative-tracking635951130.aspx

Kramer, Larry. 1985. *The Normal Heart.* New York: Samuel French.

Kraus, Cynthia. 2015. "Classifying Intersex in DSM-5: Critical Reflections on Gender Dysphoria." *Archives of Sexual Behavior* 44 (5): 1147–63.

Kreitzer, Rebecca J., Allison J. Hamilton, and Caroline J. Tolbert. 2014. "Does Policy Adoption Change Opinions on Minority Rights? The Effects of Legalizing Same-Sex Marriage." *Political Research Quarterly* 67 (4): 795–808.

Kruijver, Frank, Jiang-Ning Zhou, Chris W. Pool, Michel A. Hofman, Louis J. G. Gooren, and Dick F. Swaab. 2000. "Male to Female Transsexuals Have Female Neuron Numbers in a Limbic Nucleus." *Journal of Clinical Endocrinology Metabolism* 85 (2): 818–27.

Kruse, Michael. 2016. "My Country Accepts Me as a Woman: Hillary Clinton Was the Force behind a Little-Known Breakthrough in Transgender Rights. So Why Doesn't She Talk About It?" *Politico,* July 1. Accessed May 25, 2017. http://www.politico.com/magazine/story/2016/07/hillary-clinton-2016-transgender-rights-passport-policy-state-department-lgbt-equality-214007

Lake, Snell, Perry and Associates. 2002.July 2002 HRC Transgender Poll.

Lambda Legal. 2015. "Fact Sheet." Accessed May 31, 2017. https://www.lambdalegal.org/es/publication-category/fact-sheet?page=7

Lambda Legal. 2016. "Professional Organization Statements Supporting Transgender People in Health Care." Accessed June 4, 2017. http://www.lambdalegal.org/sites/default/files/publications/downloads/ll_trans_professional_statements.rtf_.pdf

Lambda Legal. 2017a. "Carcaño v. Cooper (formerly Carcaño v. McCrory)." Accessed November 12, 2017. https://www.lambdalegal.org/in-court/cases/nc_carcano-v-mccrory

Lambda Legal. 2017b. "Lambda Legal Lawsuit Forces End to School District Anti-Transgender Bathroom Policy." Accessed October 9, 2017. https://www.lambdalegal.org/news/pa_20170801_pine-richland-settlement

Lambda Legal. 2017c. "Zzyym v. Tillerson (formerly Zzyym v. Kerry)." Accessed October 8, 2017. https://www.lambdalegal.org/in-court/cases/co_zzyym-v-tillerson

Lamothe, Dan. 2017a. "Donald Trump Administration Delays Plan to Start Allowing Transgender Recruits to Join the US Military." *Independent*, July 1. Accessed October 8, 2017. http://www.independent.co.uk/news/world-0/america-donald-trump-james-mattis-transgender-military-a7818426.html

Lamothe, Dan. 2017b. "Transgender Ban Frozen as Mattis Moves Forward with New Review of Options." *Washington Post*, August 29. Accessed October 8, 2017. https://www.washingtonpost.com/news/checkpoint/wp/2017/08/29/pentagon-chief-mattis-freezes-trumps-ban-on-transgender-troops-calls-for-more-study/?utm_term=.fa1ce7639592

Landers, Melissa, and Gary Fine. 1996. "Learning Life's Lessons in Tee Ball: The Reinforcement of Gender and Status in Kindergarten Sport." *Sociology of Sport Journal* 13 (1): 87–93.

Lascher, Edward L., Jr., Michael G. Hagen, and Steven A. Rochlin. 1996. "Gun behind the Door? Ballot Initiatives, State Policies, and Public Opinion." *Journal of Politics* 58 (3): 760–75.

Lavers, Michael. 2013. "Herring Unveils LGBT Agenda." *Washington Blade*, April 5. Accessed January 22, 2017. http://www.washingtonblade.com/2013/04/05/herring-unveils-lgbt-agenda-gay-virginia/

Lavers, Michael. 2015. "Herring: Va. School Boards Can Ban Anti-LGBT Discrimination." *Washington Blade*, March 5. Accessed January 22, 2017. http://www.washingtonblade.com/2015/03/05/herring-va-school-boards-can-ban-anti-lgbt-discrimination/

Lavers, Michael. 2017. "Fed'l court in California latest to rule against Trump's trans ban." *Washington Blade,* December 23. Accessed January 22, 2018 from http://www.washingtonblade.com/2017/12/23/fedl-court-in-california-latest-to-rule-against-trumps-trans-ban/Lawrence v. Texas, 539 U.S. 558 (2003).

Lax, Jeffrey R., and Justin H. Phillips. 2009. "Gay Rights in the States: Public Opinion and Policy Responsiveness." *American Political Science Review* 103 (3): 367–86.

Lax, Jeffrey R., and Justin H. Phillips. 2012. "The Democratic Deficit in the States." *American Journal of Political Science* 56 (1): 148–66.

Laythe, Brian, Deborah Finkel, and Lee A. Kirkpatrick. 2001. "Predicting Prejudice from Religious Fundamentalism and Right-Wing Authoritarianism: A Multiple-Regression Approach." *Journal for the Scientific Study of Religion* 40 (1): 1–10.

LeBlanc, Steve. 2017. "15 Attorneys General Oppose Trump Transgender Military Ban." *Star Tribune*, October 16. http://m.startribune.com/15-attorneys-general-oppose-trump-transgender-military-ban/451132413/?section=nation

Lee, Jason. 2012. "Lost in Transition: The Challenges of Remedying Transgender Employment Discrimination under Title VII." *Harvard Journal of Law & Gender* 35: 423–61.

Leemann, Lucas, and Fabio Wasserfallen. 2016. "The Democratic Effect of Direct Democracy." *American Political Science Review* 110 (4): 750–63.

Leff, Lisa. 2016. "The Fight over Transgender Rights in School Restrooms Intensifies." Associated Press, February 22.

LeGaL Foundation. 2016. "Mindless Bureaucracy Temporarily Foiled as District Judge

Refuses to Dismiss a Challenge to Gender-Binary Requirement on U.S. Passports." *LGBT Law Notes.* Accessed May 31, 2017. http://www.nyls.edu/faculty/wp-content/uploads/sites/148/2016/12/LGBTLN.12.20164.pdf

Lenz, Gabriel. 2009. "Learning and Opinion Change, Not Priming: Reconsidering the Priming Hypothesis." *American Journal of Political Science* 53 (4): 821–37.

Levasseur, M. Dru. 2015. "Gender Identity Defines Sex: Updating the Law to Reflect Modern Medical Science Is the Key to Transgender Rights." *Vermont Law Review* 39: 943–1004.

Levi, Jennifer, and Bennett Klein. 2006. "Pursuing Protection for Transgender People through Disability Laws." In *Transgender Rights*, edited by Paisley Currah, Richard Juang, and Shannon Price Minter, 74–92. Minneapolis: University of Minnesota Press.

Levi, Jennifer, and Daniel Redman. 2010. "The Cross-Dressing Case for Bathroom Equality." *Seattle University Law Review* 34: 133–71.

Lewis, Daniel C. 2011a. "Bypassing the Representational Filter? Minority Rights Policies under Direct Democracy Institutions in the U.S. States." *State Politics & Policy Quarterly* 11 (2): 198–222.

Lewis, Daniel C. 2011b. "Direct Democracy and Minority Rights: Same-Sex Marriage Bans in the U.S. States." *Social Science Quarterly* 92 (2): 364–83.

Lewis, Daniel C. 2013. *Direct Democracy and Minority Rights: A Critical Assessment of the Tyranny of the Majority in the American States.* New York: Routledge.

Lewis, Daniel C., Andrew R. Flores, Donald P. Haider-Markel, Patrick R. Miller, Barry L. Tadlock, and Jami K. Taylor. 2017. "Degrees of Acceptance: Variation in Public Attitudes toward Segments of the LGBT Community." *Political Research Quarterly*, June 30. https://doi.org/10.1177/1065912917717352

Lewis, Daniel C., and Matthew L. Jacobsmeier. 2017. "Evaluating Policy Representation with Dynamic MRP Estimates: Direct Democracy and Same-Sex Relationship Policies in the U.S." *State Politics & Policy Quarterly* (Winter). Accessed November 12, 2017. https://doi.org/10.1177/1532440017739423

Lewis, Daniel C., Saundra K. Schneider, and William G. Jacoby. 2015. "The Impact of Direct Democracy on State Spending Priorities." *Electoral Studies* 40: 531–38.

Lewis, Daniel C., Jami K. Taylor, Brian DiSarro, and Matthew Jacobsmeier. 2014. "Is Transgender Policy Different? Policy Complexity, Policy Diffusion, and LGBT Non-discrimination Laws." In *Transgender Rights and Politics: Groups, Issue Framing, and Policy Adoption*, edited by Jami Kathleen Taylor and Donald P. Haider-Markel, 155–88. Ann Arbor: University of Michigan Press.

Lewis, Gregory B. 2003. "Black-White Differences in Attitudes toward Homosexuality and Gay Rights." *Public Opinion Quarterly* 67 (1): 59–78.

Lewis, Gregory B. 2009. "Does Believing Homosexuality Is Innate Increase Support for Gay Rights?" *Policy Studies Journal* 37 (4): 669–93.

Lewis, Gregory B. 2011. "The Friends and Family Plan: Contact with Gays and Support for Gay Rights." *Policy Studies Journal* 39: 217–38.

Lewis, Gregory B., and Charles W. Gossett. 2008. "Changing Public Opinion on Same-Sex Marriage: The Case of California." *Politics & Policy* 36 (1): 4–30.

LGBT Sports Foundation. 2016. "'All 50': The Transgender-Inclusive High School Sports and Activities Policy and Education Project." San Francisco: National Center for Lesbian Rights.

Light, Paul. 1984. "The Presidential Policy Stream." In *Public Policy: The Essential Readings*. 2nd edition, edited by Stella Theodoulou and Matthew Cahn, 221–30. Upper Saddle River, NJ: Pearson.

Light, Paul. 1999. *The President's Agenda: Domestic Policy Choice from Kennedy to Clinton*. Baltimore: Johns Hopkins University Press.

Lindblom, Charles. 1977. *Politics and Markets: The World's Political Economic Systems*. New York: Basic Books.

Lipsky, Michael. 1980. *Street-Level Bureaucracy: Dilemmas of the Individual in Public Services*. New York: Russell Sage Foundation.

Liptak, Adam. 2017. "Supreme Court Won't Hear Major Case on Transgender Rights." *New York Times*, March 6. Accessed June 5, 2017. https://www.nytimes.com/2017/03/06/us/politics/supreme-court-transgender-rights-case.html

Liptak, Adam. 2018. "In Narrow Decision, Supreme Court Sides With Baker Who Turned Away Gay Couple." *New York Times*, Jun 4. Accessed June 5, 2018 from https://www.nytimes.com/2018/06/04/us/politics/supreme-court-sides-with-baker-who-turned-away-gay-couple.html

Littleton v. Prange, 9 S.W.3d 233 (Tex. App 1999).

Ljunqvist, Arne, and Myron Genel, M. 2005. "Transsexual Athletes: When Is Competition Fair?" *Lancet* 366 (S1): S42–43.

Lopez, Nancy, and Vivian L. Gadsden. 2016. "Health Inequities, Social Determinants, and Intersectionality." Accessed June 15, 2017. https://nam.edu/wp-content/uploads/2016/12/Health-Inequities-Social-Determinants-and-Intersectionality.pdf

Lottes, Ilsa L., and Peter J. Kuriloff. 1994. "The Impact of College Experience on Political and Social Attitudes." *Sex Roles* 31 (1–2): 31–54.

Love v. Johnson, 146 F. Supp. 3d 848 (E. D. Mich. 2015).

Lowry, Bryan. 2016. "Kansas Weighs Proposal to Prevent Transgender People from Changing Birth Certificates." *Wichita Eagle*, May 12. Accessed May 31, 2017. http://www.kansas.com/news/politics-government/article77203467.html

Lusardi v. Dept. of the Army. Appeal No. 0120133395 (United States Equal Employment Opportunity Commission 2015). Accessed January 29, 2017. https://www.eeoc.gov/decisions/0120133395.txt

MacKenzie, Gordene. 1994. *Transgender Nation*. Bowling Green, OH: Bowling Green State University Popular Press.

Macy v. Department of Alcohol, Tobacco, Firearms and Explosives. Appeal No. 0120120821 (United States Equal Employment Opportunity Commission 2012). Accessed January 25, 2013. http://www.eeoc.gov/decisions/0120120821%20Macy%20v%20DOJ%20ATF.txt

Macy v. Holder. 2012. Appeal No. 0120120821 (United States Equal Employment Opportunity Commission 2012). Accessed January 29, 2017. https://www.eeoc.gov/decisions/0120120821%20Macy%20v%20DOJ%20ATF.txt

Madison, James. (1787) 1999a. "No. 10: The Same Subject Continued." In *The Federalist Papers*, edited by Alexander Hamilton, James Madison, and John Jay. New York: Penguin Books.

Madison, James. (1787) 1999b. "No. 51: The Structure of Government Must Furnish the Proper Checks and Balances Between the Different Departments." In *The Federalist Papers*, edited by Alexander Hamilton, John Madison, and John Jay. New York: Penguin Putnam.

Maffei v. Kolaeton Industry, Inc., 626 N.Y.S.2d 391 (N.Y. Sup. Ct. 1995).

Maine Legislature. 2000. LD 2239, SP 840, 119th Legislature. Accessed June 16, 2017. http://legislature.maine.gov/bills/search_ps.asp

Mair, Julie Samia, Shannon Frattaroli, and Stephen P. Teret. 2003. "New Hope for Victims of Prison Sexual Assault." *Journal of Law, Medicine & Ethics* 31 (4): 602–6.

Mallory, Christy, Amira Hasenbush, and Brad Sears. 2015. *Discrimination and Harassment by Law Enforcement Officers in the LGBT Community* . Los Angeles: Williams Institute. Accessed June 26, 2017. https://williamsinstitute.law.ucla.edu/wp-content/uploads/LGBT-Discrimination-and-Harassment-in-Law-Enforcement-March-2015.pdf

Maril, Robin (chief legislative counsel, Human Rights Campaign), interviewed by Jami Taylor, Washington DC, June 1, 2016.

Marimow, Ann. 2017. "Case of Virginia Transgender Teen Gavin Grimm Put Off by Appeals Court." *Washington Post*, August 2. Accessed October 6, 2017. https://www.washingtonpost.com/local/public-safety/case-of-virginia-transgender-teen-gavin-grimm-put-off-by-appeals-court/2017/08/02/4d49a254–77ad-11e7–8839-ec48ec4cae25_story.html?utm_term=.317acc678b2b

Markell, Jack (Governor of Delaware), interviewed by Jami Taylor, telephone, September 23, 2016.

Marmot, Michael. 2005. "Social Determinants of Health Inequalities." *Lancet* 365 (9464): 1099–1104.

Massachusetts Department of Elementary and Secondary Education. 2013. "Safe Schools Program for LGBTQ Students." Accessed June 2, 2017. http://www.doe.mass.edu/sfs/lgbtq/GenderIdentity.html

MassLive. 2011. "Gov. Deval Patrick Signs Transgender Protection Bill." Accessed May 9, 2017. http://www.masslive.com/news/index.ssf/2011/11/gov_deval_patrick_signs_transg.html

Mathis v. Fountain-Fort Carson School District 8. Charge No. P20130034X (Colo. Department of Regulatory Agencies, Division of Civil Rights June 17, 2013).

Matsusaka, John G. 1995. "Fiscal Effects of the Voter Initiative—Evidence from the Last 30 Years." *Journal of Political Economy* 103 (3): 587–623.

Matsusaka, John G. 2010. "Popular Control of Public Policy: A Quantitative Approach." *Quarterly Journal of Political Science* 5 (2): 133–67.

Matsusaka, John G., and Nolan M. McCarty. 2001. "Political Resource Allocation: Benefits and Costs of Voter Initiatives." *Journal of Law Economics & Organization* 17 (2): 413–48.

May, Charlie. 2017. "Republicans in Congress Quick to Criticize Trump's Ban of Transgender People in the Military." *Salon*, July 26. Accessed October 8, 2017. https://www.salon.com/2017/07/26/republicans-in-congress-quick-to-criticize-trumps-ban-of-transgender-people-in-the-military/

Mayer, Kenneth R. 1999. "Executive Orders and Presidential Power." *Journal of Politics* 61 (2): 445–66.

Mayhew, David R. 1974. *Congress: The Electoral Connection.* New Haven: Yale University Press.

McAdam, Doug. 1994. "Culture and Social Movements." In *New Social Movements: From Ideology to Identity,* edited by Enrique Laraña, Hank Johnston, and Joseph Gusfield, 36–57. Philadelphia: Temple University Press.

McAdam, Doug. 1995. "'Initiator' and 'Spinoff' Movements: Diffusion Processes in Protest Cycles." In *Repertoires and Cycles of Collective Action,* edited by Mark Traugott, 217–39. Durham, NC: Duke University Press.

McAdam, Doug, John D. McCarthy, and Mayer Zald. 1988. *Social Movements.* In *Handbook of Sociology,* edited by Neil Smelser, 695–737. Newbury Park, CA: Sage Publications.

McCammon, Holly J., Karen Campbell, Ellen Granberg, and Christine Mowery. 2001. "How Movements Win: Gendered Opportunity Structures and U.S. Women's Suffrage Movements, 1866 to 1919." *American Sociological Review* 66 (1): 49–70.

McCarthy, John, and Mayer Zald. 1973. *The Trend of Social Movements in America: Professionalization and Resource Mobilization.* Morristown, NJ: General Learning Press.

McCarthy, John, and Mayer Zald. 1977. "Resource Mobilization and Social Movements: A Partial Theory." *American Journal of Sociology* 82 (6): 1212–41.

McClosky, Herbert, and Alida Brill. 1983. *Dimensions of Tolerance: What Americans Believe about Civil Liberties.* New York: Russell Sage Foundation.

McClosky, Herbert, and John Zaller. 1984. *The American Ethos: Public Attitudes toward Capitalism and Democracy.* Cambridge: Harvard University Press.

McDonagh, Eileen, and Laura Pappano. 2008. *Playing with the Boys: Why Separate Is Not Equal in Sports.* New York: Oxford University Press.

McKinney, Jeffrey. 2005. "On the Margins: A Study of the Experiences of Transgender College Students." *Journal of Gay & Lesbian Issues in Education* 3 (1): 63–76.

Meier, Stacey, and Christine Labuski. 2013. "The Demographics of the Transgender Population." In *International Handbook on the Demography of Sexuality,* edited by Amanda Baumle, 289–327. New York: Springer.

Melucci, Alberto 1995. "The Process of Collective Identity." In *Social Movements and Culture,* edited by Hank Johnston and Bert Klandermans, 41–63. Minneapolis: University of Minnesota Press.

Messina, Ignazio. 2014. "Council OKs Buying Land to Woo Jeep; Another Unanimous Vote Adds Transgender Protections to Law." *Toledo Blade,* December 3. Accessed October 9, 2017. http://www.toledoblade.com/local/2014/12/03/Council-OKs-buying-land-to-woo-Jeep.html

Meyer, David. 2004. "Protest and Political Opportunities." *Annual Review of Sociology* 30: 125–45.

Meyer, David, and Douglas Imig. 1993. "Political Opportunity and the Rise and Decline of Interest Group Sectors." *Social Science Journal* 30: 253–70.

Meyer, David S., and Debra C. Minkoff. 2004. "Conceptualizing Political Opportunity." *Social Forces* 82: 1457–92.

Meyer, David, and Nancy Whittier. 1994. "Social Movement Spillover." *Social Problems* 41 (2): 277–98.

Meyer, Ilan H., Taylor N. T. Brown, Jody L. Herman, Sari L. Reisner, and Walter O. Bockting. 2017. "Demographic Characteristics and Health Status of Transgender Adults in

Select US Regions: Behavioral Risk Factor Surveillance System, 2014." *American Journal of Public Health* 107: 582–89.

Meyerowitz, Joanne. 2002. *How Sex Changed: A History of Transsexuality in the United States*. Cambridge: Harvard University Press.

Mezey, Susan Gluck. 2007. *Queers in Court: Gay Rights Law and Public Policy*. Lanham, MD: Rowman and Littlefield.

Mezey, Susan. 2009. *Gay Families and the Courts: The Quest for Equal Rights*. Lanham, MD: Rowman and Littlefield.

Michels, Holly. 2017. "Montana Transgender Bathroom Bill Killed in Committee; Ballot Initiative Vowed." *Independent Record*, March 27. Accessed October 7, 2017. http://helenair.com/news/politics/state/montana-transgender-bathroom-bill-killed-in-committee-ballot-initiative-vowed/article_37d2b2b6-a2c8-5b3c-98f0-b4073d19914a.html

Miles v. New York University, 979 F. Supp. 248 (S.D.N.Y. 1997).

Miller, Lisa R. and Eric A. Grollman. 2015. "The Social Costs of Gender Nonconformity for Transgender Adults: Implications for Discrimination and Health." *Sociological Forum* 30 (3): 809–31.

Miller, Patrick R., Andrew R. Flores, Donald Haider-Markel, Daniel C. Lewis, Barry Tadlock, and Jami K. Taylor. 2017. "Transgender Politics as Body Politics: Effects of Disgust Sensitivity and Authoritarianism on Transgender Rights Attitudes." *Politics, Groups, and Identities* 5 (1): 4–24.

Miller, William Ian. 1997. *The Anatomy of Disgust*. Cambridge: Harvard University Press.

Minkoff, Deborah. 1997. "The Sequencing of Social Movements." *American Sociological Review* 62 (5): 779–99.

Minkowitz, Donna. 1994. "Love Hurts." *Village Voice*, April 19, 24–30.

Minter, Shannon (legal director, National Center for Lesbian Rights), interviewed by Jami Taylor, telephone, May 24, 2016.

Minter, Shannon. 2003. *Representing Transsexual Clients: An Overview of Selected Legal Issues*. Accessed August 8, 2004. http://www.transgenderlaw.org/resources/translaw.htm

Minter, Shannon. 2006. "Do Transsexuals Dream of Gay Rights?" In *Transgender Rights*, edited by Paisley Currah, Richard Juang, and Shannon Price Minter. 141–70. Minneapolis: University of Minnesota Press.

Mintrom, Michael, and Phillipa Norman. 2009. "Policy Entrepreneurship and Policy Change." *Policy Studies Journal* 37 (4): 649–67.

Molloy, Parker Marie. 2014. "What Barney Frank Still Gets Wrong on ENDA." *Advocate*, October 1. https://www.advocate.com/commentary/2014/10/01/op-ed-what-barney-frank-still-gets-wrong-enda

Montgomery, David, and Manny Fernandez. 2017. "Texas Bathroom Bill Dies Again, Raising Republican Acrimony." *New York Times*, August 16. Accessed October 7, 2017. https://www.nytimes.com/2017/08/16/us/politics/texas-bathroom-bill-dies-again-raising-republican-acrimony.html

Montgomery v. Independent School District No. 709, 109 F. Supp. 2d 1081, 1093 (D. Minn. 2000).

Montopoli, Brian. 2010. "Dan Choi, Other Gay Rights Protesters Arrested after Chaining Selves to White House Fence." *CBS News*, April 20. Accessed November 15, 2017. https://www.cbsnews.com/news/dan-choi-other-gay-rights-protesters-arrested-after-chaining-selves-to-white-house-fence/

Moon, Emily. 2007. "California to Recognize Non-Binary Gender on State IDs." *Pacific Standard*, October 16. https://psmag.com/news/california-to-recognize-non-binary-gender-on-state-ids

Mooney, Christopher Z., and Mei-Hsien Lee. 1995. "Legislating Morality in the American States: The Case of Pre-Roe Abortion Regulation Reform." *American Journal of Political Science* 39 (3): 599–627.

Morris, Aldon. 1984. *The Origins of the Civil Rights Movement: Black Communities Organizing for Change*. New York: Free Press.

Morris, Mike. 2014. "Council Extends Rights Protection for Gays, Transgendered." *Houston Chronicle*, May 28.

Moyer, Justin William. 2015. "Why Houston's Gay Rights Ordinance Failed: Fear of Men in Women's Bathrooms." *Washington Post*, November 4.

Moynihan, Donald and Alasdair Roberts. 2010. "The Triumph of Loyalty over Competence: The Bush Administration and the Exhaustion of the Politicized Presidency." *Public Administration Review* 70 (4): 572–81.

M.T. v J.T., 140 N.J. 77, 355 A.2d 204, 205 (NJ Super. Ct. 1976).

Mucciaroni, Gary. 2008. *Same Sex, Different Politics: Success and Failure in the Struggles over Gay Rights*. Chicago: University of Chicago Press.

Murib, Zein. 2015. "Transgender: Examining an Emerging Political Identity Using Three Political Processes." *Politics, Groups, and Identities* 3 (3): 381–97.

Nagoshi, Julie L., Katherine A. Adams, Heather K. Terrell, Eric D. Hill, Stephanie Brzuzy, and Craig T. Nagoshi. 2008. "Gender Differences in Correlates of Homophobia and Transphobia." *Sex Roles* 59 (7–8): 521–31.

Namaste, Viviane. 2000. *Invisible Lives: The Erasure of Transsexual and Transgender People*. Chicago: University of Chicago Press.

Nash, Tammye. 2011. "Who Decides What's Medically Necessary?" *Dallas Voice*, June 16. Accessed June 4, 2017. http://www.dallasvoice.com/decides-whats-medically-1080315.html

Nataf, Zachary I. 1996. *Lesbians Talk Transgender*. London: Scarlet Press.

National Center for Charitable Statistics. 2008. "How and by Whom Are NTEEs Assigned?" Accessed April 28, 2017. http://nccsweb.urban.org/knowledgebase/detail.php?linkID=728

National Center for Charitable Statistics. 2014. "NCCS All Registered Nonprofits Table Wizard." Accessed February 16, 2014. http://nccsweb.urban.org/tablewiz/bmf.php

National Center for Transgender Equality. 2005. "Selective Service and Transgender People." Accessed May 31, 2017. http://www.transequality.org/issues/resources/selective-service-and-transgender-people

National Center for Transgender Equality. 2016a. "How Trans-Friendly Is the Driver's License Policy in Your State?" Accessed May 31, 2017. http://www.transequality.org/sites/default/files/docs/DL%20Grades%20Sept%202016.docx

National Center for Transgender Equality. 2016b. "Transgender Legal Services Network." Accessed September 23, 2016. http://www.transequality.org/id-documents-center/transgender-legal-services-network

National Center for Transgender Equality. 2016c. "Victory: Nevada Passes the Most Progressive Birth Certificate Gender Change Policy in the Nation!" Accessed May 31, 2017.

http://www.transequality.org/blog/victory-nevada-passes-the-most-progressive-birth-certificate-gender-change-policy-in-the-nation

National Center for Transgender Equality. 2017a. "ID Documents Center." Accessed June 2, 2017. http://www.transequality.org/documents

National Center for Transgender Equality. 2017b. "Know Your Rights: Medicare." Accessed October 8, 2017. https://www.transequality.org/know-your-rights/medicare

National Center for Transgender Equality. 2017c. "Trump Administration Says It Will Try to Legalize Anti-Transgender Discrimination in Health Care." National Center for Transgender Equality, May 2. Accessed June 26, 2017. http://www.transequality.org/press/releases/trump-administration-says-it-will-try-to-legalize-anti-transgender-discrimination-in

National Center for Transgender Equality. 2017. "Lisa Mottet." Accessed January 4, 2017. http://www.transequality.org/about/people/lisa-mottet-she-her

National Center for Transgender Equality Action Fund. 2017. "About Us." https://www.ncteactionfund.org/about/

National Coalition of Anti-Violence Programs (NCAVP). 2016. *Lesbian, Gay, Bisexual, Transgender, Queer, and HIV-Affected Hate Violence in 2016*. New York: NCAVP.

National Collegiate Athletic Association. 2011. *NCAA Inclusion of Transgender Student-Athletes*. Accessed October 9, 2017. https://www.ncaa.org/sites/default/files/Transgender_Handbook_2011_Final.pdf

National Conference of State Legislatures. 2014. "Civil Unions and Domestic Partnership Statutes." Accessed February 27, 2017. http://www.ncsl.org/research/human-services/civil-unions-and-domestic-partnership-statutes.aspx

National Conference of State Legislatures. 2016. "2016 State Religious Freedom Restoration Act Legislation." Accessed May 9, 2017. http://www.ncsl.org/research/civil-and-criminal-justice/2016-state-religious-freedom-restoration-act-legislation.aspx

National Conference of State Legislatures. 2017a. "2017 State & Legislative Partisan Composition." Accessed May 12, 2017. http://www.ncsl.org/portals/1/documents/elections/Legis_Control_2017_March_27_11am.pdf

National Conference of State Legislatures. 2017b. "State Religious Freedom Restoration Acts." Accessed May 9, 2017. http://www.ncsl.org/research/civil-and-criminal-justice/state-rfra-statutes.aspx

National Education Association. 2016. "Legal Guidance on Transgender Students' Rights." Washington, DC: National Education Association.

National Gay and Lesbian Task Force. "2014. Nondiscrimination Laws Map." Accessed February 11, 2017. http://www.thetaskforce.org/static_html/downloads/reports/issue_maps/non_discrimination_5_14_color_new.pdf

National Institute of Corrections. 2012. *A Quick Guide for LGBTI Policy Development for Adult Prisons and Jails*. NIC Accession #026702. Washington, DC: U.S. Department of Justice. https://info.nicic.gov/nicrp/node/375

National Panhellenic Conference. 2017. "Meet NPC." Indianapolis, IN: National Panhellenic Conference. Accessed May 22, 2017: https://www.npcwomen.org/about.aspx

Navarette, Carlos David, and Daniel Fessler. 2006. "Disease Avoidance and Ethnocentrism: The Effects of Disease Vulnerability and Disgust Sensitivity on Intergroup Attitudes." *Evolution & Human Behavior* 27 (4): 270–82.

NBC News. 2017a. "First 100 Days: How President Trump Has Impacted LGBTQ Rights." Accessed May 12, 2017. http://www.nbcnews.com/feature/nbc-out/first-100-days-how-president-trump-has-impacted-lgbtq-rights-n750191

NBC News. 2017b. "Trans Teen's Murder Case Raises Question: Do LGBTQ Hate Crime Laws Work?" NBCNews.com. Accessed October 6, 2017. https://www.nbcnews.com/feature/nbc-out/trans-teen-s-murder-case-raises-question-do-lgbtq-hate-n805476

Nelson, Kimberly, and James Svara. 2010. "Adaptation of Models versus Variations in Form: Classifying Structures of City Government." *Urban Affairs Review* 45 (4): 544–62.

Nemoto, Tooru, Don Operario, JoAnne Keatley, Hongmai Nguyen, and Eiko Sugano. 2005. "Promoting Health for Transgender Women: Transgender Resources and Neighborhood Space (TRANS) Program in San Francisco." *American Journal of Public Health* 95 (3): 382–84.

Neustadt, Richard. 1960. *Presidential Power and the Modern Presidents: The Politics of Leadership.* New York: John Wiley & Sons.

News Desk. 2015. "Arresting Dress: A Timeline of Anti-Cross-dressing Laws in the United States." *PBS Newshour*, May 31. Accessed June 26 2017. http://www.pbs.org/newshour/updates/arresting-dress-timeline-anti-cross-dressing-laws-u-s/

New State Ice Co. v. Liebmann, 285 U.S. 262 (1932).

New York State Division of Human Rights. 2015. "Governor Cuomo Announces New Regulations Protecting Transgender New Yorkers from Discrimination." Accessed May 17, 2017. https://dhr.ny.gov/gender_identity_regulations

New York State Governor Press Office. 2015. "Governor Cuomo Introduces Regulations to Protect Transgender New Yorkers from Unlawful Discrimination." Accessed January 5, 2017. https://www.governor.ny.gov/news/governor-cuomo-introduces-regulations-protect-transgender-new-yorkers-unlawful-discrimination

New York Times. 2015. "Milestones in the American Transgender Movement." *New York Times*, May 15. Accessed January 21, 2017. https://www.nytimes.com/interactive/2015/05/15/opinion/editorial-transgender-timeline.html

Nichols, James Michael. 2016. "This Trans Supermodel Was Outed in the '80s, Lost Everything and Became a Pioneer." *Huffington Post*, June 19. Accessed July 20, 2016. http://www.huffingtonpost.com/entry/trans-supermodel-1980s-caroline-cossey_us_575b03dce4b0e39a28ad822e

Niland, Olivia. 2015. "6 Trans Students Fighting for Equal Access to Their School's Bathrooms." *Mashable News*, October 31.

Nirappil, Fenit. 2017. "Democratic Challenger to Marshall Would Be Va.'s First Openly Transgender Lawmaker." *Washington Post*, June 13. https://www.washingtonpost.com/local/virginia-politics/democratic-challenger-to-marshall-would-be-vas-first-openly-transgender-lawmaker/2017/06/13/2cae81e4-4f95-11e7-b064-828ba60fbb98_story.html?utm_term=.2225e1c8990f8&wpisrc=nl_politics&wpmm=1

Norsworthy v. Beard, No. 14-cv-00695-JST (N.D. Ca. April 2, 2015).

North-American Interfraternity Conference. 2017. "Fraternity Stats at a Glance." Carmel, IN: North-American Interfraternity Conference. Accessed May 22, 2017. http://nicindy.org/press/fraternity-statistics/

Norton, Aaron T., and Gregory M. Herek. 2013. "Heterosexuals' Attitudes toward Transgender People: Findings from a National Probability Sample of US Adults." *Sex Roles* 68 (11–12): 738–53.

Nownes, Anthony. 2010. "Density Dependent Dynamics in the Population of Transgender Interest Groups in the United States 1964–2005." *Social Science Quarterly* 91 (3): 689–703.

Nownes, Anthony. 2014. "Interest Groups and Transgender Politics: Opportunities and Challenges." In *Transgender Rights and Politics: Groups, Issue Framing, and Policy Adoption*, edited by Jami Taylor and Donald Haider-Markel, 83–107. Ann Arbor: University of Michigan Press.

Obergefell v. Hodges, 576 U.S. ___ (2015).

O'Donnabhain v. Commissioner of Internal Revenue, 134 T.C. No 4 (2010).

O'Hara, Mary E. 2016. "Nation's First Known Intersex Birth Certificate Issued in NYC." NBC News. Accessed May 31, 2017. http://www.nbcnews.com/feature/nbc-out/nation-s-first-known-intersex-birth-certificate-issued-nyc-n701186

O'Hara, Mary E. 2017. "LGBTQ Advocates Say Trump's New Executive Order Makes Them Vulnerable to Discrimination." *NBC News, March 29.* Accessed June 28, 2017. http://www.nbcnews.com/feature/nbc-out/lgbtq-advocates-say-trump-s-news-executive-order-makes-them-n740301

Oiler v. Winn-Dixie La., Inc., No. 00–3114, 2002 U.S. Dist. LEXIS 17417.

Olatunji, Bunmi O., and Craig N. Sawchuk. 2005. "Disgust: Characteristic Features, Social Manifestations, and Clinical Implications." *Journal of Social and Clinical Psychology* 24 (7): 932–62.

Olatunji, Bunmi O., Nathan L. Williams, David F. Tolin, Jonathan S. Abramowitz, Craig N. Sawchuk, Jeffrey M. Lohr, and Lisa S. Elwood. 2007. "The Disgust Scale: Item Analysis, Factor Structure, and Suggestions for Refinement." *Psychological Assessment* 19 (3): 281–97.

Olivo, Antonio. 2017. "Danica Roem of Virginia to Be First Openly Transgender Person Elected, Seated in a U.S. Statehouse." *Washington Post*, November 8. https://www.washingtonpost.com/local/virginia-politics/danica-roem-will-be-vas-first-openly-transgender-elected-official-after-unseating-conservative-robert-g-marshall-in-house-race/2017/11/07/d534bdde-c0af-11e7–959c-fe2b598d8c00_story.html?utm_term=.54812ec114cc

Olson, Laura R., Wendy Cadge, and James T. Harrison. 2006. "Religion and Public Opinion about Same-Sex Marriage." *Social Science Quarterly* 87 (2): 340–60.

Olson, Mancur. 1965. *The Logic of Collective Action: Public Goods and the Theory of Groups.* Cambridge: Harvard University Press.

Olsson, Stig-Eric, and Anders Möller. 2003. "On the Incidence and Sex Ratio of Transsexualism in Sweden, 1972–2002." *Archives of Sexual Behavior* 32 (4): 381–86.

Oncale v. Sundowner Offshore Services, 523 U.S. 75 (1998).

Ore, Addison (former board chair, Equality North Carolina), interviewed by Jami Taylor, telephone December 20, 2016.

Orr, Asaf, Joel Baum, Jay Brown, Elizabeth Gill, Ellen Kahn, and Anna Salem. 2017. "Schools in Transition: A Guide for Supporting Transgender Students in K-12 Schools." Washington, DC: Human Rights Campaign.

Overby, L. Marvin, and Jay Barth. 2002. "Contact, Community Context, and Public Attitudes toward Gay Men and Lesbians." *Polity* 34 (4): 433–56.

Padula, William V., Shiona Heru, and Jonathan D. Campbell. 2016. "Societal Implications of Health Insurance Coverage for Medically Necessary Services in the U.S. Transgender Population: A Cost-Effectiveness Analysis." *Journal of General Internal Medicine* 31: 394–401.

Palmquist, Ian (director of leadership programs, Equality Federation), interviewed by Jami Taylor, telephone, May 23, 2016.

Palmquist, Ian (director of leadership programs, Equality Federation), interviewed by Jami Taylor, electronic communication, October 9, 2017.

Pan, Po-Lin, Juan Meng, and Shuhua Zhou. 2010. "Morality or Equality? Ideological Framing in News Coverage of Gay Marriage Legitimization." *Social Science Journal* 47 (3): 630–45.

Park, Justin H., Jason Faulkner, and Mark Schaller. 2003. "Evolved Disease-Avoidance Process and Contemporary Anti-Social Behavior: Prejudicial Attitudes and Avoidance of People with Physical Disabilities." *Journal of Nonverbal Behavior* 27 (2): 65–87.

Park, Justin H., Mark Schaller, and Christian S. Crandall. 2007. "Pathogen-Avoidance Mechanisms and the Stigmatization of Obese People." *Evolution and Human Behavior* 28: 410–14.

Patient Protection and Affordable Care Act. 2010. Sec. 18001 et seq.

Patterson, Brandon E. 2016. "Jeff Sessions Fought against Hate Crime Protections for LGBT Victims." *Mother Jones*, November 22. http://www.motherjones.com/politics/2016/11/jeff-sessions-hate-crime-law/

Pearce, Matt. 2016. "South Dakota Governor Vetoes Transgender Bathroom Bill, Saying It 'Invites Conflict and Litigation'." *Los Angeles Times*, March 1.

Peffley, Mark A., and Jon Hurwitz. 1985. "A Hierarchical Model of Attitude Constraint." *American Journal of Political Science* 29: 871–90.

Pérez-Peña, Richard. 2015. "California Is First State to Adopt Sex Reassignment Surgery Policy for Prisoners." *New York Times*, October 22, A15.

Peters, Jeremy, Jo Becker, and Julie Hirschfeld Davis. 2017. "Trump Rescinds Rules on Bathrooms for Transgender Students." *New York Times*, February 22. Accessed June 5, 2017. https://www.nytimes.com/2017/02/22/us/politics/devos-sessions-transgender-students-rights.html

Peterson, Bill, Richard Doty, and David Winter. 1993. "Authoritarianism and Attitudes towards Contemporary Social Issues." *Personality and Social Psychology Bulletin* 19 (2): 174–84.

Peterson, Karen (Delaware state senator), interviewed by Jami Taylor, telephone, September 12, 2016.

Pettigrew, Thomas F. 1998. "Intergroup Contact Theory." *Annual Review of Psychology* 49: 65–85.

Pettigrew, Thomas F., and Linda R. Tropp. 2008. "How Does Intergroup Contact Reduce Prejudice? Meta-Analytic Tests of Three Mediators." *European Journal of Social Psychology* 38: 922–34.

Pew Research Center. 2016. "Changing Attitudes on Gay Marriage." Pew Charitable Trusts, May 12. Accessed June 21, 2017. http://www.pewforum.org/2016/05/12/changing-attitudes-on-gay-marriage/

Phillips, Amber. 2016. "How Loretta Lynch's Speech Brought Some Transgender Advocates to Tears." *Washington Post*, May 11. Accessed January 21, 2017. https://www.washingtonpost.com/news/the-fix/wp/2016/05/11/loretta-lynchs-speech-just-made-her-a-hero-to-transgender-activists/?utm_term=.a4566c1f0751

Pierceson, Jason. 2005. *Courts, Liberalism, and Rights: Gay Law and Politics in the United States and Canada*. Philadelphia: Temple University Press.

Pierceson, Jason. 2013. *Same-Sex Marriage in the United States: The Road to the Supreme Court*. Lanham, MD: Rowman and Littlefield.

Pierceson, Jason. 2016. *Sexual Minorities and Politics: An Introduction*. Lanham, MD: Rowman and Littlefield.

Pierceson, Jason, and Ashley Kirzinger. 2015. "Examining Attitudes towards the "T" in LGBT." Accessed June 5, 2017. https://transgenderinclusivepolicysurvey.wordpress.com/

Pink News. 2007. "US Senate Passes Gay Hate Crimes Law." *Pink News*, September 27. http://www.pinknews.co.uk/2007/09/27/us-senate-passes-gay-hate-crimes-law/

Pinneke v. Preisser 623 F.2d 546 (8th Cir. 1980).

Plessy v. Ferguson, 163 U.S. 537 (1896).

Plumb, Marj. 2000. "Advocating for Lesbian Health in the Clinton Years." In *Creating Change: Sexuality, Public Policy and Civil Rights*, edited by John D'Emilio, William Turner, and Urvashi Vaid, 361–81. New York: St. Martin's Press.

Polletta, Francesca, and James Jasper. 2001. "Collective Identity and Social Movements." *Annual Review of Sociology* 27: 283–305.

Powers, Daniel A., and Christopher G. Ellison. 1995. "Interracial Contact and Black Racial Attitudes: The Contact Hypothesis and Selectivity Bias." *Social Forces* 74 (1): 205–26.

Prevent School Violence NC. 2009. "New Poll Shows Overwhelming Support for School Violence Prevention Act." Accessed October 9, 2017. http://preventschoolviolencenc.blogspot.com/2009/03/new-poll-shows-overwhelming-support-for.html

Price Waterhouse v. Hopkins, 490 U.S. 228 (1989).

Public Policy Polling. 2009. "NC Voters Support Bullying Bill." Accessed October 9, 2017. http://publicpolicypolling.blogspot.com/2009/03/nc-voters-support-bullying-bill.html

Public Religion Research Institute. 2011a. "Religion and Politics Tracking Survey." Public Religion Research Institute, pollster.

Public Religion Research Institute. 2011b. "Strong Majorities Favor Rights and Legal Protections for Transgender People." Public Religion Research Institute, November. Accessed April 9, 2014. http://www.publicreligion.org/newsroom/2011/11/news-release-strong-majorities-favor-rights-and-legal-protections-for-transgender-people/

Public Religion Research Institute. 2017. "February 2017 Survey." Public Religion Research Institute, pollster.

Quinnipiac University Polling Institute. 2016. "Quinnipiac University Poll, May 2016." Quinnipiac University Polling Institute, pollster. Cornell University, Ithaca, NY: Roper Center for Public Opinion Research, iPOLL, distributor. Accessed March 28, 2017.

Quinnipiac University Polling Institute. 2017. "Quinnipiac University Poll, March 2017." Quinnipiac University Polling Institute, pollster. Cornell University, Ithaca, NY: Roper Center for Public Opinion Research, iPOLL, distributor. Accessed March 28, 2017.

Ramirez, Fernando. 2017. "District Judge Makes Landmark Ruling in Transgender Discrimination Lawsuit." *Houston Chronicle*, May 22. Accessed May 23, 2017. http://www.chron.com/national/article/District-Judge-makes-landmark-ruling-in-11164317.php

RAND Corporation. 2016. "Assessing the Implications of Allowing Transgender Personnel to Serve Openly." Accessed May 23, 2017. http://www.rand.org/pubs/research_reports/RR1530.html

Ranney, Austin. 1976. "Parties in State Politics." In *Politics in the American States: A Comparative Analysis*, edited by Herbert Jacob and Kenneth Vines. Boston: Little, Brown.

Rao, Devi M. 2013. "Gender Identity Discrimination Is Sex Discrimination: Protecting Transgender Students from Bullying and Harassment Using Title IX." *Wisconsin Journal of Law, Gender & Society* 28: 245–70.

R.A.V. v. City of St. Paul, 505 U.S. 377 (1992).

Ray v. Antioch Unified School Dist., 107 F. Supp. 2d 1165 (N.D. Cal. 2000).

Raymond, Janice. 1979. *The Transsexual Empire: The Making of the She-Male*. London: Women's Press.

Raymond, Janice. 1996. "The Politics of Transgenderism." In *Blending Genders: Social Aspects of Cross-dressing and Sex-changing*, edited by Richard Ekins and Dave King, 215–23. London: Routledge.

Rayside, David, and Clyde Wilcox, eds. 2011. *Faith, Politics, and Sexual Diversity in Canada and the United States*. Vancouver: UBC Press.

Reeser, J. C. 2005. "Gender Identity and Sport: Is the Playing Field Level?" *British Journal of Sports Medicine* 39: 695–99.

Renn, Kristen. 2007. "LGBT Student Leaders and Queer Activists: Identities of Lesbian, Gay, Bisexual, Transgender, and Queer Identified College Student Leaders and Activists." *Journal of College Student Development* 48 (3): 311–30.

Republican Party. 2016. "Republican Platform 2016." Accessed June 4, 2017. https://prod-cdn-static.gop.com/static/home/data/platform.pdf

Reuters. 2016. "Louisiana Judge Throws Out Executive Order to Protect LGBT Rights." Reuters, December 14. Accessed January 22, 2017. http://www.reuters.com/article/us-louisiana-lgbt-idUSKBN1432HF

Reynolds, Andrew. 2013. "Representation and Rights: The Impact of LGBT Legislators in Comparative Perspective." *American Political Science Review* 107 (2): 259–74.

Richardson, Billy. 2016. "NC Representative Voted for HB2; Now He Says It Was a Mistake." *Charlotte Observer*, April 18. Accessed October 8, 2017. http://www.charlotteobserver.com/opinion/op-ed/article72446667.html

Richards v. U.S. Tennis Assn, 93 Misc. 2d 713, 400 N.Y.S.2d 267 (Sup. Ct. 1977).

Riley, Jenelle. 2015. "Amazon, 'Transparent' Make History at Golden Globes." *Variety*, January 11. Accessed July 14, 2016. http://variety.com/2015/tv/news/amazon-transparent-make-history-at-golden-globes-1201400485/

Riley, John. 2013. "D.C. Mayor Signs LGBT-Backed Bills." *Metro Weekly*, August 6. Accessed May 31, 2017. http://www.metroweekly.com/2013/08/dc-mayor-signs-lgbt-backed-bil/

Rimmerman, Craig. 2015. *The Lesbian and Gay Movements: Assimilation or Liberation?* 2nd ed. Boulder, CO: Westview Press.

Ring, Trudy. 2016a. "A Former Student Helped Change This N.C. Lawmaker's Mind on HB2." *Advocate*, April 15. Accessed June 29, 2017. https://www.advocate.com/politics/2016/4/15/former-student-helped-change-nc-lawmakers-mind-hb-2

Ring, Trudy. 2016b. "Trans Activist Mara Keisling Arrested at N.C. Protest." *Advocate*,

April 25. Accessed June 20, 2017. https://www.advocate.com/transgender/2016/4/25/trans-activist-mara-keisling-arrested-north-carolina-protest

Ring, Trudy. 2018. "A New Day: Trans Americans Begin Enlisting in the Military." *Advocate,* January 2. Accessed January 22, 2018 from https://www.advocate.com/military/2018/1/02/new-day-trans-americans-begin-enlisting-military

Roberts, Andrea L., Margaret Rosario, Heather L. Corliss, Karestan C. Koenen, and S. Bryn Austin. 2012. "Childhood Gender Nonconformity: A Risk Indicator for Childhood Abuse and Posttraumatic Stress in Youth." *Pediatrics* 129: 410–17.

Rochon, Thomas R., and Daniel Mazmanian. 1993. "Social Movements and the Policy Process." *Annals of the American Academy of Political and Social Science* 528: 75–87.

Roen, Katrina. 2002 "Either/Or and Both/Neither: Discursive Tensions in Transgender Politics" *Signs: Journal of Women in Culture and Society* 27 (2): 501–22.

Romboy, Dennis. 2015. "LDS Church, LGBT Advocates Back Anti-discrimination, Religious Rights Bill." *Deseret News*, March 5. http://www.deseretnews.com/article/865623399/Utah-lawmakers-unveil-anti-discrimination-religious-rights-legislation.html

Romer, Thomas, and Howard Rosenthal. 1979. "The Elusive Median Voter." *Journal of Public Economics* 12 (2): 143–70.

Romer v. Evans, 517 U.S. 620 (1996).

Rosa v. Park W. Bank & Trust Co., 214 F.3d 213 (1st Cir. 2000).

Rosenberg, Gerald N. 2008. *The Hollow Hope: Can Courts Bring about Social Change? 2nd ed.* Chicago: University of Chicago Press.

Rosenberg, Matthew. 2016. "Transgender People Will Be Allowed to Serve Openly in Military." *New York Times*, July 1. Accessed May 9, 2017. https://www.nytimes.com/2016/07/01/us/transgender-military.html

Rosenthal, Alan. 2013. *The Best Job in Politics: Exploring How Governors Succeed as Policy Leaders*. Los Angeles: SAGE/CQ Press.

Rosky, Clifford. 2016. "Still Not Equal: A Report from the Red States." In *After Marriage Equality: The Future of LGBT Rights*, edited by Carlos A Ball, 73–104. New York: New York University Press.

Ross, Janel. 2015. "Houston Decided It Had a Problem: Its LGBT Nondiscrimination Law." *Washington Post*, November 4. https://www.washingtonpost.com/news/the-fix/wp/2015/11/04/houston-decided-it-had-a-problem-its-lgbt-nondiscrimination-law/?utm_term=.7756ac1ca83c

Rothacker, Rick. 2017. "HB2 Emails Show McCrory's Complaints about Media, Joke from Moore Staff Member." *Charlotte Observer*, January 31. Accessed June 27, 2017. http://www.charlotteobserver.com/news/politics-government/article129784979.html

Roubein, Rachel. 2017. "Timeline: The GOP's Failed Effort to Repeal ObamaCare." *Hill*, September 26. Accessed October 8, 2017. http://thehill.com/policy/healthcare/other/352587-timeline-the-gop-effort-to-repeal-and-replace-obamacare

Rozin, Paul, Jonathan Haidt, Clark McCauley, Lance Dunlop, and Michelle Ashmore. 1999. "Individual Differences in Disgust Sensitivity: Comparisons and Evaluations on Paper-and-Pencil versus Behavioral Measures." *Journal of Research in Personality* 33: 330–51.

Rudacille, Deborah. 2005. *The Riddle of Gender: Science, Activism and Transgender Rights*. New York: Pantheon Books.

Ruiz, Michelle. 2016. "Can Trans Girls Be Sorority Girls?" *Cosmopolitan*, October 17.

Rupert, Maya (senior policy advisor to the secretary at U.S. Department of Housing and Urban Development), interviewed by Jami Taylor, Washington, DC, May 31, 2016.

Rupp, Leila J., and Verta Taylor. 1999. "Forging Feminist Identity in an International Movement: A Collective Identity Approach to Feminism." *Signs* 24 (2): 363–86.

Russell, Stephen T., Stacey S. Horn, Raymond L. Moody, Amanda Field, and Elizabeth Tilley. 2016. "Enumerated State Laws: Evidence from Policy Advocacy." In *Sexual Orientation, Gender Identity, and Schooling: The Nexus of Research, Practice, and Policy*, edited by S. T. Russell and S. S. Horn. New York: Oxford University Press.

Rustin, John. 2016. "Cutting Through the Liberal Propaganda on HB 2." *News & Observer*, April 24. Accessed February 27, 2017. http://www.newsobserver.com/opinion/op-ed/article73394937.html

Sabatier, Paul A., and Christopher M. Weible. 2007. "The Advocacy Coalition Framework: Innovations and Clarifications." In *Theories of the Policy Process*, 2nd Edition, edited by Paul Sabatier, 189–222. Boulder, CO: Westview Press.

Sanchez, Diego (director of advocacy, PFLAG), interviewed by Jami Taylor, Washington, DC, November 16, 2016.

Savage, Charlie. 2017a. "5 Transgender Service Members Sue Trump over Military Ban." *New York Times*, August 9. Accessed October 6, 2017. https://www.nytimes.com/2017/08/09/us/politics/5-transgender-service-members-sue-trump-over-military-ban.html

Savage, Charlie. 2017b. "In Shift, Justice Dept. Says Law Doesn't Bar Transgender Discrimination." *New York Times*, October 5. Accessed October 6, 2017. https://www.nytimes.com/2017/10/05/us/politics/transgender-civil-rights-act-justice-department-sessions.html

Savage, Charlie, and Sheryl Gay Stolberg. 2011. "In Shift, U.S. Says Marriage Act Blocks Gay Rights." *New York Times*, February 24. Accessed January 25, 2017. http://www.nytimes.com/2011/02/24/us/24marriage.html?pagewanted=all&_r=0

Schaller, Mark, and Lesley A. Duncan. 2007. "The Behavioral Immune System: Its Evolution and Social Psychological Implications." In *Evolution and the Social Mind: Evolutionary Psychology and Social Cognition*, edited by Joseph P. Forgas, Martie G. Haselton, and William von Hippel, 293–307. New York: Psychology Press.

Schattschneider, Elmer E. 1960. *The Semi-sovereign People: A Realist's View of Democracy in America*. New York: Holt, Rinehart and Winston.

Scheingold, Stuart. (1974) 2004. *The Politics of Rights: Lawyers, Public Policy, and Political Change*. 2nd ed. Ann Arbor: University of Michigan Press.

Schiappa, Edward, Peter B. Gregg, and Dean E. Hewes. 2006. "Can One TV Show Make a Difference? Will & Grace and the Parasocial Contact Hypothesis." *Journal of Homosexuality* 51 (4): 15–37.

Schildkraut, Deborah, J. 2001. "Official-English and the States: Influences on Declaring English the Official Language in the United States." *Political Research Quarterly* 54 (2): 445–57.

Schirmer, Annett. 2013. "Sex Differences in Emotion." In *The Cambridge Handbook of Human Affective Neuroscience*, edited by Jorge Armony and Patrik Vuilleumier, 591–610. Cambridge: Cambridge University Press.

Schlozman, Kay L. 1984. "What Accent the Heavenly Chorus: Political Equality and the American Pressure System," *Journal of Politics* 46: 1006–32.

Schlueter, Elmar, and Peer Scheepers. 2010. "The Relationship between Outgroup Size and Anti-Outgroup Attitudes: A Theoretical Synthesis and Empirical Test of Group Threat-and Intergroup Contact Theory." *Social Science Research* 39 (2): 285–95.

Schneider, Anne, and Helen Ingram. 1993. "Social Construction of Target Populations: Implications for Politics and Social Policy." *American Political Science Review* 87 (2): 334–47.

Schroer v. Billington, 577 F. Supp.2d 293 (D.D.C. 2008).

Schwarz, Hunter. 2015. "Obama's Latest 'Evolution' on Gay Marriage: He Lied about Opposing It, Axelrod Says." *Washington Post*, February 10. Accessed January 25, 2017. https://www.washingtonpost.com/news/the-fix/wp/2015/02/10/axelrod-says-obama-lied-about-opposing-gay-marriage-its-another-convenient-evolution/?utm_term=.74f7ddd081cd

Schwenk v. Hartford, 204 F.3d 1187 (9th Cir. 2000).

Scott, Gunner (director of programs, Pride Foundation), interviewed by Jami Taylor, telephone, June 15, 2016.

Seaton, Liz (former legal counsel, Human Rights Campaign), interviewed by Jami Taylor, telephone, November 14, 2016.

Segal, Corrine. 2016. "Oregon Court Rules That 'Nonbinary' Is a Legal Gender." *PBS NewsHour*, June 11. Accessed May 31, 2017. http://www.pbs.org/newshour/rundown/oregon-court-rules-that-nonbinary-is-a-legal-gender/

Segal, Corinne. 2017a. "D.C. Will Be First in Nation to Offer Non-binary Driver's Licenses." *PBS Newshour, June 25.* Accessed June 28, 2017. http://www.pbs.org/newshour/rundown/d-c-will-first-nation-offer-non-binary-drivers-licenses/

Segal, Corrine. 2017b. "Nation's First Known 'Intersex' Birth Certificate Issued in New York City." *PBS NewsHour, January 5.* Accessed May 31, 2017. http://www.pbs.org/newshour/rundown/new-york-city-issues-nations-first-birth-certificate-marked-intersex/

Selective Service System. 2017a. "Change of Information—Address and Personal Information." Accessed May 31, 2017. https://www.sss.gov/Home/Address-Change

Selective Service System. 2017b. "Who Must Register." Accessed May 31, 2017. https://www.sss.gov/Registration-Info/Who-Registration

Sellers, Mitchell D. 2014a. "Discrimination and the Transgender Population: Analysis of the Functionality of Local Government Policies That Protect Gender Identity." *Administration & Society* 46 (1): 70–86.

Sellers, Mitchell D. 2014b. "Executive Expansion of Transgender Rights: Electoral Incentives to Issue or Revoke Executive Orders." In *Transgender Rights and Politics: Groups, Issue Framing, and Policy Adoption*, edited by Jami K. Taylor and Donald P. Haider-Markel, 189–207. Ann Arbor: University of Michigan Press.

Sellers, Mitchell D. 2016. "Gubernatorial Use of Executive Orders: Unilateral Action and Policy Adoption." *Journal of Public Policy* 37 (3): 1–25. https://doi.org/10.1017/S0143814X16000180

Sellers, Mitchell Dylan, and Roddrick Colvin. 2014. "Policy Learning, Language, and Implementation by Local Governments with Transgender-Inclusive Nondiscrimination Policies." In *Transgender Rights and Politics: Groups, Issue Framing, and Policy Adop-*

tion, edited by Jami K. Taylor and Donald P. Haider-Markel, 208–30. Ann Arbor: University of Michigan Press.

Selmi, Michael. 2001. "Why Are Employment Discrimination Cases So Hard to Win?" *Louisiana Law Review* 61 (3): 555–75.

Selznick, Philip. 1948. "Foundations of the Theory of Organization." *American Sociological Review* 13 (1): 25–35.

Shaffer, N. 2005. "Transgender Patients: Implications for Emergency Department Policy and Practice." *Journal of Emergency Nursing* 31: 405–7.

Shapiro, Eva. 2004. "'Trans' cending Barriers: Transgender Organizing on the Internet." *Journal of Gay and Lesbian Social Services* 16 (3–4): 165–79.

Shapiro, Nina. 2016. "State's Rules for Transgender Restroom Access Set Off Debate." *Seattle Times*, January 29. https://www.seattletimes.com/seattle-news/politics/states-rules-for-transgender-restroom-access-set-off-debate/

Sharp, Elaine B. ed. 1999. *Culture Wars & Local Politics*. Lawrence: University of Kansas Press.

Sharp, Elaine B. 2005. *Morality Politics in American Cities*. Lawrence: University of Kansas Press.

Shear, Michael. 2015. "White House Hires First Openly Transgender Staff Member." *New York Times*, August 18. https://www.nytimes.com/politics/first-draft/2015/08/18/white-house-hires-first-openly-transgender-staff-member/

Sherwin, Robert. 1969. "Legal Aspects of Male Transsexualism." In *Transsexualism and Sex Reassignment*, edited by Richard Green and John Money, 417–30. Baltimore: Johns Hopkins University Press.

Shipan, Charles R., and Craig Volden. 2008. "The Mechanisms of Policy Diffusion." *American Journal of Political Science* 52 (4): 840–57.

Shoichet, Catherine E. 2016. "North Carolina Governor Issues Executive Order in Wake of HB2." *CNN*, 12 April. http://www.cnn.com/2016/04/12/us/north-carolina-bathrooms-law-hb2-executive-order/index.html

Shull, Steven. 1999. *American Civil Rights Policy from Truman to Clinton: The Role of Presidential Leadership*. New York: M. E. Sharpe.

Simon, Richard. 2007. "Hate Crime Veto Is Vowed." *Los Angeles Times*, May 4. http://articles.latimes.com/2007/may/04/nation/na-hate4

Sinfield, Alan. 2004. "The Challenge of Transgender, the Moment of Stonewall, and Neil Bartlett." *GLQ: A Journal of Lesbian and Gay Studies* 10 (2): 267–72.

Singer, T. Benjamin. 2006. "From the Medical Gaze to Sublime Mutations: The Ethics of (Re)Viewing Non-normative Body Images." In *The Transgender Studies Reader*, edited by Susan Stryker and Stephen Whittle, 601–20. New York: Routledge.

Sitek, Zuzanna. 2015. "Human Rights Campaign Not Backing Fayetteville Civil Rights Ordinance." 5 News Online, September 2. Accessed October 2, 2017. http://5newsonline.com/2015/09/02/human-rights-campaign-not-backing-fayetteville-civil-rights-ordinance/

Skiles, Kat. 2016. "#ThanksObama: 23 Important Moments for LGBTQ Progress." Human Rights Campaign. Accessed January 22, 2017. http://www.hrc.org/blog/thanksobama-20-important-moments-for-lgbtq-progress

Skipworth, Sue Ann, Andrew Garner, and Bryan J. Dettrey. 2010. "Limitations of the Contact Hypothesis: Heterogeneity in the Contact Effect on Attitudes toward Gay Rights." *Politics & Policy* 38 (5): 887–906.

Smith, Barry. 2016. "Senate Democrats Walk Out on Vote Overturning 'Bathroom' Ordinance." *Carolina Journal*, March 24. Accessed October 8, 2017. https://www.carolina-journal.com/news-article/senate-democrats-walk-out-of-vote-overturning-bathroom-ordinance/

Smith, Ben, and Maggie Haberman. 2011. "Gay Donors Fuel Obama's 2012 Bid." *Politico*, May 9. Accessed January 4, 2017. http://www.politico.com/story/2011/05/gay-donors-fuel-obamas-2012-bid-054539

Smith, Grant, and Daniel Trotta. 2017. "U.S. Hate Crimes up 20 Percent in 2016 Fueled by Election Campaign—Report." Reuters, March 13. Accessed October 9, 2017. https://www.reuters.com/article/us-usa-crime-hate/u-s-hate-crimes-up-20-percent-in-2016-fueled-by-election-campaign-report-idUSKBN16L0BO

Smith, Jackie, and Tina Fetner. 2010. "Structural Approaches in the Sociology of Social Movements." In *Handbook of Social Movements across Disciplines*, edited by Bert Klandermans and Conny Roggeband, 13–57. Boston, MA: Springer.

Smith, Mitch. 2016. "South Dakota Governor Vetoes Restriction on Transgender Bathroom Access." *New York Times*, March 2. Accessed January 18, 2017. https://www.nytimes.com/2016/03/02/us/governor-vetoes-transgender-bathroom-restrictions-south-dakota.html?_r=0

Smith v. City of Salem Ohio, 378 F.3d 566 (6th Cir. 2004).

Snow, David. 2001. "Collective Identity and Expressive Forms." Accessed November 7, 2016. http://escholarship.org/uc/item/2zn1t7bj#page-2

Snow, David, E. Burke Rochford, Steven Worden, and Robert Benford. 1986. "Frame Alignment Processes, Micromobilization, and Movement Participation." *American Sociological Review* 51 (4): 464–81.

Somashekhar, Sandhya. 2015. "Gay Rights Battle Flares in Houston over Nondiscrimination Ordinance." *Washington Post*, November 19. https://www.washingtonpost.com/national/gay-rights-battle-flares-in-houston-over-nondiscrimination-ordinanc e/2015/11/01/02282754–7f08–11e5-b575-d8dcfedb4ea1_story.html?utm_term=.da86499e9c80

Somashekhar, Sandhya. 2016. "Georgia Governor Vetoes Religious Freedom Bill Criticized as Anti-Gay." *Washington Post*, March 28. Accessed January 21, 2017. https://www.washingtonpost.com/news/post-nation/wp/2016/03/28/georgia-governor-to-veto-religious-freedom-bill-criticized-as-anti-gay/?utm_term=.687750e65dde

Sommers v. Budget Marketing Inc, 667 F. 2d 748 (8th Cir. 1982).

Sontag, Deborah. 2015. "Once a Pariah, Now a Judge: The Early Transgender Journey of Phyllis Frye." *New York Times*, August 30. Accessed January 27, 2017. https://www.nytimes.com/2015/08/30/us/transgender-judge-phyllis-fryes-early-transformative-journey.html

Sopelsa, Brooke. 2017. "Obama Selects Two Transgender People for Presidential Appointments." *NBC News*, January 17. Accessed May 25, 2017. http://www.nbcnews.com/feature/nbc-out/obama-selects-two-transgender-people-presidential-appointmen-ts-n707916

Soule, Sarah A., and Jennifer Earl. 2001. "The Enactment of State-Level Hate Crime Law in the United States: Intrastate and Interstate Factors." *Sociological Perspectives* 44 (3): 281–305.

Spade, Dean (associate professor of law, Seattle University), interviewed by Jami Taylor, telephone, November 10, 2016.

Spade, Dean. 2006. "Compliance Is Gendered: Struggling for Gender Self-Determination in a Hostile Economy." In *Transgender Rights*, edited by Paisley Currah, Richard Juang, and Shannon Minter, 217–41. Minneapolis: University of Minnesota Press.

Spade, Dean. 2011. *Normal Life: Administrative Violence, Critical Trans Politics, and the Limits of the Law*. Brooklyn: South End Press.

Spade, Dean. 2015. *Normal Life: Administrative Violence, Critical Trans Politics and the Limits of Law, Revised and Expanded Edition*. Durham, NC: Duke University Press.

Spies, Mike. 2015. "What It's Like to Be a Transgender Woman in a Max-Security Prison." *Voactiv*, April 8. http://www.vocativ.com/underworld/crime/what-its-like-to-be-a-transgender-woman-in-a-max-security-prison/index.html

Stack, Liam. 2017. "U.S. Hate Crime Law Punishes Transgender Woman's Killer, in a First." *New York Times*, May 16. https://www.nytimes.com/2017/05/16/us/us-hate-crime-law-transgender-murder.html

Stack, Liam, 2018. "Christine Hallquist on Her Primary Victory: 'It Gives the Transgender Community Hope'." *New York Times*, August 15. Accessed August 16, 2018 from https://www.nytimes.com/2018/08/is/us/politics/transgender-christine-hallquist-vermont.html

Staggenborg, Suzanne. 1988. "The Consequences of Professionalization and Formalization in the Pro-Choice Movement." *American Sociological Review* 53 (4): 585–605.

St. John, Paige. 2015a. "Inmate Who Won Order for Sex Reassignment Surgery Recommended for Parole." *Latimes.com*, May 21.

St. John, Paige. 2015b. "In a First, California Agrees to Pay for Transgender Inmate's Sex Reassignment." *Latimes.com*, August 10.

Stam, Paul (Majority Leader, North Carolina House of Representatives), interviewed by Jami Taylor, telephone, September 9, 2016.

State Library of Massachusetts. 2017. "Governor Patrick Signs Transgender Equal Rights Bill." Accessed April 10, 2017. http://archives.lib.state.ma.us/bitstream/handle/2452/125845/ocn795183245-2011-11-23.PDF?sequence=1

State of Texas et al. v. United States of America et al., No. 7:16-cv-00054-O (S.D. Tex. 2016).

Steinmetz, Katy. 2014. "The Transgender Tipping Point." *Time*, May 29. Accessed May 25, 2017. http://time.com/135480/transgender-tipping-point/

Steinmetz, Katy. 2015. "Why It's a Big Deal That Obama Said 'Transgender.'" *Time*, January 21. Accessed January 25, 2017. http://time.com/3676881/state-of-the-union-2015-barack-obama-transgender/

Stenner, Karen. 2005. *The Authoritarian Dynamic*. New York: Cambridge University Press.

Stern, Mark J. 2018. "Federal Court Emphatically Shoots Down Anti-Trans Lawsuit in Rare Ruling From the Bench." *Slate*. Accessed June 5, 2018 from https://slate.com/news-and-politics/2018/05/third-circuit-shoots-down-adfs-anti-transgender-lawsuit.html

Stevens, Matt. 2018. "Transgender Student in Bathroom Dispute Wins Court Ruling." *New York Times*, May 22. Accessed May 23, 2018 from https://www.nytimes.com/2018/05/22/us/gavin-grimm-transgender-bathrooms.html

Stolberg, Sheryl Gay, Julie Bosman, Manny Fernandez, and Julie Hirschfeld Davis. 2016. "New Front Line in Culture War: The Bathroom," *New York Times*, May 22, A1.

Stone, Deborah. 2012. *Policy Paradox: The Art of Political Decision Making*. 3rd ed. New York: W. W. Norton.

Stone, Sandy. 1991. "The Empire Strikes Back: A Posttranssexual Manifesto." In *Body Guards: The Cultural Politics of Gender Ambiguity*, edited by Julie Epstein and Kristina Straub, 280–304. New York: Routledge.

Stotzer, Rebecca L. 2009. "Violence against Transgender People: A Review of United States Data." *Aggression and Violent Behavior* 14: 170–79.

Stroumsa, Daphna. 2014. "The State of Transgender Health Care: Policy, Law, and Medical Frameworks." *American Journal of Public Health* 104: e31-e38.

Stout, David. 2007. "House Votes to Expand Hate-Crime Protection." *New York Times*, May 4. http://www.nytimes.com/2007/05/04/washington/04hate.html

Stryker, Sheldon. 2000. "Identity Competition: Key to Differential Social Movement Participation?" In *Self Identity and Social Movements* edited by Sheldon Stryker, Timothy Owens, and Robert White, 21–40. Minneapolis: University of Minnesota Press.

Stryker, Susan. 2008. *Transgender History*. Berkeley, CA: Seal Press.

Stryker, Susan, and Stephen Whittle, eds. 2006. *The Transgender Studies Reader*. New York: Routledge.

Stuart, Tessa. 2016. "17 Anti-Trans Bills That Could Become Law Next." *RollingStone.com*, March 28. https://www.rollingstone.com/politics/news/17-anti-trans-bills-that-could-become-law-next-20160328

Suffredini, Kasey (chief program officer, Freedom for All Americans), interviewed by Jami Taylor, telephone, November 7, 2016.

Sullivan, Andrew. 2009. "The Fierce Urgency of Whenever." *Daily Dish*, May 13. Accessed January 25, 2017. http://www.theatlantic.com/daily-dish/archive/2009/05/the-fierce-urgency-of-whenever/201958/

Sullivan, James W. 1893. *Direct Legislation by the Citizenship through the Initiative and Referendum*. New York: True Nationalist Publishing.

Svara, James. 1999. "Complementarity of Politics and Administration as a Legitimate Alternative to the Dichotomy Model." *Administration & Society* 30 (6): 676–705.

Tadlock, Barry L. 2014. "Issue Framing and Transgender Politics: An Examination of Interest Group Websites and Media Coverage." In *Transgender Rights and Politics: Groups, Issue Framing, and Policy Adoption*, edited by Jami Taylor and Donald Haider-Markel, 25–48. Ann Arbor: University of Michigan Press.

Tadlock, Barry L., C. Ann Gordon, and Elizabeth Popp. 2007. "Framing the Issue of Same-Sex Marriage: Traditional Values versus Equal Rights." In *The Politics of Same-sex Marriage*, edited by Craig A. Rimmerman and Clyde Wilcox, 193–214. Chicago: University of Chicago Press.

Tadlock, Barry L., Jami K. Taylor, Andrew R. Flores, Donald Haider-Markel, Daniel C. Lewis, and Patrick Miller. 2017. "Testing Contact Theory and Attitudes on Transgender Rights." *Public Opinion Quarterly* 81 (4): 956–72. https://doi.org/10.1093/poq/nfx021

Tan, Avianne. 2016. "North Carolina's Controversial Anti-LGBT Bill Explained." *ABC News*, March 24. Accessed February 27, 2017. http://abcnews.go.com/US/north-carolinas-controversial-anti-lgbt-bill-explained/story?id=37898153

Tarrow, Sidney. 1989. *Democracy and Disorder: Protest and Politics in Italy, 1965–1975.* Oxford: Oxford University Press.

Tarrow, Sidney. 1994. *Power in Movement: Social Movements, Collective Action, and Politics.* New York: Cambridge University Press.

Tausanovitch, Chris, and Christopher Warshaw. 2014. "Representation in Municipal Government." *American Political Science Review* 108 (3): 605–41.

Taylor, Jami K. 2007. "Transgender Identities and Public Policy in the United States: The Relevance for Public Administration." *Administration & Society* 39 (7): 833–56.

Taylor, Jami K. 2008. "The Adoption of Gender Identity Inclusive Legislation in the American States." PhD diss., North Carolina State University.

Taylor, Jami K., and Donald P. Haider-Markel, eds. 2014. *Transgender Rights and Politics: Groups, Issue Framing, and Policy Adoption.* Ann Arbor: University of Michigan Press.

Taylor, Jami K., and Daniel C. Lewis. 2014. "The Advocacy Coalition Framework and Transgender Inclusion in LGBT Rights." In *Transgender Rights and Politics: Groups, Issue Framing, and Policy Adoption*, edited by Jami Taylor and Donald Haider-Markel, 108–32. Ann Arbor: University of Michigan Press.

Taylor, Jami K., Daniel C. Lewis, Matthew L. Jacobsmeier, and Brian DiSarro. 2012. "Content and Complexity in Policy Reinvention and Diffusion: Gay and Transgender-Inclusive Laws against Discrimination." *State Politics & Policy Quarterly* 12 (1): 75–98.

Taylor, Jami K., Barry L. Tadlock, and Sarah Poggione. 2013. "State LGBT Rights Policy Outliers: Transsexual Birth Certificate Amendment Laws." *American Review of Politics* 34 (Winter): 245–70.

Taylor, Jami K., Barry L. Tadlock, and Sarah Poggione. 2014. "Birth Certificate Amendment Laws and Morality Politics." In *Transgender Rights and Politics: Groups, Issue Framing, and Policy Adoption*, edited by Jami K. Taylor and Donald P. Haider-Markel, 252–72. Ann Arbor: University of Michigan Press.

Taylor, Jami K., Barry L. Tadlock, Sarah Poggione, and Brian DiSarro. 2014. "Transgender-Inclusive Ordinances in Cities: Form of Government, Local Politics, and Vertical Influences." In *Transgender Rights and Politics: Groups, Issue Framing, and Policy Adoption*, edited by Jami K. Taylor and Donald P. Haider-Markel, 135–54. Ann Arbor: University of Michigan Press.

Taylor, Verta, and Alison Dahl Crossley. 2013. "Abeyance." In *The Wiley-Blackwell Encyclopedia of Social and Political Movements*, edited by David Snow. Malden, MA: Wiley. doi:10.1002/9780470674871.wbespm00

Taylor, Verta, and Nancy E. Whittier. 1992. "Collective Identity in Social Movement Communities." In *Frontiers in Social Movement Theory*, edited by Aldon D. Morris and Carol McClurg, 104–29. New Haven: Yale University Press.

Tee, Nicola, and Peter Hegarty. 2006. "Predicting Opposition to the Civil Rights of Trans Persons in the United Kingdom." *Journal of Community and Applied Social Psychology* 16 (1): 70–80.

Texas v. U.S., No. 7:16-cv-00054-O (N.D. Tx. August 21, 2016).

Theno v. Tonganoxie Unified School Dist No. 464, 377 F. Supp. 2d 952 (D. Kan. 2005).

Theodoulou, Stella. 2013. "In Search of a Framework to Understand the Policy Process." In *Public Policy: The Essential Readings, Second Edition*, edited by Stella Theodoulou and Matthew Cahn, 123–33. Boston: Pearson.

Thompson, A. C., and Ken Schwencke. 2017. "Federal Agencies Are Failing to Report a Range of Crime Statistics to the FBI's National Database." *Pacific Standard*, June 22. https://psmag.com/news/federal-agencies-failing-to-report-to-fbi-national-database

Thompson, Ian (legislative representative, American Civil Liberties Union), interviewed by Jami Taylor, telephone, June 8, 2016.

Tilly, Charles. 1978. *From Mobilization to Revolution.* Reading, MA: Addison-Wesley.

Title IX of the Education Amendments of 1972, 20 U.S.C. A§ 1681 et. seq.

Tobia, P. J. 2015. "Defense Secretary Carter Opens All Combat Jobs to Women." *PBS Newshour*, December 3. Accessed July 5, 2016. http://www.pbs.org/newshour/rundown/watch-live-defense-secretary-carter-to-lift-ban-on-women-in-combat-jobs/

Tran, Stevie V. 2012. "Embracing Our Values: Title IX, the Single-Sex Exemption, and Fraternities Inclusion of Transgender Members." *Hofstra Law Review* 41 (2): 503–43.

Transgender Law Center. 2015. "State of CA and Transgender Law Center Reach Historic Settlement over Trans Prisoner Health Care." August 7. Oakland, CA: Transgender Law Center. https://transgenderlawcenter.org/archives/11861

TRICARE. 2016. "TRICARE to Expand Access to Mental Health Care and Substance Use Disorder Treatment." Accessed June 4, 2017. https://tricare.mil/About/News/Archives/09_29_16_MHSUD?sc_database=web

Trotta, Daniel. 2016. "U.S. Transgender Woman's Journey Turns into Constitutional Fight." Reuters, June 17. Accessed May 9, 2017. http://www.reuters.com/article/us-usa-lgbt-idUSKCN0Z30ZZ

True, Nicole. 2012. "Removing the Constraints to Coverage of Gender-Confirming Healthcare by State Medicaid Programs." *Iowa Law Review* 97: 1329–62.

Truman, David. 1951. *The Governmental Process: Political Interests and Public Opinion.* New York: Alfred A. Knopf.

Ulane v. Eastern Airlines, 742 F.2d 1081 (7th Cir. 1984).

Underwood v. Archer Management Services, Inc., 857 F. Supp 96 (DDC. 1994).

United States Citizenship and Immigration Services (USCIS). 2004. "HQOPRD 70/6." Accessed May 31, 2017. https://www.state.gov/documents/organization/82784.pdf

United States Citizenship and Immigration Services. 2009. "HQOPS AD09–03 HQ70/8." Accessed May 31, 2017. https://www.uscis.gov/sites/default/files/USCIS/Laws%20and%20Regulations/Memoranda/Petitions_Transsexual.pdf

United States Citizenship and Immigration Services. 2012. "PM-602–0061." Accessed May 31, 2017. https://www.uscis.gov/sites/default/files/USCIS/Outreach/Feedback%20Opportunities/Interim%20Guidance%20for%20Comment/Transgender_FINAL.pdf

United States Citizenship and Immigration Services. 2017a. "PM-602–0141." Accessed May 31, 2017. https://www.uscis.gov/sites/default/files/USCIS/Laws/Memoranda/2017/2017–1-19ChangeGenderDesignation-PM-602–0141.pdf

United States Citizenship and Immigration Services. 2017b. "Adjudicator's Field Manual \ Chapter 10 An Overview of the Adjudication Process.\ 10.22 Change of Gender Designation on Documents Issued by USCIS." Accessed May 31, 2017. https://www.uscis.gov/ilink/docView/AFM/HTML/AFM/0–0-0–1/0–0-0–1067/Chapter10–22.html

United States Department of Education. 2016a. "Characteristics of Private Schools in the United States: Results from the 2013–14 Private School Universe Survey." Accessed November 13, 2017. https://nces.ed.gov/pubs2016/2016243.pdf

United States Department of Education. 2016b. "Dear Colleague Letter on Transgender Students." Accessed June 28, 2017. https://www2.ed.gov/about/offices/list/ocr/letters/colleague-201605-title-ix-transgender.pdf

United States Department of Health and Human Services (HHS) Office of the Secretary. 2016. "Nondiscrimination in Health Programs and Activities; Final Rule." *Federal Register* 81: 99.

United States Department of Housing and Urban Development. 2012. "HUD Secretary Donovan Announces New Regulations to Ensure Equal Access to Housing for All Americans Regardless of Sexual Orientation or Gender Identity." Accessed July 14, 2016. http://portal.hud.gov/hudportal/HUD?src=/press/press_releases_media_advisories/2012/HUDNo.12–014

United States Department of Housing and Urban Development. 2016. "HUD Issues Final Rule to Ensure Equal Access to Housing and Services Regardless of Gender Identity." Accessed January 21, 2017. https://portal.hud.gov/hudportal/HUD?src=/press/press_releases_media_advisories/2016/HUDNo_16–137

United States Department of State. 2017a. "Apply for a Passport in Person." Accessed June 1, 2017. https://travel.state.gov/content/passports/en/passports/applyinperson.html

United States Department of State. 2017b. "Gender Designation Change." Accessed May 30, 2017. https://travel.state.gov/content/passports/en/passports/information/gender.html

United States Social Security Administration. 2016. "How Do I Change My Gender on Social Security's Records?" Accessed May 30, 2017. https://faq.ssa.gov/link/portal/34011/34019/Article/2856/How-do-I-change-my-gender-on-Social-Security-s-records

United States Social Security Administration. 2017. "Corrected Card for a U.S. Born Adult." Accessed June 2, 2017. https://www.ssa.gov/ssnumber/ss5doc.htm

United States v. Carolene Products Co., 304 U.S. 144 (1938).

United States v. Morrison, 529 U.S. 59 (2000).

United States v. Windsor, 570 U.S. ___ (2013).

University of Illinois, Springfield Survey Research Office. 2015. "2015 Attitudes towards Transgender Supportive Policies Survey." UIS SRO Qualtrics, pollster. Accessed March 28, 2017. https://transgenderinclusivepolicysurvey.wordpress.com/

Ura, Alexa. 2017. "Texas House Approves Bathroom Restrictions for Transgender Students." *Texas Tribune*, May 22.

Ura, Alexa, Bobby Blanchard, and Todd Wiseman. 2017. "Following North Carolina's Lead, Texas GOP Unveils So-called 'Bathroom Bill.'" *Texas Tribune*, January 5.

Ura, Joseph Daniel. 2014. "Backlash and Legitimation: Macro Political Responses to Supreme Court Decisions." *American Journal of Political Science* 58 (1): 110–26.

Vaid, Urvashi. 1995. *Virtual Equality: The Mainstreaming of Gay and Lesbian Liberation.* New York: Anchor Books.

Vaid, Urvashi. 2012. *Irresistible Revolution: Confronting Race, Class, and the Assumptions of LGBT Politics.* New York: Magnus Books.

Valentine, David. 2007. *Imagining Transgender: An Ethnography of a Category*. Durham, NC: Duke University Press.

Vanden Brook, Tom. 2018. "Transgender Military Academy Grads Could Join Ranks Quickly, Expert Says." *USA Today*, January 17. https://www.usatoday.com/story/news/politics/2018/01/17/transgender-military-academy-grads-could-join-ranks-quickly-expert-says/1040908001/

van Kesteren, Paul, Louis Gooren, and Jos Megens. 1996. "An Epidemiological and Demographic Study of Transsexuals in the Netherlands." *Archives of Sexual Behavior* 25 (6): 589–600.

Veterans Health Administration. 2013. "Providing Health Care for Transgender and Intersex Veterans." Accessed June 4, 2017. http://www.va.gov/vhapublications/ViewPublication.asp?pub_ID=2863

Vielmetti, Bruce. 2016. "Transgender Suit against Kenosha School Advances." *Milwaukee Journal Sentinel*, September 19. http://www.jsonline.com/story/news/education/2016/09/19/transgender-suit-against-kenosha-school-advances/90706692/

Virginia Governor's Office. 2014. "Governor McAuliffe Signs Executive Order Number 1 Prohibiting Discrimination Based on Sexual Orientation or Gender Identity." Accessed January 22, 2017. https://governor.virginia.gov/newsroom/newsarticle?articleId=2561

Vozzella, Laura. 2017. "McAuliffe Bans State Contracts with Firms Engaged in Anti-LGBT Discrimination." *Washington Post*, January 5. Accessed January 22, 2017. https://www.washingtonpost.com/local/virginia-politics/mcauliffe-bans-state-contracts-with-firms-engaged-in-anti-lbgt-discrimination/2017/01/05/5f701dc0-d35f-11e6–945a-76f69a399dd5_story.html?utm_term=.a1d216083645

Wald, Kenneth D., James W. Button, and Barbara A. Rienzo. 1996. "The Politics of Gay Rights in American Communities: Explaining Antidiscrimination Ordinances and Policies." *American Journal of Political Science* 40 (4): 1152–78.

Wald, Kenneth, and Allison Calhoun-Brown. 2010. *Religion and Politics in the United States, 6th ed.* New York: Rowman and Littlefield.

Warshaw, Chris, and Chris Tausanovitch. 2015, "Replication Data for: Representation in Municipal Government." doi:10.7910/DVN/AXVEXM, Harvard Dataverse, V1, UNF:6:mXEw2QBZgkDHZxXsLke1QQ==.

Weiss, Jillian T. 2013. "Protecting Transgender Students: Application of Title IX to Gender Identity of Expression and the Constitutional Right to Gender Autonomy." *Wisconsin Journal of Law, Gender & Society* 28: 331–46.

Weissert, Will. 2016. "Speculation Mounts on Race between Top 2 Texas Republicans." Associated Press, December 28.

Welch v. Brown, No. 15–16598 (9th Cir. 2016).

Welkos, Robert. 1993. "The Secret of 'The Crying Game': Don't Read Any Further if You Haven't Seen This Film." *Los Angeles Times*, February 18. Accessed January 3, 2017. http://articles.latimes.com/1993–02–18/entertainment/ca-292_1_miramax-films

West, Candace, and Don Zimmerman. 1987. "Doing Gender." *Gender & Society* 1 (2): 125–51.

Westbrook, Laurel, and Kristen Schilt. 2014. "Doing Gender, Determining Gender: Transgender People, Gender Panics, and the Maintenance of the Sex/Gender/Sexuality System." *Gender & Society* 28 (1): 32–57.

Wheeler, Lydia. 2017. "ACLU Sues Trump over Transgender Ban." *ill*, August 28. Accessed October 6, 2017. http://thehill.com/regulation/court-battles/348242-aclu-sues-trump-over-transgender-ban

Whitaker v. Kenosha Unified School District No. 1 Board of Education, et al., No. 16–3522 (7th Cir. 2017).

White House. 2007. "Statement of Administration Policy H.R. 1592—Local Law Enforcement Hate Crimes Prevention Act of 2007." Accessed January 23, 2017. https://georgewbush-whitehouse.archives.gov/omb/legislative/sap/110–1/hr1592sap-h.pdf

White House. 2009. "President Barack Obama's Inaugural Address." Accessed January 25, 2017. https://obamawhitehouse.archives.gov/blog/2009/01/21/president-barack-obamas-inaugural-address

White House. 2011. "Presidential Memorandum—International Initiatives to Advance the Human Rights of Lesbian, Gay, Bisexual, and Transgender Persons." Accessed January 23, 2017. https://obamawhitehouse.archives.gov/the-press-office/2011/12/06/presidential-memorandum-international-initiatives-advance-human-rights-l

White House. 2013. "Inaugural Address by President Barack Obama." Accessed January 25, 2017. https://obamawhitehouse.archives.gov/the-press-office/2013/01/21/inaugural-address-president-barack-obama

White House. 2014. "Executive Order—Further Amendments to Executive Order 11478, Equal Employment Opportunity in the Federal Government, and Executive Order 11246, Equal Employment Opportunity." Accessed January 22, 2017. https://obamawhitehouse.archives.gov/the-press-office/2014/07/21/executive-order-further-amendments-executive-order-11478-equal-employmen

White House. 2015. "Remarks by the President in State of the Union Address| January 20, 2015." Accessed January 25, 2017. https://obamawhitehouse.archives.gov/the-press-office/2015/01/20/remarks-president-state-union-address-january-20–2015

White House. 2016a. "Obama Administration Record for the LGBT Community." Accessed January 30, 2017. https://obamawhitehouse.archives.gov/sites/default/files/docs/lgbt_record.pdf

White House. 2016b. "Remarks by the President at PBS NewsHour Town Hall Discussion with Gwen Ifill for Elkhart, IN Residents." Accessed January 30, 2017. https://obamawhitehouse.archives.gov/the-press-office/2016/06/02/remarks-president-pbs-newshour-town-hall-discussion-gwen-ifill-elkhart

White House. 2017a. "President Donald J. Trump Will Continue to Enforce Executive Order Protecting the Rights of the LGBTQ Community in the Workplace." Accessed May 9, 2017. https://www.whitehouse.gov/the-press-office/2017/01/31/president-donald-j-trump-will-continue-enforce-executive-order

White House. 2017b. "Presidential Executive Order on the Revocation of Federal Contracting Executive Orders." Accessed April 14, 2017. https://www.whitehouse.gov/the-press-office/2017/03/27/presidential-executive-order-revocation-federal-contracting-executive

White House. 2017c. "Presidential Memorandum for the Secretary of Defense and the Secretary of Homeland Security." Accessed October 7, 2017. https://www.whitehouse.gov/the-press-office/2017/08/25/presidential-memorandum-secretary-defense-and-secretary-homeland

White House. 2017d. "President Obama's Farewell Address." Accessed January 30, 2017. https://obamawhitehouse.archives.gov/Farewell

Wiggins, Charles, and William Browne. 1982. "Interest Groups and Public within a State Legislative Setting." *Polity* 14 (3): 548–58.

Wikileaks. 2016. "Rocco: Would You Please Forward This for Me, So It Finds Its Way to Secretary Clinton." Clinton Emails. Accessed January 21, 2018. https://wikileaks.org/clinton-emails/emailid/26530

Wilchins, Riki (executive director, True Child), interviewed by Jami Taylor, telephone, November 2, 2016.

Wilchins, Riki (executive director, True Child), interviewed by Jami Taylor, e-mail correspondence, March 19, 2017.

Wilchins, Riki. 1997. *Read My Lips: Sexual Subversion and the End of Gender.* Ithaca, NY: Firebrand Books.

Wilchins, Riki. 2002. "A Woman for Her Time: In Memory of Stonewall Warrior Sylvia Rivera." *Village Voice*, February 27. Accessed July 7, 2016. https://web.archive.org/web/20060619094746/http://www.villagevoice.com/news/0209,wilchins,32645,1.html

Wilchins, Riki. 2004. *Queer Theory, Gender Theory: An Instant Primer.* Los Angeles: Alyson Books.

Wilcox, Clyde. 1990. "Religion and Politics among White Evangelicals: The Impact of Religious Variables on Political Attitudes." *Review of Religious Research* 32 (1): 27–42.

Wilcox, Clyde, and Barbara Norrander. 2002. "Of Moods and Morals: The Dynamics of Opinion on Abortion and Gay Rights." In *Understanding Public Opinion.* 2nd ed. Edited by Barbara Norrander and Clyde Wilcox, 121–47. Washington, DC: CQ Press.

Wilkinson, Willy. 2006. "Public Health Gains of the Transgender Community in San Francisco: Grassroots Organizing and Community-Based Research." In *Transgender Rights*, edited by Paisley Currah, Richard Juang, and Shannon Price Minter, 192–214. Minneapolis: University of Minnesota Press.

Williams Institute. 2011. "United States Census Snapshot: 2010." Williams Institute, UCLA School of Law 2011. Accessed June 13, 2017. https://williamsinstitute.law.ucla.edu/#mapwrap

Wilson, Angelia, and Cynthia Burack. 2012. "'Where Liberty Reigns and God Is Supreme': The Christian Right and the Tea Party Movement." *New Political Science* 34 (2): 172–90.

Wilson, Meagan Meuchel. 2014. "Hate Crime Victimization, 2004–2012—Statistical Tables. NCJ 244409." Washington, DC: U.S. Department of Justice, Office of Justice Programs, Bureau of Justice Statistics.

Wisneski, Hope (regional field director, Human Rights Campaign), interviewed by Jami Taylor, telephone, October 19, 2016.

Witten, Tarynn, and A. Evan Eyler. 1999. "Hate Crimes and Violence against the Transgendered." *Peace Review* 11 (3): 461–68.

Witten, Tarynn, and Evan Eyler, eds. 2012. *Gay, Lesbian, Bisexual, and Transgender Aging.* Baltimore: Johns Hopkins University Press.

Wood, Curtis. 2011. "Understanding the Consequences of Municipal Discretion." *American Review of Public Administration* 41 (4): 411–27.

Wooten, Amy. 2008. "Congress Drops Hate-Crimes Bill." *Windy City Times*, January 1. http://www.windycitymediagroup.com/gay/lesbian/news/ARTICLE.php?AID=17078

World Professional Association for Transgender Health. 2012. "Standards of Care for the Health of Transsexual, Transgender, and Gender-Nonconforming People, Version 7." *International Journal of Transgenderism* 13 (4): 165–232.

World Professional Association for Transgender Health. 2016. "Position Statement on Medical Necessity of Treatment, Sex Reassignment, and Insurance Coverage in the U.S.A." Accessed June 4, 2017. http://www.wpath.org/site_page.cfm?pk_association_webpage_menu=1352&pk_association_webpage=3947

Wright, John. 2003. *Interest Groups and Congress: Lobbying, Contributions, and Influence.* New York: Longman.

Yoshino, Kenji. 2006. "Sex and the City: New York City Bungles Transgender Equality." *Slate*, December 11. Accessed January 28, 2017. http://www.slate.com/id/2155278

Zaller, John. 1992. *The Nature and Origins of Mass Opinion.* Cambridge; New York: Cambridge University Press.

Zapotosky, Matt, and Sarah Pulliam Bailey. 2017. "Civil Liberties Groups Decry Sessions's Guidance on Religious Freedom." *Washington Post*, October 6. Accessed October 7, 2017. https://www.washingtonpost.com/world/national-security/civil-liberties-groups-decry-sessionss-guidance-on-religious-freedom/2017/10/06/cd5cfcde-aaa7–11e7–92d1–58c702d2d975_story.html?utm_term=.8aa059f4d9a5

Zhou, Jiang-Ning, Michel A. Hofman, Louis J. G. Gooren, and Dick F. Swaab. 1995. "A Sex Difference in the Human Brain and Its Relation to Transsexuality." *Nature* 378 (6552): 68–70.

Zivi, Karen. 2012. *Making Rights Claims: A Practice of Democratic Citizenship.* New York: Oxford University Press.

Zucker, Kenneth, Peggy T. Cohen-Kettenis, Jack Drescher, Heino Meyer-Bahlburg, Friedemann Pfäfflin, and William Womack. 2013. "Memo Outlining Evidence for Change for Gender Identity Disorder in the DSM-5." *Archives of Sexual Behavior* 42 (5): 901–14.

Zucker, Kenneth, and Anne Lawrence. 2009. "Epidemiology of Gender Identity Disorder: Recommendations for the Standards of Care of the World Professional Association for Transgender Health." *International Journal of Transgenderism* 11 (1): 8–18.

Zucker, Kenneth, Anne Lawrence, and Baudewijntje P. C. Kreukels. 2016. "Gender Dysphoria in Adults." *Annual Review of Clinical Psychology* 12: 217–47.

Zzyym v. Kerry 2016 U.S. Dist. LEXIS 162659.

About the Authors

Donald P. Haider-Markel is a professor of political science at the University of Kansas. His research and teaching is focused on the representation of interests in the policy process and the dynamics between public opinion, political behavior, and public policy. He has authored or coauthored over sixty refereed articles, multiple book chapters, and several books on a range of issue areas, including civil rights, criminal justice, environmental policy, and terrorism. He coedited *Transgender Rights and Politics: Groups, Issue Framing, and Policy Adoption* (University of Michigan Press, 2014) with Jami Taylor. He has been recipient or co-recipient of grants from the EPA STAR program, the National Science Foundation, and the American Psychological Foundation.

Daniel C. Lewis is an associate professor of political science and faculty fellow of the Community Policy Institute at Siena College. He is the author of *Direct Democracy and Minority Rights: A Critical Assessment of the Tyranny of the Majority in the American States*. His research on gay and transgender rights policies and direct democracy has also been published in *State Politics & Policy Quarterly, Public Opinion Quarterly, Political Research Quarterly, Political Psychology, Politics, Groups and Identities*, and *Social Science Quarterly*. He also contributed two chapters to Taylor and Haider-Markel's edited volume, *Transgender Rights and Politics*.

Jami K. Taylor is a professor of political science and public administration at the University of Toledo. She conducts research related to LGBT rights and on public service motivation. Her LGBT related work has appeared in *State Politics & Policy Quarterly, Administration & Society, American Review of Politics, Public Opinion Quarterly, Political Psychology*, and *Politics, Groups* *and Identities.* She also coedited *Transgender Rights and Politics: Groups, Issue Framing, and Policy Adoption* (University of Michigan Press, 2014) with Donald Haider-Markel.

Other Contributors

Ryan Combs is an assistant professor of Health Promotion & Behavioral Sciences and a Commonwealth Scholar at the University of Louisville School of Public Health & Information Sciences. He received his PhD in Politics from the University of Manchester (UK) and has taught in the disciplines of Public Health, Politics, and Gender Studies. His qualitative and community-based research explores the impact of health policies and practices on marginalized populations. Using that knowledge, he and his team develop, implement, and evaluate culturally competent public health interventions. Dr. Combs has several years of experience conducting research in partnership with stakeholders such as community members, patient groups, policymakers, and practitioners.

Andrew R. Flores is an assistant professor of political science at Lorry I. Lokey Graduate School of Business and Public Policy at Mills College, and he is a Visiting Scholar at the Williams Institute at the UCLA School of Law. His research has appeared in edited volumes, political science blogs, and peer-reviewed journals such as *Public Opinion Quarterly*, the *American Journal of Public Health, Political Research Quarterly, International Journal of Public Opinion Research, Political Psychology, Politics Groups and Identities, Research & Politics*, and *Transgender Studies Quarterly*. Flores's primary research interests are related to how attitudes form and change about stigmatized social groups, namely, lesbians, gay men, bisexuals, and transgender people. He also examines the relationship between public opinion and social policy, and the effects of LGBT-inclusive policies.

Patrick R. Miller is an assistant professor of political science at the University of Kansas. His areas of specialization in American politics include political psychology, public opinion, electoral behavior, political communication, and survey and experimental methods. His current research interests focus on political identities, partisanship, political civility, and civic engagement. He has published in journals such as *Political Psychology, Journalism & Mass Communication Quarterly, Political Research Quarterly*, and *Politics, Groups, and Identities*. He received his doctorate from the University of North Carolina at Chapel Hill, also receiving a certification in survey research methodology there from the Howard W. Odum Institute for Research in Social Science.

Jason Pierceson is a professor of political science at the University of Illinois, Springfield. Pierceson's teaching and research interests include public law and the politics of gender and sexuality. He is the author of several books, including *Courts, Liberalism, and Rights: Gay Law and Politics in the United States and Canada* (Temple, 2005), *Same-Sex Marriage in the United States: The Road to the Supreme Court and Beyond* (Rowman and Littlefield, 2014), and *Sexual Minorities in Politics: An Introduction* (Rowman and Littlefield, 2016). In 2011, he was the Fulbright Visiting Research Chair in American Studies at the University of Alberta.

Mitchell D. Sellers is a visiting assistant professor of political science at Colorado State University. His research interests fall broadly into the field of state politics and policies, in addition to executive-legislative relations. His research on policy diffusion, executive orders and transgender rights has appeared in several scholarly outlets, including *Political Research Quarterly*, *Journal of Public Policy*, and *Administration & Society*. He also contributed two chapters to Taylor and Haider-Markel's edited volume, *Transgender Rights and Politics*.

Barry L. Tadlock is an associate professor in Ohio University's Department of Political Science. He received his PhD from the University of Kentucky (1995). Tadlock's research interests include LGBT politics, Appalachian politics, and welfare policies. He coedited (with Ellen D. B. Riggle) *Gays and Lesbians in the Democratic Process: Public Policy, Political Representation, and Public Opinion* (Columbia University Press, 1999). His work has appeared in the following edited books: *LGBTQ Politics: A Critical Reader* (2017), *Transgender Rights and Politics: Groups, Issue Framing, and Policy Adoption* (2014), *The Change Election: Money, Mobilization, and Persuasion in the 2008 Federal Elections* (2011), *The Politics of Same-Sex Marriage* (2007), *The Sociology of Spatial Inequality* (2007), *Communities of Work: Rural Restructuring in Local and Global Contexts* (2003), and *Rural Dimensions of Welfare Reform; Welfare, Food Assistance and Poverty in Rural America (2002)*. His work has appeared in the following journals: *American Review of Politics, Politics, Groups and Identities, Political Psychology, Public Administration Quarterly, Journal of Children and Poverty, Public Opinion Quarterly, Politics and Policy, Affilia: Journal of Women and Social Work*, and *Legislative Studies Quarterly*.

Index

Note: Page numbers in italics refer to illustrations and tables.